ONCE AROUND THE SUN

Once Around the Sun

Justin Brooks Atkinson

HARCOURT, BRACE AND COMPANY

NEW YORK

Illustrated by DON FREEMAN

ONCE AROUND THE SUN

JANUARY

January

NEW YEAR'S DAY. The new year comes in with a sting. New York is alarmed. Rain falling at a freezing temperature has covered the sidewalks with a hard glaze. Speaking over the city radio the Mayor personally warns motorists to keep off the icy streets. The Weather Bureau forecasts a heavy snowstorm tonight.

Our apartment, high above the streets and huddled back from the Hudson River, is like a tiny refuge scooped out of the heart of the storm. As the scud flies by on an icy gale, I look out at the wild weather through the rattling windows, sheltered and content. I wish I could also look into the round of seasons that is already swinging back north in our direction and that always keeps us headed forward through the long, many-colored corridor of the year. Every year is packed with a treasure of ordinary experience. I think I shall keep a book of days to chronicle one year in the endless revolution of the universe—one human cycle in the myriad of cycles that reaches out an unimaginable distance into time, space, and poetry. Let me try to put together a microcosm of type, ink and paper—the small change of civilization. "A day is the epitome of a year," Thoreau said. A year is the epitome of a lifetime. A lifetime is the epitome of eternity. As the winters weigh on our shoulders and the springs lighten our hearts, we go on grinding up and storing away little fragments of eternity —idly sauntering through the seasons, looking, working, studying, talking, thinking, dreaming.

At the moment, the year looks bright. There are icicles on the cornices of the apartment house across the frozen street, and our thermometer is sheathed in ice. But standing at the window and watching the cold tempest sweep across the broken surface of the river, we are warm and we begin the new year triumphantly. The worst can happen; occasionally it does. Not many of us in America are prepared for it, for we do not believe it in our bones. We cheerfully assume that in some mystic way love conquers all, that good outweighs evil in the just balances of the universe and that at the eleventh hour something gloriously triumphant will prevent the worst before it happens. In the austere light of the world's experience our optimism is naïve. When wars and depressions strike us down we are shocked, incredulous, and unprepared. But cautious calculations bore us; they have such a dismal appearance and sound. To Americans optimism is a more congenial attitude. It may be even more than that: it may be creative. For all that I know at the moment, "Happy New Year" may be nothing less than prophecy as the world begins one more journey around the sun.

2. Nothing matters except the human race. "Every good artist has two subjects—man and the hopes of his soul," said Leonardo da Vinci. Every city has one purpose—to promote the well-being of its citizens. The fabulous skyscrapers, the modern apartment houses, the rapid transit system, the limpid water drawn through tunnels from reservoirs over a hundred miles away, the garish wonder mart of Broadway, the museums and concert halls, the luxurious department stores, the great universities and even the flaming grandeur of the sunsets over New Jersey—they have no value unless they add a cubit to the stature of our people. We live poorly here, packed into cramped and dehumanized "living space," as it is called by the merchandisers, and without a margin for the amenities of living. We are bricked in. We are all serving life sentences. Even the rich can hardly do more than rent space in standardized buildings to keep warm and dry and arrange their possessions; and the poor huddle together in medieval squalor. There is not another large city in the world, excepting London, where people are walled in so grimly and channelized so mechanically in their daily migration and removed so completely from the normal comforts of back-yards for gardening and front porches for lounging. Life in New York is almost disembodied.

Yet from all over the world ideas pour into New York day and night throughout the year like pulsations in an electric current. Raise a voice in Java and New York hears it. Fire a shot in Palestine and one hundred New Yorkers spring to arms. Dancers in India, orchestra leaders in Italy, actors in Dublin, writers in

London, make pilgrimages to Gotham and are welcome. There are no lonely geniuses here. Every man with an idea has at least two or three followers. We give houseroom to the people of all nations. The Chinese study here. The Syrians are in business. Europeans find sanctuary in every apartment house. German is the second language of Riverside Drive. And so the vast mechanical and material equipment of the city is not vanity and the great buildings are not empty, for people use them. And they are the kind of people who are interested in many things. People not only hear new ideas but act on them promptly—no doubt without reflection or prudence. We live poorly. But we are constantly reminded that we are alive. It is a vivid city, harshly compact, but roofed with dreams.

3. After a day of rain and sleet we awaken to a crystal world. The ice on the trees, shrubs, buildings, and snow reflects the sun. The daylight gives an impression of exploding. The eye can hardly absorb it. For the second day our apartment house is unheated. The snow-choked streets have blocked the fuel delivery trucks, and we have nothing but "gas logs" (a hideous counterfeit) to warm one side of the interior coldness. But the ice-burnished world outside the windows gives the day fresh and exultant vitality. The ice not only etches the trunks and branches of the trees, but reaches down among the waste tangle of the dead grass and invents intricate patterns of glitter. Grass that was hardly noticed yesterday has been transmuted into a heap of jewels today. The whole world is wearing a royal robe of dazzling brightness.

4. Since night workers reverse the normal working schedule, they are sometimes pitied for the sacrifice they make to the city's convenience. Although the pity is well meant, it is wasted. For the leisure hours of those of us who work at night come at the time of the day when there is sunlight and brightness indoors and out. Most people have to plunge into the city's working maelstrom with obscene haste when they have scarcely washed the sleep from their eyes and before they have had time to digest their breakfasts. The subway crowds are morose in the morning rush hours.

Most of the night workers miss the dawn. When I occasionally have to get up at seven-thirty or eight, which seems early to me, the city looks fresher than at any other time of day, and I regret that I cannot regularly participate in it. But we night workers have other compensations that tip the scales in our favor. We begin our day with leisure in broad daylight and we can shake the sleep out of our heads slowly and painlessly. We have the city at our disposal when most people are lashed to the treadmill. We can saunter along the water front at high noon or walk through the streets in a mood of relaxed inquiry. Although many of us have to work in the afternoon, the pressure does not begin until night. Afternoon work seems to be borrowed time—free from urgency. And when we go to work earnestly at night we are not interrupted, for the day workers are out of the way and do not distract us. To complete the cycle, we do not have to rush to bed when we are through work because we do not have to rush to get up in the morning.

This is the life of the sybarite, and should be envied rather than pitied. I am not referring to the "lobster shift," which works from midnight to eight in the morning. That is drudgery.

5. For seventeen years, seven days a week, Joe Berman has efficiently presided over his newsstand at the corner of Eighty-sixth Street and Broadway. He opens it before five in the morning. Mrs. Berman, wearing a smart hair-do and a Persian lamb coat, relieves him for an hour at breakfast and for two hours in the afternoon and wishes that he would take things easier. But with the exception of this interlude of relief, Joe is alert and on duty until six-thirty. Today is one of his cruelest days. The temperature is 16° and a freezing wind rushes wildly up the two blocks from the river. Joe has an electric heater that keeps his feet from freezing, but the front of the stand is open to the weather. He wears a Navy pea jacket and woolen cap and stands behind a pile of magazines. Although his customers suffer in the cold, Joe is smiling and business-like and makes no complaints. He is used to the weather. Having been outdoors for so many years, he is probably in more vigorous health than most New Yorkers.

Piled high with newspapers and flanked with magazines, Joe's stand radiates intelligence throughout the neighborhood. It is the university of Eighty-sixth Street. Being a merchant Joe sells the comic books and squalid story magazines as well as the newspapers, reviews, and intellectual magazines; and he knows all of them, including the Russian, Yiddish, German, and French language papers. He carries and gives prominent display to the *New Times*, which is published in Moscow. If you are interested in ideas, art, politics, racing, or news, you can hardly get along without Joe, who has the information you need. In the morning and evening the stand is blocked by hurried customers. But it attracts browsers also. Three or four people seem to be loitering in front of it and looking over the stock any hour of the day. Joe is a quiet, soft-spoken man who talks pleasantly when he is spoken to and is a mine of information about the publishing business. Since he rarely leaves his corner, it is surprising that he knows so much in detail about the people and business methods of the local newspapers. He gives me more informed gossip about the *Times* than I get for myself.

Mr. and Mrs. Berman have raised two sons and a daughter on the profits of the stand. After having been discharged from the Army, the sons helped with the stand—tall, strong young men with good manners and a thorough knowledge of the neighborhood and the business. About a year ago they bought a stationery store farther up Broadway. Trained by their father, who is one of the most reputable merchants on the West Side, they are doing well and are prepared to carry on the Berman tradition. Mrs. Berman worries about Joe. "How much longer can he keep going like this?" she asks anxiously. "He doesn't rest right. He always has the stand on his mind. When he is home he is always thinking of coming back. When it is cold he worries about me standing here, and comes back before he is supposed to. What can you do?" she inquires with a hopeless roll of the eyes.

Once a year Joe does drop everything. On Yom Kippur the business collapses. No papers are delivered to any of his customers, and a stranger sells the papers in front of the stand. There is no use complaining, for Joe is not interested and has no apologies or explanations to make. Furthermore, the same thing will happen next year. I never realize how much energy and stimulus the stand contributes to the neighborhood until Yom Kippur closes it tight.

On the one day when Joe is not standing behind his counter, the neighborhood is flat.

6. The feast of Epiphany, which commemorates the baptism of Christ. This is an important religious day, the significance of which most Christians have forgotten. On the eve of Epiphany, springs and rivers are blessed, and holy water stored up for the next year's baptisms. For many years the birth of Christ was also celebrated on this day. But some time in the fourth century the birthday of Christ was separated from Epiphany for the most practical of reasons. In Bethlehem the priests had to celebrate the Virgin birth in a cave at dawn, and then hurry thirteen miles away to the river Jordan to celebrate the baptism. Since they did not have time to celebrate both occasions properly, they appealed to the Pope to look into the Jewish archives and find the date of Christ's birth. After the destruction of Jerusalem in 69 A.D. the archives had been sent to Rome. The Pope found the date of December twenty-fifth for the day of Christ's birth in the works of Josephus, it is said.

The Festival of the Three Kings is also celebrated on this day in some parts of the West. Although the Greek Orthodox church which follows the old calendar does not celebrate Epiphany until two or three weeks later, the Greek priests in New York bless the waters at the Battery in a bold ceremony that introduces a little practical showmanship to a sacred ritual. After the services at the Little Church of St. Nicholas on Cedar Street, the bishops and their congregation march down West Street to the Battery behind a clangorous and rousing brass band. After the bishop blesses the waters and tosses the cross into the harbor, several members of the congregation, dressed only in swimming trunks, plunge into the icy water and compete in a scramble to recover the cross. When the ice is packed around the pier, the bishop moves out into open water in a police launch and the swimmers dive off another. This is a picturesque ceremony that derives from Greece, where the winter waters are not so icy. Probably it is a charming custom in Greece. Like so many other things, it is sensational in New York.

7. It is better to win a war than to lose it, but not much better. Everyone dies a little when his neighbor is killed. No society is sound and vigorous enough to sustain death on the staggering scale that wars make inevitable. No one can win a war. There are survivors but no victors. It releases pestilences that infect everyone who is left. Since the nature of war is evil, it sows seeds of hatred, destruction, and suspicion everywhere and contaminates the moral life of those who think they have won as well as those who have lost. For the evil goes deep and produces epidemics of intolerance and witch-hunting, assassination of character, mass repudiation of intelligence, the murder of philosophy, surrender to despair, the abased acceptance of one more war as inevitable. Two world wars have written identical items in the Doomsday Book of America. How many times must they be repeated? After each war there is a little less democracy to save.

8. At about eight in the evening, Orion's belt of three stars rides at an angle above the grimy, frowzy cavern of Eighty-fourth Street. Through the city smoke it is dingy—nothing like so brilliant as it appears to be three miles out to sea or in the crystalline air of the Catskills. But it is one of the major splendors of the sky, dramatic in shape and size and jaunty in the rakish angle it forms with Eighty-fourth Street. Even through the sooty exhalation of the city, the great nebula is visible and glows like a luminous spot of cloud. Walk farther down Eighty-fourth Street and you can see Sirius sparkling like a great jewel over the shadowy roof and television aerials of a tenement.

At the top of the constellation there is a red star, called Betelgeuse, almost directly above Eighty-fourth Street. You might not notice it unless you looked for it deliberately, the street lights are so much more conspicuous. But the light I see from it tonight started on its long journey to Eighty-fourth Street in the time of John Milton, when Eighty-fourth Street was way uptown.

There are other things about Betelgeuse worth giving a passing thought to on the way downtown to the theater district. It has a diameter three hundred times bigger than our sun. Its candlepower is twelve hundred times that of the sun. And ancient as it is—much more ancient than the human race—it has not yet settled down to calm old age. It keeps on restlessly flaring up and dying down. At its maximum brilliance it has a diameter of nearly four hundred million miles, in contrast with the eight-thousand-mile diameter of the earth. When it subsides to minimum brilliance its diameter is about two hundred and ninety million miles. The difference between the two is about one hundred and ten million miles, which is greater than the distance between the earth and the sun.

But a difference of one hundred and ten million miles in the diameter of Betelgeuse is not noticeable from Eighty-fourth Street. As I hurry down to West End Avenue, all I can notice is that Betelgeuse is there and that winter is here and that nothing I see on Broadway tonight is going to make much difference. But the lights on Broadway will be so powerful that I can read by them and recognize the faces of my friends. For all its stupendous brightness Betelgeuse does not give light enough for that. We must recognize the realities, especially if they dazzle us.

9. Above the clatter and rumble of the traffic in Times Square, the diapason of the *Queen Mary's* whistle spreads a triumphant canopy of sound. The traffic noises are bedlam—nervous, petty, sharp, impatient. But the voice of the *Queen Mary* is grand. The tone is deep and round; the volume is tremendous as it pours down the cacophonous canyons of the city. At sea the *Queen Mary's* voice can be heard over a range of twenty miles. It cannot be heard that far in the city, where tall buildings block it and toss it back. But when the *Queen Mary* is ready to go to sea she speaks plainly enough to be heard by thousands of landlocked citizens in New York and New Jersey. No other sound so thoroughly belittles our city.

10. Although Broadway begins at the Battery and goes straight upriver to Albany (Albany Post Road) the citadel that the Tin Pan Alley music-makers serenade is the open pleasure mart between Forty-second and Forty-seventh Streets. Even by day the motion picture theater marquees glow with light, impatient for the darkness. At night Broadway explodes with light. Animated electric signs of colossal size and meaningless design crown the

rooftops of the lower buildings and fill this monstrous canyon with garish radiance. It spills glare on the upturned faces of the crowds choking the sidewalks. It flares up in the sky like the glow from a blast furnace. Most of New York's carnival energy is concentrated in this slovenly canyon, where the light is pitiless, like a continuous flash of lightning.

To some people Broadway at night is shocking—cheap, strident, depraved. They regard it as the apotheosis of vulgarity. "An angry carbuncle on the face of the city," a puritanical English visitor says. Even the merchants of the Broadway Association, worrying about the depreciation of property values, view with alarm this pitchman's bazaar with its gaudy spectacles and blowzy wares. But every day a million and a half people take the light treatment of Broadway. They trudge slowly up and down the packed street and glance with a kind of bemused curiosity at the blazing signs that surround them—flashes of news from all over the world nervously whirling around the slender Times Tower, a sheet of water pouring down the luminous wall of the Bond store's sign, and rings of steam automatically puffing out of the face of a stupendous Camel cigarette smoker on the east bank of Times Square. Nothing like this ever went on night after night and year after year on such a monstrous scale in any part of the world.

In the first chapter of Genesis it is written that the Lord "saw the light, that it was good." For light is frank and revealing. Ever since Genesis was written, people have been seeking light. If Broadway were shadowy and furtive in the gloom of the night, the moralists might have some reason for misgivings. But the tremendous bath of light on Broadway gives the evening strollers a feeling of elation. No wonder people of all classes and races pour into Times Square when the time comes for celebrating.

11. Through the window adjoining this desk, I glance at the Hudson River innumerable times every day. To watermen it is the North River (which on old charts distinguished it from the "South River" or Delaware River). To geologists it is an estuary. But to us it is the fabulous Hudson River, pouring into the Bay. It is the most glorious thing we have in Cosmopolis. Everything else has succumbed to the need for living and office space and the paraphernalia of a remorseless city. But the Hudson has remained

unconquerable all these centuries and still lives an active, independent life as it rolls through an industrial jungle. A mile wide
at this point, it keeps open a broad rivery avenue in the desperate,
ruthless scramble for space which we silently wage in this dense
corner of America.

To have the Hudson at our doorstep is to be enriched every
hour of the day. It is a kaleidoscope of beauty—lightly tinted with
greenish blue when the sun awakens it in the morning, but varying all day: a delicate maculated floor of shining silver when the
sun moves into the south and a pool of flaming red when the sun
drops down behind the Weehawken cliffs. At night it is a strip
of velvety black between garlands of lights on both banks.

The Hudson is not only beautiful but useful. We are a salt-
water port. We have a tide of six feet in some parts of the year.
And living here by the river we have direct connections with such
inland ports as Albany, Buffalo, Cleveland, Detroit, Chicago,
Milwaukee, Fort William, and Montreal. Facing downstream we
also have connections with London, Naples, Suez, Batavia, Singapore, Hongkong, Shanghai, Yokohama, to say nothing of San
Francisco and Seattle. We are in close touch every hour of the
day with all parts of the world, and have reason always to remember that there is nearly two and one half times more water
surface than land surface in the world. We are comfortably close
to the great facts of geography.

Downriver a mile to the south from my apartment windows the
great express liners of the Atlantic dock and undock on their private schedules. But since the Hudson channel is dredged to a
depth of twenty-seven feet to Albany, freight ships frequently
rush by this window with a curl of white water at their stems,
most of them flying the American flag, but others flying the banners of maritime nations all around the world—the red ensign of
Great Britain, the hammer and sickle of Soviet Russia, the flags
of Norway, Denmark, Sweden, France, Greece, Portugal, Poland,
Spain, Honduras, Panama. I have seen them all on their lawful
occasions by glancing out of the window.

12. Even at night the Hudson River is beautiful—less triumphant now, because the water is like a strip of polished blackness, but it is festive with lights. A row of lights crowns the Wee-

hawken cliffs, and bright lights at the water edge mark the steamship piers. Downstream a cluster of bright lights illuminates the
Weehawken ferry slip. Although the river water is invisible, it
catches the lights on a burnished surface and romantically repeats
them. In the night the ferries look like royal barges—rows of gay
lights swiftly, silently crossing the river. Although the passing
ships steam by like hulking shadows in the darkness, their range
lights tell you how they are headed. There is hardly an hour when
brilliantly lighted tugs are not busily and expertly at work. Sometimes they study the river with searchlights that cut a sharp, white
gash through the darkness. I have seen them still at work at three
or four in the morning. When the barge canal closes in December the long tows no longer lumber slowly upriver. But the
city tugboats, towing a barge or two or hauling a dead ship, pass
in the night, green side lights showing on the upriver course, two
or three lights on the short mast at the stern and warm round
lights showing from the galley and engine room. We are on the
edge of great waters here.

Being a mature river, the Hudson decided its course of action
millions of years ago and has never given trouble to the people
who live, work, or play beside it. It never overflows in the spring
freshets. It does not run wild, tearing trees out by the roots, destroying the land or undermining buildings that have incautiously
put down their foundations close to the water. People upstate on
the Mohawk River feel anxious in the spring when the savage
flood waters rise. But you can trust the Hudson. It is benign as
well as beautiful. Having scoured a deep gorge through the hills
and one hundred thirty-five miles into the sea long before men
were fishing and hunting here, it has no more work to do and lays
a path of unhurried blue inland water through the shrill and
tangled metropolitan area where millions of people have an endless amount of work to do. "Take it easy!" the Hudson seems
to say. It is the city's only civilized friend at court.

13. "Mild for the season," says the Old Farmer's Almanac
for today, forecasting as usual by witchcraft. How "mild for the
season" differs from "the January thaw," which is scheduled for
the twenty-third to the twenty-seventh, I don't know. But the
temperature today rises to 55°, which is indeed mild for the

season. The air is still and misty. The sun is bright. The Hudson
is silken in texture, rippling when a ferry or tugboat steams by,
but otherwise silent, as though it were keeping its own inscrutable
counsel. The whole city seems lost in reverie. I visit the tugboat
dispatcher's shack on Pier 43. Not a tug, barge, or ship is tied up
to that pier or the adjacent pier. The dock is empty. During the
two hours I am there the telephone does not ring once, and no
one comes in except the fuel man collecting empty cans. A French
freighter goes upriver, creasing the lustrous surface of the water
as she steams by, and an American freighter goes down, sliding
quietly through the sunny warmth of the afternoon on her way
to Shanghai, which must be six long weeks away. Excepting for
occasional tugs, which seem to gather the river up in a hump
where their propellers grip the water, and the gaunt-looking ferries,
there is no other traffic on this great estuary that floods through
the largest port in the world.

When you consider the great investment of materials and equipment that lines both of the river banks—pier structures, derricks,
railroad spur tracks, to say nothing of manpower—it is astonishing
how idle the water front can be. I take the Christopher Street
ferry to Hoboken and the Hoboken ferry to Barclay Street to see
just how much activity there is in this section of the harbor. A
Dutch freighter is loading in Hoboken. The *America* is taking
stores at her pier in the Chelsea district. Lying at downtown piers,
there are, in order, a Belgian freighter, an American freighter for
Porto Rico, an Argentinian freighter just in from Buenos Aires,
a United States cruiser moored at Canal Street, a coastwise steamer
laid up, and two Isbrandtsen freighters taking cargo for foreign
ports. But two-thirds of the piers are empty, closed and quiet.
Looking out of the river I see nothing in the shimmering bay except three tugs moving barges through the sun-shot haze. "Mild
for the season," as the Old Farmer's Almanac expresses it. Not
many people are working today. Even the herring gulls are languid
and indifferent.

14. Among the luxuries of modern life, the morning newspaper gives me the greatest pleasure. For five cents from my
pocket, it provides me with a wealth of knowledge and thought.
I sit here by the south window in a soft chair, reading the reports

of my sentinels who have gone over the world once lightly for me, and will do so again tomorrow. I am royally comfortable at home. I have just eaten well in a warm, sunny room. Throughout the rest of the day I can read anything I please, talk to anyone who will listen, and say anything I like. But the newspaper sentinels have been scrambling for news in uncongenial places where travel is primitive and exhausting, the food is poor and, more than likely, people speak their minds cautiously—in China, which is broken and poverty-stricken; in Russia, which is insecure and hostile; in India, which is ridden with taboos and superstitions and is starving; in Germany, which is ruined; and in other parts of Europe, where it is difficult to keep clean, warm, well-fed and clear-headed.

The mechanical and human organization that brings these bulletins to me at fabulous speed is ingenious, intricate and expensive. If it were not done every day and night with incredible dispatch and efficiency, no one could imagine that it could be done. It is the product of years of labor and enterprise by thousands of alert newspapermen who have solved one problem at a time and built a service year by year—always digging deeper, always expanding, always taking on wider areas of human endeavor. Although the job is humanly impossible, it is done every day by reporters, editors, printers, pressmen and distributors who know how. The collective industry that has gone into it is almost incalculable. But it does not tax my strength when I read it. It asks nothing of me but a pleasant hour or two of my time. Every morning when I get up, I open the door and pick up the four newspapers that are waiting there. What I read is available to more than three million people every morning.

15. When a playwright becomes successful he settles down to a busy and fascinating life in the microcosm of Broadway. For Broadway is one of the best places in which to learn and practice the craft of playwrighting. Nearly a hundred new plays turn up here in the course of a season. Good and bad, they are worth studying. Moreover, Broadway is a compact, voluble community in which plays are fiercely searched, analyzed and discussed by a multitude of keen minds absorbed in the lore of the theater. Nothing in the writing or acting of a drama escapes the sharp

eyes that Broadway turns on its own product. From the point of view of craftsmanship Broadway offers a stimulating course of instruction.

But a serious writer needs more than craftsmanship in the composition of a play. He needs material; he needs material sorely. He must draw on the experience of human beings—either his own or that of other people. In this respect Broadway is virtually destitute. It is an eccentric and closed community that has very little concrete information about the life of the world. It is dependent upon information and experience brought in from the outside. President Lowell of Harvard once explained how universities acquire so much learning: "The freshmen bring a little in and the seniors take none out, so that it accumulates throughout the years," he said.

Something of the same situation applies to Broadway. Young people bring their own experience to Broadway from all parts of the country and from all groups of society. But for the most part they are isolated from the normal experience of ordinary people as long as they isolate themselves on Broadway. For the creative writer this can be a fatal experience. He cannot write illuminating plays about life from seeing other plays or from listening to the gossip that sputters around Broadway. At some time or other he must renew his association with people. Even books are not primary sources. There is no substitute for people.

16. If New York were not celebrated for more materialistic wonders, people would travel here to admire the splendor of the sunsets over New Jersey. They are regular events of transcendent splendor. A savage might be frightened by them, for they have the flaming grandeur of primordial catastrophe. They fill our western sky with tongues of fire. Since we understand the science of sunset colors we can admire them with equanimity. There is a commonplace practical reason for their barbaric magnificence. The industrial plants, railroad locomotives and steamships of New Jersey send up a thick cloud of sullen smoke that rolls across the Palisades, showers us with specks of grit and soot, and breaks up the light. The blue rays, which have a short wave length, are widely scattered. But the red rays, which have long wave lengths, pierce the barrier of smoke and come through to us. When the

sun gets low in the western sky, the light of the sun comes to us at a long angle through the whole width of the New Jersey smoke bank, and all the color except red is diffused. Our sunsets are, therefore, abnormally red. Our days end violently—the great western arch of the sky incarnadined as if the day had taken fire.

This afternoon the sun is transmuted into an enormous orange sphere when it slips behind the smoke above the Jersey shore. I can look at it with unprotected eyes as it sinks out of sight through the smoke, gas and fumes of a huge industrial bastion. For another quarter of an hour the clouds in the west are banks of crimson. South and north of the sunset pit the clouds are washed with blue, and blue swims on the placid surface of the river. Between the celestial blue of the river and the crimson of the sky the long crag of the Palisades wall is like a deep blue band dividing the firmament from the waters. Presently the Weehawken Boulevard lights come on, the jewels on the crown of the imperial Palisades.

Tomorrow's sunset will be quite different, for the sunset pattern is infinitely varied. The western sky never repeats a design. From day to day it retains nothing but its immutable magnificence.

17. Birthday of the illustrious Benjamin Franklin, 1706. Nobody has ever better represented the triumph of humane letters. For even in his old age, when he was everywhere recognized as a sage, he never lost the common touch, and was shrewd enough to represent America in the bewigged court of Louis XVI without a wig and with a staff instead of the customary diplomatic sword. Franklin was consumed with Yankee lust for personal success when he was young. He was thrifty and industrious, which are tepid virtues. But he was a printer, and printing is the most enlightening of the trades, since it deals with facts and ideas and reaches out to many people. It stimulated him and stored up wisdom in his mind. And when he became personally successful he did not settle back into stupid affluence like a rich merchant or banker, but rapidly expanded in many new directions—all of them humane in principle. He had an inquiring, reasonable mind and he saw things in terms of life on earth.

Moderation being one of his principles, and part of his formula for personal success, he was no radical. He always hoped that the

American colonies would not have to rebel against the king, who
stood for a stable society he respected. But when the break became
inevitable, largely through the influence of hot-heads, Franklin
made the choice of a reasonable and courageous man, and labored
for revolutionary victory as earnestly as he had worked for com-
promise. "We must hang together or hang separately," he said
with his usual pithy humor.

A revolution never had a wiser and more tolerant advocate.
During the age of reason he was the most eminent man in Europe
and he was also a prophet recognized at home. His homely good
sense could not be ignored anywhere. Nothing interested him
more than human beings. Although he made use of people by
skillful exercise of his native wit, he put everything he knew at
their disposal unselfishly. During a period when he was absorbed
in great intellectual and political affairs he still had time to write
a treatise "Concerning the Causes and Cure of Smoky Chimneys."
An ambitious Yankee, who was not above petty scheming, Franklin grew by natural processes, like an oak tree, into the patriarch
of the age. In his smallness as well as his greatness, he was all
American.

18. Temperature 28°. Barometer 30.40 and rising. On a nippy
though sunny afternoon Dyckman Street is preoccupied with city
affairs. Housewives are testing the fruit by pinching it, or buying
groceries. A red-faced picket solemnly paces back and forth before
a saloon where the barkeeps are on strike. Children are roller-
skating; old men are loitering in a warm corner protected to the
north. Several young men are fascinated with a new motorcycle
that is shining with chromium and has a battery of five lights on
the handle bars. They take turns noisily racing up and down the
street. Two miniature seaplanes circle above the river and practice
landing and taking off. Busy and compact, the city pushes up to
the riverbank where the New York Central freight trains clatter
slowly north or south on city business.

Fifty feet west, however, the influence of the city yields to the
influence of the moon, which governs the tides of the Hudson
River. When the tide starts running out, Spuyten Duyvil Creek,
which flows past an ancient Indian camping site, sends a raft of
city debris into the Hudson—sticks and boxes, an old Christmas

tree, electric light bulbs, boxes, and cans. Swirling out and in to the tide current, this stream of refuse floats out towards the sea and, at about four knots, slides into the molten silver of the sunshine on the south stretch of the river.

Long before the white men started navigating the Hudson three centuries ago, long before the Indians fished here and dug clams, the black ducks wintered on the Hudson under the lee of the forested headlands of the Palisades. Some things change almost imperceptibly if at all, and the ducks are part of the life that is timeless. They are swimming here today, as preoccupied with their affairs as the busy citizens of Dyckman Street, and as oblivious of history. One pair is picking over the refuse that sweeps out of Spuyten Duyvil Creek, floating rapidly downstream and then flying back like two black missiles as fast as the little seaplanes. But most of the ducks are floating in long rafts on the Jersey side of the river. They are restless and noisy, chattering to themselves. When they leap into the air, the sun catches the silver under their wings. When they glide back to the river, using their wings as brakes, they toss up two tongues of water that reflect the sunlight swiftly and brilliantly. The Indians have gone, but hundreds of black ducks come back to the pleasant winter quarters their ancestors chose many centuries ago.

19. At dinnertime Venus comes from behind the dark loom of the apartment house across the street into the arch of open sky above the river and moves down the west into the horizon. A clear beacon, like a powerful lighthouse, it is the most sisterly of the planets and the one people notice with most delight. It is almost the same size as the earth. It is a third of the way closer to the sun, and on that account gives off twice as much solar radiation. Under favorable circumstances it can be seen by the naked eye at noontime—a tiny white ball in the cerulean sky. It shines with such glory that it lays a beam of reflected light on the river like the moon. It is so large that it casts a shadow.

Venus resembles the earth in size, mass, and density of atmosphere, with a heavy bank of luminous clouds. Some kind of life on Venus is probable, the astronomers say. My mother saw the last transit of Venus on December 6, 1882. Be prepared for the next on June 8, 2004. In the meantime it adorns the sky with clear and limpid light and keeps our little system of planets neighborly.

20. At midnight the most cheerful place in town is the waterfront area in the Fifties. Above the dingy, frowzy, wind-swept neighborhood rise the floodlighted funnels of three ocean-going steamships—the three red funnels of the *Queen of Bermuda*, the two scarlet funnels of the *Mauretania* and the three heroic scarlet funnels of the *Queen Mary* towering into the black sky. Since the *Queen Mary* is to sail at 12:30, great rolls of puffy brownish smoke are billowing out of her funnels and are borne across the city by the icy west wind. Land was created to provide a place for steamers to visit. When they are in port they are ceremonial after the style of visiting royalty. They put on their best manners: they wear their flags and at night they proudly illuminate the immaculate paint patterns of their funnels. But sooner or later they escape from the city, with the bright images of foreign ports in mind; and as soon as they have made their way out through the Narrows into the wide loneliness of the tumultuous sea, they haul down all the flags except the company pennant, douse the floodlights and race, pitch, and roll through the days and nights of the roaring winter ocean.

Nothing man has built can equal the beautiful sentience of these modern steamers. They are independent, self-sufficient, and free. Unlike our brilliant hotels, they are not dependent on foundations driven down to bedrock or the innumerable services that buildings use—like water systems, power lines, and fire departments. Unlike a hotel, they are completely mobile and carry within their holds the powerful machinery that can drive their huge bulk twenty or thirty miles an hour on trackless courses hundreds of miles removed from the lane. They have to be designed so delicately that the great weight they carry is perfectly balanced; and is transmuted out of dead weight into life and buoyancy—weights acting on each other until the whole ship talks, groans and whispers and eagerly reaches ahead. None of the great structures men have built come alive like the ocean-going steamers that pierce the storms and dance on great waters. They deserve the veneration of all landsmen when they rest for a day or two at the foot of the quarrelsome cross-streets of the city. Although they poke their sharp noses close to city avenues, they are remote and detached, sublime, and free.

21. Although American culture is not highly esteemed in many parts of the world, American plays and books are only a little less popular than American goods. Many of our novels, dramas, and books of thought are hospitably received abroad; and, of course, there is always a consistent demand for our industrial goods. I am deliberately associating our literary products with our industrial products because, I think, they are both integral parts of the same culture. They cannot be considered separately. What a man does is as much a part of his culture as what he thinks. For a culture is the sum of all the activities of all the people who compose the nation; and in a democratic society there is no arbitrary difference in rank between the doers and the thinkers. Character is a stronger influence in a society than intellect, and character is the common element in all spheres of life. We all live together and eat from the same granary (which is probably the fundamental source of a national culture); and the scholar or littérateur does not categorically outrank the farmer and the mechanic. Quite the contrary: the scholar and the littérateur lose their usefulness to a society and become nothing more than barren symbols if they are arbitrarily dissociated from the farmers and mechanics.

Americans have always resented and resisted authority. The tradition of scholarship as a separate and rather exalted department of life has never taken a firm hold on American culture. In the early days of American history we were less interested in attracting members of the genteel classes than farmers and artisans — carpenters, masons, blacksmiths, and husbandmen. They could bring immediate relief to a primitive colonial territory that was being developed in a hurry and that instinctively was taking its art, literature, and scholarship from abroad. But the separation of the thinkers from the doers has never been accepted in America. For the life of man and nature is the primary source of thinking, dreaming and creating; and art and scholarship are bogus unless they derive from life directly.

Contact with life is the first principle of thinking and creating. Contact with libraries, museums, lecture halls, and theaters is hardly more than the secondary stage. For unless art and scholarship are constantly renewed in the streets and fields, the basic errors in thought and the idle whims of imagination can never be discovered or corrected, and theories, books, and plays will have treacherous foundations. The separation of the thinker from the doer weakens the whole structure of society. During the war in China I remember being amazed and baffled by the social division of a group of young Chinese officers who were studying veterinarianism. They wore the long white coat of the scientist and carried fountain pens, notebooks, and textbooks. But they would not touch the animals. They left the animals to the privates and noncommissioned officers. Social customs that are probably thousands of years old inhibited them from working directly on the raw material they were studying.

This little vagary of vanity followed China's ancient systematization of classes, which venerates the scholar, gives him unusual social prerogatives, relieves him of many of the routine chores and associations of daily life, and saps his personal independence. In the painful process of modernization, China will inevitably destroy this old departmentalization of social life and release the energies of the educated people for the good of the nation and the world. Thousands of young Chinese, and many of their elders, have already broken through the old barriers and superstitions. In America we lack almost entirely the classical tradition. But I wonder from the pragmatic point of view whether this may not be a good thing and whether it does not foster the flexibility and optimism of American life.

22. Let's not underestimate the value of the material part of a national culture. To look down on it disdainfully is to eliminate from good society the vast bulk of the population. Without a sound materialistic underpinning, the rest of the culture is hardly more than an empty pretense or a whimsical fairy story. People have to be fed, which is the province of the farmers. People have to be housed, which is the province of the building mechanics. Since people also like to be fastidious about their personal habits, keep warm in the winter, keep their food fresh in the summer, and move as quickly and easily as possible from one place to another, the plumber and the manufacturers of heating plants, re-

frigerators, and automobiles perform useful functions in society. Taken together with the millions of trained people they employ, as well as the farmers, they constitute the largest group in the country.

Since the process of manufacture includes many thousands of minute mechanical operations, industry has a low esthetic rating. The whole of industry is sometimes thoughtlessly dismissed as a kind of odious and inhuman routine and the American civilization is ticked off as "machine-made," as though it were mediocre and soulless. But there is a flaw in that thinking: a confusion of the process with the creative idea. For machines are not stillborn monsters or examples of perpetual motion. Behind every machine stands a man who imagined it for a particular use in modern life. Men made the machines. The basic idea may have been as valuable and enriching as the basic idea of a book or play—indeed, it may have been of greater value, for the ideas of many books and plays are poverty-stricken. As a product of human creative energy, the high-speed newspaper printing press is something particularly worth respecting. It is daring in conception, ingenious in design, and perfect for what it is intended to do, which is to give fast and wide expression to information and opinion. Although it is made of steel, it is a thoroughly human enterprise. A human being imagined it; a great many human beings have made the drawings and moldings to build it. Human beings operate it and keep it in repair. There is nothing soulless about it: it is charged with human energy and spirit. Deprive it of human beings for a few hours and see how long it will do its work. It is a tool that expresses part of the human spirit, like the piano, brush, crayon, and scalpel.

In its useful forms, materialism also is a product of spirit. The drive of a culture impregnates it and radiates from it. In wartime the central idea of a national culture is expressed through it directly, for the energy of all the people is concentrated on transmuting materialistic goods and weapons into a living defense of the nation. Materialism is decadent and degenerate only if the spirit of the nation has withered and if individual people are so unimaginative that they wallow in it. The machines that are now in existence and working efficiently are part of the capital wealth of the nation. But the imagination, skill, ingenuity, and energy that have gone into them are part of the national culture.

23. Since America has instinctively resisted the dissociation of art and scholarship from the elementary functions of society, I think our plays and books radiate the energy and imagination of the people. They are part of the mass culture. There is no such thing as "closet drama" which is too refined for the general public. Coterie art has no real importance or significance. Scholars are not venerated as a social class, but are under the same compulsions as other people to demonstrate their value as good citizens and neighbors by their understanding of human beings. Officers of the government have no prestige beyond what they earn for themselves by intelligent leadership and good conduct in office. Instead of being a badge of honor, the word "congressman" may even be a term of opprobrium. Criticism of public officers is often so bitter and malevolent that sensitive and high-minded people hesitate to leave the protection of private life and expose themselves to the savagery of political opponents. Although the disciplines of democratic culture are fundamentally wholesome, they are frequently painful and often unfair.

It is significant of our culture that our only indigenous philosophy is the pragmatism of William James and John Dewey, which evaluates ideas according to their usefulness. Pragmatism suits American thinking, and is probably the workaday philosophy of many of those Americans who hunger after idealism in their thinking. Americans are not much impressed with theories. Economically the country has outgrown its youth, but its culture represents a logical development from the independence, enterprise, and willingness to work that characterized the pioneers who settled here two or three centuries ago. The culture is still youthful. American literature is only a century and a half old, and perhaps less than that; and American drama is less than a half century old. By and large, American art represents the mass culture of the country. Nations with a culture developed out of the classical tradition are often troubled or confused by the impulsiveness—in fact, the violence—of the culture that comes from America. But they are also inclined to like, not only the machines and the industrial goods, but the books and plays. These are different aspects of the same thing. That is the fundamental point: Everything American, whether it is thinking or doing, pours out of the same reservoir of energy. God made both man and matter and is reported to have been equally pleased with both. At the time, that is; there has been no authoritative bulletin from Him since the time of creation.

24. Sun sets at 5 P.M., twenty-four minutes later than on the shortest day of the year, which was only a month ago. Although I was not aware of the figures until I looked them up in the almanac, I have been aware for a week that the days seem brighter, the nights less ferocious, and that something cheerfully progressive is happening in the universe. The brightness of the south is beginning to slip under the frozen bitterness of the winter. It is almost like an animal sensation. Although our minds may not be alert to it, our bones absorb it and the rhythm of the seasons circulates through our bloodstream. This worn and wrinkled planet is dipping mercifully towards the sun and we are toasting our frosty shins before the distant fires of spring.

25. "Tree sparrow" is a thankless name to fob off on so genial a bird. Like "ground sparrow" and "house sparrow," it is almost a term of opprobrium, especially for a bird that is not much given to perching in trees. The tree sparrow deserves our gratitude. In this latitude, where winter is generally brown and withered, when it is not cruel and icy, the tree sparrow is the most buoyant spirit in the landscape. As you march across the wasteland in Bronx Park, listening to the hiss of the wind in the dry grass or the winter creak of naked branches, sometimes a contralto twitter warms the air. If you follow it, you find the ground in that direction alive with tree sparrows, feeding busily in the grass or alighting experimentally on the crest of fragile weeds, where they swing as they pick the seeds. They are an active congress. When company comes, two or three of the more curious birds perch in some leafless bush, and, turning toward you, reveal the dark spot in the center of the unstreaked breast. Even in a storm, when the driving snow fills every corner of the day, the tree sparrows keep together, reaching for the tall grasses, tracking the snow, and still conversing.

That sweet, liquid chatter and the modestly fluted double note are no more desultory than the chickadee's prattle. The song spar-

row has only a dull "chink" for such weather; the junco is no
musician, and the occasional white-throated sparrow is generally
silent. But winter suits the tree sparrow's disposition. Coming
south from Northern Ungava or Newfoundland, where he attends
to his domestic affairs, he finds nothing in the New York winter
to depress him. On warm, sunny days, in some sheltered pocket,
he has a long warbling serenade for whoever may be passing. Excepting the Carolina wren, who sometimes makes the Palisades
ring, the tree sparrow has the finest of the winter voices. There
is a promise of bluebird rapture in it. While the best singers are
in the south, the tree sparrow preserves the tradition. He is no
commoner than the juncos or the song sparrows who spend the
winter here, but by virtue of his disposition he is the winter sparrow. "Winter sparrow" should be his name. His special genius
should be celebrated.

26. Temperature 5°. By noon it rises to 12° and snow and
sleet come racing down on a northeast wind. There are about four
inches of powdery new snow on the ground by midafternoon—cut
sharp in windrows, clear, soft, silent. Riverside Park has been
abandoned to the storm. There are no footprints in the snow on
the walk beside the river. After three weeks of freezing weather
the river is choked with ice which is swimming rapidly downstream, driven by the tide, current, and the wind simultaneously.
Herring gulls ride on the ice beside the streaks of open water.
Although the bald eagles have returned to the river, I have never
seen them south of the George Washington Bridge, and I see
nothing but herring gulls today. A dingy lighter, a brown ferry
off-course and two tugboats are steaming cautiously through the
grinding and groaning ice floes. It is a dark day, hung all around
with swirling gray clouds. Late in the afternoon the *Queen Elizabeth* roars several signals of warning as she gets ready for sea. I
cannot see that far downriver in the smother of the storm. But
for a half an hour I can follow the story of her departure in the
jargon of her steam whistle—the long clamorous notes as she backs
into the stream, the staccato bellow when she has backed far
enough, the anxious barks when she wants the tugs to help swing
her downstream, the final imperious signal to stand clear as she

gets under way with her own engines. By evening she will be racing through the lonely winter seas to England.

27. The most frightening aspect of government, if you want to think about it seriously, is the fact that we are ruled by mortal men. None of them is a superman; none is a prophet, oracle, or clairvoyant. Sometimes we innocently regard them as greater people than ourselves. Standing in awe of the office of President we unconsciously identify the office with the man. We see his picture every day; we read his name several times a day; we occasionally hear his voice delivering judgments on matters that vitally concern us. He has more power more conspicuously than most people in the country. There is an aura around the President. In our imagination we develop an oversize figure in harmony with what we think a President should be.

Alas, he is as you and I—fallible and bewildered. No one can solve the affairs of the world. Those that are known are incredibly complicated and interdependent—the political, economic, scientific, human, and spiritual all entangled and interwoven. Pluck at one thread, and other threads appear; one knot leads to another. But many of the problems of the world are not even known. Although the President is advised by experts, the experts are fallible, too, lacking information on vital problems in their own fields. In a dynamic world nothing is final.

We need supermen to rule us—the job is so vast and the need for wise judgment is so urgent. But, alas, there are no supermen. Those who rule us are like you and me. It is a frightening situation.

28. We shall never need another revolution in this country. The revolution we had was the fundamental one, and the democratic tradition it founded contains within itself the seeds of its own growth and fruitfulness. In the course of three centuries that include the industrial revolution, the expansion of capitalism, and the spread of communism, democracy has adjusted itself to changing conditions and sunk deeper and deeper into the lives of people and nations. It is not a scientific rationalization, which Marxism professes to be, but a basic moral and pragmatic principle. As the animating force of constitutional government, it began not in

1776 or 1787, but on May 31, 1638, when the Reverend Thomas
Hooker told the General Court at Hartford, Connecticut, that
"the foundation of authority is laid in the free consent of the
people." The democratic constitution that evolved the next year
from that declaration of principle withstood every shock of military and economic crisis until it was superseded a century and a
half later by a federal Constitution founded on the same theme.

Constitutional democracy does not guarantee capitalism, which
is an economic system, not a moral principle. Under democratic
government, capitalism has stimulated enterprise and raised the
standard of living. But democratic government has warily kept the
capitalistic system under control—regulating and restricting it in
the public interest and setting up socialistic projects, like dams,
waterways, forest preserves, housing developments, soil conservation, and T.V.A., to safeguard the national welfare. No one dis-
putes the right of democratic government to regulate capitalism.
For the logic of capitalism is to own everything and take control
of the country and its people. Democracy can dominate any economic system, including socialism or communism. It has a genius
for progressing with the times.

In 1848 Karl Marx, a German with little experience of liberal
institutions, believed that the workers ("toilers," in the sentimental
jargon) could not move forward without a violent revolution. But
by 1872 he understood that in some cases the objective could be
reached without a revolution. "We do not deny," he said, "that
there are countries like England and America, and . . . I might
even add, Holland, where the worker may attain his objects by
peaceful means." Being a moral principle, and not a pseudoscientific dogma, democracy has fallen heir to the unfathomable
resources of philosophy and religion with a seasoning of homely
poetry stirred into it.

29. Thomas Paine, born on this day in 1737, in Thetford,
Norfolk, England, son of a staymaker. America used him when
he was needed and repudiated him when he had been used, for
there is a streak of cruelty in all ambitious societies. Even in those
days we boorishly shucked off people of strong personalities as
soon as they began to bore us. A man of pure motives and ideal-

istic character, Paine was unprepared for America's latter-day intolerance for one of her earliest friends and advocates.

In November, 1774, Paine escaped from the grinding poverty
of England to America, which was fertile ground for a person of
his passion and talents and where he immediately became a man
of influence. Rebellious and belligerent, America was in the proper
mood to respond to his militant rationalizations against hereditary
government. In January, 1776, he published *Common Sense*,
which in simple though burning style set forth the principles of
the Revolution and called for "an open and determined Declaration of Independence." His pamphlet of fifty pages was a sensation. It anticipated the Declaration of Independence by six
months. A crusader who instinctively took part in the cause he
advocated, Paine attached himself to Washington's army during
the war and became the chief propagandist of the Revolution.
For his series of pamphlets entitled *The American Crisis* ("These
are the times that try men's souls.") were propaganda, designed to
arouse the support of the people. A brilliant rationalist, Paine
could turn the most hopeless situation to the advantage of America. His first *Crisis* pamphlet was read to all Washington's soldiers
around the campfires just before they crossed the Delaware to
attack the Hessians at Trenton. To Americans his flaming in-
volutions of logic were inspiring and one of the most effective
weapons used in the war. To the British they must have seemed
specious, cunning, and frantic. Intellectual combat and inquiry
were Paine's whole life. He had dedicated himself to it, and in
most cases gave all his royalties from books and pamphlets to
various causes. He was a dedicated crusader and, as nearly as
possible, gave his works to the people.

After the American Revolution he threw himself with equal zeal
into the French Revolution, *The Rights of Man* being his chief
contribution to the intellectual principles of that great upheaval.
"My home is where freedom is not," he declared. He championed
the Haitian revolution of Toussaint L'Ouverture. He gave Napo-
leon a plan for invading the British Isles, as well as a small financial donation. He was one of the earliest fighters against
slavery. In 1793 he published the first part of *The Age of Reason*,
which ridiculed and derided the mythology of the Bible. Although
he was a declared deist, this iconoclastic book raised a storm of
hatred against him. He was denounced as passionately as he had

been praised seventeen years earlier. Most of America never forgave him this attack on its religious faith. The election commis-
sioners in New Rochelle, where he had a farm, took away his
franchise on the grounds that he—the burning torch of the Revolution—was not an American. He died in poverty, June 8, 1809,
in a lodging house on Fulton Street. His tombstone on his farm
in New Rochelle was vandalized and desecrated. To this day no
one knows where his bones lie. Twenty years after his death William Cobbett, the British pamphleteer, furtively dug up his skele-
ton, secretly took it to England and stored it temporarily in a
warehouse. But it was lost before it could be reburied with the
honors Cobbett thought Paine deserved.

In the thirty-five most active years of his life Paine mightily
stirred many thousands of people, stirring them angrily against
him in the end. In America the outbreak of hostility to him may
not have been caused solely by his scornful broadside against the
Bible. Perhaps the mood was as much against him after constitutional government had been established as it was for him in the
insurgent days of the Revolution. He never changed; he was always
on the offensive. But America was tired of war and trouble. Perhaps it got more and more irritated with an old man who never
stopped finding crises and disturbing the peace.

30. For what it is worth, one should remember that the most
useful pipes for steady smoking are produced in America and England. They are designed for heavy duty—decent and respectable
in shape, capacious enough for a smoke of ample length and ab-
sorbent enough to transform the foul sludge of smoking into a
deep brown, redolent companion. Although French brier is the
standard wood, I was never able to buy in France a pipe as sound
as the ones America and England produce. Nor do Russians make
pipes that a man can rely upon for steady duty. Those I acquired
by necessity in Russia were made of a wood that tolerated tobacco without actively sympathizing with it; and the shafts were
so tiny that they clogged easily and could not be cleaned. Chinese
pipes seem to be influenced by opium smoking; they hold only a
few whiffs, as though tobacco were a coarse drug that had no
philosophical creativeness. Chinese pipes regard smoking as an
interlude and not as a full-time occupation. With the use of

American and English pipes a man can saturate not only his body but his mind and spirit with the glorious elixir of tobacco. It seasons the facts that are heavy and releases the ideas and impulses that are naturally buoyant. With an American or English pipe in the mouth, smoking becomes something more than an idle pastime: it becomes a form of constructive social activity. Is it merely an accident that the nations that produced the Magna Carta and the Declaration of Independence and that preserve most reverently all the civil liberties also produce the most useful tobacco pipes? Whatever the reason may be, the fact is that pipe smoking is best where civil liberties are most highly prized and respected. I should like to believe that pipe smoking helps preserve freedom in a world that has not yet learned what freedom is. In fact, I think I shall believe it. I am smoking a pipe at this moment.

31. Attending a performance at the Negro Theatre, I am one of two or three white people in a group of about one hundred Negroes. This is the reverse of the situation with which I am more familiar downtown, where white theatergoers outnumber Negroes by about the same proportion. There is no tension of any kind. I take a place in the audience as I would anywhere with no restraint. But between acts and after the play is over, no one even sees me. The Negroes are in groups of their own, talking and laughing with their friends. When I move about they look through me as if I were not there. When I leave, a place is imperceptibly made for me in the crowd by people who give no indication of being aware that I am alive. The attitude is neither cordial nor uncordial. It is not even neutral. It is nothing; it does not exist. No doubt this is precisely the attitude of downtown audiences towards the few Negroes scattered throughout the house. We do not crowd them nor make way for them. There is neither friendship nor hostility in our manners, which are elaborately, cunningly, imperceptibly evasive.

All this is the negative aspect of racial animosity. Behind it lie one hundred and fifty years of ignorance, fear, cruelty, and superstition. Ahead of it lie centuries of friction and misery. There will be no solution in our time.

FEBRUARY

February

FEBRUARY SESSION of the county grand juries begins. Before eleven o'clock more than a hundred men and women silently collect in a large courtroom downtown in Centre Street, take off their overcoats, and wait rather morosely. We have been caught by the summons that comes about every thirteen or fourteen months. No matter when it comes, it finds us unprepared, unwilling, and affronted. But the style in which it is written is explicit and ominous. The summons mentions penalties that sound alarming. The mood of the courtroom is portentous. Uniformed guards patrol the courtroom. The clerk is grave and vigilant. At eleven o'clock he starts reading our names in a slow, precise and imposing voice that rumbles with authority and warning. Only a reckless man would dare intrude matters of personal convenience into this solemn assembly. When the clerk has registered the names of all the people present, he puts their slips in the ballot wheel, turns it over a few times and calls the names he draws in a voice that sounds like an awful prison sentence. Aware of all the sins we have ever committed, and silent about all the laws we have broken (I occasionally smoke on subway platforms), we meekly take our respective places in the jury seats when our miserable little names are boomed across the room. Being selected for a jury is a chastening experience. After taking the oath on the battered Bibles kept in stock, and listening to the judge's charge, we retire to our respective jury rooms to begin a month's service in the administration of democratic justice.

The grand jury is one of the most venerable institutions in the judicial system. Justice cannot be administered democratically without it. The grand jury does not try cases. It authorizes legal accusations: before a defendant can be tried on a criminal charge the legal evidence on which the county will base its case must be presented to a grand jury. The prospective defendant can appear before the grand jury if he wants to and can bring witnesses to support his case if the grand jury consents. After all the evidence has been heard the witnesses, the attorneys, the stenographer, and the court attendants leave the room. Behind closed doors the members of the jury discuss the evidence informally. If the grand jury thinks that the uncontested evidence argues a presumption of guilt on the part of the accused, it votes an indictment (known as a "true bill"), and thereby gives consent to a formal trial in a regular court. If the grand jury is not persuaded by the evidence, it finds "no bill" and the accused is dismissed.

Since the evidence in most cases is simple, real and clear, the grand jury is usually convinced that the accused should be brought to trial. But occasionally the evidence is neither complete nor convincing, even when the accused does not appear; and in defense of a private citizen, the grand jury of private citizens does not permit a trial. In this way the grand juries introduce a decisive democratic influence into the administration of justice at the beginning and at the top; and erect a formidable hurdle over which careless or unscrupulous attorneys have some difficulty in crossing.

Although composed of citizens, grand juries have quasi-judicial functions. Apart from their function in the court they can and are supposed to investigate the administration of the prisons, the conduct of the police, the alertness and integrity of the justice department, the honesty of elections, the conduct of public officials, and any crime, whether or not it is formally presented by the department of justice. Grand juries have the right and also the duty to inquire into anything bearing on the honest conduct of public business. And since the grand jury represents the people's interest in the administration of justice it has a number of autonomous rights: individual grand jurors cannot be held to account for their votes or opinions in the jury room; nor can they be coerced or instructed by the courts, attorneys, or police. The jurors have complete immunity under law for their official actions.

Being a "body of citizens" they outrank the people's servants. Grand juries can call any public official to appear for questioning and for inquiry into official business, and can use the county apparatus for the purpose.

Since the grand jury interposes the judgment of ordinary, disinterested citizens between the accused and the district attorney's office, some political organizations have tried to eliminate the grand jury system or devise ways of circumventing it, for it keeps the district attorney and public officials under observation. Without the grand jury system the citizens would have no control over flagrant or organized abuses of justice, coercion of citizens by corrupt or dictatorial departments of justice, or political domination of the courts. In this huge city with its formidable bureaucracy and unscrupulous political organizations, a "body of citizens," representing all businesses, professions, races, and religions, has the responsibility and the authority to guard the public's interest in the conduct of public affairs.

Now we settle down to the month-long grind of appearing in the jury room every morning at eleven, and for two hours listening to, inquiring into, and judging the human frailties of the law, on the one hand, and the human frailties of fellow-citizens, on the other. Neither one is above suspicion.

2. Groundhog Day. Although we pride ourselves on our realistic modern thinking, the superstition of Groundhog Day is one we are reluctant to let go. Like our ancestors, who thought the world was flat, we go through the ancient make-believe every year of speculating on the length of the winter according to the weather on this day. Today is cold and sunny. The groundhog ("woodchuck" in more familiar terminology) could have seen his shadow today and in accordance with the myth would have crawled back into his warm hole. According to the old legend, there are therefore six more weeks of winter ahead of us. But as a matter of crude fact the woodchuck has already been poking out of his hole on warm days for the last two or three weeks. He does not wait for Groundhog Day if the weather is right. We all know that Groundhog Day is a myth, but we enjoy it annually. It gives the illusion of breaking up the long expanse of winter.

The myth is very old, indeed. Ancient Egyptians thought that bears were weather prophets; Europeans, wolves; English, otters. The early English settlers in America substituted the groundhog for the otter. People everywhere enjoy believing things that they know are not true. It spares them the ordeal of thinking for themselves and taking responsibility for what they know.

3. Today the winter-sealed Great Lakes and the frozen wheat-fields of Canada have fastened an icy grip on New York. We are wincing from a biting northwest gale. On Riverside Drive it is wild and freezing. A man can hardly turn the corner into it. Although it cannot be seen, it is tangible—like a flying wall of numbing coldness. It wails around the windows, making boreal music in a deep and inhuman tone. When I hear the wind I can feel the steel and brick structure of our apartment house trembling.

None of the Algonquin Indians would recognize the carefully landscaped river margins of the Riverside Park of today. But this northwest wind would seem familiar to them. And the broken ice that rushes downriver when the tide is ebbing and that packs against the eastern shore would still be a familiar landmark. Nothing from their civilization remains except some birds and the New York weather. Today has its frigid ancestry in the wind-bitten misery of the Algonquin Indians.

4. What we all need is more knowledge. The current world is shocking and violent, and we are likely to judge it on moral grounds. But the chief source of the evil everywhere is ignorance. We are ignorant of the Russians and Chinese, and they are ignorant of us. Despite the long years of intimate association and a common language, we are ignorant of the English and they of us. Out of ignorance they and we are constantly developing moral arguments to establish our respective national superiorities. The Yankee is ignorant of the Southerner, and the Middle Westerner is ignorant of the New Yorker. The Gothamite is ignorant of the people of the Bronx, who in turn are ignorant of the natives of Staten Island. None of us knows what is going on under our noses.

We tolerate differences of opinion in people we know; for, knowing them, we realize that they are like us essentially. They, too, work, play, marry, raise families, and worry; and they, too, complain of taxes and the White House. We tolerate differences of opinion in people who are familiar to us. But differences of opinion in people we do not know sound like heresy or plots; and, since they cannot be balanced against personal knowledge of the human aspects of the people, they sound alarming. There is a greater area of agreement throughout the world than any of us know. There are deeper reservoirs of good will. Most of the differences about which we grow belligerent do not exist except in the vast penumbra of common ignorance. Knowledge is the godfather of morality.

5. Although trade ranks below scholarship, art, and all the professions in all the ancient and many of the modern codes of social standing, it is the most civilizing of human occupations. It is the unrecognized agent of good will. It provides a solid basis for the peace of the world. Ideas moving across national boundaries raise suspicions and stir up trouble or resistance. Religions and customs divide the world into distrustful camps. But food and goods are the only things that can cross the borders of countries peacefully—arousing nothing more pernicious than curiosity and discussions about value. The manganese ore we import by the shipload from the Black Sea ports of Russia does not create political crises in America. The natural rubber that we buy from the Malays and Javanese does not make Moslems out of Americans. Anyone in any part of the world, whatever his morals may be, will gladly eat a can of Columbia River salmon or wear a pair of U. S. Army boots.

Trade has an honorable record in the history of civilization. It has been good for everyone. In the second century the Chinese gratefully learned from Persian traders how to cultivate alfalfa, grapevines and walnuts. The great hot, dangerous, sandy, tempestuous Gobi desert divided the Far East from the Near East and Europe. But traders, eager for a profit, crossed it and took glass to China from Greece and Rome and stimulated the art of porcelain there. From China Europe got peaches, apricots and medicinal herbs. The Arabs learned the art of making paper from the Chinese in the second century. Rome grew luxurious with silks brought from China, and the Old Silk Road into China is still traveled after all these centuries and still has an honored name.

America could not exist without foreign goods. Although we like to think that we are independent, we are virtually dependent on foreign countries for coffee, bananas, cocoa, shellac, tin, antimony, cadmium, manganese, chrome, nickel, asbestos, mica, quartz crystals, natural rubber, silk, diamonds, burlap, and cordage fibers. Nor have we enough sugar, oil, wood pulp, lead, zinc, and copper to supply our own needs. To keep our industries running, and to pay our politicians and professional calamity-howlers, we need the cushion of exports to foreign markets—about 10 per cent of our total production. That is the margin between normal prosperity and anxiety in this country.

Our automobiles and industrial goods are the soundest ambassadors we send abroad. The good trader will do business with anyone who will trade in return. Trade is the one thing both parties can agree on, and it is the soundest basis for wholesome foreign relations.

6. Queen of the neighborhood is Mrs. Rabinowitz, the plump, smiling, animated wife of the tailor. Mr. and Mrs. Rabinowitz work all day in a narrow, dim shop heaped up with other people's clothing. But Mrs. Rabinowitz is a lady. Her manners are good because she is friendly and likes to know everything that is happening in the vicinity. She sits at the sewing machine without being a slave to it. She tints her gray hair with blue and wears a ribbon in it. Although life has not been lavish with the Rabinowitzes, they can take satisfaction in what they have accomplished. Their son is a practicing dentist with a family of his own, and he came through the war safely. Their daughter is a highly paid silk buyer for a store in Washington.

Mrs. Rabinowitz is a cheerful little lady with a motherly attitude towards her customers; and the neighbors also drop in for gossip. Like many naturalized Americans, Mrs. Rabinowitz has a somewhat intolerant attitude of national, even regional, possessiveness. She says that she does not like Orientals or Europeans. She likes Americans but not southerners, she says. But she knows a southerner who wants to be an actor. Since he naturally is penniless, I know that out of the kindness of her heart Mrs. Rabinowitz does extra work on his clothes that she does not charge him for. "He's a very good-looking young man," she says, "and in that business he must always look well, mustn't he, dear?"

7. To Staten Island by the noon ferry. I would rather ship to
Java, Celebes, or South Africa. But the twenty-four minute voyage
at eighteen knots to the tidal port of St. George is a pleasant
substitute. Riding the ferries down the ocean channel we have
salt water under us, hissing at the stem, flaring back in a white,
foamy wake astern. The clang of the warning bell, the resonant
jangle of the loosened shackles, the blast on the whistle, the
vibration of the engines as the ship undocks, and the final grind
of the propeller when it finally takes hold—these are nautical
symbols that are always pleasant, for they mean departure from
land.

Up forward the wind is freezing. When we leave the protection
of the land the bow of our vessel is swept by a blast from the icy
northwest, and the passengers seek the lee of the main cabin.
Presently we round the outer reaches of Governors Island; and
setting a course a little west of south, we settle down to the
voyage to Staten Island, the bow waves leaping angrily to either
side, the cabin windows rattling, the decks pounding and grinding from the vibration of our powerful engines. An express vessel
in the passenger trade, we rapidly overtake the slower tugboats
and gasoline barges headed on the same course; and we show our
heels to the *Santa Isabel*, bound for Guayaquil, and the *Argen-
tina*, bound for Rio, which are sailing a course just east of ours
this noon. When we are well away from the land we pass the
gaunt and lumbering channel buoys, their clanging bells lazily
and dolefully sounding a lonely warning to mariners. Twenty-five
or thirty herring gulls follow us, searching our wake for food
churned up by the propellers. About half way on the course we
silently pass a sister ship headed in the opposite direction—a fine,
able, sturdy, well-found liner that steams briskly through the sun-
shot water. Approaching port after a safe voyage through clear
weather and a calm sea, we pass comfortably east of the dangerous
ledge marked by the Robbins Reef Lighthouse and accurately
charted in our sailing directions. Reducing speed we slide easily
into our company dock, making fast without scraping a fender.
After discharging our passengers in an orderly manner and putting their baggage ashore we prepare for the return voyage through
the inland sea to the island of Manhattan.

In comparison with other voyages this is a short one. But the passengers see almost as many landmarks as passengers do on larger vessels that have spent several days at sea. The patient Statue of Liberty, towering silently above the harbor mist, and the forest of skyscrapers leaping out of Manhattan look as dramatic from one deck as from another.

8. "The good old days" never existed. Today is as good as or better than any of them. In every age "the good old days" were a myth. No one ever thought they were good at the time. For every age has consisted of crises that seemed intolerable to the people who lived through them, worrying and wringing their hands. The first twenty years of my life, which concluded with the first world war, look tranquil and innocent to me now. But the things I remember, most of them vaguely, seemed like calamities to people at the time—the Spanish-American war, the death of Queen Victoria, the assassination of McKinley, the eruption of Mt. Pelée, the San Francisco earthquake, the financial panic of 1907. I can remember reading, but not believing, an article by Flinders Petrie that predicted a catastrophic European war in 1914. Those years were full of alarms and crises, and I worried then more than I do today. For sheer horror and destruction the world has never experienced anything like the second world war, which may indeed mark the beginning of the end of civilization. But we who survived have absorbed it. Even after this shattering experience, I do not envy my father who was spared it but was riven by other anxieties and troubles every day of his life.

9. Despite the numbers of the house sparrows and the starlings, the bird of the city is the herring gull. I can see forty-two herring gulls from my window at this moment. The herring gull is handsome and accomplished, and would be an object of wonder if he were rare. He has a snowy white body, which gleams brilliantly in the sunlight on the water front, and a beautiful gray mantle with black wing-tips. If he is not the most brilliant flier, he is the most accomplished and versatile. Usually he loafs alone on slow wing-beats up and down the river or across the bay. But when he is racing towards something to eat he can go swiftly. By stretching his wings skillfully he can practically stand still in a wind, lazily rising and falling on the air currents. He can also dive like a hawk, and even fly backwards, though this maneuver is clumsy and slow. Scientists photograph and study the flight of the herring gull to learn about the principles of aviation. He is the ideal of airplane designers. They would like to manufacture airplanes that could fly with the ease, grace and versatility of the herring gull.

The gull has thoroughly adjusted himself to the city. It suits his needs. A scavenger, he lives off the sewage in the rivers and harbors. He rides the waves in all weather. He sits on old posts, generally facing the wind, or the mooring buoys; or he blandly rides on floating boxes and timbers or the ice floes. He follows the Staten Island ferries by the tens and twenties, diving into the wake, wheeling over the top deck or planing in the air currents set up by these fast-moving vessels. Particularly in the mornings and evenings, he leisurely crosses the city from the East River to the North River, sometimes stopping in the Central Park lake for a sip of fresh water. But he does not nest in the city. In April or early May, all the breeding birds leave the city to nest on islands along the New England coast or the fresh-water lakes of New York and New England, where they have seclusion. They return in August to spend the autumn and winter among the ferries, tugboats, and barges of the harbor.

At various times of the year we have gulls of other species—the laughing, black-backed, ring-billed, Bonaparte, and, sometimes, the glaucous, and Iceland gulls. But the herring gull is our most common sentinel of the river and harbor. Living so close to Cosmopolis, he has acquired some of the burly boredom of the water-front characters.

10. "Brother" is the most sublime word in the English language. It denotes love and respect freely given without obligation. Friends have similar qualities of loyalty and esteem. But in brothers the bonds are deeper and the understanding is more profound. Nor does understanding between brothers have to be renewed by frequent demonstrations of affection, for it is permanent year after year and unspoken clear across the globe and possibly into eternity. The finest world that people can imagine is

the brotherhood of man. When all men are brothers the golden age will begin.

11. A young man comes into the office, throws off his coat and sits down comfortably. Tipping back his head and smiling with complacent condescension he establishes an exalted place for himself in a troubled world. The President is stupid, he says. The State Department does not know "what it is all about." He stopped believing anything he read in the newspapers in 1939, he says. His boss is a gentleman but old-fashioned. The company he works for is a good one but conservative. He may not be able indefinitely to adjust his more enterprising personality to company practice. "We will decide how well we like each other after a few more months," he observes. There is no social or cultural life in the small town upstate where he lives. His wife may not be able to adjust herself permanently to such an unimaginative town. After about an hour of similar observations about the general inequality of the world, he leaves. I hope he never returns.

12. Lincoln was born this day in 1809. Father Abraham! Lent, which began yesterday, is only a little more devout than this day, which is sacred in the American calendar. For Lincoln endowed the American tradition with a religious character that came out of the patient, sorrowful nobility of his private soul. Every year the newspapers and the radio broadcasters pause for a few minutes to express the country's devotion to a common man who has become a saint. For there is something of Father Abraham in all of us today and it is the best that is there. Whatever other immortality he found when his worn days were ended, he is passed on from generation to generation in the faith of Americans.

It is difficult to account for the wisdom, insight and humility of this lonely man without invading the sphere of religion and believing that he was divinely inspired. Washington had moral grandeur; he had strength and purity of character. Jefferson had grace and understanding. But these are treasures that can always be found in the frame of our world. Much of Lincoln belongs there, too. "I confess plainly that events have controlled me," he said, and on sufficient practical evidence, too. But there was more to Lincoln than that: spiritual awareness in the midst of an ordinary political campaign; homely good taste in all his associations; patience, mercy, sympathy, humanity, faith. There was a harmony in him tuned to something finer than anything I am aware of in this world. Father Abraham, the soul of the American dream!

13. The Hudson is completely covered with loose ice floes now. Where the tugboats push through it they leave a black lane curving through a white surface. The ice floats down to us from Haverstraw Bay. When the wind is from the north and the tide is making, the ice chokes the river from one shore to the other. There is a tradition that the North and East rivers "froze over" in Revolutionary times—as if the cold were deeper long ago. I have never seen our river frozen over, even in the winter of 1934, which was the coldest on record; and I should think that the tides every day would prevent solid freezing. The tugboat men say that both rivers occasionally "freeze over," and the oldest say that they can remember such occasions. But "freezing over" means to them a heavy collection of closely packed ice floes over which a man can jump and pick his way from one shore to another. One of them remembers a winter in which men could cross the East River in this fashion, but none of them remembers the North River choked solidly. I am skeptical of the tradition that these arctic-looking rivers have frozen solid in one great sheet of ice in New York. The tide rises and falls too high twice a day. In modern times there have always been too many steamers breaking up the ice as they navigate the river. The tugboat men say one steamer upriver and one downriver every day is enough to keep the river open to Newburgh.

14. Take Eighty-fourth Street as the meridian: Procyon now stands directly overhead at eight in the evening. The winter stars are slipping down the sky, already making way for spring and summer. Orion stood overhead in the first half of January. But now it has moved over beyond the housetops on the south side of the street. Sirius has moved up from Amsterdam Avenue to West End Avenue (my astronomy is a neighborhood affair). In a gap left by an apartment house that is being torn down, Sirius

sparkles so brightly that, at first glance, it looks like the landing lights of an airplane. It is hard to think that anything that bright can be fifty-one million million miles away.

By comparison Procyon is much dimmer. It is a steady white light on which an Eighty-fourth Street navigator can take his bearings and plot a straight course to the Broadway subway. Procyon (which means "Leading Dog") is the brightest star in the little constellation called Canis Minor. The term "leading dog" derives from the fact that Procyon rises a little earlier than Sirius (the "Dog Star") and so leads it into the winter night. It is ten and a quarter light years away (the sun reckoned at zero). It is ten times brighter than the sun, about twice as big and about twice as hot. It is advancing towards us at the rate of two and a half miles a second, though fortunately it is still a long distance away.

North of Procyon, and apparently sailing above Eighty-fifth Street, are Castor and Pollux, the twins. In another month Procyon will be over the south rooftops, and Castor and Pollux will command Eighty-fourth Street. The patches of sky visible here are small. But the stars that move through them are like the hands on the great clock of the universe, and we can always tell the month by looking at them.

15. There is no use complaining because the spring returns to this austere latitude so sluggishly. But this much can be said: It returns to Moscow more swiftly than it does to New York, and this has many charming advantages. In Moscow you have the sensation of rushing out of winter into spring at a tremendously joyous speed. Moscow lies at 56 N. latitude; New York, at 40.45 N. latitude. Since Moscow is so much farther north it has longer nights than New York in the dead of winter and longer days at the height of summer. Moscow therefore loses daylight much more rapidly than New York in the autumn, but it gains daylight much more rapidly after the winter solstice. Today Moscow has nine hours and forty-one minutes of daylight, and New York, ten hours and thirty-four minutes. But in the first fifteen days of February, the length of the days in Moscow has increased fifty-nine minutes in comparison with only twenty-eight minutes in

New York. In other words, Moscow has recovered thirty-one more minutes of daylight than we have in the same period.

In practice the sensation is very dramatic. In Moscow I had resigned myself to a long, dark winter which would have no end. But in February it occurred to me that the sun was getting up much earlier in the morning than I was expecting. The days arrived before I was prepared to meet them. After daydreaming about the situation for a few weeks I remembered that since Moscow is far north, the transition from winter to summer would therefore have to be much swifter every day than in New York, and I made a few astronomical computations.

The coming of spring is breath-taking in Moscow. It sweeps in at high speed as though drawn out of the Ukraine by swift horses. Your enthusiasm and expectations leap rapidly out of darkness into radiant sunlight. If you are a New Yorker you can hardly keep pace with the season. In Moscow spring, coming with a burst of light and glory, rapidly transforms the whole structure of daily life. This violent tempo of the seasons must have an influence on the Russian temperament.

16. No doubt about it, the most lethal theater audiences are those dominated by smart and fashionable people. They bring nothing into the theater except shallow, distracted minds and tired emotions. Professional egotists, they are only casually interested in the play. They cannot lose their identity in the ideas of an author, and they have only a shrill emptiness where the imagination should be. Although they have had more social experience than most people, their manners are rude. They are the rudest people who go to the theater. They come late and noisily, ignore the play, and disturb the rest of the audience. Having no regard for public safety or for the property of other people, they light matches and cigarette lighters during the performance, and between acts they smoke in the aisles and drop lighted butts on the carpets. Children brought up in the streets have a finer sense of behavior in public places than the smart people of the international set. Travel, wealth, education, and wide acquaintance have taught them nothing but arrogance. They can wreck a play by staring at it without knowledge, understanding, or sympathy. For

they have nothing to give. They are the unburied dead, brushed, combed, richly dressed, and expensively embalmed.

17. Entering Riverside Park at Eighty-fourth Street, I hear the thin chirp of a wintering sparrow. The shrubbery is full of dingy English sparrows who are as restless as a gang of young hoodlums. But under the shrubbery I see one quiet sparrow with a white line over the eye and a grayish-white napkin under the throat; he is scratching in the mud under the thicket, a member of the group, but detached in spirit. He is a white-throated sparrow. Possibly he has been here all winter without my having seen him, for he is inconspicuous and muted. But when the spring comes north in the next month or two it will transfigure him into one of the loveliest and most poignant singers in the north mountains. Now he is a white-throated sparrow, but then he will be a Peabody bird, shaking out his sad lyric among the dark spruces—"Old Sam Peabody, Peabody, Peabody, Peabody," the last cluster of notes in a minor key.

The thrushes are finer singers. In the mornings and evenings the hermit thrushes praise God and magnify Him forever. But the white-throated sparrows have a sweet, sad song that can be very nearly transcribed in the notes of the human musical scale; and they tell the story of the northern woods, which is pure, but lonely. Their song is the perfect sylvan reverie. It lasts most of the summer—getting a little sadder and weaker after the middle of July.

Now, in the damp chill of the New York winter, one vagrant white-throat is patiently searching in the mud for seeds that have dropped from the shrubbery. It is a strange place for him to be. The company he is keeping seems uncongenial. His plumage and markings are duskier than they will be six weeks from now when the yellow close to the eye will give his head a gayer look. He is virtually silent now. He is like a cello in its case put away in a closet, capable of rich sound but silent until awakened. In a few weeks spring will transfigure the white-throated sparrow into melody.

18. Nothing big is clean all the way through. And the great city, which keeps its head in the golden haze that surrounds the skyscrapers, tries not to see the dirt on the pavement and in the backyards. The city is too big. No organization can manage or control it now. Most of our streets most of the time are filthy with trash and fruit rinds. The city still pours tons of raw sewage into the river where it stinks and churns back and forth on the tides. Many of the school buildings have been obsolete for years. Some of them lack inside toilet facilities in a civilization founded on good plumbing, and some of them are as dried-out and inflammable as tinder. The schools are overwhelmed with children; the children for whom the schools are built are what the schools arc lcast ablc to handlc. Many of our tenements have no heat, no hot water, and no insidc toilcts. Large sections of the most valuable water front in the world are a shambles—crumbled and deserted or immobilized by the bloody tyranny of murder and crime. The streets are choked with traffic, or lined at both curbs with thousands of parked automobiles that cannot be driven because the streets are jammed. Although it is unlawful, as well as dangerous, to park automobiles overnight in the streets, there are not enough garages to house a quarter part of them. Attempts to solve the chaos of travel remove the chaos to other places. For the great, rumbling, battered, aging, impetuous city is too gigantic to solve the problems it creates, and it hardly keeps ahead of paralysis. The monuments to modernism—the steel skyscrapers, colossal building projects, scientific sewage treatment plants, the great bridges and tunnels, the superb parks—are hardly more than clean islands in a stagnant bog of decay and disorder. The incredible city is incredibly muddled.

19. Temperature 56°. For three days the thermometer has risen above fifty, and the deep, dirty, snowbanks have almost vanished. The reprieve from winter has come virtually unnoticed, although it is sensationally merciful. During the past six weeks we have been imprisoned in snow and cold, the thermometer touching zero briefly. Because of the ice in the river, the snow that has been choking the streets and the long period of freezing weather, fuel has been difficult to get delivered and thousands of

houses have been unheated. The house in which we live has been heated only in the mornings and evenings. Hundreds of thousands of New Yorkers have been uncomfortable and many have been suffering.

There should be a flood of joy up and down the streets as the thermometer rises and people can relax again. But we have short memories for discomfort. It is hard now to remember the cutting wind off the river or the iciness of my workroom or the numbing chill of the living room, although that was only three days ago. When a man is well fed he cannot remember the sensation of hunger. When a man is warm he cannot remember the numbness and pain of the cold.

20. People are all right. The world is full of trouble and alarm. But there is no real trouble with people taken on their own level as human beings. If we could live as neighbors—that is, purely on social terms—the problems of the world would be trivial. We all know from personal experience that the people of America are sound. Russia and China are the only other countries where I have lived for any length of time. The people there were as sound as Americans. They were friendly and fair; in some cases they were hospitable and open-hearted. As a correspondent I traveled widely in China, much of the way on horseback and foot into primitive villages and through areas infested with bandits. The few things I had with me were almost priceless there—a watch, a blanket, a raincoat, shoes, fur gloves, aluminum cooking kettles. I could not cautiously stand watch over my possessions which were in other hands during the days. But in two years I never lost a thing. On the contrary, I acquired gifts that I hardly knew what to do with. In three difficult years overseas in China and Russia I can recall nothing but kindness and good will from ordinary people.

"There's something wrong somewhere," as a troubled character says in a Saroyan play. It is not the people.

21. To Asbury Park to hear the thunder of the surf and smell the salt water. Two hours after they leave New York, southbound steamers pass Asbury Park a couple of miles offshore. This has been a cold day with a biting wind from the north. Among the

steamers heading south, the *Santa Clara* is throwing out a snowy bow wave as she steams eagerly towards the oily warmth and the gorgeous blue of the Caribbean. In New York harbor with the towering buildings and the Statue of Liberty as standards of measurement, the *Santa Clara* looks small. But off Asbury Park she looks enormous—tall and bulky against the steel-blue sky. Steamers pass in twos or threes all afternoon, some of them hull down and showing only a vagrant stain of smoke across the horizon. Once during the evening the lights of seven ships are visible simultaneously—all drawn as by a magnet towards the sun-drenched south.

Tomorrow and tomorrow and tomorrow! Tomorrow the *Santa Clara* will pass the tossing cockle-shell Diamond Shoals lightship off Cape Hatteras (the graveyard of the Atlantic) and then, heading a little west, she will slide blandly into southern waters off the Carolinas and Georgia. On the third day she will be steaming along the yellow coast of Florida, hugging the shore to escape the north pressure of the Gulf Stream; and the world she enters then will be idyllic—the sea and sky stained a rapturous blue, the sun bright, hot, and soothing. Today the crew, bundled in wool, try to avoid the icy wind. But two days from now those who are off watch will be luxuriating in the wind, as though it were holy water, and will be lounging at the rails in their under shirts, letting the sun bake and brown them.

The boardwalk in Asbury Park creaks with frost. Towards evening a snowstorm sweeps in from the sea and drifts softly against the shops and the summer arcades.

22. Washington's Birthday. The first break in the city's routine since New Year's Day, it delights millions of people who have hardly had time to look up from their desks for eight weeks. Broadway is choked in the afternoon and evening with cheerful people, and the theater treasurers begin to smile. The carnival spirit is cautious but it is genuine. There are formal patriotic exercises around the statue of Washington at the Treasury Building. But this is a pagan holiday. Not many hearts are stirred by memories of the founder of the nation, who wore himself out in the service of his countrymen.

Among our immortals there have been men with more brilliant

minds, finer imaginations, spiritual perceptions, and more social independence than Washington. Others had the great idea before they drew him into it. But even now we cannot too often thank God for the moral grandeur of the Virginia planter who stood almost alone through those bleak years, nearly deserted by his own countrymen. "I have almost ceased to hope," he wrote when, after five disastrous years in the field, there was no reason to expect anything but failure. But with the honor of a gentleman of character he went on, carrying in his pride the seed of a free country. When he addressed the unpaid and rancorous troops at Newburgh he began: "Gentlemen, you will permit me to put on my spectacles, for I have not only grown gray but almost blind in the service of my countrymen." Yet how long America kept calling for him—for the Constitutional Convention and eight long years as President. Even after he had at last wearily and gratefully retired to Mt. Vernon to enjoy the only life he loved, the country in a panic sent for him again to organize a new army, leaning with childish confidence on his native grandeur. No one dared to be without his support. Let us always renew our faith in men by remembering the long and freely given service of this tenacious, earnest, upright gentleman—the aristocrat who built the foundation of a democracy.

23. To look on art reverently as a holy thing outside the sphere of ordinary life is to miss its real significance. Discussions of art frequently assume that art is confined to the theaters, concert halls and museums. But that is making a parochial subject out of a form of human expression that began around the savage camp-fires and in the caves of primitive man and that still runs through every department of life—the art of government, the art of law, the art of education, the art of speech. In varying degrees we are all artists, practicing the supreme art of living, according to our abilities. For art is moribund unless it is firmly rooted in our common heritage and growing out of the needs of human beings. Yeats once said that the church mass "would lack authority were it not descended from savage ceremonies taught amid what perils and by what spirits to naked savages." Art must be an integral part of life if it is to survive. Sooner or later the world discards art

that no longer expresses human fundamentals, as it has discarded the bogus ostentation of the McKinley period in architecture.

It would be extravagant to declare that every man is an artist. Many men are obtuse and stupid. But many are genuine artists, despite the fact that they do not think of themselves in that role. Taking the raw materials of mind, emotions, and body they have created characters that have form and radiance. Out of disorder and jangle they have made something coherent that expresses the interest they have in living. If that is not art, what is? Although they may not be geniuses, they are craftsmen in their homely medium. To vary M. Jourdain's ingenuous discovery, they have been living art all their lives without knowing it.

There is no need of making the requirements sublime. If we keep them simple they are easy to recognize as we walk around the city streets, where we can find evidences of people who are making something out of whatever is at hand and giving it the imprint of their characters. In a row of slovenly dwellings, for example, you may discover one house where plants are luxuriating in the light at the window. They bring growth and grace into a morose environment. At Christmastime a row of candles flickers in one window in a dingy tenement: an old bit of folklore is setting someone apart from the commonplace. There is an imaginative garage man uptown who transcends the oily clatter of his trade by hanging paintings on the walls of his garage and discussing them with enthusiasm if you stop to glance in. A tugboat skipper stretches a white awning topsides in the summer, thus turning his battered craft into a Hudson River yacht.

Most of the coal barges that lumber back and forth across the North River are as grimy as their cargoes. But some of them are conspicuously clean, with tidy curtains hanging at the windows and gaily colored paint on the housing. They are romantic variations on the common noun "barge." In one of them a mechanic and his wife ride the local waves. He has rigged a radio mast like those on ocean liners and constructed a triple-mouthed fog horn that pugnaciously faces forward as though it intended to warn the *Queen Elizabeth* to pull out of the way. That barge skipper may have delusions of grandeur, but he enjoys himself. He has an idea that pulls things into a pattern for him and gives his humdrum life an amusing rapture.

24. Fine art, of course, requires more passion than that, and also an idea that is more widely illuminating. But the difference is one of degree rather than of kind. For they are also artists who have sufficient enthusiasm to take whatever materials are at hand and give them shape, direction, significance and meaning. It is said that the colored patterns in the feathers of birds are the product of superfluous energy, i.e., energy not consumed in the routine work of feeding and flying. Flowers that are sturdy bloom more brilliantly than flowers that are weak. Fruit on trees comes from abundance of energy. And so it is that some people have, for one reason or another, more physical and spiritual energy than others, and some of them use their energy to express spontaneously their pleasure in being alive. That is art.

In an ideal state men might gratefully squander all their energy on work. Making something, accomplishing something are the most profoundly satisfying joys of being alive. But for millions of people work is a precarious occupation, hard to find and meagerly rewarded; it is the basic chaos of the modern world. And in an industrial civilization most of the work that is available does not wholly satisfy normal aspiration. In large-scaled production a man's mechanical activity has no visible relation to creation; he has an imperfect sense of participating in a whole process. A carpenter building a hencoop derives a deeper satisfaction from work than one of the hands who is tightening bolts on an automobile or one of the office workers in a huge corporation. When the hencoop is finished it belongs to the carpenter more intimately than it does to the man who hired him; and if the carpenter has done an honest journeyman's job, he can enjoy it every time he passes by.

As things go in this world, the carpenter on a small job that he can mentally encompass is a lucky man, for his mind and hands are employed on one of the useful arts. But millions of people have to look outside their daily chores to fill the emptiness of their workaday lives. Let it be acknowledged at once that they do some remarkable things by way of compensation. That is the primary source of the amateur theatricals that keep thousands of people faithfully rehearsing after hours all over this broad land. That is the source of the amateur choruses that endure a proud director's contumely all winter. Out of frustration has come the passion for amateur photography that conjures beauty out of the most unlikely places and lets as much light into the hearts of photographers as it does into the lenses of their cameras. When people are blocked off in one direction they overflow in another and make something beautiful or vital, or both, out of material that is lying idle.

For art is not a separate chamber of life or the exclusive property of cultivated people. It goes down through the whole structure of life. It is the words we speak and the clothes we wear and the friendships we cultivate in passing and the stamp of individuality we give to our homes. The savages began it with the dance. Although civilized people have refined it into myriad forms of common and high expression, they have not civilized it out of their systems. And the raw materials of art are the commonest property we have at our disposal—mind and heart, eyes and hands. "What a piece of work is a man!" Hamlet exclaimed. Man is not categorically a work of art. But millions of people make art out of him by keeping their imaginations alert and taking up the slack in the day's living. There is nothing occult about art.

25. Although a home is intimate and personal, it is a piece of property. The relationship of the tenant to the owner in New York is a property relationship that reveals the unwieldy size, the boorishness and greed of this gigantic city. The tenant wants a home, as warm, attractive and comfortable as possible, and he pays the money that makes the property valuable. But the owner is interested chiefly in the real estate market. Some people have lived for twenty-five or thirty years in the aging, crumbling, depressed apartment house where we have lived eight years. But they have no rights or privileges except by recourse to the law which tempers but does not remove the tyranny of property over individuals. Most of us do not know who the owner is at any particular moment. I lived here seven years before I set eyes on the landlord. For the building has been sold several times to people gambling for a profit. Since the owner's only interest in the building is the value it may have in a fluctuating real estate market, the agent, the janitor, the porters, the elevator men are not interested in it as a community home for the tenants. No one is responsible; no one cares. We pay the bills to keep the property running, but we live here on sufferance in a dirty, deteriorating building owned by absentee speculators who do not know who we are. Except in rare cases, residential tenants in New York City are pawns in a real estate gamble that has eliminated the human being. There is a price on the head of every tenant who wants a home.

26. Outside a large downtown building there is a uniformed guard whom many people regard as whacky. Standing erect with his hands in his uniform pockets he sings all day in a round, deep, resonant voice—musically competing with the grinding traffic. There is an ironic twinkle in his eyes. His greetings to the people he knows are ironically formal—"How do you do, sir. Lovely weather, sir," with just an edge of mockery. Day after day, week after week and year after year he plays a part amid the jangle of the streets where everyone except him is in a hurry. He preserves a mock heroic standard through the seasons which never seem to touch him. Singing with a great and rolling volume he isolates himself from the madness that rushes by him. Behind that rubicund mask of official affability, who knows what he is thinking? I don't, but I doubt that he is whacky.

27. There is one sweet compensation for the harshest of the seasons: the evenings are long. When the sun sets at 5:44, the night spreads over the city before 6:30 and we shut out the world with lamps, newspapers, magazines and books. Outdoors the automobiles are still speeding up and down the highway; and the heavy passenger busses grind along the Drive, groaning to a stop when the traffic lights change, wearily getting under way again when the green light winks on. In our apartment, which seems to be the lighted eye of the universe, we are warm and comfortable, and occasionally we can stay here all evening. Time, which is so impatient during the day, immerses us in the soft silence of the night—effortless and soothing, with an endless margin of good will. It is personal. Nothing can separate it from me. I can squander it by making profligate use of it—poking into savory corners of the newspapers that ordinarily I have to skim, looking through pamphlets that accumulate during the week, getting a bellow of anarchism in one and a scream of alarm in another (all the pamph-

lets sent to me seem to be revolutionary) or subsiding into the capacious comfort of a book. Oh, I have all the universe at my disposal in the winter evenings I spend at home. I can watch the play at the Globe Theatre, where the acting is big, round, and booming and the audience is saturated in wonder; I can listen to the grandiloquent talk in Gough Square off Fleet Street; walk up Fairhaven Hill in Concord; round the Horn in the *Pequod*—one of the madmen hunting the evil whale; or I can clamber breathlessly up the malevolent cone of Mt. Everest, the rocky slabs on the summit all fiendishly pointing downward. I am tossed loose in the universe—testing the mineral elements of Aldebaran, sledding through the mindless, shrieking cavern of the Arctic to the North Pole, hunting the blue tiger in Fukien Province, or steaming cautiously up the Madeira River to Porto Velho to deliver a cargo of English coal. The ceilings are only ten feet high in my apartment and the walls are not much farther apart. But the space is limitless in the winter evenings, the thoughts are bold, the phrases pithy, the men are brave and mighty and their deeds are heroic. Like the bird of dawning, they delight the long winter evenings at home.

28. At the completion of its tour of duty the grand jury is discharged by the presiding judge, who convened us on the first of the month. We have acted on one hundred and fifty-six cases, forty-one of which we have dismissed. We have ordered a fresh investigation of one case that is suspiciously ambiguous. In the one hundred and fifteen cases where we have found indictments, the defendants will now stand trial before formal trial juries and will have a chance to defend themselves under the protection of the criminal law. Most of them will be convicted, I believe, because the evidence is explicit and decisive.

But most of us feel prouder of the forty-one cases that we have dismissed, for this is the point in the criminal system where the judgment of citizens is most humane and wholesome. We have dismissed these cases for a number of reasons. In many of them the evidence was weak. In others the plaintiff appeared to be no better than the defendant, the pot pursuing the kettle by law. In a few we decided that criminal prosecution would not solve the problem. Two or three of the defendants we thought were sufficiently punished already by the grim process of arrest, arraignment, and imprisonment. Some of the crimes seemed to us to be too trivial—or, in one or two cases, too hilarious—for criminal prosecution. The reasons for dismissing cases have been various—in most instances rational, but often purely human, expressing the sympathy of one human being for another who is in distress and needs forgiveness more than punishment.

The law is no better than the people who administer it. But the law would not be as wise as it is if juries of citizens did not bring to bear on it the common sense and normal good will of the layman. Our jury did not know much about the law. But it was composed of businessmen and professional men, some who have retired from active life, and two alert and sensible women designated as "housewife." As a group we may not know much law but we know a lot about the frailties and passions of human beings. Everyone in daily life carries such a heavy, mixed burden on his own conscience that he is reluctant to penalize those who have been caught. Most indictments in a grand jury are voted without a sense of vindictive rectitude. Not many grand jurors feel grand when they leave the jury room.

MARCH

March

The annual warning has been posted: Income taxes due in fifteen days. In government some mistakes are basic and fundamental, like the power to tax and the protective tariff. Although we know that they are irrational and throw everything else out of balance, we cannot correct them now, for a vast structure of customs and business is founded on them. In science the principle of entropy means that accidents cannot be corrected. If a boulder falls off a mountain and crashes into many fragments below, there is no power in nature to reassemble the pieces and restore the boulder to its original position. The accident is permanent. Nature must construct a new and presumably inferior balance on the basis of what is left. It is so with the power to tax. The single tax on land values is logical and equitable, and could produce all the revenues the nation needs on a rational basis without robbing those who do not share in the increase of values. But by the time the single tax was formulated as a theory, the state was already deep in the pockets of the defenseless and had already given special recognition to land owners and had established a society on the basis of privilege and protection. Nothing can be done about it now without ripping out the foundation of our society.

Relatively our society is free. But the steady expansion of the state in response to successive crises has constructed a predatory tyranny that we dare not recognize, it is so terrible. Now the tax collector has access to our private affairs, reaches into the vitals of business and into the seclusion of the home, sits in judgment on our earnings and expenditures, and arbitrarily decides how much he can safely carry away. The power to decide has passed from us to him.

For the sake of self-respect we pretend that the tax collector is honest and applies his authority equitably in the public interest.

In point of fact he is unscrupulous. Operating on the principle that the public is crooked, he resorts to blackmail, intimidation, and slander. Since the power of the state is greater than that of most individuals, even the honest citizen finds that the burden of proof is on him and that, at cost of money and convenience, he has to defend himself against a furtive tyranny. Every citizen is at the mercy of petty officials cloaked in a little brief authority. The situation is so monstrous that you who read these lines think that I am exaggerating. You do not want to believe that you are helpless. You regard those who resist abuses as eccentrics or subversive. But the power to tax is the power to rule, and it has passed out of your hands. We cannot do anything fundamental about it now. The time for decision was centuries ago. Relatively we are still free, for we can tell the truth about the tax collector, who is prying into our private lives at this moment, keeping a dossier on individuals and shaping our destiny in society. But our freedom is no more than relative. By giving ourselves over into the hands of the tax collector and countenancing methods he has learned from the gangsters, we have submitted to the despotism of contrivers, bullies, informers and crooks. From the moral point of view this is so frightening and degrading that I do not want to think about it because I cannot do anything about it now.

2. In the back of every mind these days, there is a terrible thought: man has ingeniously devised the means of his own destruction. This is only an idea, but it has given everything in life the illusion of being temporary. Perhaps the sunrise this morning was the last one and New York is going through the slow dance of its last day. With a few atomic bombs men can demolish the achievements of thousands of years of thought, work, and dreams. In less time than it takes to write this paragraph, doom can crack wide open and devour in one savage flame everything nature and man have created. Our little thoughts, our pleasures, troubles and plans, lie thin on the surface of this terrible knowledge that primeval chaos is less than a second away. If anything is left, the citizens of some future state may put together a few fragments of records and find that our civilization began to go to pieces in 1945 when intelligence lost control of the world.

Why do we keep on planning for the future and educating the

children? Is it merely an old habit, the dying momentum of the
ages? No doubt it is. But it is also an act of faith growing out of
experience. Men have survived so much horror and violence and
have hung on to existence so tenaciously that no one knows what
powers of endurance, accidental or intelligent, men still may have.
For centuries men have been picking up the pieces and beginning
again. The facts of the atom bomb are catastrophic—perhaps final.
But those of us who are not yet dead have unknown powers of
endurance. There is still one more chance.

3. Temperature 8°. After a soggy snowstorm, the northwest wind
clears the skies and blows us another tingling winter day with a
cold blue sky. The river is again half-choked with broken ice that
sparkles in the brilliant sunlight. Shaken out of our vernal dreams
by the cutting whiplash of winter weather, we turn up our coat-
collars and, grumbling bitterly, hurry along the ringing pavements
in the icy wind.

But I can see that the back of winter has been broken. Although
the day is bleak it is deluged with light, which is the decisive fac-
tor. Believe what you see, not what you feel at this time of year.
Daylight has increased an hour and twenty minutes since the
shortest day of the year. Today the sun sets at 5:56. Surveying
the visible world from my window on the river, I have a homely
gauge that shows how swiftly the season is moving. In January
the sun sets behind a church steeple in Weehawken, west of the
ferry landing. But today it goes down in a flare of flame behind
a tall apartment house a mile farther north on the New Jersey
boulevard. By measuring with my eye the distance between the
church steeple and the apartment house I can see how far the
season has moved while we have been shivering. That is a dramatic gauge of solar distances—sounder than the thermometer,
more authoritative than the ice floes in the river. The great decision is being made in the south and it is a good one. The north
is losing jurisdiction.

I wonder whether there may not be another human sense that
recognizes the change of the seasons. Is not this immortal rhythm
born into us? Is it not the seed of millions of years in human experience, which gives us the ageless expectancy and keeps us facing
forward? Although our ordinary senses are frozen today, more

rigidly than in most days of the winter, we know in our hearts
that there is not much winter left and that presently the buds
will be swelling, the catkins lengthening, and the forsythia blooming. Did we learn this last year, or millions of years ago when our
forebears were squatting in stinking caves?

If we did not have this universal knowledge in our bones and
flesh, the change of the seasons might seem portentous and frightening, particularly in the autumn when life seems to die all around
the landscape, the light dwindles and the warmth goes out of the
days and nights. But no one is worried. We do not learn to have
faith in the universe by personal experience. It is born into us. I
may have learned in the caves of Europe millions of years ago
that today's arctic weather is merely covering the retreat of winter; and that if I survive today I can rejoice tomorrow.

4. Soma Morgenstern observes that anti-Semitism is most virulent in places where there are few Jews. New York proves his
point. Of the 4,770,647 Jews in America, 2,035,000 live in New
York City, and thus compose about 20 per cent of the metropolitan population. The result is that there is less anti-Semitism in
New York than in any place in America. For anti-Semitism is superstition founded on ignorance. When the ignorance disappears, the
prejudice disappears also and that is what is happening. No one
can estimate what the Jews have contributed to New York. Other
groups match them in business and finance. But no group could
duplicate or provide substitutes for the gifts they have brought
to art or for their brilliance as thinkers, students of affairs, and
philosophers. They have enriched the life of New York; they have
kept it alert, broadminded, flexible, and hospitable to ideas. New
York would quickly lose its drive, its spontaneity, and its cosmopolitan flair if the Jews were not every day pouring warmth and
vitality into it. They have superstitions, too, which contribute
some ancient strains to the tribal folklore of Cosmopolis. I would
not want to live in New York without the counsel and friendship
of Jews.

5. During the blustering March weather the coziest refuge I
know along the water front is the tugboat dispatching office on

Pier 43 at Christopher Street. It is a tiny, corroded metal shack equipped with a stove huge enough to keep the temperature at ninety unless a northwest gale is sweeping off the river. Prosperous business enterprises are never so hospitable. The watchmen at the U. S. Lines and Grace Line piers are cold-hearted and adamant. I have never been able to establish friendly relations with either of these prosperous organizations. But by good fortune Pier 43 has been deteriorating for years. It used to be one of the city's recreation piers, i.e., it had a gay overhead deck where families in the neighborhood could take the river air in warm weather. But when the overhead structure became unsound it was "temporarily closed for emergency repairs" and remained in that state for about twenty years, when the overhead deck was dismantled and carted away. The shipping pier used to be a busy place. Freight steamers from Hudson, Catskill, Kingston, and Newburgh used to bring apples, hay and country provender there every morning and take express goods upriver every night. But the combination of motor trucks and good trunk roads gradually destroyed the river freight service —incidentally increasing costs of transportation about 300 per cent. The river freight ships and their country crews have long since disappeared. The shack at the end of the pier has also dwindled. It was originally a solid, metal building in three sections—full of desks, offices, telephones, and storerooms. As the business of the pier shrank, the shack grew rustier and rustier. Ultimately, a heavy snowstorm broke down the east section. Temporary repairs sealed off the two remaining sections so that they could still be used. By spring the shack management had concluded that the most practical solution would be to dump the wreckage of the collapsed section into the river. This was done successfully and furtively at night. In due course the second section broke down under the weight of another heavy snow. Following established precedent, the management disposed of the second section in the same fashion. This left one section—rusty, rickety and drafty, but somehow cozier than the entire original building, and I have spent many warm and pleasant mornings there in good company.

6. In the great days of Pier 43 Captain William Westervelt used to pilot his tugboat, the *William Westervelt*, around the

harbor on important business with a crew consisting of his son and some agreeable friends. But at the age of seventy-one he has swallowed the anchor. When his tug is not lying alongside, someone else steers her in the service of the Meseck Towing Line, a big corporation. Captain Westervelt is now in command of the shack, playing poker and taking part in the conversation with the same iron-lunged voice that he used to hurl out of the windows of the pilot house of his tug. The tug was built in 1896 at Noank, Connecticut, for the brilliant White Star Line. She was queen of the harbor tugs in those days. Now her engines are obsolete and use vast quantities of water. But they are still powerful. She also has an oak bottom. "That's the best part of her now," says George, an old Westervelt crony. "She's hard under the water, but I guess she's getting soft on top. Don't lean too hard on them deck rails."

Broken-down business is more hospitable than business that annually shows a smart profit.

7. The water front is frontier country, and the work done there is rough, heavy, and dangerous. You might expect the longshoremen, who do the work, to be hard to discipline, like the old frontiersmen. On the contrary, they are the most thoroughly disciplined—"cowed" might be the best word—of any of the heavy workers in the city, and they are subject to the humiliation of a primitive hiring system, known as the "shape-up." As I come into West Street this noon, a shape-up is in formation in the street before one of the U. S. Lines piers. About one hundred longshoremen are drawn up in a wide semicircle. They are meekly watching the stevedore at the pier gate who is picking a gang to work a cargo ship that has just come in. The signals the stevedore gives to the men he chooses are too fast and small to be recognized by people like myself who do not understand them. But as the stevedore, a paper in his hand, rapidly picks his gang, groups of four longshoremen fall out of formation and, with their working clothes under their arms, walk with a loose gait into the pier shed. They can work; they can take home five or six dollars tonight. They have presumably made some private and elusive agreement to kickback a dollar or two to the stevedore who has the authority to hire them. When the full gang has been chosen, those who remain in the shape-up formation saunter away morosely, gather in

idle groups on the street corners, or drift into the saloons. Victimized by racketeers who control the water front, the burly longshoremen are the most helpless laboring people in the city. They can move mountains of cargo but they cannot take care of themselves. The shape-up is the most degrading human spectacle in New York. In appearance as well as in fact, it retains the peonage relationship of worker to master.

Walking down the water front I can see some of the things America is shipping to foreign countries today—cotton for Gothenburg, Fords for East London, Durban and Lourenço Marques, steel rods for Piraeus, small automobiles and trucks for Bremerhaven, Fords and jeeps for Santos, Fort de France and Guanta, a red fire engine for Maracaibo, four-inch steel tubing for Paramaribo. All this cargo will pass through the hands of water-front brigands who get rich while the longshoremen do the work. Although the ships and the cargo machinery are modern, the working conditions are medieval.

8. Several sharp and ardent people are discussing politics with nervous desperation and the future of the world looks catastrophic. The more we talk the grimmer the prospect seems to be. But the room is filled with an almost mystical emanation of calm, patience, and reassurance. For Beauford Delaney, an artist and son of a southern Negro preacher, is in the room—listening, smiling, and wondering. No one knows exactly how Beauford lives. Pegging away at a style of painting that few people understand or appreciate, he has disciplined himself, not only physically but spiritually, to live with a kind of personal magnetism in a barren world. He lives in a battered rookery in Greene Street. But he lives in an aura of splendor. The one room he inhabits he has painted white—walls as well as ceiling, and also the barrel-shaped stove that keeps him warm when he can afford coal in the winter. Coming up the dark stairway you suddenly walk into magnificence when you enter his room. His personality is the same. His eyes are bright, his lips smiling, and his voice is deep, warm and melodic. He dominates any group he joins. Although other people in the group may have sharper minds and more abundant information, Beauford has the authority of a prophet. Everyone feels relaxed and secure when he is around. He is humorous and gentle. When

he speaks, his words rise out of many long, pinched years of lonely meditation. The words are vague; the ideas are amorphous. But he radiates goodness so abundantly that everyone instinctively defers to him. There is no safe defense against simple goodness.

9. Since 1667 the stone manor house with its steep roof at Tottenville on Staten Island has been looking out at the silvery bay. This is the venerable house where Franklin, Rutledge, and John Adams heard and rejected Lord Howe's proposals for peace in 1776. The house now looks grand, as though it were proud of the history it contains. But the world in which it stands has changed from provincial to cosmopolitan and the pleasant country seclusion has evaporated. The view across the bay is ruggedly industrial now. There is a great railroad bridge across the Raritan River mouth; the monstrous rumble of the trains thunders across the shining, flat water. Modern industry has invaded and contaminated the vast bay. A huge tanker, the *Louisiana Sun*, lies at anchor today, just outside the channel. She is taking on galley stores; she is warming up her engines, and a cloud of yellowish smoke pours out of her funnel and sweeps across the water on the south wind. I can hear the master of the ship giving querulous orders over the voice amplifier. A police launch tears out of the Kill and heads around the island. Planes are drumming through the sky. Since this is the oil depot of New York, the stones on the little beach are covered with black scum. The beach is also strewn with grapefruit rinds, old automobile tires, and the hideous trash of a callous city.

But if the manor house notices, it must take comfort in the shore and sea birds that still come and go as if nothing had happened and as though nothing more imposing than naval barges ever invaded these quiet waters. The birds are the symbols of timelessness. A bufflehead—not much bigger than a robin—is placidly swimming a few yards offshore, diving for shell fish or rising half out of the water on lazy wings. There are a number of other ducks offshore—scaup, a few goldeneyes, and a number of old squaws just coming into their nuptial plumage. Some of them already appear to be mated, for they swim and dive in pairs. There is a dead baldpate lying limp on the shore, probably a victim of the oil on the water. Herring gulls fly leisurely out of the Kill. And here comes a small, mild gull patrolling the beach and flying not more than ten feet over my head as he follows the south end of Staten Island. He is a Bonaparte gull, still in winter plumage. He is the smallest and most beguiling of the gulls.

At length, the *Louisiana Sun* ponderously ups anchor with the sharp rattle of the chain coming link by link inboard. With a white explosion of water under her counter as the propellers take hold, she swings into the ship channel and bellows a departure signal that awakens the drowsy echoes. The little bufflehead does not notice her. Although she displaces ten thousand tons, she does not intrude on his ancient empire of sun, water, air, and shell fish, and he serenely bobs up and down on the little waves that lap ashore from the propellers. The ancient manor house still stands solid amid the old trees on the lawn leading to the water edge.

10. Having been summoned for the quarterly check-up by Dr. S. M. Frank, the compassionate dentist, I appear unhappily but dutifully at his office. A solid, white-haired, Dickensian professional man, he greets me at the door with a mixture of paternal hospitality and sympathy. "Have you been comfortable?" he inquires, meaning, "Have you been free of toothache?" After I have sat down in the chair and he has washed his hands, he proceeds gently to the preliminary examination, occasionally emitting thoughtful sounds of reassurance, and occasionally expressing tentative doubt. A convinced scientist, he never jumps to conclusions. Using magnifying glasses, he looks more carefully and experiments with one of his thousands of instruments; he takes X-ray photographs, and makes a diagnosis, balancing what he sees against what he knows. Two or three times a year he decides on immediate action. While he is assembling his equipment, I gloomily resign myself to what is inevitable, consoling myself by thinking that in another hour I shall be released to mingle happily with the society of free men.

For the pain and expense of dentistry are crosses that nearly everyone has to carry through life. No part of the body has failed so completely under the unnatural strains of modern civilization and the sophistication of modern food as the teeth. I rarely need medical attention. But I need the care of a dentist three or four times a year; and although my teeth are as good as the average, there is hardly a tooth in my head that has not been repaired. This is the common experience of people who look after their teeth as regularly as possible. Hardly one of us is free from some dental defect or of decay that will result in a defect soon. Over the myriad centuries of civilization nothing in the body has broken down so disastrously.

The only compensation is the knowledge and skill of the dental profession. While I ruefully submit to the whirl of the drill, I am also grateful for Dr. Frank's mastery of his profession and devotion to science. In his late middle years he is still in love with dentistry. He reads the dental journals, attends the professional meetings, talks and lives dentistry and loves to speculate on experiments to control decay by introducing chemical solutions into the water supply or into cleansing compounds. He enjoys the discipline and the stimulus of the scientific method—cautiously judicial but not without hope. Being in close contact with human beings every day of his life, he seasons his knowledge with personal sympathy. His science is sweetened with philosophy

11. After a few bland days during which a faint tinge of green has been hurrying over the beaten grass in the park, we angrily tumble back into winter again. A powdery sleet comes rattling out of the murky sky and covers the streets and walks with crunching rime. The automobiles are fringed with icicles. This might have been exciting in November; it is disheartening now when we are all hoping to climb over the rim of winter into the garden of spring.

On this day in 1888, the people of New York were not so much disappointed as astounded and alarmed. For the great blizzard began about midnight, continued through the next two days and did not clear until the fourteenth. After three cold, wild days, New York was paralyzed. The word "blizzard" had come into use only a few years previously. After 1888 it became a common noun, for nature had violently confirmed it. The temperature was low—variously reported at four below zero or eight above; the northwest wind reached a velocity of eighty-four miles an hour, and forty inches of snow fell, interlaced occasionally with flying pellets of ice. Drifts measured as high as twenty feet where the wind caught the snow.

In spite of the tempestuous and freezing weather, thousands of people automatically started to go to work on the morning of the twelfth (which was Monday). But not many got to their offices, and most of those who did could not return home until Wednesday. For all forms of transportation broke down. There was a fatal wreck on the elevated railroad. Some hacks and a few sleighs kept on making their way slowly through the center of a few main streets. Some people managed to walk in single file along some of the sidewalks. But after fighting the blizzard with varying success on the first day, most people abandoned New York until the storm was over, and stayed where they were indoors.

Despite the suffering, people were also elated; there was a streak of holiday excitement around town. For, with a few exceptions, people survived the most deadly weather New York had ever endured. They had further evidence of the stupendous fortitude and ingenuity of human beings, who are unconquerable as a race. There was not a man in New York as powerful as that wild blizzard, which kept on coming as though it meant to annihilate the city. But, again with a few exceptions, every man was still here and in high spirits after the blizzard had blown out to sea. People were elated because they knew in their bones that the most frightful storm the city ever had could not destroy them. It confirmed what they had learned in the gray dawn of history when men were living in caves.

12. Primitive societies have communal dances and festivals. Advanced societies are hardly more than standardized work-camps unless they, too, have some communal activities that draw people together for imaginative experiences. Being simple and human in its method, the theater is ideal for this purpose. For it is not good theater unless everyone understands it and responds to it. It is a simple exchange of ideas and emotions from one human being to another—specifically, from the actor to the audience.

Culture should include the whole man—that is, the man who not only earns his living in an office or factory or on a farm but also reads books, looks at paintings, listens to music, goes to the theater and wrestles with ideas. For all these are aspects of modern living, equally important and equally illuminating. Nobody is fully alive who cannot apply to art as much discrimination and appreciation as he applies to the work by which he earns his living.

The value of the theater to a community lies here. It is a vivid and vibrant expression of truths and ideas—satire, comedy and tragedy; and it helps to make life whole. For the most part, the theater is entertainment, which is something everybody is hungry for. But sooner or later every theater tires of a steady diet of entertainment and starts peering inside human beings, where the greatest mysteries and wonders of the world are gathered. For about three thousand years dramatists have been peering inside human beings without solving the mysteries or exhausting the wonders, and this process is likely to go on for a few years more. It is a good thing to have a theater in the neighborhood to find out what is going on in the hearts and minds of men and women everywhere.

13. Count me among the most delighted votaries of the philosophy of resistentialism, a product of the alert and sardonic minds of modern British thinkers. "Resistentialism" refers to the stubborn resistance the universe offers to normal and rational human behavior. In the vernacular it means "You can't win," although the scholars naturally prefer the esoteric term. Everyone, whether he knows it or not, is a victim of resistentialism. For instance, the sure way of bringing on rain is to wash and polish the car. Wait fifteen minutes for a bus: invariably three turn up together, all full. Or take a more vivid example: if I step into the bathtub, the telephone rings. This is the most carefully co-ordinated example of resistentialism that I know. This morning the telephone rings just an instant before I step into the bath. After answering it, I feel incautiously elated over having frustrated resistentialism for one day. Then I step happily into the tub. Almost at once, the doorbell rings! Resistentialism!

Since resistentialism is a new scientific philosophy, the British resistentialist school is at present merely collecting, correlating, and evaluating the evidence. Several years will elapse before there is sufficient evidence on which to base a search for the source and the metaphysical motive of this constant subtle warfare against human beings. But I know the motive for the bathtub and telephone sequence. It is an attempt to murder me without breaking the law. If a man who is immersed in a tub of warm, soapy bath water touches an electric light fixture or telephone instrument, he electrocutes himself. The law would classify this as death from accidental causes. But all trained resistentialists know that it would be premeditated murder. There are mysterious, invisible forces in nature that are maliciously at war with normal, high-minded people. We may as well recognize the fact and try to identify it. Never plant a garden during a spell of sublime weather. After a garden has been planted, the first crucial weeks will be too cold and wet or too hot and dry. The best way to ensure a late frost is to set out tomato plants late in May. The best way to attract deer is to fill a garden with succulent vegetables. These are homely examples of resistentialism.

14. There is no resistance in the air this morning. The temperature is 52° at 10 A.M. The wind is from the south; the sun filters through a lazy haze that softens the view and wraps the city in warmth. Instead of rushing mechanically to the subway, I walk down beside the river in the hope of hearing a song sparrow in the park. Yes, there he is! In a bushy hollow, which the sun fills with warmth and gentleness, a song sparrow pours out his cheerful melody in praise of the spring, rolling back the winter, rolling back the city, rolling back the centuries. Probably he has spent the winter scratching in the leaves of the frost-bound park. But this is the first day on which he has tipped back his head and sung with rapture. Fifty yards away a freight train is rattling through the railroad tunnel—the mechanical clatter coming out through the gratings; and on the highway almost overhead the traffic is sweeping by with a hiss of rubber on cement. But the song sparrow is lost in his own ecstasy, apparently oblivious of everything alien to it. He keeps on singing a long, varied melody that overlays the heavy sounds of the city. He is singing down the walls of the city like the seven trumpets of ram's-horns that blew down the walls of Jericho.

There is only one small cake of ice in the river, floating placidly on the glossy water, like something that has been lost from a forgotten season.

15. Andrew Jackson, "the old Indian scalper," "the old hero," born this day in 1767. To this violent, explosive southerner we owe practical democracy. He put into practice the philosophical idealism of gentlemen. They were shocked when it happened. Full of contempt for the blazing manners of a turbulent frontiersman who had literally fought his way up from squalor, John Quincy Adams refused to accompany him to his inauguration. When Jackson was inaugurated, the mob took over Washington, stormed the White House, stood with muddy boots on satin-covered furniture and nearly crushed the new President.

To trained and educated statesmen, accustomed to decorum in the capitol, this outburst of popular enthusiasm seemed like a catastrophe. Many of them were sincere and high-minded. But they had never had an opportunity to learn that democracy is men as well as principles. Jackson brought into our system the direct action of Americanism. "Let the people rule," he had said and he meant it. He had been a fighter since his youth. He fought in the Revolution when he was thirteen. He fought Indians; he fought and defeated trained British troops in the War of 1812 and he fought at least three duels, at least once "killing his man." He hated wealth and power. He opposed Washington when he was in Congress; he broke the control of bankers over the funds of taxpayers. He shook the genteel traditions out of government. He made the White House inhabitable for Abraham Lincoln, who enriched and inspired the popular American tradition.

16. The cult of gentility masks our life with a thin, contemptible veneer of politeness and respectability. (Automobiles are not "greased"; they are "lubricated.") Perhaps that is why we are satisfied with a performance of *Antony and Cleopatra* in a decorous, intellectual tone suitable for an afternoon in a library. Antony as a scholar, Cleopatra as a rather mature graduate of Wellesley College—this soothes the public and preserves a middle-class illusion that the classics are refined and that Shakespeare was a gentleman who associated with only the best people and wrote beautifully out of books.

Shakespeare is the most passionate and tumultuous of poets. But the cult of gentility has turned him into an intellectual so that respectable people may feel safe in his presence. This is the great spiritual swindle of our culture. Most of the Shakespeare productions on Broadway are too refined. The scenery is too imposing. The costumes are too splendid and immaculate. The acting is too studious and respectable. You would think that Shakespeare were written by a college graduate for bachelors of arts exclusively, and that every big scene were an intellectual problem. Shakespeare is played as though he were Ben Jonson, who was a university man. We have accepted Dryden's pallid and snobbish assumption that "Shakespeare is scarce intelligible to a refined age."

17. St. Patrick's Day, when the whole of New York wears a broad grin and feels festive. When I go into the barbershop I am greeted with convivial smiles, although I am not Irish, and most of the barbershop personnel is Italian, Jewish, and Negro. "I thought you would be parading today," Harry sings out jocosely, although he does not think any such thing. "They got a fine day for it," he adds, with a dutiful murmur about "the luck of the Irish." At the office I find a dried shamrock in an envelope, sent to me by an Irishman I do not know as reward for an article he liked. "It is a sacred relic," he says. "One of my nephews in Ireland has sent it to me." Although business goes on as usual, the spirit of the day is turned over to the Irish. This is the only day of the year on which we exuberantly celebrate a foreign country. It would be as much as a politician's life is worth to refuse to review the St. Patrick's Day parade on Fifth Avenue. The Mayor takes the salute as though he were the Irish ambassador. The Cardinal keeps open house in St. Patrick's Cathedral, as though Roman Catholicism were the official city religion. Everyone is good-natured on St. Patrick's Day. A kind of humorous madness sweeps across the city. Perhaps it is because everyone has a warm spot in his heart for the Irish, who have a special talent for life in America and live together here more amicably than they do in Ireland. The Irish in New York love Ireland passionately like émigrés cruelly torn away from the fatherland. But they are also the most loyal New Yorkers and would never dream of leaving the city. The St. Patrick's Day parade is a cheerful masquerade, like a family reunion. On one day of the year the Irish pretend that they are not dyed-in-the-wool New Yorkers.

18. Nothing society can do assuages the pain caused by the death of a relative or friend. Society is aware of the pain, and has found ways of accepting it and respecting it. The professional funeral directors have developed techniques that are merciful at the time when the pain is sharpest. The undertakers are thoughtful, unobtrusive, and impersonal. Their solemn manners, which look comic to wags who have never had the devastating experience of death in the home, are comforting, like a soft buffer against the breeziness of normal life.

Society treats death with honor and solemnity. The funeral attendants wear formal clothes. The funeral coach is immaculately polished. The automobiles in the procession are the best that are available—comfortable, quiet, and imposing; and city traffic respectfully gives way to funeral processions. In some funerals an expensive flower vehicle precedes the procession—displaying in the public streets the abundance and quality of the floral gifts. As tokens of the respect people have for the one who has died, the flowers soothe the pride of the grieved ones who are left.

But the stately ceremony of funerals and burials does not ease the pain and does not mask the terrible helplessness of the mourners. Style is no triumph on these crushing occasions. And when I see the splendor of modern city funerals, I remember compassionately the battered poverty of a country funeral I once saw in an obscure village in the Philippines and the ragged, forlorn, wretched funerals in the backlands of China. Tribal customs are the same everywhere. There is not much difference. Whether the funeral is elegant or primitive, the awful fact of death is identical. Society is helpless against this cataclysmic confrontation with nothingness. The most society can do is for a day or two to shield those who are left from the insistent clamor of life.

19. "Yes" is the creative word that unlocks doors and opens alleys into the future, and it has the whole weight of humanity behind it. The pioneers said "Yes" and made their way to the Pacific. The idealists said "Yes" and founded a free nation. Watt

said "Yes" and built the steam engine. The railroad builders said "Yes" and laid rails across a wild country. Edison said "Yes" and lighted the world. Emerson said "Yes" and wrote the philosophy of a new nation, and Whitman transformed "Yes" into a mighty roar of exultant affirmation. Say "Yes" to the seedlings and a giant forest cleaves the sky. Say "Yes" to the universe and the planets become your neighbors. Say "Yes" to dreams of love and freedom. It is the password to utopia.

20. The astronomers confirm what we have all been divining: spring has officially arrived. The day and the night are of equal length all over the world today. In New York the sun rises at 6:03 and sets at 6:12.

In confirmation of the almanac, the temperature rises to 71° this afternoon. Most of us do not quite dare leave off our coats, but soon wish that we had, for the walking is hot. There is a great holiday feeling all through the town. Everyone moves outdoors and has leisure. The benches in the center of Broadway are filled with idle people basking in the sun. People sit on the front stoops, reading or gossiping; the children are playing in the streets. Along the water front red-faced, frowsy drunks sleep on the sidewalks or against bulkheads. Saloons keep their doors open, letting out the fragrant odors of liquor and the sound of laughter and conversation.

In the lower bay the herring gulls seem to be less numerous than they were a month ago. Perhaps they are already on their way to their breeding grounds. There are a number of terns (probably common terns) sweeping lightly through the air like pieces of forked white paper caught in spirals of air. They fly more joyously than the gulls and write the characters for "spring" in the air currents of the harbor.

21. Samples of the spring conversation in the dispatching shack on Pier 43. George, a deep-voiced mariner who began in sail but long ago swallowed the anchor:

"I can't drink the way I used to. I feel it in my legs the next day. Liquor ain't as good as it used to be before prohibition. I can't take more than twelve drinks without feeling it. I went into the White Horse the other night with four dollars. Over at a table I see Martha and she invites me to sit down and have a drink. Then I stand her to a drink and then she stands me to a drink. Suddenly she says, 'George, let's get drunk.' I don't know what got into her, because I never see her drunk before. She had ten dollars and I had four. We borrowed five more from the barkeep, so that made nineteen in all. She was drinking scotch, and me rye. We sat there drinking until about three in the morning, and I could hardly get home and felt awful all the next day. Martha's rich. I guess she's got twenty-five thousand dollars. When the liquor was good I could keep on drinking without ever feeling it. I don't drink any more."

After a silent interval, another lounger in a ruminative mood addresses a direct question to me: "Did you ever do any gold prospecting?" I have to confess with a flush of shame that I never did. "I did in California about the time of the earthquake," he says. "Another feller and I went into the mountains. We followed a mountain lion's trail for two days. But you can't catch them without a dog, you know. No, we never saw any gold. There were some pretty veins, though."

22. The glory of the theater is the power it has voluntarily to command the best work that individual artists and artisans can bring to public attention. No one can appear at his best in the theater unless everyone else conspires with him sincerely—not only the playwright and the actor, but the director, the scene designer, the costume designer, the lighting expert, the scene builder and painter, the stage hands, and even the audience. No one of these can create the magic of theater unless all the others work together in a common enterprise.

If the theater were an exact science it would be easy to draw up an exact table of dramatic values. Without the playwright, obviously, there would be no play for the actor to work with. Ergo, as one of the oldest actor-dramatists used to exclaim, the playwright comes first in the hierarchy of theater values. But in practice the scale of values is not that logical. For the theater is not a science but an art, and many actors are much greater artists than many playwrights. Since actors have learned the art of the theater by personally facing an audience—projecting a character through the intangible medium of movement and voice—many of them have a deeper instinctive knowledge of the theater than the playwright who works in seclusion with paper and pencil. The theater is not belles-lettres but one of the public arts, and the actor is the person who represents the theater in public. He can destroy a play by not understanding it or by not being able to express it lucidly. But in practice, more actors save faltering playwrights than the other way round. As professionals, they are likely to be more gifted in the creation of theater; and in the best instances they are artists. For acting is not the mechanical reproduction of a character by an automaton but the impact of an actor's art and personality on the art of a playwright.

23. "Call this a govment! A man can't get his rights in a govment like this. Sometimes I've a mighty notion to just leave the country for good and all. Says I, for two cents I'd leave the blamed country and never come a-near it agin."

That's the way Huckleberry Finn's pap talked when he had a skinful of Missouri liquor. But that's also the way most Americans talk even when they are cold sober. For it has always been an axiom of American life that the government is crooked. "A fine Congress, made up of cutthroats and thieves!" the Albany *Gazette* exclaimed scornfully in 1806. This is still one thing that we can all happily agree on, whether we are Democrats or Republicans. It is the one grievance all of us have in common.

There are two ways of accounting for the American's rancor about his government. In the first place, it gives him a heady feeling of importance. No matter how incompetent he may be in looking after his own affairs, he can easily convince himself that he is competent in the affairs of state. He diverts all the bitterness of his personal life towards the government—holding the government responsible for his personal failure. Since the government cannot take the time to talk back to him and defend itself, and since everyone he knows agrees that the government is crooked and stupid, he comes to think of himself as part hero and part martyr. Blaming the government for his misfortunes takes a great burden off his conscience.

In the second place, it is not the function of a government to solve the private problems of individual people. Looking after the commonweal, it should protect them from injustices which they cannot control by themselves, but it is no substitute for intelligence and initiative. Since the government is composed of people, it is no better than people—no better, to be precise, than average people. No government of human beings—democratic, socialist, communist, fascist, or monarchial—can put the world in order and save people from suffering and anxiety. The affairs of the world are too complicated to be understood by anybody. The most we can expect is an occasional government that moves in the direction of freedom. Principle and good will are creative: the most we can expect is an occasional government animated by men of principle and good will.

Nothing wholly admirable ever happens in this country except the migration of birds.

24. Gotham's shad fishermen are getting ready. From rowboats, towed into position by motor launches, they are setting up the long twenty- and twenty-five foot poles to which they attach their nets. Ocean steamers pass up- and downriver in the channel, and myriad tugs skip helter-skelter across the river all day and night on modern business. But still the ancient art of fishing goes on every year by professional fishermen who live on the banks of an ancient river. In a week or two the shad will come rushing out of the Atlantic upriver to fresh water where they spawn. Foul as the river is with sewage and waste industrial products, the shad come every year by the millions, following some overwhelming, immutable instinct. Although the Hudson fishermen haul a million dollars' worth of shad out of the river in a good season, the shad are always abundant. I can see the fishermen from my windows raising the net twice a day on the west side of the river off Edgewater.

After living for one or two years in fresh water, the young shad plunge more than one hundred miles downriver into the vast coldness of the Atlantic. Loafing on the end of a pier I once happened to see a migration of young shad to the sea. In a great silvery, swift, wriggling mass they came on like a desperate cataract in waves. I watched for an hour, but the power of the multitude never slackened. There were millions more to come, and some were still passing down the next morning. That was the most immortal thing I ever saw in New York.

25. After being confined for four months in the shrill city O. and I make our first trip to the country and open the old house for another year. It is like jailbreak. Snowbanks still lie in the hollows and on the mountains. But the winter is broken and the country is busy laying the foundation for the season. Robins never feel so important as they do in the spring. Just back from winter quarters, they are eager to be seen and admired. They look enormous in the barren branches of the maples and they speak with a tone of truculent authority. But the bluebird is the poet of spring. Since our bluebird box was empty for two years in succession some time ago, I wonder every year whether it is tenanted again. There is no sign of the bluebird today as we drive into the dooryard and move into the house. As soon as we are settled I go out under the box and rap on the locust trunk. Yes, there he is! He leaves the box, flashing his calm, sweet blue against the lifeless brown of the landscape. Perching in another locust, he puts his feathers in order like someone who has been interrupted and is annoyed. He looks at me peevishly. I have a feeling that I am not starting the new season tactfully and may lose a guest I value. But after a curt interval, his throat swells; and that warm, contralto meditative warble pours out and flows through the whole landscape and opens a new country year with a word of praise, forgiveness and confidence. This is the most celestial sound of our spring. Now I am certain that the months ahead will be rich and gentle and that the foundations of life are solidly rooted in the long truth of the centuries.

There is an enormous amount of work to be done indoors and out before we are in control of the house and the dooryard and before we can start on the new projects we have thought about during the winter. The song of the bluebird is a blessing on the grass, the foliage and the flowers that we shall joyfully share during the next few months; and the work I have to do is not drudgery but a small part of the whole creation. At sundown three deer— two does and one buck—walk to the middle of the field behind the house and graze there at leisure. They seem to know that the house is open again. But they have not learned to fear us yet. Alas, that is something we never have to teach them.

26. God rested on the seventh day. Since everything He had made during six epochal days was "very good," He could rest with equanimity. The heavens and the earth being finished, He had completed the preliminary job of the grand experiment. Unfortunately, the experiment has not worked out very well. God must have noticed its innumerable imperfections. But one of its accidental perfections is that, in the middle of the twentieth century, most of us can rest on the sixth day in a state of demoralized shiftlessness. Sunday deserves honor; it is the day that God sanctified. But Saturday is the work day that has been mercifully forgotten and weeded out of the week's routine. I gratefully celebrate it with the three sublime negations: Shave not, bathe not, wear thou not the necktie. Although these things are virtuous in themselves, they are the preliminary symbols of the working day in civilized society where everyone has to conform to certain arbitrary standards. Dispense with them, and you declare a holiday. There is much to be done on Saturdays—painting the kitchen, tidying the yard, walking at random, reading for pleasure, talking with people who are wise and supple enough to agree. But these are pleasant pursuits that can be indulged most heartily by the unshaved and unbathed who have foresworn the necktie. Of the things that seem "very good" on the Lord's day, the memory of an aimless Saturday is the best. No one but God has reason to be satisfied with the week's work, and there must be times when He has His private misgivings.

27. Although unskilled labor has a low social and economic rating, it has a tradition, too. You do not distinguish yourself as an unskilled laborer unless you bring some ability to it. It needs a good back, muscles and wind. But it also needs training and experience. A first-rate unskilled laborer knows a thousand professional secrets. If he is digging a ditch, he knows how to use his back and leg muscles to save his arms. He knows the best way to stand. He knows the rhythm that will help him do the most work without exhausting his strength before the day is over. He

knows when to pick and when to dig. He knows how big a hole he must start on the surface in proportion to the depth he has to go, for he knows that he needs more room to shovel the deeper he goes. There used to be a man in our neighborhood in the country who could dig himself out of sight before lunchtime. He enjoyed considerable honor in town.

Don't condescend to unskilled labor. Try it for half a day first. Try chopping wood. Try splitting logs, and observe how easily a good man can make a stubborn log burst open by biting into the right places with his ax. Even though you have good muscles and a strong back you will be astonished by the difficulty of this kind of work, and you will wonder how anybody can dig, lift, or chop all day and return to the job refreshed and ready at seven or eight o'clock the next morning. There are not many first-rate bankers or industrialists. Nor are there many unskilled laborers of first-rate quality.

28. Easter Sunday. When the women came to the sepulcher at sunrise, the angels said: "He is not here, but is risen." It is written that the women received this miraculous news with fear and great joy. The joy is obviously less ecstatic now, but every year it is revived throughout Christendom. This is the great Christian day of the year. For even now people hope that death can be transcended. Man who has evolved so fabulously from protoplasm may yet, through creative force of will, finally triumph over death as Jesus did—thus confirming the poetry of the Scriptures. The music of the spheres may not be a dirge but a lyric.

It has always seemed to me that we observe Easter abominably. Nothing could poison the religious wonder of Easter much more contemptuously than the custom of dressing ostentatiously for the religious services. From the sepulcher at sunrise to the fashion parade on Fifth Avenue is the boorish measure of our denial of Christ—from innocent wonder to cynical worldliness. On Easter Sunday our churches are crowded with the heathen who mock their Lord with finery. The Easter flowers, which are holy, and the Easter music, which is pure and glorious, can roll the stone away from the sepulcher. But the Lord is greeted by congregations of coxcombs and egotists who have publicly renounced the humility of this teaching.

The Easter festival is closely allied with nature which, being a renewal of life, gives Easter natural validity. According to the venerable Bede, the word "Easter" derives from "Eostre," who was the Anglo-Saxon goddess of spring. The calendar for Easter was set in 325 A.D. by the Council of Christian Churches in Nicaea, and was governed by the fact that the pilgrims needed moonlight for their travels to Easter celebrations. Easter comes on the first Sunday following the Paschal Full Moon which occurs on the twenty-first of March or during the next month. The Paschal Full Moon is the fourteenth day of a lunar month reckoned according to an ancient ecclesiastical computation; it is not the real astronomical full moon. The date of Easter thus varies as much as thirty-five days between March twenty-second and April twenty-fifth. Never having accepted the Gregorian calendar, the Russian Orthodox church usually celebrates Easter on a different date. The Eastern and Western Easters coincided in 1865, but not again until 1946.

The Russian people celebrate Easter more devoutly than we do. The services, with magnificent clerical processionals and a concert of Gregorian chants, are profoundly beautiful and moving. They are the supreme religious observance of the believers who pack the churches to worship with almost hysterical fervor. No other Russian public demonstration arouses the people to such a pitch of faith and feeling. During the Easter season the familiar greeting between Russian friends is: "Christ is risen," and the polite response is: "He is risen, indeed."

29. Although the city is organized for the convenience and comfort of people, the country people came through the last winter better than we did in the city. The city was wrecked by the snow and cold; fuel was scarce and for a while could be bought only on the black market. Naturally the country people who burn wood were warm all winter. But in spite of the long distances that fuel trucks had to go through snow-choked roads, the people who burn oil were never cold. Everett Matthews says that once he had only one more day's supply in his tank. But at four on the next morning the truck from Catskill, twenty-two miles away, drove up and filled his tank again. There is a greater sense of community responsibility in the country. The people know each other and rarely let each other down. But in the city even the human relationships tend to become mechanized. Although the city is organized for people, it is surfeited with people and bored with them and accepts only impersonal and group responsibility.

30. The revolution that everyone longs for would be simple, and yet it would be complete. It would begin in the hearts of men and women all over the world, and it would start acting this moment on the universal principle: "Therefore all things whatsoever ye would that men should do to you, do ye even so to them, for this is the law and the prophets." This line covers everything in every field of activity everywhere. It is the genius of the Christian religion, which took it from Jewish laws, giving it a positive rather than negative accent. The same thought appears in Buddhism and Confucianism. Like most really inspired observations it represents simple common sense and is practical.

The organization of modern life is too complex to be understood by anyone. No one can learn enough to put it in order. But amid the rubble of the centuries this is the one golden idea that could transmute our broken, despairing century into a mansion of enlightenment and well-being. If everyone began this morning to live by the oldest idea in history the world would be green and golden tonight.

31. On walking into a basement barbershop I have not visited for six months, I do not recognize it. Like all first-rate barbershops, it was faultless six months ago—tiled in white glaze, the basins and fixtures immaculate, the heavy, complicated barber chairs clean and comfortable. But the management was tired of its familiar perfection. It has installed new chairs that cost four hundred and fifty dollars each, and has spent forty thousand dollars on redecoration—a new variation of barbershop perfection. Not long ago the customers had to accept higher fees to meet what the management described plaintively as higher wages and cost of operation. Although we were thoroughly satisfied with the splendor of the plant, it now appears that we are contributing forty thousand dollars to build a new plant with blue interior

decoration. This is labeled "modernization," and it consists partly in scrapping expensive equipment that is efficient and in perfect working order. Anyone except an aggressive business engineer would label it "waste."

For business is not only an art and a science but a hobby. Managers like to play with their enterprises. Change is a sort of merchandising fetish. It is not necessarily an improvement. Indeed, it is sometimes a step backward. The bank where I have an account has just spent over one hundred thousand dollars on a sleek renovation; but the tellers who bear most of the burden of dealing with the customers now have less room to work in than they had before. At the cost of several million dollars one of the department stores has recently constructed a building less comfortable and inviting than the one it had before.

Modern America frequently makes changes that are progressive and constructive—like the modern railroad equipment which is not only more comfortable but more efficient. But change for the sake of change is adolescent restlessness. In the instance of most new automobile models, it is a colossal national swindle that makes it impossible for a driver to see what he is doing. Every responsible driver knows that new models become increasingly difficult to drive safely. Not being able to see the right-hand side of his car he has to guess how much clearance he has there. And for more than a decade new cars have been built so low that they cannot be driven safely on muddy or snowy country roads. Automobiles are designed to look irresistible in show windows; they can be driven at maximum efficiency only on paved highways. They are designed chiefly for people who do not need them. Not every change is an improvement, and some of them are not designed to be improvements. They are designed to sell things that are not wanted or needed.

APRIL

April

"Whan that I here the smale foules singe,
And that the floures ginne for to springe,
Farwel my studie, as lasting that sesoun!"

THOSE WERE the vagrant spring thoughts that flashed through Chaucer's mind more than five hundred years ago. They are valid for New York in the twentieth century. From now on the intellectual life of New York will be fitful and tepid. For the forsythia bloomed in the park this morning—all at once, like a golden affirmation, strewing a treasure of wealth across the scrawny landscape. And for another six months no one will beat his brains out as earnestly as he did during the winter. The finest part of the theater season is over. The opera has closed. The concert season is frittering out, and the most imposing art exhibitions are finished.

Although the business of the city goes through the familiar motions—too settled in a fixed rhythm to stop—the universities and schools have the grace to close for a spring recess and throughout the summer. It shows how much wisdom the institutions of learning have. For no one can keep his nose in a book or think consecutively when the forsythia unfolds its splendid banners. Many people who think they are accomplishing something of consequence today are merely creatures of habit. The sun and the forsythia are laughing at them. "And the earth abideth forever."

2. In a line that sounds ironic but represents a conviction, Bernard Shaw says: "The moral for conquerors of empires is that if they substitute savagery for civilization they are doomed." The most staggering event in modern times is the swift suicide of Germany under Hitler. Even now it is hard to realize what happened. Not so many years ago Germany had a glorious civiliza-

tion that enriched the world. Think of her poets and composers; her philosophers and scientists; her surgeons and medical schools; her theaters and actors. Her industries and railroads compared with the greatest in the world. Her artisans and craftsmen were among the best. As a maritime nation she ranked high, with some of the fastest and finest ships, and she operated them with skill that was almost peerless. Germans had and acted on advanced ideas. As for her armies, they were at one time the most powerful in the world, and they were manned by people who believed in armies and liked them.

What happened? Although we know the facts, they still seem incredible. For a great nation that in some respects led the world went down in a fiery, bloody catastrophe with the dazzling speed of an exploding comet and lies in ruins—spiritual as well material. *Sic transit gloria* under the insane leadership of an ignorant mystic who brought down a shining civilization in the crash and flame of a modern cataclysm. Even the victors have not yet recovered from that moral disaster.

3. Supposing you want to go to Iloilo or Cebu amid the heat and placid loveliness of the Philippine Islands: you have a wide range of ships to choose from in the harbor just now: the *Fernmoor, Ivaran, Pioneer Tide, Staghound, Steel Scientist, Johannes Maersk*—all loading this week. There are many more ships bound for the Philippines and the China coast that might accommodate you to Iloilo or Cebu if you make inquiries of the agents. If you decide rather to go to Cheribon or Samarang in Java, which is the most enchanting island in the world, you have a very remarkable choice of ships during the next three weeks: *St. Cloud Victory, Sumatra, Florence Luckenbach, Edgar F. Luckenbach, Rondo, Mentor, Cape San Diego,* and *Legion Victory.* Unfortunately, you cannot get through to Bangkok without transshipping. The sandbar thirty miles south of the city cannot be crossed by deepwater vessels. You will have to change ships at Singapore or Saigon—a regrettable though tolerable inconvenience.

4. If philology were an art instead of a science, the word "humor" would be derived from the Latin "humanus," for it is the most chastening of human attributes. No one is thoroughly human without humor enough to have a working sense of proportion and to get along without crises and quarreling. But "humor" is one of the capricious words that roguishly turn up in strange places after a wayward history. It is derived from a Latin word meaning "moisture" or "fluid." In ancient physiology it referred to one of the four basic fluids (blood, phlegm, choler, and black bile) that were thought to govern a person's temperament. There could be ill-humor as well as good humor. Ben Jonson's *Every Man in His Humor* meant "Everyone According to His Own Temperament."

But now "humor" refers specifically to the recognition of ludicrous and absurd things in life, and differs from "wit" in the human warmth that makes it glow. Thackeray thought that it was a mixture of love and wit. John Burroughs regarded it as "the wit of the heart." Never trust the judgment of a man whose association with other men is not enlightened with humor. Specifically, don't trust the judgment of a man who does not regard humor as an essential part of the alembic of life, for he is a fanatic and is impervious to normal human relationships. Humor is not merely the telling of funny stories. It recognizes the vast difference between life as we imagine it and life as we live it, and between the fanciful and imposing impressions we have of ourselves and what we actually are. From a disinterested point of view these differences are as tragic as they are comic. And people who perceive them tragically are likely to jump out windows, or hang, or shoot themselves from a terrible feeling of mortification—like Hitler who brought half the world to ruin. But the humorous man recognizes that absolute purity, absolute justice, absolute logic and perfection are beyond human achievement and that men have been able to live happily for thousands of years in a state of genial frailty. "Dost thou think, because thou art virtuous, there shall be no more cakes and ale?" Trust only the men who laugh with relish. I trust Shakespeare more than Corneille, Mark Twain more than Henry James, Robert Frost more than T. S. Eliot, Ernest Hemingway more than Thomas Mann. They do not expect to vanquish folly from the world overnight.

5. Sidney Phillips pops in for the evening, and almost instantly everyone is laughing. Everyone feels gay and brilliant when he is around. He laughs clear down to his feet. In fact, Sidney is living proof of the fact that the fastidious George Meredith did not know what he was talking about when he delivered his celebrated lecture on comedy. Meredith inveighed against people who laugh too much: "Whom we may term 'hypergelasts' [a pompous word!]; the excessive laughers, ever-laughing, who are as clappers of a bell, that may be rung by a breeze, a grimace; who are so loosely put together that a wink will shake them." There is something almost inhuman in Meredith's distaste for them. Can there be excessive laughter? Can people have too good a time, too vast an appreciation of the ludicrous, too much gusto for joking and revelry? For the ability to laugh comes out of moral strength and the courage to face the sublime muddle of human affairs; and those who can laugh are those who have faith enough to go on.

Some things that some people laugh at do not seem funny to others. Laughter can be stupid and cruel. Not everything that is obscene is funny, though some people are stupid enough to think so. But laughter is social; it breaks down the prison walls that people build around their souls to protect their vanity or to hide their fears and sorrows. It is the open sesame to the human race. There is nothing more triumphant than an evening of laughter. Look at those who have been laughing together: they go home weary but in a glow of good spirits, still laughing in their minds, and supple enough to face tomorrow without cracking. They are friends. They have inherited the earth. God would not dare trust the earth to people who are churlish or surly. For they have not learned how to let the poison out of their systems and they would infect the flowers, the trees, and the people.

6. On this day in 1917 Congress declared war on Germany. No one has referred to it today, but it has governed a good deal of what we have been doing and thinking. We think we act independently but we are saturated in all the past evils, and today was partly shaped and weighted in 1917. April 6, 1917, was a cloudy day; the noon temperature was 45°. After a number of American ships had been torpedoed, an unsophisticated, cocky nation ac-

cepted the responsibilities of a world power. "The world must be
made safe for democracy," President Wilson said in a phrase that
has become part of the common speech and was published in the
next day's newspapers. We did not make the world safe for democracy, although 130,274 Americans gave their lives then, and
310,979 gave their lives in the second world war, fought for the
same principle. Embittered by the chaos and brutishness of the
modern world, there are people who still believe that we should
never have joined forces with the British and French in 1917,
since the fruits have been so sour and evil. There is no point now
in looking back ruefully at a never-never world of dreams. In 1917,
acting on the principle of self-protection, we innocently thought
we could make the world safe for democracy by helping to win
a war. Now we know that the world will never be safe for democracy until we have created democracy here in the image of the
first dream and until we have demonstrated to the world that
freedom is simple, normal, and natural.

Under the pressure of a great decision in 1917, President Wilson
said: "We are at the beginning of an age in which it will be in-
sisted that the same standards of conduct and responsibility for
wrong done shall be observed among nations and their governments that are observed among the individual citizens of civilized
states."

We are still at the beginning of that age; it is not yet formed
or coalesced. But that is still the great social principle. "Good
neighbors" was the phrase the next war president used to express
the same idea. American instincts still lie in that direction and
always will, for they have the authority of human experience.

7. In literary composition there is only one fundamental principle: clarity. Nothing else is as vital as that. Force, eloquence,
euphony, variety, and passion are admirable or beguiling. But unless they are founded on the hard core of clarity they are bogus
and contemptible. Literary composition is not an artificial exercise, but an expression of mind, and the only mind worth respecting is the one that is clear. Since writing is pure mind, it has no
sensual or social satisfactions. The composer has the pleasure of
hearing sound. The artist can enjoy color and design. The actor
and the dancer perform in terms of motion. All these arts are in

varying degrees social. But writing has to be done in solitude, and the marks a writer makes on paper are only arbitrary symbols, scratched out of mind, with no esthetic satisfactions.

Good writing comes out of a mind that is clear. There is no good writing that is not clear. There is no clear writing that is not good.

8. In the northern latitudes where our week-end farm is located the raw time of year yields reluctantly to the climbing sun. While the sap drips into the buckets and the sap-house chimney chokes with wood smoke, the bleak mountains can still shake snow out of the clouds and cover April mud with immaculate whiteness. "Sap snow" is what the neighbors call it. At bedtime the sky is dark; the wind is damp and blustering; the thermometer hangs at the freezing point. Spring is perceptibly backsliding. By morning the ground is pure white, the tree trunks plastered on the windward side with the clinging mortar of winter, the shrubs dressed in fleeciness and the spruce branches packed deep in soft glory. Usually the sap snow is dissolved by midmorning amid a steady dripping from the eaves. But sometimes, as today, it covers the thawing ground to a depth of five or six inches and packs into hard, keen drifts where the wind drives furiously around the buildings. Under foot the ground is sopping wet. Where the white surface is broken with footprints the brown stain of mud quickly appears, and the water is running brightly in the ditches. But the fields that only yesterday were responding to the April sun have gone back to sleep under winter covers.

A sap snow discourages the birds. They have just begun to feel at home. About three weeks ago the first robins turned up joyfully out of the south into the "untillable hills" and scurried with excitement through the trees where they flourished last summer. For days, the bluebirds, uttering their warm contralto serenade, have been sitting on the doorstep of last year's box, discussing the new season. But the sap snow drives them to cover. It buries their food and destroys their enthusiasm. The robins, bluebirds and song sparrows search mournfully along the edges of the barnyard where the snow has melted or venture on to the barn floor where the dried grass seed is thick. It is bare picking for a bird who has spring in his heart. Fortunately, the cold is not killing. A sap snow can hardly last more than a day or two. For greater influences are at work: the sun is mounting higher every day, warmth is almost imperceptibly accumulating during the lengthening days and the friendly balm of the south is steadily creeping northward. The sap snow is winter's last fling—beautiful and guileless. When it melts, the earth looks and feels richer, and the first warm day seems wholly luxurious.

9. Civil War closed by the surrender of Lee to Grant near Appomattox Courthouse on this day in 1865. The deaths in the field had exceeded 498,216 counting the dead on both sides—more Americans than were killed in both world wars, which is something most of us have forgotten. Since Americans had been killing Americans, this was the most terrible calamity that has ever swept through the country. Although it was concluded long ago, and very few men who fought in that war survive, it has left wounds that have never healed. Indeed, the two world wars have not wounded America so deeply nor left so much agony to trouble our memories. The North, having won on the battlefield, has largely put the Civil War out of mind. But the South still lives in the bloody memories of the War Between the States, still grieves, still suffers and is still embittered. When I was in Oxford, Mississippi, in the spring of 1942, investigating the impact of the second world war on an independent community, one friendly and genteel lady assumed that the war I was to write about was the Civil War; that was the one that lay heaviest on the hearts of a few of the older people. To them the "Oxford Greys," who had a gallant record in the Confederate Army, were still the most illustrious soldiers Oxford had ever mustered.

The Civil War held the Union together. The Union will probably always remain that way, which will be a blessing. But the fervent concord in which the South and New England established American independence will never return. Between the North and the South stands this awful memory now, occasionally breaking out into rancorous feeling. For the Civil War was not concluded at Appomattox. The hatred was too fierce. The fighting was too exhausting. Too many Americans fell in the field. The noblest of the Americans was assassinated.

10. Critics Circle meets at the Algonquin Hotel to choose the best new plays of the season in three categories. Since this is the most important and illuminating act of the season in criticism, nearly every member is present and on time, too, although critics are highly individualized people and normally do not associate as a group. They have disagreed too long, too passionately, and too publicly to be good companions. There are too many skeletons in everyone's closet. But they have long since agreed on the virtue of taking a formal annual poll of the best plays of a season, since it is the one positive contribution they can make to the drama. After a number of stormy years the Circle has found a way to choose the best plays without curbing the free choice of the individual members, i.e., the play in each category that wins the most votes in one round of signed ballots becomes the choice of the Circle. No one is coerced, proselytized or even influenced by his neighbors; and everyone's individual choices are published. It took many years of suspicion and acrimony to find this simple solution to every critic's natural objection to accepting a group verdict different from his own. To ask a critic to change his vote is to challenge his ability as a critic, and to give credence to the myth that opinions can be "right" or "wrong" or that the opinions of the majority are shrewder than the opinions of individuals. One brilliant iconoclast, like Bernard Shaw, may turn out to be vastly more creative than a whole roomful of amiable conformists.

Members of the Circle ask only two things: (1) to have the full right to personal opinion and (2) not to have to associate socially. After the votes have been taken today in a workmanlike manner, one member proposes that the Circle meet regularly once a month at luncheon. A feeling of panic sweeps across the room. The prospect, not of talking to a critic, which is enviable, but of listening to a critic, which is unbearable, alarms everyone. The motion is voted down with a roar of horror and outrage.

11. Critics represent an authority that no intelligent man recognizes. That is the comic thing about them—authority without franchise, the form without the substance, dignity without respect, law-giving without the consent of the governed. For the truth is that there is no such thing as being right about a work of art.

There can be nothing more decisive than opinions. Criticism of a work of art works both ways—against the art and against the critic. What he writes reveals his mind and heart as intimately as it reveals the work of art he is criticizing. In his opinion of your play or novel you see the indecent exposure of his character. Not only his knowledge but his prejudices are there—not only his alertness but his ignorance. Washington Irving said the New York critics are "the most presumptuous, arrogant, malevolent, illiberal, ungentlemanly, malignant, rancorous, villainous, ungrateful, crippled, invidious, detracting, fabricating, personal, dogmatic, illegitimate, tyrannical, distorting, spindle-shanked moppets, designing villains and upstart *ignorants*." That is, Washington Irving thought so. But since he was a critic, he cannot be trusted. He would have to be overruled on the basis of an ostentatious literary style.

12. About three years after First Class Private Adelbert E. Gallt died in battle, the following public notice appeared in the Middleburgh *News:* "In loving memory of our son, Pfc. Adelbert E. Gallt, who was killed in action, March 28, 1943. 'Time heals all wounds,' folks say to me. They neither know or care. Time only makes the awful hurt more cruelly hard to bear. God gave His son, the Bible says. But I am human, not divine. I do not think the world was worth that precious son of mine.—Mother and Father!"

The human candor and the private agony of this public statement are final. No one can answer it, no one can comfort the parents; no one can beguile them into believing that honor and glory overweigh the death of a son on the battlefield. I think this is the most unanswerable public statement I have ever seen. All of us who are alive stand convicted of a monstrous crime, and there is nothing we can do to atone for it. For whom does the bell toll? It tolls for you and for me. We have stood by piously while a young man was killed for a cause he never created. I don't know how the war could have been avoided. As a nation based on moral principle, we had no choice. But I hope I never meet the grief-stricken parents of Private Gallt. For normal compassion is irrelevant and supercilious; and nothing I know or believe would have any validity in their presence. There is no man honest enough to meet them on equal terms, inspired enough to soften their pain and wrath, or noble enough to invade their loneliness.

13. Thomas Jefferson born this day in 1743. As a young man in his thirties he imagined, more clearly than anyone else, what a free nation might be. A philosophical idealist, with a lawyer's practical training, he declared "that all men are created equal," which is something that the world soon learned, has never forgotten, and has never ceased trying to prove. Having stated the philosophy of a free nation at the age of thirty-two, he put it into practice as President at the age of fifty-seven. His two predecessors in that high office had suspected that he was a theorist with radical ideas that would lead to licentiousness and anarchy. For his imagination was nimbler than theirs; and he believed with his head as well as his heart that, given freedom, men could govern themselves. He proved it in two enlightened administrations that completed the revolution against monarchy. Without the purity of faith that he poured into our national institutions as the chief executive, the cynicism of more practical men might have destroyed the principles of a new nation. He was romantic, artistic, idealistic and modest; he was a student and a dreamer. Although practical men did not wholly trust those qualities, he preserved them in action as the chief executive of the land. After a century and a half the Jeffersonian principles are still the fountainhead of American liberalism. "Life, liberty and the pursuit of happiness"— these three; and the greatest of these is liberty.

14. Come April, come the circus. In a jangled world it is one of the cheerful absolutes. At 8:30 in the vast maw of Madison Square Garden, the spotlight flashes on the handsome bandmaster, who is dressed in a dazzling white suit with expensive gold braid. The brass band, a peerless carnival instrument, lets go with a terrific blast (incidentally, turning "Some Enchanted Evening" into "Slaughter on Eighth Avenue"); and after three solid hours of pandemonium and terror the audience is happily exhausted and unable to speak, think or dream. Whether it is good or bad is beside the point. For the sheer size of the circus is the thing that makes it immune to criticism. Habitual theatergoers may think

that the showmanship is loose and ponderous, the clowns lost in the shuffle, the spectacles naïve and some of the material obsolete. Nearly everything the circus does, the theater could do with more finish and brilliance; for in the theater, time and space are used efficiently. But that has nothing to do with the case. For when the circus is over everyone knows, by golly, that he has seen a show and some great performers. Any one of them would be sensational enough to head a theater vaudeville show. But the circus prodigally tosses them all into the ring and garnishes them with the aerial performers who must make every performance a masterpiece or have their necks broken. A leap in the air that is almost perfect is not good enough for these people. Everything they do has to be completely perfect or—you know what! Golly!

It is the genius of the circus to waste everything extravagantly—wasting clowns by sending them in droves once around the ring, wasting acts by letting several perform simultaneously, wasting individual floats by burying them in an endless, gaudy procession. There has to be too much of everything—too many alluring señoritas (or so it says in the program) tapping too many irrelevant xylophones, too many harlequins, too many horses, bears, dogs, and elephants, too many pompous words in the circus vocabulary. Everything has to be done in the grand manner with spectacular flourishes. And no doubt one of the chief attractions is the circus organization as a community. It not only puts on a three-hour show twice a day with hundreds of performers, costumes, props, animals, automobiles and tractors, but it has the effrontery to pack everything and everybody into railroad trains more than a hundred times a season and travel fifteen thousand miles all through the country, setting up tents in most of the cities, providing meals for fourteen hundred people and feed for the animals, attending to laundry and repairs and keeping everyone in good health and spirits for months. The circus costs about fifteen thousand dollars a day to operate. In New York it pays ten thousand dollars a day rental to the Madison Square Corporation. No, it can't be true. No one can do the things the circus does every day. Compounded insanity!

15. The *Titanic* foundered on April 15, 1912, at latitude 41° 46 minutes North; longitude 50° 41 minutes West, off the

Grand Banks. Seven hundred and six people were saved; fifteen hundred and seventeen were lost. New York was horrified the next day by rumors of this incredible catastrophe. Even now New York cannot forget it, for every day thousands of New Yorkers take their bearings on the *Titanic* Memorial Lighthouse on top of the Seamen's Church Institute in South Street. The death of the *Titanic* has left a permanent scar on the conscience of our port. Lifeboat drill today on every passenger-liner visiting New York harbor derives from the *Titanic* disaster. The shadow of the *Titanic* still haunts us.

The *Titanic*, safest ship of her time, was on her maiden voyage from Southampton to New York. For three and a half days the sea had been remarkably smooth and the atmosphere clear. On her previous twenty-four hours she had traveled five hundred and forty-six miles and was steaming at twenty-two knots. Reports of ice had started coming in over the radio at 2 P.M. on April 14. There were several messages, particularly from the *California*, which reported ice in the evening: "We are stopped and surrounded by ice." To this the *Titanic* operator had irritably replied: "Shut up. I'm busy. I am working Cape Race." At 11:30 P.M. when the two ships were about ten miles apart, the *California* operator went to bed, leaving his radio unattended. The night was clear and cold, with no moon, but with brilliant starlight.

At 11:45 the *Titanic* ran at top speed into a huge iceberg that ripped a gash three hundred feet long in her bottom and sides. The impact was not great enough to alarm the passengers or to awaken many who were asleep. Living in warmth and luxury on an "unsinkable" ship, those who were awake did not take the accident seriously at first. But water started pouring in in huge quantities in the lower part of the ship. Within half an hour the officers knew that she was sinking. They sent out radio calls for help; the deck crew fired emergency rockets, and started filling the boats, "women and children first." Men on board the *California* saw the lights and rockets, but unaccountably made no investigation and moved off on the east course, although they might have saved all or most of the *Titanic*'s people. Captain Arthur Henry Rostron, of the *Carpathia*, was fifty-eight miles away, but immediately turned about and started coming through the ice under forced draft towards the scene of the disaster. After all the *Titanic*'s sixteen boats had gotten away, carrying only 706 of the 1,176 people they might have accommodated, the steamer settled by the head and, with her lights still burning, rose almost perpendicular and, amid the crash of loosened machinery, slid into the cold sea at 2:22 A.M. Hundreds of the people who had remained on board were left floating in the water where most of them soon died. The *Carpathia* came up through the night and ice too late to save them. Having been efficiently organized by her master, who had foreseen everything, she picked up all the survivors in boats and cared for them. She was engaged in this errand until after sunrise when the *California* came up belatedly and continued the useless search for survivors. The *Carpathia* then headed for New York where she arrived four days later.

This terrible calamity distressed the world. In the most harrowing way, it revealed several weaknesses in the design and equipment of the most costly vessels of that time: that watertight compartments were not watertight overhead; that ships did not carry enough lifeboats to accommodate everyone on board; and did not organize crew and passengers for the use of lifeboats; and that radio sets were not continuously manned. As a result of the *Titanic* disaster every ship now carries enough lifeboats to hold everyone on board; crews have to practice lifeboat drill at frequent intervals; passengers are assigned to specific life boats when a voyage begins and have to participate in lifeboat drills, and radio sets have to be manned continuously or equipped to pick up S O S signals automatically. Atlantic ships have to follow tracks that keep them reasonably south of the ice fields. And during the ice season, the ice fields are patrolled by ships in accordance with an international agreement, and information about ice is supplied thoroughly to all ships in the vicinity. By intelligent organization the danger from collisions with ice has been eliminated as completely as possible.

16. Although I am confined behind the dingy city walls just now and bound by the cords of many duties, spring insists on being recognized. When I wake in the morning in a room that looks out winter and summer on the same blank, decaying brick masonry, I hear the laughing gulls cackling and screaming as they circle over the rooftops. At breakfast time, while the heavy busses are groaning down the Drive and the ash truck is clattering at the

littered curb, I hear the flicker shouting from the Park—"wick-wick-wick-wick," as if it were his duty to tell the thousands of Riverside Drive dwellers that spring is here and this is no day to go to the office. A black drake and his infatuated duck, who obsequiously keeps two paces behind him, are swimming just north of the yacht basin, their domestic arrangements settled for the season. Two yellow palm warblers, the first sentinels of this dainty and enchanting race, drop from the black branches of a hawthorn to the black pavement beside the river; and while preoccupied city strollers go by, lost in thought, the warblers skip nimbly along the margins of the sidewalk. The human race and the warbler race pass close by without touching, neither one appearing to recognize the other.

At dinnertime the busses, heavy with office-workers going home, labor noisily up the little hill, the gears grinding and the exhausts coughing. Everyone, including the motors and the gears, is bored and weary. But the robin, sitting in one of the maples across the Drive, is singing his long, sweet evening song in a key much more exalted than any of the city voices. Looking back over the day's events, he is relaxed and content, he is grateful for the evening and he makes music that comes through our south windows at dinnertime. It is a meditative song evoked out of river, grass, trees and the sunset and it concludes the day magnificently.

17. Even the Hudson River looks different now. The water looks the same, but the traffic that swims on it looks gayer and more relaxed. The black diesel yacht of the Engineer Corps, which remained in service until mid-November, has returned to the small boat basin. The "round Manhattan" excursion boats are in service again on Saturdays and Sundays. Freshly painted in gleaming white, they look handsomer than they will be in midsummer. Now the State Barge Canal is open, connecting New York by water with the Great Lakes and the vast interior of Canada. At night I hear the anxious panting of the steam tugs and feel the heroic drumming of the diesel tugs as they pull their barges upriver—the running lights glittering like diamonds against the rich blackness of the water. After lying up all winter at Pier 43, the Farrell tugs are in service again. They have a charter to haul molasses to Buffalo—$11.50 a ton from Philadelphia and

$8.50 a ton from New York. It will take fifteen days for each unit of barges to make the round trip from New York to Buffalo— night and day through the water gorge in the Hudson Highlands under the stars and sun and then up the Mohawk River and across the north of the state to Lake Ontario. The world is open again and both the blossoms and the barges are moving north.

18. Go down Pine Street three blocks to the water front. From the cramped, dark soullessness of the area where money is handled you emerge rapidly into the clear sunlight. Over the rim of a pier barrier the yellow masts of a steamship rise, and the white letter- ing on the pier shed says: "India, Straits, Far East." You are lucky to get out of the financial district so swiftly and safely. West of Pearl Street the gloomy banks and austere office build- ings hide from the sun and house millions of pieces of paper. But east of Pearl Street, two blocks of warehouses and workshops form a *cordon sanitaire*, and the culture is marine on South Street. The signs say "Tackle blocks," "Fishing Supplies," "Wall Rope Works," "Whitlock Cordage Company." Farther down towards the tip of the island rises the Seamen's Church Institute, culmi- nating in a cross and a miniature lighthouse. The clock strikes ship's bells.

The waterside is hardly glamorous. Barges, tugs, Coast Guard harbor craft lie up there aimlessly. A dead Liberty ship has been rusting there for more than a year. Sometimes a Norwegian steamer comes in for a few days. Two small Honduran craft have been lying there for nearly a month, and today a large steamer from Uruguay, flying the Uruguayan flag, which is rare in this port, is tied up in a vacant slip. Some of the seamen are painting the funnel blue and white. Canal barges, with huge rudders and tillers, are moored there. Lace curtains at the cabin windows keep the pier-head drifters from looking in. But sometimes the master of the barge, smoking a pipe, comes up the ladder to toss a bucket of slops overside and to look over the neighborhood.

Seamen temporarily on the beach stand in knots or sleep in the doorways along the street. Some are in pea jackets left over from the Navy or the wartime Merchant Marine. Some are in khaki- colored cotton trousers and jumpers, and some are splendidly dressed with colored shirts and matching ties for going ashore.

Some are bleary and red-faced. But most of them are sharp and able—Americans, Swedes, South Americans, Norwegians, the Negroes and whites mingling affably.

The seamen's bookshop in a narrow store near the ferry house looks after their intellectual needs. *Seamen's Law* has just been republished in a dollar edition. The window is full of textbooks—Knight's *Marine Engineering*, Riesenberg's *Standard Seamen's Manual*. As a kind of frivolous border to the serious fare, the window has a series of paper-covered pamphlets: *French Stories of Love and Passion, One of Cleopatra's Nights, How to Make Love.*

At the noon hour the saloons are as quiet and contemplative as a gentleman's club.

19. When people talk about how much better life was in the good old days, I like to think about automobiles. In the good old days the stage-driver devoted a long, tedious day of about fourteen hours to driving to Catskill and back from the town where we have a farm, and it was a four-hour train ride from Catskill to New York or an overnight boat ride downriver. The good old days are over. But in these days, which are less celestial, I can drive from the city to the country between breakfast and luncheon, carrying all sorts of baggage and odds and ends with no trouble. On several occasions I have made the round trip between breakfast and dinner.

This seems to me an extraordinary achievement, not only mechanically but spiritually. My life has more range because of the automobile. That is a demonstrable fact and not a sentimental opinion. I can season the business of the city with gardening, brush-cutting and work in the carpenter shop on week ends through most of the year. This is what the automobile has contributed to my life, and I am grateful; and I do not look back enviously at the days when my mother and father, sisters and brother, devoted a long, nerve-wracking day to getting to the country once a year and another day to getting back. We had to rise at four o'clock to make all the stage, boat, and train connections. In those days we snatched desperately at the country. Now we drive comfortably from door to door in a few hours.

Since automobiles are sold by the design and color of the bodies, there is a vast heap of nonsense and mumbo-jumbo in automobile culture. But I admire the perfection of the motor and machinery. Although I know nothing about machinery, the motor always starts when I need it and keeps on going, fast or slow, uphill or on the level, as long as I am on the road. I can drive a car as well as a mechanic. All this has happened in my lifetime, and I think it is miraculous and I am glad I am living in the motor age when I can get to the country without having to organize a complicated and worried safari.

There were 34,373,002 motor vehicles registered in the United States last year.

20. There is no fundamental difference between walking in the city and walking in the country. The physical technique of walking may be less mechanical in the country. But seeing is the chief virtue of walking everywhere, and there is as much to see in one place as another. Along the city streets the faces, the shops, the fruit, the newsstands and the buildings are the abstracts and brief chronicles of the times and supply a rich library for reading and thinking. There is a reason for every item posted along the street—a hope fulfilled or a hope vanquished, a dream crumpled by experience, a piece of luck or a blow of misfortune. The Indians walked here. The Dutch burghers did business here; the English cut down the trees and planted crops. America has dug, built, and organized a nation in these streets and buildings, strewing the debris everywhere carelessly, wearing out and rebuilding, buying, selling, going to school, playing stickball, and raising families. We rub elbows with a million destinies every time we walk down a street.

I confess that Central Park is the only part of the city where I do not like to walk. It is the best the city can do in an admirable attempt to keep a few hundred acres open. Thousands of people use it gratefully. But it is counterfeit country; and to me insipid and less refreshing than the vibrant thunder of the traffic across Brooklyn Bridge or the tension and loquacity of the garment center, where the rights of man are fiercely argued during the lunch hour.

To walk is to be free. It is escape from the system of telephones, subways, office and routine; and it is foreign travel only a few blocks from home. I never see anything on my daily migration to and from work by subway. But if I walk to the office I see hundreds of people I never saw before. To a person who works in the Times Square area, the Wall Street area or the Foley Square section are like separate cities and Mott Street is like a foreign nation. You have to walk to see these places. You have to keep your feet on the ground.

21. On this day in 1838 thousands of New Yorkers crowded the Battery wall and hundreds put out in rowboats to see the first steamer that crossed the North Atlantic. She was the *Sirius* and she had come across under steam-power in sixteen and a half days at eight and a half knots average speed.

As if that were not enough excitement for one day, a second steamer stood into the harbor a few hours later—the *Great Western* which had been built especially for the London-New York trade. She had left London three days after the *Sirius* had left Cork, and must have made a shorter passage since there was little difference in their speeds. In fact, the two vessels, which were rivals, had raced each other down the Thames on the day the *Sirius* left London, and the *Sirius* had won.

Nineteen years earlier, in 1819, the American-built *Savannah*, a full-rigged ship with steam paddle wheels as auxiliary, had sailed from Savannah to St. Petersburg, Russia, and return. But she was essentially a sailing ship, and the steam auxiliary was removed after the round trip. The first steamship to cross the Atlantic was the *Conde de Patmella*, which steamed from Liverpool on October 20, 1820, to Lisbon and then to Brazil. The records of this ship are scant and vague. The *Sirius* and the *Great Western* appear to be the first steamships to have crossed the North Atlantic without relying on canvas; and they inaugurated the famous North Atlantic passenger trade. The *Sirius* carried ninety-four passengers.

Morally, the *Great Western* should have had the honor to open that trade. She was designed for it. On her trial trip she had caught fire, and the accident had delayed her maiden voyage. In the meanwhile, a rival line chartered the *Sirius*, which had been built for coasting, to make two voyages to New York to beat the *Great Western* in that trade. Although the *Great Western* arrived in New York a few hours later than the *Sirius*, she was in the trade for a long time and for years was the only steamship in

the North Atlantic. She made seventy voyages. Her fastest west-
ward passage was twelve days, nineteen hours; eastward, twelve
days, seven hours.

To judge by a story in the *Evening Post*, the next day New
York went mad with excitement, as it has done on many other
occasions. Thousands of people rushed to the Battery to gape,
and many hired rowboats to pull around these epochal vessels.
"The practicability of establishing regular intercourse between
Europe and America is considered to be solved by the arrival of
these vessels," the *Evening Post* declared prophetically.

22. About this time of year many city men discover that they
are not husky enough for the country. This happens every year,
but it is always surprising. Since this is a warm, windless day in
the country, I plunge enthusiastically this morning into the annual chore of raking the lawn and gathering the dead leaves
from under the shrubs and hedges. It is one of the easiest spring
jobs—tedious but light. But after a couple of hours I discover,
much to my annoyance, that my back aches, my wind is getting
short, and my eyes are beginning to focus with difficulty. There
are about twenty-five or thirty wheelbarrow loads of trash to be
rolled off the yard every year. I am an exhausted man after I have
carried away seven. Writing newspaper articles and walking along
the water front are no training at all for pottering in the country.
Since the work has to be done, I keep on with it in a sort of
trance, although my body and my mind hum and vibrate with
fatigue. And, to make matters worse, I am continually discovering
new things that must be done—holes to be filled with top soil,
ant hills to be removed, dead branches to be sawed out of old
trees. I have no time to waste on getting my muscles tuned up.
Everything has to be done now, without delay. I must plant a
garden, paint the living-room woodwork, clean the grease off the
wood-working tools in the shop, finish the bathroom cabinet that
I let go last year, clean the garage, clean the cellar, burn trash on
the first wet day when fire will not spread, dump crushed stone
in the hollows of the driveway—all this before I can set to work
on the main project of the season, which is a rear porch.

Every year city men burst enthusiastically into the country, expecting to begin where they left off the previous autumn. But

they forget how long it takes to get muscles working again. "Stoop labor," as it is pungently labeled in the South, shatters the morale. From previous experience I know that I shall sleep tonight like a man who has had a bad accident. When I wake up tomorrow morning I will be in a daze, like a man coming out of a coma. It's a good thing I don't have to begin the season by chopping down trees and sawing logs. I am reminded of this because two of the neighbors today have been drawing logs, some of them sixteen inches in diameter and all of them ten feet in length. God knows how heavy those logs must be. But they don't exhaust my neighbors half as much as the rake and wheelbarrow have exhausted me and broken my spirit.

23. This is commonly celebrated as the birthday of William Shakespeare. The Shakespeare Society has its annual dinner and members of the Players Club gather around the statue of Edwin Booth, the illustrious Shakespearean actor, in Gramercy Park. The selection of today as Shakespeare's birthday is hypothetical. All that is known certainly is that on April 26, 1564, William; son of John Shakespeare, was baptized at Stratford. It was the custom at the time to baptize children about three days after they were born. Not much is known factually about the personal life of the king of writers in English. We cannot satisfy our curiosity about his private life; and, in fact, we do not know with certainty whether he was happily married or not. But as an honest writer of incomparable abundance, Shakespeare drew his spiritual image with great candor in the poetry he wrote for more than a quarter of a century, with a passion and a virtuosity unequaled by any other writer in English and perhaps in any language.

He had a winning personality. He had grace, wit and humor and loved the excitement of the town as well as the savors and delights of the country. Although he was decently modest, he took pleasure in the success his talents brought him and happily accepted the social structure of the England of his day. Halfway through his career something staggering happened—no one knows what it was—that detached him from the easy gaiety of his youth and plunged him into melancholy. He became aware of the wildness of human nature—evil, greed, treachery, intrigue and murder. Overwhelmed by the disasters of human affairs, he wrote the most tumultuous tragedies in our language. Gradually he recovered his normal good humor and concluded his career with sweetness and fancies that forgive without forgetting the boorishness of the world; and he retired to Stratford to live with his married daughter and enjoy four years of comfort and leisure amid the green beauties of his youth. By that time he had said nearly everything worth saying about nature and her fretful little children—and said it, moreover, with force, eloquence, and richness of imagery beyond anything any other man has poured out of his soul. He had the supreme gift of the great writer: the dual capacity to see human beings objectively in all their frailty and the compassion to pity them as friends. He did not disassociate himself from any experience and did not look down on anyone. Although he dealt in ideas he never expressed them abstractly but seasoned his lines with the sweat, stink, laughter and revelry of human society. No one knows how much our lives nearly four centuries later have been shaped by this singing monarch of literature.

24. First day of Passover, which continues seven days for Reformed Jews and eight days for Orthodox. The festival begins at sundown with the *Seder*, or Passover feast, at which unleavened bread is eaten and the story of the Passover is told at family dinners. When the Lord struck down the first-born in the land of Egypt he passed over the houses of Jews. Following His command, Moses and Aaron had instructed the Jews to smear lamb's blood on the two door posts and the lintel to distinguish their houses from those of the Egyptians. When the Egyptians found that their first-born had been killed, Pharaoh told Moses and Aaron to take their people and their flocks and leave Egypt. In their haste the people took their bread before it was leavened, "their kneading-troughs being bound up in their clothes upon their shoulders." Six hundred thousand Jews, not counting the children or the mixed multitudes that went with them, and also their flocks and herds, passed out of Egypt from Rameses to Succoth. The day was set for perpetual commemoration by the Lord's instruction as recorded in Exodus:

"And this day shall be unto you for a memorial; and ye shall keep it a feast to the Lord throughout your generations; ye shall keep it a feast by an ordinance forever. Seven days shall ye eat unleavened bread; even the first day ye shall put away leaven out of your house: for whosoever eateth leavened bread from the first day until the seventh day, that soul shall be cut off from Israel. And in the first day there shall be a holy convocation, and in the seventh day there shall be a holy convocation to you; no manner of work shall be done in them, save that which every man must eat, that only may be done of you."

The Jews were delivered from bondage out of Egypt about 1,450 years before Christ. After 3,400 years the Jews of New York are devoutly following the ancient teachings of Moses and Aaron today, repeating the story of the Passover and observing the sacred ritual before sitting down to the family feast. Thousands of their kinsmen abroad have still not been delivered out of bondage and have not yet crossed over to the free land.

25. The birds possess the woods and fields of our country home. It is their empire; they praise it with song. While I am working around the house on uninteresting spring chores, the birds exult throughout the neighborhood. A pair of phoebes is building over the dining-room door, and a pair of robins over the back door. Meadowlarks are feeding in the back field, stopping now and then to sing. In the wild field across the road a field sparrow is singing in the warm sunshine, and further on a flicker is alternately screaming and drumming. Purple finches pour out their rhapsodic song in the old spruces. There are birds everywhere—goldfinches, red-winged blackbirds, chickadees, downy woodpeckers, white-breasted swallows, a sparrow hawk, crows, Peabody birds, song sparrows, bluebirds, vesper sparrows—I did not realize there were so many. The land is wider awake than I had realized. For the shad-bush is in bloom. Tomorrow the tulips will flower. Wild strawberries have begun to blossom. The birches have begun to open tiny, delicate, yet fully formed leaves.

"Let's get away from the place," I say to O., who is indoors making curtains; and we walk down to the spruce lot where the trees are thickly budded. From a long distance away comes the soft, tremulous coo of a mourning dove. High on a dead tree a brown thrasher is singing interminably—sheer praise of the hillside in a long, chatty conversation-piece. Out of the leafless valley comes the thoughtful evening song of a hermit thrush; another

answers and still another farther away. It is too early for the wood
thrush, and the hermit is probably a migrant bound north to
deeper woods and higher mountains. But on this warm, still hazy
day when the earth is stretching and stirring, the goodness of
creation has overcome his reserve, and he lifts his voice to the
encircling hills. It is the most glorious wild voice in northeast
America—unsocial, but devout and pure. No other song has so
much depth and nobility. Although the hermit is a migrant in
our spruce lot, we are the intruders when he sings.

26. Jean Jacques Fougère Audubon (John James) born on this
day in 1785 in Santo Domingo. Knowing the value of a noble
river he spent his last years on the bank of the Hudson on the
edge of New York City. He was the son of a French naval officer
and Mlle. Rabin, a Creole of French parentage. When Lieutenant
Audubon returned to France, his wife happily received the child
of another woman, and brought him up with affectionate indul-
gence. A handsome, vain and versatile boy, he loved drawing birds
near his home in Nantes. When he was eighteen his father sent
him to America to learn English and business. Settled on a farm
near Philadelphia, he began one of the most amazing and creative
careers in the odyssey of America.

Young Audubon had the good fortune to marry Lucy Bakewell,
who lived near by in a well-to-do household and had the character
and fortitude to balance his genius. As a business man Audubon
was a failure. By the time he was thirty-four years of age and the
father of two sons, he had lost all his own and his wife's money,
had been imprisoned for debt, had no home and no prospects.
For both his wife and himself, this was a shocking experience;
neither one of them had ever been so harshly expelled from the
world. The next six or seven years tested their valor. Making a
vocation of his lifetime avocation, Audubon decided to draw the
birds of America life-size and from life and to publish them. Never
for a moment doubting the value of this stupendously ambitious
enterprise, Mrs. Audubon relieved her husband of the support of
the family by taking jobs as governess or teacher wherever she
could. Audubon began seven years of wandering in the American
wilderness, supporting himself by drawing portraits for a night's
lodging, teaching art, French, dancing and music—meanwhile col-

lecting birds all through the southeast and drawing them. His only assets were his unconquerable spirit, his genius as an artist, his extraordinary physical stamina, and his wife's devotion to him and his project.

America, absorbed in the exhausting labor of founding a nation, did not have the leisure to appreciate what he was doing. In 1826 he went to England with his drawings. Many people there recognized his genius and he rapidly became a celebrity—partly, no doubt, because with his long, greasy hair, he looked like a frontiersman from a wild, new country. In England he began a new and equally wearing chapter in his career. He had the good fortune to discover a highly talented engraver, Robert Havell, Jr., who could make fine plates from his drawings. With no resources except his spirit and genius, Audubon thus began publication of the immortal *Birds of America,* which took twelve years in the press and cost more than a hundred thousand dollars to produce. In addition to supplying all the art, he had to peddle the book and supervise the business arrangements. The subscription price was one hundred seventy-four pounds in England and one thousand dollars in America. The completed work included four hundred and thirty-five plates, representing "over one thousand individual birds, as well as thousands of American trees, shrubs, flowers, insects and animals."

Every plate had to be colored by hand. Sometimes there were fifty people employed in the coloring process. During the twelve years many of the original subscribers canceled their orders and some of them, including the King of England, never paid. The number of perfect sets produced was between one hundred and ninety and two hundred. Audubon once said that he lost twenty-five thousand dollars on the enterprise, although his bookkeeping was never exact; and since he was penniless when he began, it is difficult to see where he got twenty-five thousand dollars to lose. Now the *Birds of America* is recognized as a heroic artistic achievement. It was also a pioneer work in American ornithology and added many new species to our check list.

Nor was the *Birds of America* a studio job. It was the fruit of years of labor in the woods, fields, and swamps. At a time when transportation was primitive, Audubon crossed and recrossed Pennsylvania, Ohio, Kentucky and Louisiana, visited Texas, descended the Ohio and Mississippi several times, covered Florida and New England, visited Labrador and Canada, and in his old age pushed up the Missouri and got into the Yellowstone. In 1841 he bought about thirty-five acres of land in what is now Washington Heights, and built a two-story house on the shore of the Hudson River between what is now One Hundred and Fifty-fifth Street to One Hundred and Fifty-eighth Street. That was before the railroad was built on the shore line. There was good fishing in the Hudson then. Once, Audubon and his boys caught near their home a sturgeon eight feet long and weighing two hundred pounds.

Audubon died at the age of sixty-seven on January 27, 1851. Owing to the Civil War, improvident business management and perhaps the cupidity of some publishers, the Audubon estate fell to pieces during the next decade. At the age of seventy, Mrs. Audubon had to start teaching school again and continued for five more years. She outlived her husband by twenty-three years of penury, and also outlived both her sons. She died at the age of eighty-six after a lifetime of hard work, great valor, and heroic devotion.

27. Daylight-saving time begins. Tonight the sun sets at 6:51 standard time, but 7:51 by daylight-saving time, and this gives not merely the illusion but the fact of a long, leisurely evening. We dine by the brilliant light of the declining sun; after dinner the gold of the west keeps on flooding across the bright Hudson and pouring its natural refulgence through the burgeoning maples and plane trees on Riverside Drive. The sun has come a mighty distance north since the winter. At Christmas time it set close to a church steeple in Weehawken, southwest from the window of my workroom. On March fifth it had swung north to a tall apartment house that I can just see out of the corner of the window. But today it sets too far north over Edgewater for me to see from here. There are still nearly two months before summer begins. But already the sunset has migrated from one New Jersey city to the next city upriver without any apparent political consequences. Wait until it enters Bergen County!

For the past week the laughing gulls have been whirling over the river—screaming a mirthless, sardonic "ha, ha, ha." Most of the heavier and sedate herring gulls have gone north to their breeding grounds. The abundance of the laughing gulls is more than casually gratifying. They had all but deserted New York a quarter-century ago. For a half-century or more they had been slaughtered for the millinery trade, and they became rare in New York. But since the commercial slaughter of birds for their feathers has been prohibited by law, the lively and noisy laughing gulls have become common again. A great flight of them in 1921 was considered notable enough to be recorded by one of the Museum of Natural History ornithologists. Now they come whirling up the river in great numbers during the migration season—screaming with enthusiasm as they wheel and dive through the air.

28. If the New York subways did not exist, no one would be able to imagine them. No one could conceive of such barbarism and animal brutality day after day in a dungeon. Hogs get better care in transit, for hogs are worth so much a pound and it pays to take care of them. But a human being in the New York subway is only a malevolent encumbrance that must be gotten out of the way as quickly as possible before another avalanche of malevolent encumbrances can swarm down the steps and choke the platform. When the subway was invented to solve the traffic problem, no one ever imagined that people would be so frantic, desperate, and brutalized.

John Kieran says that man is the only animal tough enough to endure torture in the subway day after day: "If a rhinoceros or a lion had to make that journey every day he would die of nervous prostration within a week. No wild animal could stand it." No man could stand it daily unless he had been conditioned to it over a period of time and had not learned to go through it in a state of insensibility. Twice a day we do penance in the Inferno, automatically withdrawing from civilization until we climb up to the street level again. If we thought about the subway we would be terrified and go insane. We have to regard it, like bodily elimination, as something necessary but mechanical and revolting.

29. The opinions of the aristocrat are absolute and icy. He categorically rejects everything that does not satisfy him completely. He is dogmatic and arrogant and traditional. Into the wastebasket with everything that does not repeat to him every-

thing he already knows! No wonder aristocracy gets paler and more futile every generation. It cannot be enriched or renewed from outside its own arid kingdom.

To reject life is to build walls and construct a graveyard for the mind and spirit. To be lacking in perception and understanding is to die. To raise abstract intellectual barriers against creation and love is to be already dead in spirit. Aristocracies commit suicide, for they live by illusions. The most fatal illusion is the settled point of view. Since life is growth and motion, a fixed point of view kills anybody who has one. This applies also to Marxists, Communists and any group that adheres to a specific rigid program. Both the aristocrats and the Communists are fatal to progress and creation.

30. In 1789 George Washington was inaugurated as first President of the United States on the balcony of Federal Hall, located on what is now the corner of Wall and Nassau streets. Every year this momentous episode in our national life is re-enacted in costume by self-conscious citizens on the steps of the Treasury Building on the same plot of land. On April 30, 1789, the city was packed, several thousand visitors being added to the thirty thousand residents. Apparently, everyone understood the solemn importance of founding a new government. After having been formally notified of his election by the Electoral College, Washington had made a journey of several days by carriage and on horseback from Mt. Vernon through Baltimore and Philadelphia to New York. It was everywhere a triumphant processional. At Elizabethport, New Jersey, he entered a magnificent barge especially built for the occasion and was rowed up the bay to Manhattan by thirteen ship's masters in white uniforms and black caps.

Inauguration day began with a broadside from the guns at Fort George near Bowling Green. Beginning at nine o'clock all the church bells rang for a half-hour. People attended church services "to implore the blessings of Heaven upon the new Government, its favor and protection to the President and success and acceptance to his administration." The procession of soldiers and federal, state and city officials began at noon at the Cherry Street home of the President, who rode in a state coach drawn by four white horses. There was a band of bagpipers. The procession came

up Broad Street to Federal Hall, where it arrived at about one
o'clock. Washington entered the hall with his hat in his hand.
He wore a suit of dark brown material that had been manufactured in Hartford. The suit had metal buttons ornamented with
eagles. He wore white stockings. There were silver buckles on his
shoes. His hair was tied back and powdered. He wore a sword with
a steel hilt.

The balcony was dressed for the inauguration with red and
white curtains. At the last minute the officers discovered that they
had neglected to provide a Bible. Chancellor Livingston, a Mason,
sent to his lodge for the big Bible in use there. When everything
was ready Washington stepped out on to the balcony where he
was received with cheers from the packed streets and the windows
of the neighboring buildings. He put his hand on his heart and
bowed. Chancellor Livingston read the oath of office, which Washington repeated phrase by phrase, adding, "So help me God" at
the conclusion. The flag was raised on the steeple of the hall; the
cannon were fired at the Battery, the church bells were rung again,
and the crowd cheered.

Then Washington returned to the Senate Chamber to deliver
his inauguration address. He was noticeably nervous and ill at
ease. In the course of the address he asked God's blessings "to
concentrate to the liberties and happiness of the people of the
United States, a government instituted by themselves for these
essential purposes." He excused himself from making specific rec-
ommendations to Congress, as prescribed by the Constitution. He
said that he hoped that "no local prejudices or attachments, no
separate views nor party animosities will misdirect the compre-
hensive and equal eye which ought to watch over the great as-
semblage of communities and interests." After his speech, he went
on foot to a service at St. Paul's Chapel, and then home in the
state coach.

The evening of Inauguration Day was especially festive for the
entire population. Most of the houses were lighted up with candles
in the windows. There was a display of fireworks which Washington observed from the home of Chancellor Livingston. The display concluded with thirteen skyrockets and thirteen cannon vol-
leys in honor of the thirteen original colonies. The streets were
so crowded that no carriages could be driven through them. Wash-

ington returned on foot at ten o'clock to his house on Cherry Street.

So, the first President of the United States took office. No other President has been so devotedly and gratefully received by all the people.

MAY

May

I N Moscow those who have not been jailed or assassinated by their own leaders are today marching in a triumphant processional through the Red Square under the Kremlin walls. Many people are also marching for Soviet Russia down Eighth Avenue in New York. Like the arctic lemmings, they are marching to their own destruction. All the Communists in America and the American votaries of Soviet communism whom I know are motivated by abnormal circumstances and are seeking refuge in a mystic dogma expressed in pseudoscientific jargon. One is trying to escape the bitterness of a painful youth. One is a Negro, trying to escape race persecution in America. One is abnormally vain and wants to feel superior to ordinary Americans. One is a cynic who is bewildered by his riches and needs negative security to sustain his cynicism. One is turbulently emotional; he has wrecked his personal life and the personal life of others and needs some remote, mysterious security to lean against. One is physically grotesque and needs to lose himself in a sanctimonious myth that is impersonal. One feels guilty because he has never suffered. They are a psychiatric, more than a political, problem. In one degree or another they are unable to cope with the complexity of democracy and its myriad choices. To escape what they cannot control or understand they turn towards a rosy illusion, vainly hoping to be saved from themselves by a barbaric system in a secretive foreign land.

2. This is Easter for the Russian Orthodox church. O. and I are invited to an Easter supper with some Russian actors and writers who are now American citizens. They left Russia about twenty years ago when the Soviet regime began to gather the artists into the tyranny, and regiment them as servants of the

state. Russians as a whole are warm-hearted and hospitable, overflowing with generosity and good will. Love of the homeland is
possibly deeper and more passionate in Russians than in most
nationals. When they turn away from the land of Pushkin, Dos-
toievsky, Chekhov, and Tolstoy, they abandon something of wild
and brooding grandeur that has spread throughout the world and
added several golden cubits to the stature of the soul. The re-
nunciation of Russia is painful to Russians. Here they are, twenty
years later, still fervently Russian, but American citizens now with
families, homes and jobs, pouring into our national life some of
the flaming vitality of the humane Russian spirit. We should be
proud of these people. They have made sacrifices that few of us
have to make. They have proved to us that some of the things
we believe about our national life are true and work out as we
had hoped they would. Coming from a foreign land, they often
have a sharper perspective on American life than we do. Since
Russians are sociable and humane, they see things in our national
life that we overlook or underestimate. They revitalize and enrich
America.

3. To most city people the rain is a nuisance. It impedes them
with rubbers, raincoats, or umbrellas. Goods have to be covered.
The newsstands have to withdraw their newspapers and magazines
to places that are covered, and the newsdealers have to huddle
inside their coops. The air in the subways seems to be more choking than usual. The water runs down to the train platforms and
stands in pools. A damp steam fills the subway cars. Trade falls
off sharply in all the big department stores. Since the New York
water supply comes from up-state through one hundred miles of
tunnels, New Yorkers have a false illusion of self-sufficiency and
do not associate rain with the water they drink or bathe in.

But to those of us whose hearts are in the country at this time
of year a spring rain brings a cheerful feeling of confidence, gratitude, and security. To wake to the sound of rain dripping at the
bedroom windows and of automobile tires hissing on the wet
pavement is to feel thoroughly contented. The spring flowers, the
summer vegetables, and the autumn harvest are being covenanted
for and sanctified. This is part of the process of creation. The trees
in the park look greener than they did yesterday. The soot and

grime have been washed off them and the leaves are breathing cleaner air.

Since we work at the office behind opaque glass and under artificial light, one day looks like another, winter or summer, fair or foul. The engineers and architects have scooped an area out of nature, sealed it and neutralized it. The only signs of rain are the umbrellas, raincoats, and rubbers in the cloakroom. But perhaps our work will be a little cleaner and more tranquil today because the soot is washed out of the air, the city clatter is a little muffled, and the pace is not so driving and shrill. It is a light spring rain, soft but drenching. It permeates the roots of Cosmopolis as it waters the roots of trees and it softens the texture of a steel, brick and concrete city built to nullify the annoyance of the seasons.

4. On this day in 1626 Peter Minuit landed in New Amsterdam from the Dutch sloop, *Little Sea-Mew* ("Muwtje"). He probably landed on a gravelly beach at what is now Battery Place where an Indian trail began and wound north to the present Westchester.

Glancing out of the window today, more than three centuries later, I happen to see the *Queen Mary* coming slowly up the river to her berth. In the soft, gloomy murk of a rainy day her white work shines with pride and splendor and she emerges from the fog, high and formal, like a modern city on a hill. Clouds of oily smoke solemnly ruffle out of her towering scarlet funnels; and swept by the cold east wind, the smoke hangs a tawny curtain across the river to Weehawken. I can see eleven tugs massed on her starboard bow or pulling at her port quarter to heave her around in the slack water before she can slide into her berth at Fiftieth Street. She has brought 1,851 passengers from England in less than four days. Peter Minuit arrived with a handful of colonists—we don't know how many, nor do we know how long the *Little Sea-Mew* was pitching and rolling on the violent surface of the sea. But his enterprise plotted the compass bearings for the *Queen Mary*.

5. In midafternoon a small, white sloop ties up to a buoy near the Seventy-ninth Street yacht basin. Three men on board unship

the tall mast and secure it on deck. She turns out to be the Swedish
sloop, *Monsunen* ("Monsoon"), which left Gothenburg ten months
ago, sailed down the Baltic Sea, out through the English Channel,
down the coast of Europe and North Africa to Cape Verde Islands, west to Martinique and north to Florida and New York.
She is twenty-three feet over-all and carries a thirty-foot mast with
one huge sail. She steers with a tiller. She carries no auxiliary engine. The *Monsunen* must be smaller than the early ships that
visited this country from Europe, and her long voyage, following
the wind tracks, compares favorably with the bravest of the pioneer voyages. Columbus' *Santa Maria* was ninety feet in length—
about three times as long as the *Monsunen*. The *Monsunen's*
longest sea voyage was twenty-two days from Cape Verde Islands
to Martinique. Columbus' longest open sea voyage was thirty-three
days. As these figures suggest, men of modern times have not only
built great steamships that nobly represent the mechanical age,
but have also marvelously improved the small wind ships. We can
beat pioneer men on their own terms.

The crew of the *Monsunen* consists of three Swedish amateur
sailors—a teacher in a trades school, a mechanic and a house-
painter. Their voyage to the new world fulfills a romantic dream.
In every port except New York they have found people full of
enthusiasm for their adventure. They have been received as guests;
port dues have been suspended in their favor and repairs made
free on their sloop. In Havana admirers painted her free. In Florida the sailors were given a new nylon sail. But New York, which
is used to everything and bored by a good deal of it, charges the
Monsunen two dollars a day to tie up at the yacht basin. After
spending months at sea and after battling one furious North Atlantic storm off Cape Hatteras, the men of the *Monsunen* regard
the placid boorishness of New York as an anticlimax.

6. On May 6, 1626, Peter Minuit, agent for the Dutch West
India Company, bought Manhattan (the island of hills) from the
Reckgawawancs or Manahatin Indians. He paid goods to the value
of sixty guilders or twenty-four dollars, worth about two hundred
or two hundred and fifty dollars today. This was a legal transaction.
That is what gives it so much significance. For white men had
been familiar with the Manhattan site for a number of years.

More than a century earlier (1524) Giovanni da Verrazano, sailing for the King of France, had entered the harbor; and, responding to the invitation of the Indians, landed at what was then the tip of the island, probably on the place that is now the corner of Battery Place and Greenwich Street. He piously placed the land and bay under the protection of St. Anthony, miracle-maker. The French were soon busy at fur-trading along the river. Hudson arrived in the *Half Moon* on September 12, 1609. Acting on his reports the Dutch came to Manhattan soon afterwards. In 1613 Captain Cornelis Jacobzen May, in the sloop of two hundred and sixty tons, *New Netherland*, brought thirty families of Walloons and French people, and landed eight of his men to bivouac on the island. Like his French predecessors he was chiefly interested in the port at Albany. Immigrants began to arrive in the following months with cows, sheep and horses. Fort Amsterdam was staked out on the site of the present Custom House.

Peter Minuit appears to have been a fine and able man who administered his colony justly. In March, 1632, he was recalled by the Dutch States General, charged with having shown too much partiality towards the patroons on the Hudson and Delaware, who were accused of not having lived up to their agreements by trading with the Indians on their private account. Peter Minuit next appears in 1638 as leader of a Swedish attempt to set up a colony on the west shore of Delaware Bay, near the present site of Wilmington. After he had built Fort Christina, the Dutch warned him to stop colonizing and leave. He disregarded their threats, strengthened the fort, stocked it well with food and ammunition, and started home for reinforcements. While his ships were stopping at the island of St. Christopher in the West Indies, Minuit lost his life in a hurricane. The Swedish colony lasted until 1655 when Peter Stuyvesant captured the five hundred colonists with a force of seven warships and seven hundred soldiers.

The Dutch colony of New Amsterdam lived on in sufferance to the British who wanted it to complete their holdings from New England to Virginia. In July, 1664, the merry Charles II blandly conferred all the land from the Connecticut River to Delaware Bay on his brother James, Duke of York and Albany. British warships crossed the Atlantic, picked up several hundred eager New Englanders at Gravesend Bay, and, sailing up to the Battery, called on Peter Stuyvesant to haul down the Dutch flag. On September

8, 1664, New Amsterdam surrendered and the British colors were raised. In honor of James, Duke of York and Albany, the name of New Amsterdam was changed to New York.

According to an English landowner in 1670, New York was a beautiful place of brick and stone buildings roofed with red and black tile and it gave off a "fragrant smell" that could be perceived at sea before sailors could see the land.

7. More than most large cities, New York is anchored to the past. The future will be only a variation on the present. Nothing except a major catastrophe can change its fundamental appearance now. Cities in the West and Southwest with a third of New York's history are relatively unhampered by the past. They are still developing and spreading into new areas—building new art museums and theaters, new civic centers, new newspaper plants, new boulevards, new bridges, new suburban villages with a coherent plan and integrated architecture. The future in the new cities is crowding the present and great things can be done.

Some new things can be done in New York. The worst of the past can be destroyed and replaced, as it has been on the East River. But the emergencies are always so great that there will never be enough margin to build a modern city. No matter how many new schools are built, most of the old ones will be obsolete. We cannot tear down the Public Library and build a new one large enough and inviting enough for the people of today. We are anchored to the moldy Natural History Museum. We cannot seem to get rid of the archaic Metropolitan Opera House or Carnegie Hall. We cannot tear down the dismal and uncomfortable theaters and build new ones suited to the modern age. Here and there unusual circumstances will produce modern buildings—like Rockefeller Center, which originated in philanthropy, and the United Nations district, which a new idea about the world required.

But the basic pattern of New York was set years ago. We can never shake loose from the past as Dallas and Houston, San Francisco and Seattle do every day of the year. Although New York generates a mighty current of modern ideas, they are acted upon more decisively in Cincinnati and Salt Lake City than in New York. We can never unburden ourselves of the past. Our future is mortgaged to history.

8. Since there was a south wind last night Central Park is full of migrating birds this morning. City-pent though we may be, we can associate with them. For many birds that migrate during these spring nights find temporary sanctuary in the Park, which is one of the few green islands in the solid masonry of Manhattan. Amid the trash, broken bottles and litter of the Park, some of the wild birds spend the day—nervously feeding in the flowering trees and the bushes. In fact, about three hundred and seventy-two different species have been found there by amateur observers through the years. The migrants do not sing much. When the park begins to fill up with people the birds are no doubt uneasy; it is not the wild region it appeared to be when they discovered it at night. But against the surrounding roar of the city which increases in volume and clangor as the day awakens, and under the drumming of the transport planes crossing the city, Baltimore orioles and chewinks are singing this morning, and occasionally I hear the gentler and more puzzling spring songs of migrating warblers. In two hours before breakfast I recognize twenty species but there are probably at least ten more that I do not know or do not see. Only the experts can sort out the females from the males and name all the uncommon birds that stream through the city.

The most distinguished visitors this morning are three white-crowned sparrows. They are strikingly beautiful with patrician white heads streaked with black bands. They are the most elegant of the sparrows. In another two or three weeks they will probably be nesting in the woods of Canada, where they will sing. But my favorite today is the magnolia warbler, which has the extravagant beauty of a bird you would expect to find only in rich tropical forests. He is about five inches long; you would not notice him unless you were searching the trees. He is gorgeously striped with black, white and bright yellow in a handsome pattern. His throat, upper breast and sides are bright yellow streaks with narrow black lines. He sings a little tentatively this morning as though he were talking softly to himself as he hunts along stems and leaves for ants, plant-lice and insects. He, too, is on his way north, though probably not so far north as the white-crowned sparrow. But for a day or two in transit he squanders his innocence and beauty on a worn park in the heart of the city. Probably his ancestors streamed over these tiny hills when the Indians were hunting there. Possibly he does not understand what has happened.

9. Some of the correspondence that comes to my office desk is difficult to answer satisfactorily. For example, a diligent student engaged in an erudite project asks for the "esthetic criteria" that govern the criticisms I write for the *Times*. He is beating his brains out on the philosophy of art. "Our principal concern," he writes, "is to investigate, both by semantical and empirical analyses of art criticism, the validity of art criticism, and especially, the problem of 'relativism' in esthetics. At the moment, we are concentrating upon the origin and possible 'objective justification' of primary and secondary esthetic criteria and the definitions from which the latter might emerge."

In a nutshell, that is the problem. Since it is written in academic jargon impossible to translate into the common tongue of uncloistered men, the temptation is to dismiss it as pretentious humbug. But what the gentleman is asking rather learnedly is: "How do you get that way?"—a question a lot of people, including myself, would like to see answered.

Great bodies of knowledge can be and have been systematized, which is something worth doing, since it relieves future generations of the necessity of beginning at the bottom. It saves time not to have to discover by personal investigation that the world is round and travels around the sun and has a very cozy relationship with an agreeable system of planets. Copernicus and Galileo have saved us a lot of annoyance by doing this preliminary work for us. It would be illuminating to extend the same accumulation of knowledge to the field of art appreciation. For this is the one place where sheer anarchy still prevails. In the appreciation of drama there is one basic problem: "Is it good or is it bad?" But this is a question that so far has defied systematization and that has to be answered afresh every time a new play opens and by everybody who sees it. In art there is nothing right or wrong but thinking makes it so. There are no concrete rules that specify the virtues and vices of a drama, and there are no authorities learned enough to give the magic word.

10. If there is no accounting for taste, there is no disputing it. In your opinion of a drama you may find people who agree with you, and you can build up a strong case for your side by bringing them together and screaming in unison. But there is no one who knows art in the sense that Galileo knew that the earth revolves around the sun. In the course of centuries educated men have come to regard Aeschylus, Euripides and Shakespeare as great dramatists. But this may be nothing more than a myth or a cultural conspiracy. If you do not think that they are great, you are under no compulsion to accept the cultural tradition. And you will not be wrong in the sense that you will be grotesquely wrong if you do not believe that the earth moves around the sun.

Everyone may look for and expect one thing from a drama or any other work of art—stimulation. Whether it is comedy or tragedy, vaudeville or musical drama, it stimulates you if it moves you to laughter or tears. Nothing is a good drama for you—even Shakespeare—if it does not enter into your imagination. That is the only possible test. Dutiful appreciation of art is a form of cant that should be despised, and boredom is a thoroughly legitimate form of criticism.

But this, of course, begs the question. In the appreciation of art you are on trial as much as the artist. You have as much to give as the artist, and the failure may be yours and not his. Although every man is a king when he enters the theater, his response to what he sees on the stage is not capricious. There is a reason for it. Every man brings his own heritage, character, environment and personal experience into the theater with his hat and coat; in short, he brings certain gifts and certain prejudices. What he thinks of the play represents a mingling of his personality with the materials of the drama—in fact, the adventure of his soul among masterpieces, which was Anatole France's definition of criticism. If the theatergoer is literal-minded he may not like an imaginative play. If he is imaginative he may be dissatisfied with naturalism. You can bet your boots that someone is going to dislike something, no matter how good it is.

11. Discovering the basis for critical responses to a work of art is therefore a staggering problem. Let's not even think about it.

It involves not only an analysis of the work of art but the analysis of everyone who sees it—a job in mass psychiatry terrible to contemplate. What is it in the souls of men that responds so profoundly to *Hamlet*, *When We Dead Awaken*, or *The Death of a Salesman?* On the other hand, why do some people come away from such plays untouched and scornful? In a physical sense they look at the same play but they do not see the same things in it. This is horribly unscientific.

In every creative work of art there is one unfathomable mystery —the personality of the artist. The ultimate truth about him cannot be isolated, identified, or explained. In that respect he is like the universe, of which he is a part, and no doubt that is why he is creative. We have had some very imposing lawgivers in the drama from Aristotle to Dryden to Dr. Johnson. But none of the laws they promulgated with so much assurance can explain why Shakespeare was a greater dramatist than Ben Jonson, despite the fact that Jonson, wearer of the learnèd sock, had studied the rules in college. The problem of esthetics is not one of subject matter or technique, but of human character, and the essential life force in human character is still a mystery. The only rules that apply are too general to be pertinent.

Although it would be convenient to codify art, one may be forgiven for resting one's head on the pillow of doubt. In this sort of situation George Santayana is a good man to have in the house: "I think that common sense, in a rough dogged way, is technically sounder than the special schools of philosophy, each of which squints and overlooks half the facts and half the difficulties in its eagerness to find in some detail the key to the whole." But, alas, Santayana is a poet, which leaves us where we were before and leaves the diligent student without a satisfactory answer.

12. St. Tammany's Society, or the Independent Order of Liberty, was founded on this day in 1789, thirteen days after Washington had been inaugurated. What has become one of the most sordid political organizations in America was founded by William Mooney, an upholsterer in Nassau Street and a friend of Aaron Burr. The first officers consisted of a brewer, carpenter, goldsmith, tavern-keeper, printer, grocer, broker, butcher, merchant, chairmaker and shoemaker. Socially Tammany was in opposition to

the aristocratic and hereditary Order of the Cincinnati. Although naturalized Americans could be members of Tammany, only native-born Americans could hold office. In 1805 the title was changed to Tammany Society, or Columbian Order.

At first Tammany seems to have been a convivial society that met once a month at Martling's Long Room at Nassau and Spruce streets for drinking and Indian mumbo-jumbo. There is a verse by Fitz-Greene Hallock which celebrates that aspect of the society:

> "There's a barrel of porter in Tammany Hall,
> And the buck-tails are swigging it all the night long;
> In the days of my youth 'twas a pleasure to call
> For a seat and a pipe with the jovial throng."

Tammany also used to hold noisy and rollicking parades every year to the picnic grounds. One year the anniversary was concluded with a play called *Tammany* which was produced at the John Street Theatre with President Washington and some of his cabinet in attendance.

Tammany openly entered politics in 1800 to elect Burr president of the United States. A year earlier the Federalists had carried New York with a majority of nearly one thousand, which was huge for that date. Tammany got to work in the same spirit that still characterizes the society, and carried the city for Burr. In the electoral college he and Jefferson were tied for the presidency. The House of Representatives had to make the final choice, and selected Jefferson. Burr was the first of New York's political bosses and Tammany was his organization. Although the Society has lost its early carnival and convivial nature, it has never shaken off the political spirit it inherited from Aaron Burr.

13. At 8:30 Coast Guard Cutter 64306 leaves Pier 9 for her morning anchorage patrol. Backing out into the East River she heads out towards the Federal anchorages off Governors Island and at the mouth of Gowanus Canal to see that the ships are anchored in the proper places and that the traffic channels down the Bay are unobstructed. She is a bright and able little craft— sturdy and kindly looking in the tradition and spirit of the Coast Guard. Designed like a miniature tug, she is driven by a sweet-toned diesel motor of one hundred and sixty horsepower. She

dances lightly on the lively water of the harbor; stinging pellets of spindrift rushing back from the bow strike the windows of the wheelhouse where we stand. The ship-to-shore radio is chattering coast guard business bulletins to all the craft that are policing the vast harbor. Our cutter, which is in command of a young chief bosun's mate, is ordered to keep an eye out for another cutter that has disappeared into the industrial jungle along Kill Van Kull, where the steel bridges interrupt radio communication.

Although Cutter 64306 is a harbor craft and ties up at the coast guard mooring basin every night she has a life of her own as soon as she gets under way. We have left the land; we are on our own. The bosun's mate smokes a pipe as he stands at the wheel, peering out at the passing blue-water vessels. The engineer hands up mugs of coffee from the galley. One of the crew is sleeping in a bunk in the deep well of the fo'c's'le, visible down the companionway from the wheelhouse. By ten o'clock, when we are checking on a ship anchored in Gravesend Bay, the appetizing odor of frying onions is coming out of the galley. At noontime we tie up to the towering hulk of a barge in the tide-race of Kill Van Kull and the crew of four and their passenger sit down to a meal below. We have steak, boiled potatoes, succotash, asparagus tips, baked apples, and more mugs of coffee. The coffee pot is never off the stove.

After dinner we resume the patrol out through Arthur Kill and around Staten Island, taking notes on the shipping, hailing the lost cutter and another picket boat, looking for obstructions in the channel and for any infractions of the harbor rules. There are none. It is an uneventful cruise of sixty miles, monotonous to the four boys who make it once or twice a week in alternation with other anchorage patrols up the East and North rivers. But they are glad to indulge their passenger who enjoys the cruise through the busy Kills, the long view across the endless ocean between Sandy Hook and Long Island, the romantic spectacle of a French and an American freighter dropping rapidly down Ambrose Channel, a near view of the shad fishermen raising their nets off the island and the gallery of snaky-necked cormorants perched along the weirs, fat and lazy from the fish they have already eaten. At 3:30 we come up through Buttermilk Channel and return to Pier 9 with a sheaf of reports about the daily traffic of New York harbor. We have another mug of coffee to settle our marine affairs.

14. At last the ground is ready for planting the kitchen garden on a week end in the country. The earth is mellow, i.e., damp without being wet, and warm under the sun. The garden was plowed last autumn. It was harrowed with a tractor ten days ago. With a wheelbarrow full of garden tools, fertilizer and seeds, John Whitbeck and I start preparing the ground today with a thorough raking, and before noon we plant peas, beans, beets, lettuce, radishes, onions, and corn. We will plant potatoes and other stuff at intervals for the next six weeks.

It is exhausting work. It requires stooping and kneeling and pulling grass roots and handling the dirt. But every year it is almost a religious day. For planting dry seeds and reaping green vegetables is the annual miracle. The planting of the kitchen garden is as sincere and devout an act of faith as I know. "And God said, Let the earth bring forth grass, the herb yielding seed, and the fruit tree yielding fruit after his kind, whose seed is in itself, upon the earth: and it was so . . . and God saw that it was good." We all know the general principles of garden cultivation: sun, air, water, and soluble elements in the soil germinate the seed which flourishes and yields green vegetables. But still we do not know anything about the first act of creation, except what the first chapter of Genesis tells us.

These are days that are ecstatic with life. Life is bursting all around us in song and blossom. While we are grubbing in the dirt and trying to pull out the quack grass by its roots, the heavy fragrance of the lilacs pours across the road from the dooryard, and the oriole, robin, catbird, song sparrow, house wren, chebec and bobolink weave around us a vibrant web of song. They have eggs in their nests and they are ecstatic. Full of the common joy, they are uttering some in the manner of Dr. Donne. They are the "fowl that may fly above the earth in the open firmament of heaven," which God created on the fifth day. As John and I stoop over the friable dirt, we participate in the annual miracle, which passeth understanding. No wonder primitive people try to appease the gods with music and mystic rites when they put seeds in the ground. Chinese beat drums and ring bells in the fields where they are planting. For they cannot understand what produces the green wealth of the cultivated fields. And neither do I. We are laying up riches for the summer and autumn. Kneeling is the natural posture for putting seeds in the ground.

15. Of all the household arts, painting is the easiest and pleasantest. Almost anybody with the slightest mechanical facility can paint chairs, tables, and the woodwork, and get immediate pleasure out of it. For color, pleasurable in itself, quickly transforms things that are old and battered into things that give new delight. Browns and greens used to be respectable colors; they are modest, and, moreover, they hide the dirt. But modern people are keen enough to enjoy bright colors—yellow, blue, red, which are gay and brilliant. Almost anybody nowadays can begin life all over with a cheap brush and a can of ready-mixed paint from the store. What is old and grimy glows with clean, youthful beauty when it is painted with a jaunty color.

But even painting—simple though it is—has its code of values. Alas, that's where the drudgery comes in. For a paint surface needs a foundation—like a house, a bird bath or a clothes-pole; and foundations are drudgery because they do not show and give no pleasure. If you are painting new wood, you must give it two and possibly three coats, for the foundation coat merely treats the wood. There is nothing more tedious than repainting and repainting. By the time you can enjoy the finishing coat you are bored and peevish from having gone over the same surface before.

If you are painting wood that has already been painted, you must scrape, sandpaper and wash until you have a smooth and tactile surface. This is one of the most disenchanting jobs around the house. It is dirty. It is slow. It is stubborn. It keeps the house upset, sometimes for several days. The more you learn about painting, the more difficult it becomes. Good craftsmen are men without temperament. They have patience and probity. They can wait for the pleasure of finishing a job.

16. Last evening Sophocles' *Oedipus Rex* was acted with the usual humility. Why? Since it reveals fundamental aspects of the mind of the ancient Greeks, it has valuable historical significance, like the Acropolis, for we need to know something about their mental habits. I cannot read the original Greek verse, which is

said to be majestic, although none of the English translations seems majestic to me. Most theatergoers cannot read ancient Greek. Why do they stand so much in awe of classical Greek drama? I suspect that is one of the cultural illusions that hangs over from generation to generation. For the anguish of Oedipus is only an artificial gesture, based on spiritual assumptions that have not been valid for nearly two centuries. I suppose that cultivated Greek people took the ancient Greek gods seriously, although that is hard to believe. For their gods were capricious and whimsical. The curse they laid on Oedipus and the tangle they made of his life were no more than rather contemptible conceits in a mindless fairy tale. To submit today to gods of this ignoble breed, as Oedipus has to do, is to acquiesce in a colossal fraud. I am not purged with pity and terror, but irritated by the hang-dog stupidity of the Greek point of view.

Children delight in these gratuitous horrors based on fairy stories, but adults should have more independence of mind. To me *Oedipus Rex* does not represent a calmly ordered civilization of golden means, but the mannered ritual of a primitive religion that no one believes. There is great wisdom and remarkable knowledge in Socrates, Plato, Aristotle, and Thucydides. The thoughts about thinking of the Greek philosophers confirm many thoughts that we have today and show the long panorama of intellectual life. But the reverence for Greek drama is fetish worship. We go on piously propitiating the ancient Greek gods, although we no longer believe in them, and in fact, know that they never existed. The medieval miracle and morality plays, rude and superstitious as they are, are closer to the spirit of modern men and speak in the tongue of men and angels. For the God they reverence represents love and is not class-conscious.

17. The lilacs are definitive. When the lilac blooms begin to glow with their pinkish blue, the capricious part of spring is over and the settled weather begins. Fruit blossoms are magnificent; the apples and the pears, the haws, the wild cherries and the wild plums sweeten the landscape and brighten the corners of fields and the bottom of the cow lanes. In the spring you are pleasantly aware of fruit trees that you hardly notice in the summer. "Oh, I didn't know there was an apple tree beside that wall," you reflect

when the carcass of an old tree bursts into pink and white blossoms in May. Fruit blossoms are fragile and drop in the wind and
rain. Their season is over before you have really enjoyed it. But
the lilacs are more durable. The lilacs spend ten days coming to
bloom, bloom with tropical abundance and perfume the air lux-
uriously, and the blossoms still retain a friendly echo of color a
fortnight later when spring has acquired momentum. In this part
of the country we cherish the lilac as the chief blessing of spring
and we praise it with religious devotion. We surround ourselves
with lilacs on the tables indoors as though they were holy flowers.

In point of fact, the lilac is the most democratic of shrubs. It
lives long and companionably in the dooryard, leaning out from
the house and holding its canopy of blooms against the second-
story windows. It surrounds and embraces the house. Long after
a house has fallen into the cellar the lilac bush goes on blooming
faithfully every year in memory of lost generations. The lilac out-
lives the beams and the loose cellar walls, and like something immortal, raises its handsome panicles every spring in overgrown
fields where there is no longer any sign of a building. The lilac is
an Asiatic and Eastern European shrub, a member of the olive
tree family. There is a legend that a Yankee sea-captain brought
the first lilacs from India to New Hampshire, and that the multitudes have sprung from that stock.

If we love the lilac, it is equally true that the lilac loves us.
Thrust a lilac twig in the ground and it will become a bush and
after a decade it will reward us with blossoms. There are about
two hundred different species of lilac in colors ranging from pure
white to crimson. But the common lilac blossoms with a color that
has become standard in color charts. For a man would as soon
doubt the virtue of the lilac as of the sun, moon and stars; and
he would instinctively celebrate the building of a house by reverently planting a common lilac in the dooryard.

18. Amid the springtime grace and glow of Plymouth, New
Hampshire, in the foothills of the White Mountains, Nathaniel
Hawthorne died in his sleep sometime in the night of May
eighteenth or the morning of the nineteenth in 1864. No one
was present when he reached the end of his days. He was sixty
years old. That solitary release from a life that had already begun

to elude him concluded a shy, furtive, strangely romantic American literary career. Although he was not religious, he was a Puritan in his introspection and his passion for moral judgments. He had the Puritanical horror of sin—particularly of egotism. When he graduated from Bowdoin College, he was determined to become a writer. Although America was expanding and acquiring momentum, he took no part in progress and did not share the enthusiasm. For twelve lonely years he read, dreamed, looked, and scribbled in an upstairs room in a house in Salem. In search of themes and characters, he listened to the tales of old men and women, loafed in saloons and in coach stations and wandered idly through New England and as far west as Detroit. Storing up material for writing, he kept copious notebooks of the things he had seen and heard; and these became the ballast for the dark, supernatural romances he wrote in a dark, melodious style.

He began to earn his living as a writer by hack work. He edited the *American Magazine of Useful and Entertaining Knowledge*—writing most of the stuff he edited; and he compiled *Peter Parley's Universal History*. From 1839-41 he earned his living as a weigher and gauger in the Boston Custom House; and in 1845 he returned to Salem as surveyor of the port. An odd, unsocial, timid person—the end of a vigorous Puritan line—he slipped through the landscape and lived to himself. His marriage to Sophia Peabody was the happiest event—perhaps the only happy event—of his life; and behind the mask of seclusion that he turned towards the world, he lived a warm, rich, sometimes joyous domestic life. Thoreau, whom he knew as a neighbor in Concord, was conducting an austere, one-man rebellion against the social economy of America. Hawthorne was a rebel, also. But he rebelled by analyzing and exposing the sinful characters of the heroes of his unworldly romances, which had roots in the things that people knew and saw but which drifted off into supernaturalism. He was our first artist in prose fiction. The art is so pure and the knowledge of men so profound that external events do not affect his writings. Lacking the egotism of his time, he modestly wrote our first literature of the troubled spirit.

19. By temperament and experience the man of letters is poorly suited to an active political life. He is, or should be, personally disinterested, which is fatal to success in a skilled trade founded on maneuvering for gain. By temperament he is also easily bored, which is a malady in any public life. He is likely to have a sense of humor, which is a handicap.

Being principally interested in the life of man, however, he cannot be indifferent to politics, which intimately affect the life of man, and might dominate it if men are not constantly vigilant. In consequence, the man of letters is being frequently drawn in. Milton was a political pamphleteer as well as the second greatest poet in English literature. Swift wrote about politics so savagely that he is still a force in Irish thought. Sheridan gaily dabbled in politics, having one good Parliamentary speech to his credit. The deeper Tolstoy probed into the life of man the more he became involved in politics. Ibsen began as an epic poet and concluded by writing plays of social and political significance. Shaw did pamphleteering for years. Although Yeats was the most mystic of modern poets, which should disqualify him from any life of action, he was at one time a working statesman in a country where a poet is an imposing figure. A. P. Herbert annoyed the English ruling class by getting himself elected to Parliament; presently he annoyed them further by putting through a bill to modernize the marriage laws. In spite of their temperamental handicaps, men of letters have always taken political stands, sometimes getting themselves elected to office and honorably acquitting themselves.

In the democracies that survive, writers are drawn into politics because the future of their profession is at stake. Without the individual freedom they now enjoy they cannot work at their craft. They have ample evidence of what can happen. When the artist becomes the servant of the state he retires as high priest of the life of man, most of which lies outside the province of the state and politics. Even in this country it is necessary to keep this truth in mind. For there is constant pressure here from special pleaders; the writer is urged to believe that politics and economics are the basic laws of life, and he is invited to drop whatever he is doing and pitch in. But it is the writer's job to minister unto the whole man, not merely to a political being; and the subject of man in conflict with or in pursuit of his destiny involves a great many things that cannot be bought, sold or legislated. Man falls in love without the advice and consent of his district leader. His friends are people of his own choosing; and, like the woman he marries, they are the deepest influence in his life. His life in nature is the product of his own perceptions: economics and politics cannot influence his love of sea, land, and sky, or deprive him of the glory of sunlight. When he dies he passes completely outside the jurisdiction of government, which, incidentally, is one of the pleasures of mortality. For the life of man has enormous latitude, and the most vital parts of it burn in the hearts and minds of private individuals. The essential impulses in it are a private contract between man and God. Politics hardly scratch the surface.

20. Most writers do not think of themselves as men of influence on the thought and morale of the community. But dictators attach a flattering importance to all forms of art. They require not merely the silent acquiescence of writers and artists, but their active support. It is not enough for the writers of the Soviet Union to remain neutral politically. They must take an active part in the political control of the state by praising their leader, glorifying the political system and urging the people to make greater sacrifices for the state and work harder at the forge, lathe, plow and desk. For the leader must control not only the means of production but the minds and souls of the people. Since it is difficult to make everyone love him, the leader is not really secure until everyone else in the world is dead.

Although dictators have demonstrable political cunning, their taste in art and letters is appalling, and their influence on art and thought is boring. Hitler very quickly reduced German art and thought to a level of stupefying mediocrity. Mussolini flattened out Italian art. As soon as his influence was removed, Italy underwent a notable artistic renaissance. Although a dictator can bottle up or pervert the creative impulses of a country, he cannot kill them. Get rid of him and the genius of his country blossoms again.

Since Stalin is the ablest of the dictators, he has obliterated the culture of his country more thoroughly than Hitler and Mussolini swept away the art of their countries. It is true that Stalin is cursed with gifted composers who seem to be constitutionally unable to write popular melodies all the time. Stalin suspects that their talents are perverse. He would be happier if their tastes were as dull as his.

Being an intangible art, music is hard to fit into a political pattern. Something original or inspired is likely to creep in before a vigilant dictator realizes what is happening. But in literature, drama and journalism, which are written in terms of the common speech, Stalin has been totally successful. He has reduced them to the level of whining sanctimoniousness. In view of the brooding beauty of Russian drama and literature before the Revolution, Stalin's success in destroying them is one of his mightiest achievements. No man of ordinary strength could wreck so much national genius.

21. In the Wall Street area the buildings, dedicated to money and power, are massive and grim and as grave in appearance as a checkbook. Most of the work done there is with pieces of paper—innocuous in themselves, but symbols of decision and authority. I suspect that the clerks and bookkeepers trapped in that dark and ponderous area do not like their work. For there is no part of the city where the noon hours are enjoyed so gratefully. For so imposing a section of the city the street traffic is light. It cannot compare with the roar and jangle of the Times Square traffic. Uptown people take their lunch on the run. But downtown they pour hatless into the streets, saunter along the sidewalks, loiter on the street corners or in front of stores and restaurants, relax in the Trinity churchyard or on the hundreds of City Hall benches, browse in the bookstores, scowl into the sunshine and dream. The tempo is torpid. Don't count on these benchers and loungers for the revolution. At noontime the custodians of capital are too ruminative for action. Overhead where the office spires swim in the golden haze business may be brisk and important decisions made. But the streets are heavily laden with daydreamers.

Look at the stores in the neighborhood if you want to know what these guardians of wealth are daydreaming about. In Chambers Street are the small-boat chandleries, well stocked at this time of year with ship's paint, spar varnish, and cordage. In Park Row, the hardware store of Patterson Brothers is jammed with customers buying wood-working tools, brass hinges, prepared paints, nails, screws and shelf-brackets, or handling the "week's special" in cross-cut saws. None of the clerks in Patterson Brothers' emporium can begin to guess at the number of people who make purchases there every day. Every item, of which there are thousands, is fascinating and worth taking home to play with. Between Broadway and the North River piers there are hundreds of stores for seeds, tomato plants, pansies, and forget-me-nots already in flower, or lawn mowers, rakes, hoes and smartly painted labor-saving tools for the conscientious suburbanite. Although Wall and Pine streets are sober, the little hill running west to the ferry terminals is bright and gay with small articles that can be wrapped up and taken home with the evening newspaper. Close down Wall Street and the whole financial district, and the thousands of clerks who work there would not miss it. At this time of year their hearts are far away.

22. In view of the power that money has in our society, it is an astonishingly impotent thing. It cannot do anything of value for the individual or the nation. It cannot plant a garden, build a house, cook a meal, navigate a ship, write a play or symphony, or paint a picture. It is merely a utilitarian medium of exchange— more convenient than barter for goods and services. By law and custom it has been artificially endowed with the ability to reproduce itself through the institution of interest. At one time in history, all interest was usury and unlawful. But for centuries, the charging of interest has been lawful and the term "usury" applies only to "exorbitant" interest which, under certain circumstances, is unlawful. For society has found that it still has to protect itself against interest. Without arbitrary control by the state, money would eventually own the world.

Since money is in itself impotent, it has to be protected by the law and given some rights equivalent to those of human beings. This is an arbitrary extension of human authority into the inanimate world, and has no basis in philosophy or morality. As if aware of its shaky foundations, money assumes an attitude of grave respectability, like a whore who is trying to escape her past. Banks try to look aristocratic. The counting-house is formal and discreet. Bankers are expected to dress soberly and behave with decorum and face the world with caution. Even though they cannot afford it, they are expected to live like the privileged classes in comfort and with style. They are abject conformists. By behaving with respectability they compensate themselves for the awful fact that they cannot do practical and useful things, like the plumber or carpenter; and also for the fact that their ability to make money out of money has no validity except in the law.

Being impotent, money clings more desperately to its rights under the law than industry, merchandising, or service. It cannot afford to forgive or to forget. It must insist on the bond. Otherwise, the devastating fact might leak out that it is not good for anything and that the power it has is hollow and artificial.

23. At 9 P.M. the Great Dipper stands directly overhead, with Cassiopeia crowding the north horizon. This is the reverse of the positions they occupy in November, and it is the farthest distance the Great Dipper travels from the north. The winter sky is falling down the west horizon—Castor and Pollux and Capella dipping out of range before midnight; and the summer sky is rising. Vega— the prophet of summer—is already high in the east. Arcturus, the fourth brightest star in our heaven, reaches the meridian at 10:15. During the night every mate standing watch on every ship in the North Atlantic and North Pacific will get a "fix" on Arcturus, which is one of the most obliging beacons. Further south in the constellation of Virgo, the white heat of Spica burns a hole in the sky. This, too, is a good star for navigation, and many watch officers at sea will hang on to it tonight.

The Little Dipper is standing on its head tonight, holding up the North Star, which we regard as the immutable pivot of our sky. But nothing is absolute. Between the Little and the Great Dipper there is a faint star, Thuban, which was the Pole star in the days when the Pyramids were built. There is a dark gallery in the Great Pyramid with a small aperture that, at the time it was built, framed Thuban, which the Egyptians regarded as the immutable pivot of their sky. Five thousand years ago the sky seemed to turn around Thuban. But the earth is not a perfect globe. It bulges at the equator, and the gravitational pull of the sun is therefore irregular. In the course of centuries our north pole keeps swinging towards a different corner of the sky. Once it was Thuban. Now it is Polaris. In another five thousand years it will be a point in the constellation of Cepheus. Wait twelve thousand years and it will be a point in Cygnus. Tonight Cepheus and Cygnus in the northeast horizon appear to be modestly unaware of the distinction that is in store for them. What interests me is this: At some time in the future the North Star will be so obviously superseded as a practical pivot that the loyalties of star-gazers will have to be transferred to another star now lying to the east. But how will the change be made? And will the popular Sunday newspaper supplements present it as something alarming and as further evidence of doom?

24. A new worker has come to the city to begin his adult career. At the moment the city is not impressed. He has a job. But he has no place where his wife, his two children, and he can live. The available accommodations are small and uninviting; the rents are higher than he had supposed, and the landlords are not sure that they want him. As a beginner he cannot guarantee them all the security they require. No one really wants him in New York. The new worker has no rights in our preoccupied commu-nity. Everybody is busy or looking for a settled prospect.

But he comes to the great city bearing gifts. He has behind him a good family which has given him moral character. He has a good mind, a talent for working with people and friends who admire him and regard him as one of the nation's assets. Most valuable of all, he has a dream. Ever since he was a boy he has wanted to be a lawyer. When he was in early grade school he explained in a classroom theme why he wanted to be a lawyer: "Many times I have known inocent (sic) people to be convicted on false charges. This is a very common happaning (sic). Death has even overcome some inocent (sic) prisoners. May be I shall save somebody who is not guilty from one of these unjust con-victions." That was what he dreamed twenty years ago. Since then he has finished public school, gone through college, devoted another four years of his life to defending his country, and now he has finished law school. Unwilling to wait while the world was obliging enough to make a place for him, he had the good sense to marry a navy nurse at the end of the war; and as an earnest of their faith in life and society, they have two children.

The new worker and his family are bringing qualities above price to New York. New York is about to acquire something that will strengthen and prosper the future. For the character of our future depends on acquiring thousands of enlightened men and women of courage and idealism, drawing, as usual, on the richness of the rest of the country.

At the moment, however, New York has no place where they can live in health, good humor, and contentment.

25. On this day in 1803, Ralph Waldo Emerson, the Concord sage, was born in Boston. To this grand old parson and poet we owe a great deal of the democratic faith. Independence from monarchy had been won on the battlefield. Under the leadership of Jefferson, Madison, Franklin, and Washington, democracy had been written into the law; and by the time Emerson graduated from Harvard College, political democracy had begun. Believing in all this with the purity of a religious man, Emerson saw what it meant in the hearts and minds of all kinds of Americans, in scholarship, religion, art, farming, commerce, civil relations. He could see no end to progress and enlightenment. As he phrased it, he believed in "the infinitude of the private man." Conservative people who had not yet thrown off the culture they had defeated in the Revolution, considered Emerson a radical. After listening to his interpretation of the spirit of the brave new world in religion, Harvard College shut the gates against him until, by sheer force of goodness, he was recognized as respectable in his old age.

He was a mild man to arouse so much rage in other people. He was a preacher, descended from a line of Boston preachers, all of whom were eminently respectable. He had had a sickly youth; his health seemed dangerously frail. He was a sedate person, prudent and modest in his habits. But he had a surprisingly resonant voice; and after retiring from the ministry because of conscientious scruples against administering the sacrament, he became an illustrious lecturer and carried the gospel of American democracy throughout the East and Middle West—encouraging people, enlarging their minds, awakening their spirits, appealing to their independence, self-reliance and strength. "Trust thyself," he said. "Accept the place divine providence has found for you, the society of your contemporaries, the connection of events." He prepared the ground for Thoreau and Whitman, who built the foundations under his dreams. For the inspiration he gave to others he drew from God and nature and reading in his library. A mild man, he

was a little shocked by some of the coarse uses to which his
thoughts were put. For his thinking had a sweep and fire far beyond his personal experience. But having said that everything alive
is good, he could not retreat into parochial respectability, nor
deny the noise and tumult of America.

26. After huddling all winter at their Forty-second Street
berth, the Hudson River Day liners are plying the river again.
Festive and gay with flags fore and aft and all around the ship,
these white steamers are a seasonal portent as certain as the forsythia and lilacs, for they mean that the holiday season has
opened. Only one of the four steamers, the 1,721-ton *Peter
Stuyvesant*, built in 1927, is driven by a propeller. The others are
old-fashioned side-wheelers, ideal for river work. Two of them are
venerable ships. The *Hendrick Hudson*, 2,847 tons, and still the
queen of the fleet, was built in 1906. The *Robert Fulton*, which
steams daily to Indian Point and Bear Mountain, was built in
1909. She has a walking-beam and three slender stacks in an odd
row set across ship. Incidentally, she carries the steam-whistle
that once served the *Mary Powell*, the finest steamer that ever
plied the Hudson. The *Alexander Hamilton*, 2,367 tons and sister
to the *Hendrick Hudson*, was built in 1924. Between them they
carry nearly a million and a half passengers a season to the mid-
river recreation points and upriver to the country. Built for outdoor enjoyment, they have wide, long decks and family state-
rooms with unobstructed views of the river. They also have an
unparalleled record for safety; the management has paternally
anticipated the wild vagaries of excited vacationists.

Since they were built in Chesapeake Bay or Camden, the ships
have all had one brief coastal voyage. But after arriving in New
York they have been confined to the Hudson River, which they
have mastered. They are steered by the most experienced Hudson
River pilots, perched high above the madding vacation crowd in
roomy pilot houses. The job of steering these long ships up the
snaky river channel through currents, tides, occasional fog, and
uncertain winds is not simple; and the ships have to make at least
four landings a day. At least four times a day they have to be
brought alongside a pier and tied up to bitts and bollards. Sometimes a pile is broken or a plank crushed. But there have been no

serious accidents. And in spite of capricious river and weather conditions these happy ships ably maintain their schedules. They are cheerful ships to see on any part of the river and it is pleasant to hear the thunder of their paddle-wheels in the river gorge. When our apartment windows are open on summer evenings we can hear the rumble of the downriver ships returning to their midtown berth.

27. Herewith I formally notify Congress and the Supreme Court that I will not answer official questions respecting my political beliefs or affiliations or any of my opinions concerning art, religion, culture, or friends. I will permit no government organization or authority to invade my private life. I will discuss these matters informally with anyone—even with government representatives when they are off duty; and any time the President wishes to invite me for cocktails and a chat I will happily accept. Since I take an almost ribald delight in gossip and personal affairs I shall expect government representatives and the President to tell me as much as I tell them, for I am interested in their private opinions and affairs, which may, indeed, be more creditable than mine. I wish to learn from the experience of others, and I am a very garrulous person in convivial society. But I herewith warn Congress and the Supreme Court to conduct their affairs in the future on the premise that I will not be investigated formally. Some rather ambiguous customs give Congress the right under law to ask me impertinent questions without protecting me from libel or slander, and the Supreme Court has sanctioned this practice by not judging it. But I do not recognize it. My personal bill of rights exempts me from it. In matters of opinion and intellectual judgment Congress in mass has less intelligence than a dog. It is riddled with ignorance, prejudice, and political cunning. The intelligence of the Supreme Court is higher, but, like all human institutions, fallible. Even if it were infallible, I would not recognize its authority respecting my opinions, but if it were infallible, of course, it would not question them, and the argument would disappear. The government has not quartered any soldiers in my house during times of peace. I commend the government for scrupulously obeying the law in this respect. But I put Congress and the Supreme Court on notice not to inquire

into my private opinions, which are dangerous because I believe
in America. I also warn them not to send me to jail. I should be
more dangerous incommunicado there than I am here at my
writing-table where I can speak my mind freely and defiantly and
contribute copiously to the normal boredom of society.

28. As we drive through the country, near New York or in the
Catskills, I keep hearing everywhere the thin, squeaking song of
the blackpoll warbler. If I hear ten or fifteen in the course of one
day, there must be millions of these warblers that I do not hear,
migrating north across the country. Towards the close of the
warbler migration they are everywhere in an abundance that staggers the imagination. Only people who listen for bird notes hear
the blackpoll. Like the notes of the Savannah and grasshopper
sparrows, the song of the blackpoll is only a faint and unmusical
sound that hardly stirs the consciousness of the ear. And since he
is so tiny a bird and hides so successfully in the tops of the trees,
few people ever notice him. Although I have never seen more
than five or six blackpolls, I always know when they are around
for two reasons: 1. When I was first interested in birds thirty-
five or forty years ago, I saw one in the top of the oak tree that
brushed our attic windows. He stayed there a long time. When he
tipped back his head to sing, I could associate the bird with that
"cob-web thin" and feebly passionate sound that carries so far
and composes his song. If I had not seen him singing, I might
never have known that the "tsee, tsee, tsee, tsee" he utters is a
bird song. 2. Some years later amid the wind-stunted spruces on
the cone of Mt. Washington, I heard that elfin sound again, and
soon found a blackpoll on a spruce tip, apparently reveling in the
austere loneliness of those lordly heights. It seemed to me pathetic
that he should feel so rhapsodic about so dreary a neighborhood
of beaten trees, weather-beaten rock, fog, haze, and wind. How
feeble are his requirements of life if this bleak environment gives
him ecstasy.

He nests in the spruce forests of Labrador and Alaska (to which
the top of Mt. Washington is climatically equivalent) and reaches
up into the Arctic zone. But he winters in South America; and
on the migration route, millions of blackpolls fly several hundred
miles across the Caribbean Sea. Now that I hear the wavering

song of the blackpoll again, I realize that there is rapture in it. In the middle of his faint serenade there is a vibrant measure of ecstasy. Even this plain, secretive little creature who lives so much to himself is intoxicated by the warmth and splendor of the spring. When the quiet of the countryside is scratched by blackpoll singing, the migration season is almost over.

29. Ten years ago he was a normal human being. Since then he has made four million dollars—net profit. He is haunted. His eyes look terrified. He is restless and worried. He thinks he has found a way to run up his four million to eight or ten by plunging recklessly into a new venture which will yield a fabulous profit if the public obligingly falls in with his plans. But he has less confidence in himself now than he had ten years ago. There was nothing at stake then: now four million dollars are in jeopardy. Hoping for a stray word of encouragement, he sits down in my office to tell me the plan. But he cannot sit still. He twists in his chair, puffs nervously on a chain of cigarettes and pulls out charts and blueprints designed to visualize the new operation. He is trying to convince himself. Eight or ten million dollars would be better than four million. But the four million might vanish as quickly as it came. He is frightened and unhappy. Four million dollars has taken possession of him.

30. Memorial Day. Although the common lilacs are just beginning to fade, the white lilacs are at the peak of their glory, like a celestial Easter flower; and the spirea is in bloom. In memory of the soldiers and sailors who now lie silent and unseen in the cemeteries or who died at sea, nearly every house in the state shows the American flag on the porch or at an upstairs window; and children still too young to know the anguish of death on the battlefields, are dressed in white and are marching to the music of a brass band in the company of veterans in uniform. This day was set aside in 1868 by the commander in chief of the Grand Army of the Republic, for decorating the graves of the soldiers in the Civil War. Are we never to outgrow this day of respect and memories? Must we go on forever sowing the broken seed for national mourning?

When I was a boy the men and women who joined the Memorial Day parade laid flowers and posted flags on graves that were already a half century old. The Civil War veterans were already beginning to forget the anguish. Memorial Day was a time for reunion in the G.A.R. hall after the parade to the cemetery. The veterans of the Spanish-American War, who also took part in the parade, had very little to forget. To us boys, who ran beside the band, envied the youngster who helped carry the bass drum and marveled at the blue and gold uniforms, the service in the cemetery was an inexplicable drawing together of the elders, like a cabala. It seemed like a spiritless anticlimax to a splendid martial ceremony. Hanging around on the fringes of the service, we were impatient for the parade back to the veterans' hall. The dead had already buried the dead—long before we were born; the war was swallowed up in the past, part horror but mostly heroism, and we innocently imagined that every veteran in the parade had fought at Gettysburg. We were not mournful; we were excited. As the ranks of the G.A.R. veterans thinned year by year, we assumed that Memorial Day would drop out of the calendar or become a holiday for the first revels of the summer. How little we knew! After 1917 we became the veterans, and after 1946 thousands of other Americans had things to remember with sorrow and reverence. Now the grass has to be cut and the flowers tended on hundreds of cemeteries in Europe and on islands in the Pacific. I remember a tiny American cemetery in the wretched interior of China where hardly a man is learned enough to read the English characters on the markers, and no one comes with flowers on Memorial Day. The memories are bitter on this day of national observance. Too much youth has been lost too many times. Too many homes are desolate. Too many hearts are grieving.

31. On this day in 1819 Walt Whitman was born in West Hills, Long Island. Five years later his family moved to Brooklyn, where he attended the public schools. After working in printing offices and at newspaper desks he published the first edition of *Leaves of Grass* in 1855. After reading it, Emerson "hailed him at the beginning of a great career." For America had acquired her greatest native singer. Lying on the beach in Orient on the sea-beaten shores of Long Island Whitman dreamed of expressing in poetic form "my own emotional, moral, intellectual and esthetic Personality in the midst of, and tallying, the momentous spirit

and facts of its immediate days, and of current America." The second half of that pronunciamento is important. Although Whitman sang of himself with an egoism seldom equaled, he sang of himself as a democratic American. Sixty-six years after constitutional government had been founded, he was intoxicated with the stupendous idea of a free country of equal men and women, enriched by immigration from abroad. Everything took on fresh significance from this lyric point of view—ordinary men and women going about their workaday affairs, crossing on the cosmic Brooklyn ferry, cutting wood, mining gold, digging potatoes, writing poems, and making love. A great democrat, he discarded as useless for his purposes the poems of Europe, Greece, and Rome which had been conditioned by social organizations in which he did not believe. "Does not the best thought of our day and Republic conceive of a birth and spirit of song superior to anything past or present?" he inquired. If that is braggart, so was Walt Whitman and America. But it was not vain boasting. For by some miracle he had caught the great, exultant fact of democracy, and he sang for comradeship, for love, good cheer, content and hope. It was not pretense. He knew the ideal uses of literature, and he always worked towards the grand subject of the ages: "In the center of all, and object of all, stands the Human Being, towards whose heroic and spiritual evaluation poems and everything directly or indirectly tend, Old World or New."

If the good gray poet with his abundant beard and long hair were alive today, he would be the bard of One World. Even then he knew what must be, and he saluted it exuberantly. "Salut au Monde!" he shouted:

> "I see the steppes of Asia,
> I see the tumuli of Mongolia, I see the tents of Kalmucks and Baskirs,
> I see the nomadic tribes with herds of oxen and cows,
> I see the table-lands notch'd with ravines, I see the jungles and deserts,
> I see the camel, the wild steed, the bustard, the fat-tailed sheep, the antelope and the burrowing wolf."

All this and much more he saw in the deep bowl of the heavens as he lay on the yellow beaches of Long Island.

JUNE

June

SINCE THE STANDARD CONTRACT for employing actors expires on May 31, the theatrical season is officially over today. The transition from one season to the next is not visible to the naked eye. Every production that is earning a profit will continue as long as that rare and happy situation continues, and all the actors now employed in them will continue to draw pay checks at the end of the week. Profitable productions have no problems that cannot be solved speedily, for a profit is such a rare thing in the theater that everyone eagerly conspires to preserve it.

People who are not familiar with the business of the theater can hardly imagine the chaos it is in. Those of us who are familiar with it are constantly astonished that the commercial theater survives. Variety, scandal-sheet of the theater business, estimates that $6,500,000 has been invested in the last theater season. Of that colossal sum, Variety estimates that $4,535,000 has been lost. Of the sixty-three regular commercial productions, forty-eight have been financial failures. There have been a number of uncommercial productions by co-operative groups of actors who want to act for the good of their souls. It is safe to assume that all the uncommercial productions have been financial failures.

The business record of the season has therefore been catastrophic. But it has been one of the finest seasons I can remember. There were three works of art. Three of the productions have been creative expressions of some of the immortal truth about humanity. In comparison with the total amount of work that has been done by—let us estimate roughly—three thousand experienced theater people, this seems like a pitiful record of achievement. But a genuine work of art has a value that cannot be estimated, since it transcends all commercial considerations. Three works of art in one season comprise a fabulous treasure. What is the value to you of a play that adds a cubit to your spiritual stature and enriches your knowledge of man and God? It permanently widens your capacity for happiness. It stretches your soul. From the point of view of an inquiring theatergoer, four and a half million dollars (of other people's money) is a trivial price to pay for three works of art.

2. Lucky is the neighborhood that has bobolinks dancing in it. For the bobolink behaves as though spring had been invented for his special pleasure, and for more than twenty years he has lived joyously in our back field in the country. He has a conspicuous carnival costume—black below, white with buff stripes on the wings and back and a handsome buff patch on the back of the neck. His song lacks the beauty of the thrushes'. There is a metallic quality in it. But it is long, lyric, and irrepressible and it sprays the neighborhood with a cascade of wild music. The male bobolinks arrive in our country in the middle of May with enormous enthusiasm. Since late March they have been flying steadily from their winter quarters in southwest Brazil; and they behave as though this long journey had been worth-while. Their delight in our spring meadows is ecstatic. They dance all day—shooting into the air and sprinkling music over the fields, or perching conspicuously on the tops of trees and singing with rapture. There are always several families in the fields around our house. During the mating season there is hardly a minute in the day when they are not singing. Even on rainy days their singing is undiminished. No one else serenades the spring with such joy. No one makes so much of a carnival out of the growing season.

Towards the end of July the nuptial plumage fades into an undistinguished brown. By September the decorative bobolink has become the drab rice bird of the South Atlantic states; and when rice was a big crop there, the rice bird was a menace. "Beaters" had to be employed in the rice fields to shoot and drive the birds away. The annual damage they did to the rice crop was estimated at two million dollars. Millions of rice birds were killed every year to keep them out of the fields. They were shipped to the market like pheasants. But rice is no longer a big crop in that area, and the birds are now protected by law. By late autumn they take off from Florida over the Caribbean and arrive in their winter fields east of the Andes where they spend about five months feed-

ing and relaxing. They cover about eight thousand miles a year
in their migrations. I am glad that they never forget our lush
spring meadows. It is a happy day for all of us when the bobolinks arrive and enclose us in a sparkling network of song

3. Like art and religion, old friendships endure without motive
or advantage. External events seem to have very little effect on
them. Today Gilbert and Ada Gabriel, our oldest friends, spent
their thirtieth wedding anniversary with us. We have not seen
each other for three months. But nothing has been lost; nothing
has depreciated in value. As soon as they drive in the yard, the
old warmth and gaiety begin again, and we settle down to an
appreciative and convivial visit, some of it serious, some of it
hilarious, but all of it comfortable, sincere, and affectionate.

We are very different people with different experience, points
of view and personality, and different systems of friends. There
have been periods, especially during the war, when we have been
separated for years and wholly concerned with our individual affairs. I do not doubt that we have all disappointed each other at
times. In similar circumstances other friendships have imperceptibly ended. But the Gabriels and we have enjoyed each other
too long, we have seen each other through too many anxieties, we
have taken delight in too many of each other's pleasures to pay
much attention to anything specific that happens now. Nations
rise and fall, administrations come in and go out of office, newspapers fail, books succeed, and everything changes. But our friendship goes on, like the ivy the Gabriels planted when they built
their house and that now covers one end of it in a deep bank of
tenacious greenness. Having gone through the feverishness and
instability of youth together we now talk of spending our old age
with each other.

For we know all about each other and the score is good. In
middle age people lose the rapture and animation of youth. But
while visiting with the Gabriels on their thirtieth anniversary I
am mercifully unaware that anything has been lost. It seems to
me that we have always been like this together—talking politics,
discussing art, comparing household notes, gossiping and guffaw-
ing. We are middle-aged now. But the friendship is young. Perhaps old friendships have a vitality of their own.

4. Someone from the suburbs has brought into the office today the first rose of the season from his garden. It is tenderly received by the staff, put into a glass of water and displayed on our office table. Although the office represents work, and work is supposed to be drudgery, most of us would rather go to the office than not. The office is a remarkably interesting place, full of interesting people, most of whom, being married and parents, are full of problems and experiences. There is a lot of work to be done, some of it under pressure. But the office is well organized for work. Every part of the organization works expertly under pressure at the critical moments of the day and night. And it is not an organization of robots. Every pivot in it has personality. Even the copy boys, most of whom are just beginning in our shop, collect and deliver copy in styles that vary from friendly to automatic. When I am racing through my stint at midnight and anxiously engrossed in what I am doing, I am always aware of the individual who silently collects the copy from my desk although I scarcely see him. He is like a good nurse in a hospital, busy, quiet, efficient but friendly.

But the work is only a small part of the office, which is also a social place. It is riddled with gossip. Our day's work at the telephones and typewriters is affected by many intangible outside influences. A sick wife upsets the equilibrium of the staff. A birth wrecks things for days. Of course, all our office births are normal, successful, and brilliant, and mother and child progress famously.

Don't tell the union, but most of us spend more time in the office than is necessary or legal. It is more hospitable than a saloon, and the conversation is funnier. I am glad we can get into the office free, and stay as long as we like. For it would run into money to pay for the companionship and chaffing of the normal working day.

5. Today the locust petals are fluttering down from the week-old blossoms and accumulating in soft, white drifts along the driveway. Their brief, entrancing garland season is over. The black locust leaves out later than the other shade trees. When the foliage of the maple trees looks dark and thick and fairly well settled for the season, the black locust is just coming into bloom.

It is a member of the pea family. Hundreds of delicate, cream-white blossoms hang like garden-party lanterns from the sharply twisted branches of the shaggy-barked tree. In a day or two the air is laden with heavy, sweet perfume, and the bees work by the thousands in the blossoms. The hummingbird moves swiftly from flower to flower, gathering the sweets in his long bill, his wings buzzing like an insect. But this is the carnival season for the bees. The amber locust honey is the clearest and most delicately flavored of the year. In the flowering season the hum of the bees lasts from early morning until after sundown. On the one day when the blossoms are at their height, the hum of the bees over-whelms all the other sounds out of doors. It sounds like an old-fashioned trolley car passing at high speed. Never again, I believe, do the bees work so frantically in shock-troop brigades. Yesterday they were working hard, but today only a few of them are clearing up their great project for the year.

When the black locust reaches maturity, it has a certain hard, resolute majesty. But it is not an altogether likeable tree. It is brittle, and it constantly strews broken twigs over the lawn. It is so prolific that it is almost like a weed; it is so heavily armed with thorns that it angrily resists anyone who tries to cut a young locust thicket. Since it grows rapidly it overwhelms trees that grow slowly, like the spruce—steals sunlight, absorbs most of the nutri-ment in the soil and, I am told, emits a noxious gas that kills other young trees. The race of the black locust to take over un-cultivated fields has the implacable speed and voracity of an armed invasion. But once a year the black locust in its only beguiling mood hangs out its nodding, white lanterns and sweetens the countryside. The blooms are edible. Some people fry them in deep fat and regard them as a delicacy.

6. In a hundred years the human race has changed in many ways, but the race of woodchucks has remained unaltered. The woodchuck we see feeding in the fields this evening near the shop is identical with the one Thoreau saw in Concord on May 8, 1860. Thoreau's sketch of the woodchuck he saw on that day is vivid and accurate: "I see a woodchuck in the middle of the field at Assabet Bath," Thoreau wrote. "He is a heavy fellow with a black tip to his tail, poking about almost on his belly, with a great

heavy head. He is very wary, every minute pausing and raising his head, and sometimes sitting erect and looking around. He is evidently nibbling some green thing, maybe clover. He runs at last with an undulating motion, jerking his lumbering body along and then stops near a hole." Exactly! The woodchuck we see this evening is identical. Throughout the centuries nature remains the basic standard, for the changes in nature are slow and imperceptible.

Since the time when Thoreau saw and described his woodchuck, which cannot be distinguished from ours, the human race has changed remarkably. Clothes are gayer and more comfortable, manners are easier, ideas are more tolerant and flexible, the standards of living have improved and, on the whole, people are less provincial. If we could step back into Thoreau's Concord, we would find the people odd and quaint, like figures in a museum. We would be curiously aware of many differences. But the woodchuck of Concord would look the same and behave the same as the one we see today. We would not be aware of any difference in period in the trees, flowers, birds, fish and animals.

7. The kindest and gentlest man in our country village is Charles Jenkins. He is seventy-four years of age now, and his lameness cripples him a little more seriously every year. When he was a boy he cut a cord in one foot, which has always made his walking unsteady, and in his old age he has more difficulty than ever in getting around. But his loyalties remain unchanged, his good will shines steadily and he never forgets his friends. As we come and go in the spring and autumn Charlie keeps an eye out for us. If he does not meet us in the village he drives up to the house with many expressions of welcome and sociability. "Glad to see you all well," he says. "I'll stay by you," he says reassuringly. "I'll look in tomorrow." Like as not he gives us a chicken for Sunday dinner.

Charlie is a Negro, son of a Hudson River steamboat cook. In his youth he and another Negro boy, John Whitbeck, were adopted by a white doctor and his wife. When the old folks died they left the house in the village and some other property to both their wards, who have lived there ever since and kept the house in good repair and the grounds attractive. It would be too much to say that they have never experienced race discrimination in this town. There is a certain reserve in some of the neighborhood associations. John and Charlie never take the initiative in social matters, for they do not invite resistance. But on the whole this odd adventure in race equality has been remarkably successful; and both Charlie and John are important members of the village. The village could hardly get along without them.

Although Charlie is naturally less vigorous than he was ten or fifteen years ago, he is still active, and can mow a lawn if he has to. "I have always worked and always expect to," he says sweetly and patiently. He is more than a little proud of his sound health. He takes a sort of moral pride in it. Perhaps in some obscure way it is his revenge for the shadow of race prejudice that has always lurked in the back of his mind and tested his character. When one of his contemporaries is ill Charlie feels considerably superior, and virtuously recalls that he has never taken more than a few tea-spoonfuls of medicine in his life and has always worked hard and kept going.

"We'll get her, we'll get her," he says when he is trying to do something that is really beyond his strength. Willingness and ability to work are the standards by which he judges the quality of people. "He's a good worker," is the finest thing he can say of anybody. A good worker commands his admiration and loyalty. Charlie now spends most of his time roaming slowly around the town in his car, taking someone to the station, delivering milk and mail, making life a little more agreeable for people who need help. He is so kindhearted that everybody rushes to him with little troubles, and he never turns his back on anyone. Through native strength of character Charlie maintains a tranquillity and spirit of good neighborliness that are unequaled here. He is the most Christian man in town.

8. The drumming in the chimney is the chimney swift. Although the chimney is in use on cool days when the flue is choked with wood smoke, the swifts stick their nests of twigs there every year; and when the eggs hatch the birds fill the chimney with cheeping and chattering. When they come and go the flue roars with the vibration of their wings and the soot tumbles down on the hearth. For birds that live so close to the family hearth, they

are antisocial. We can catch glimpses of their activities by laying a mirror against the back of the fireplace. But from dawn to dark the chimney swift lives in the sky, hawking, racing, veering and swooping at incredible speed. The falcons may fly faster, but not much faster and perhaps not so fast. No one knows exactly. The chimney swift never perches out of doors. His day is spent in sweeping through the upper air for insects, which provide his food, and also, I suspect, for fun and enjoyment. In the evening he races through the sky in the company of other swifts from the neighborhood. You have to watch sharp to see him dive into the chimney; after circling around it, flying over it, skimming across it and indulging in other gay maneuvers he disappears into it so swiftly you are not sure that he has gone.

Long spells of rainy weather are hard on the swifts. Rain washes the air clean of insects. It also dissolves the sticky saliva with which the swift cements his shell-like nest to the flue.

There has been no rain recently. Probably we can look forward to lively fireside company for two or three weeks more.

9. Among our major blessings, let's not overlook the English language. It is versatile, vigorous, and lyric. It can say anything. Of modern languages, only Russian, as far as my knowledge goes, equals or exceeds English in music, variety, and subtlety. Like English, Russian is a sturdy language, but it can also express familiarities of affection and family loyalty that are austere and self-conscious in English. Like English, again, Russian can convey the eloquence of poetry.

But no one can be impersonal about his native language. It contains the history of his race. It is no accident that the English language is eminently practical, that it expresses exact facts and is useful in science, industry, and economics. It derives from the Anglo-Saxons, who were practical people with a native capacity for looking after themselves. In *Beowulf* the language was not lovely, although it was plain and forceful. By the time of Chaucer it had acquired beauty. Within the next three or four centuries it reached the peak of beauty and vigor. The fiery magnificence of Shakespeare, the grave simplicity of the King James Bible, and the melodious nobility of Milton are still the grand treasures of our language. The purity it had then was natural; the use of words was pithy. The language had the tang of homely living.

After Milton, the language became a conscious art. It drew more and more from southern Europe and the Near East, where there was a tradition of learning and culture. Addison, Steele, and Dr. Johnson were writing a bastard jargon that valued form above content. The language grew further and further away from the lives of people. The great stylists of the nineteenth century— Lamb, De Quincey, Carlyle, Macaulay—were artificial writers. In fact, Carlyle wrote gibberish which is virtually unreadable today. Some of his American contemporaries were writing sincerer English—Thoreau, Whitman, and Melville, for example. Like *Beowulf*, these three Americans were writing close to human experience. For language does not come out of books. It comes out of the mouths of people. By listening to the conversation of ordinary people, Synge wrote some of the most glorious prose ever put into English. The crowning beauty of English is its strength and simplicity. There are only two words of more than one syllable in this line from the King James Bible: "Glory to God in the highest, and on earth peace, good will toward men." But nothing else for centuries has set so many hearts ringing. Even the most uneducated people understand it because it is frank and true.

10. Even totalitarian governments need the support of public opinion. They look secure, remote and powerful to us, but they long for the spontaneous "Aye." Although they have the police power to do whatever they wish, they put a high value on the illusion of public approval. They need the respectability that only the consent and good will of the public can provide. For the infallibility of Stalin is no more than an intellectual postulate unless the public recognizes his genius. He must be cheered by the masses in person. They must see him and he must personally acknowledge their enthusiasm with a smile and salute, as he does at stated intervals in the Red Square. For the forms of legitimacy are particularly important to governments that treat their people like rather worthless cattle. Stalin and his associates have the power of life and death over their people. Thousands have been assassinated to keep the government in office; millions have been rounded up by the police and sent off to the penal labor camps.

Stalin and his associates are safe now unless they betray each other. This is not security enough. Without the appearance of public consent their dictatorship looks exactly like what it is—a bloody tyranny. But if it appears to have behind it the awe and love of the people it gives the illusion of being benevolent paternalism.

If the public did not have to be wooed the administration of a totalitarian state would be much simpler. The forms have to be scrupulously, even fearfully, observed. There has to be a constitution, guaranteeing more rights than any other constitution does. There have to be elaborate court trials in which the enemies of the people are fearlessly denounced, persuaded to confess and then sacrificed to the gods of wrath. Newspapers have to be filled with praise of the government and expressions of obsequious devotion from the people. Thousands of party workers have to associate with the people. At safe and convenient intervals, public elections —complete except for the privilege of choice—have to be held to endorse the candidates who are officially regarded as deserving. Totalitarian governments are obsessed with public opinion, for they are in desperate need of respectability. And the wellsprings of respectability are not the lords, dukes, teachers or bishops, but all the people of all kinds who do the work of the world. Even the man who is swindling them longs for their approval. He appeases them with ceremony and festivals. The protection of a vast army of secret police does not give him security. Having once led the people to revolution he knows how terrible they can be when they are choking the streets and building barricades.

11. At the Greasy Spoon on Broadway, the day begins without enthusiasm. No one is glad to see anybody else at breakfast time. The cashier by the door gives a contemptuous· glance at anyone who comes in; to him it is a matter of indifference whether or not you take breakfast there. Along the windows there are a few white-topped tables. But if there are any vacant stools at the counter, you will not be waited on at the tables. There is no margin of elegance at the Greasy Spoon. Climb up on a stool, lean morosely on the counter and stare at the bill-of-fare posted on the wall. It has not changed for years. At first you may suspect that the counterman is deliberately ignoring you. Perhaps he is; perhaps he wants to assert his importance before acknowledging yours. But presently

he drops a knife, fork, spoon, and paper napkin in front of you
so swiftly that it looks like an accident and he looks at you with
faint hostility. He does not acknowledge the order except the one
item he has to bawl into the kitchen. Otherwise, he gives no indication of having heard it or of intending to act on it. His attitude is one of sullen disinterest. But in a few minutes your breakfast starts accumulating, item by item, before you, with the check
flung down at the end with a gesture of surly dismissal.

Since people must take food occasionally, the Greasy Spoon is
in the business of supplying it as though it were merchandise, and
the food is of satisfactory quality. But no one enjoys serving it and
no one enjoys eating it. The customers are just out of bed; they
are heavy-lidded and resigned to a day that is going to be no better
than yesterday or the day before. They are literally breaking fast
before lunging angrily into the hot, humid, overstuffed downtown
subway train. In a peevish daze they glance mechanically at the
morning newspaper; they are not interested in it or in anything
else. The general spirit of the Greasy Spoon is just right for early
morning; it wishes that it had never been born.

12. Today I open the ventilating louvres at each end of the
blind attic above my room in the country. Circulation of air
through the attic helps to cool the upstairs rooms. For the attic
gets fiercely hot when the sun beats on the roof. Before we opened
ventilating ducts there ten or fifteen years ago the attic was like
an oven all summer, and the upstairs rooms were five degrees
warmer than the rooms downstairs. Now we sleep comfortably except in the hottest weather. Making these four small, triangular
openings under the eaves was a simple job. But for about one
hundred and twenty-five years no one who lived in this house
had taken the trouble to make them. People were born, lived and
died without enjoying relief from heat accumulated in the attic.

There is a sentimental American superstition that old houses
were well built. The old manor houses were well built with dry
and sturdy cellars, heavy oak beams and fine oak floors. But houses
of solid construction were rare exceptions in colonial days or in
the first era of the republic. In this neighborhood, at least, the ordinary houses were poorly built. The foundations were loose and
the cellars wet. Ells were built on foundations laid on the top of

the ground. Every house in this region has been tossed and heaved
by the frost every year of its life. Although our house is the product of average workmanship, the walls were almost incredibly por-
ous until we re-sided them. The original outside layer was of thin,
unbeveled boards lapped and nailed to the studding. There was
nothing between the clumsy, makeshift siding and the plaster of
the interior. Since the north and west winds streak across this hill
savagely in the winter, I don't know how the people who lived
here in the first century of the house managed to keep warm unless
they burned an enormous pile of wood every day. The outside
walls of the house now consist of one layer of flat boards, a layer
of building paper, and beveled siding, which makes a good wall,
though not the best.

I do not look back with reverent admiration on the early settlers
in these mountains. They were shiftless house builders. Granted
that we have materials that were not available a century ago, the
old settlers suffered cold and heat through lack of initiative. Notice those "fine, old beams." They are cracked. The tenons, which
are about half the size of the beams, have to carry all the weight.
Half of the "fine, old beam" is wasted. The pioneers used their
backs more than their heads.

13. Every summer I rediscover one of the fundamentals of human activity. It is easier and more satisfying to work with the
hands than the brain. In the country it is more natural to mow,
hammer, saw, dig, and paint than to put words on paper; and the
results are more enjoyable. Nothing a man writes can please him
as profoundly as something he does with his back, shoulders and
hands. For writing is an artificial activity. It is a lonely and private substitute for conversation, which is social and stimulating,
since it draws excitement and magnetism from the personalities
and ideas of the other people in the room. In comparison with
conversation, writing is abstract, austere, slow, colorless, exhausting—and, most of all, lonely. When the house is full of people
and also surrounded with odd jobs that need doing, I have to make
nothing less than a heroic decision to retire into an empty room
and sit down to write. Nor is writing a pleasant afterthought to
a busy day. You can plunge into physical work after finishing a
job of writing. But you cannot plunge into writing after finishing

a job of physical labor. Writing needs all the freshness you can bring to it. Writing needs your best thought, energy and enthusiasm.

Physical labor is like dissipation. It is an escape from the elusive things. It is completely engrossing. Although it is physically exhausting, it is a release from nervous tension; and the exhaustion is soothing, like the tranquil aftermath of a thunderstorm. And I confess that I enjoy inordinately the fruits of my physical labor. They flatter my ego. I become lord of the manor. During the past week I have built and painted a bathroom cabinet, fixed a door that did not close tightly, set out four clothes posts and braced the cross-pieces, freed the kitchen drain that was plugged, and mown the lawn. I cannot remember writing anything that gave me such a bland sensation of accomplishment. It will be weeks and maybe months before I cease taking pride in the way the cabinet doors fit. They are real and simple. They are constructive. They completely solve the problem of keeping dust out of the shelves and of helping to give the bathroom a single, immaculate appearance. Writing is never that complete, useful, final or beautiful.

14. Flag Day. Every house in the village is flying the Stars and Stripes. On New Year's Day, 1776, Washington raised the Continental or Grand Union flag on Prospect Hill outside Boston. Although the Continental flag had thirteen stripes it showed the British Union Jack in the upper left corner, for even the Revolutionary army had not completely thrown off its emotional ties with England. But the flag adopted on this day in 1777 by the Continental Congress made a complete break with old ideas and introduced thirteen stars in a blue field. Between 1794 and 1818 one more stripe as well as one more star was added for every new state. In 1818 there were twenty states and therefore twenty stripes. Since the flag was becoming unwieldy, Congress voted to revert to thirteen stripes and represent the number of states by stars.

The first American flag ever raised was over Fort Stanwix after the bloody battle of Oriskany, August 6, 1777. By ingenuity, enterprise and stubbornness, some American rebels had routed a mixed force of Tories, British soldiers, and Indians in a terrible pitched battle in the woods. Among the British stores the Americans captured five British flags. Although there were no American flags available, apparently the design of a national flag was already known in the woods of New York State less than two months after Congress had adopted it. Elated over the victory at Oriskany, the Americans improvised one out of a white shirt, a blue jacket and stripes of red torn from the petticoat of the wife of a soldier. Having been sewn together the flag was then raised above the captured British standards.

No doubt every man loves best the flag of his native country. This is one of the natural loyalties that go deeper than reason. But in all modesty it seems to me that the American flag is extraordinarily vivid. The colors combine brilliance with loveliness, and the design is dynamic. When seen abroad by a foot-loose American it is a thrilling sight. After sloshing down the Burma Road for three cold, wretched days during the war I saw an American flag on a staff outside Tali, where five American soldiers were posted. I cannot sort out the different elements in the emotion that suddenly possessed me—relief, hope, eagerness, confidence, with some prospects of a bath and clean food included. State seals are grave, but flags are gay and lively. They symbolize a million human impulses and ideas that cannot be analyzed or spoken.

15. After two or three years of stubborn labor, the settlers on our farm over a century ago cleared seven acres at the break of the hill. Out of the wilderness they created a cultivated field with a pleasant slope and a beautiful view. They were putting a solid foundation under their future. When I took possession of the farm the old field was worn and almost imperceptibly slipping back into the wild. With the friendly co-operation of several neighbors it was planted in 1935 to about nine thousand Norway pine seedlings that came from the nursery neatly tied and packed in a small box. For two or three years after the seedlings were planted it was almost impossible to find them again. They were so tiny that they were lost in the tangle of weeds and grass. Now the seedlings have grown into a young pine forest. The trees are twelve to fifteen feet high. The trunks are six to eight inches in diameter and are covered with rough bark. The branches are long and bushy, and so intertwined that I have to push a way through as if I were not father of the forest but an intruder. Already the

ground under them is soft with needles. A forest in miniature is
growing there. Fair land that bore hay and crops for more than
a century has begun to slip over the edge of civilization back into
the wilderness, back into the silence and loneliness of history. No
man controls it now.

The Norway pine is a handsome tree. The lumber is inferior
to that of the white pine. But the Norway pine has long needles
and an aura of abundance. Now that the roots are settled it grows
two or three feet a year, for the trees are so closely spaced that
they all race for the sunlight. The leaders have already grown a
foot this season. Although the mature leaves are dark green, the
new growth in the spring is light and willowy. All the new shoots
reach towards the sky. As you look down the hill the thousands
of new shoots give an impression of lift and rise as if the little
forest were eager to leap into the blue of the sky and tie the earth
to the heavens with a living bond of greenness. Foxes and woodchucks live all through the pine lot, and the deer have worn paths
through the trees. The sparrow hawk hunts through it. The Maryland yellow-throat nests there. The great crested fly-catcher behaves as though he were the resident monarch. Partridges and
pheasants occasionally raise families there. They have forgotten,
if they ever knew, that this green empire that hums and sings in
the wind was once a cultivated field where farmers laboriously
cropped the land in the heat of the summer. In a rock pile in the
center of the young forest, two tines from a wheelrake and the
blade of a broken plow are rusting. They are aging relics of a dead
civilization.

16. It is difficult to find a bird that is neither interesting nor
beguiling. But the house, or English, sparrow (really a weaver)
admirably fulfills these specifications. He is not only lacking in
charm, but he swarms across the world like a scourge, driving out
other birds, wantonly destroying the eggs of other birds, and in-
festing the city like a pest. With his vivid black throat, the male
is more distinguished than many of the other sparrows. But his
only note is a dull and irritating "cheep." He is dirty. The house
sparrow nest is only an accumulation of waste material, and the
house sparrow's habits are filthy. Like gangs of hoodlums, house
sparrows usurp bird baths and bird houses and fight other birds.

It would be pleasant to have wild birds in the city. But the house sparrow has learned the worst traits of the city and debases the normal spirit of bird life.

The house sparrow has conquered the world by aggressiveness and numbers. In Europe, Africa, Persia, India, Russia, and China the house sparrow is thoroughly established like a true internationalist. He has lived in America for about a century. Eight pairs were introduced in 1850 in Brooklyn by some directors of the Brooklyn Museum in the hope that the house sparrow would exterminate caterpillars and insects. More were imported in 1852, and those that survived were released in the Greenwood Cemetery. For the next twenty years others were imported in Portland, Maine, Peacedale, Rhode Island, Boston, and New Haven and many other places in the United States and Canada. Within a quarter of a century house sparrows had spread across the country to San Francisco. They spread from the cities to the country. They killed native birds by driving them away or appropriating their nests. Birds that nested in holes, like the house wrens, purple martins and cliff swallows found themselves evicted from their nests and began to disappear. By 1887 people who had welcomed the house sparrow were trying to exterminate him, fearing that our song birds might not survive. Michigan paid a bounty for dead house sparrows. Attempts were made to poison them in the winter when few of our song birds were around. Now the house sparrows seem to be decreasing, especially in the cities where the automobile has replaced the horse and the streets are now clean of horse manure, which used to be the house sparrow's chief food supply. But he is still abundant in Riverside and Central parks, and firmly established in the country. Although the house wrens are flourishing, the cliff swallows and purple martins have never grown in numbers again. Probably the unlovely house sparrow has permanently replaced these gentler and more beautiful birds.

17. It is easy to share the bobolink's ecstasy just now. Almost anyone would like to sing in praise of June fields. Although men are living anxiously from day to day, the wide fields are flourishing with their normal expectations and rising to the peak of springtime glory as though nothing mattered except the turn of the season. The lush green of new grass is sprinkled with white by

the blossoming daisies; a sheen of gold sweeps across it where the hawkweed is in bloom. Color will not be so abundant in the fields again all season.

To the farmer the color is a mixed delight. When his fields maculate the green with careless banners of white and gold he concludes that they are running out and must be plowed and seeded before another year. Although the pink of the clover pleases him, the white of the fleabane, wild caraway and yarrow show that the stand of grass is thinner than it ought to be on a well-worked farm. But the farmer is the original nature lover, since he puts her principles into practice; and perhaps he, too, will be forgiven for marveling at the extraordinary wealth of the flowing grasslands. Life often seems stale and meager in the parts of the world men have set apart for their own uses. Where men do not much intrude, vitality wells up from the roots. Out of the brown earth the sunlight engenders wonderful colors that give a man a heady feeling. When the June fields are at the height of their splendor it is worth walking around them to try the different angles of light that mass the colors, changing the scattered white of the daisies into pure radiance and transforming the greenish yellow of the hawkweed into a solid gold that a painter might hesitate to copy.

No wonder the bobolinks overflow with song. Sometimes they sing from the topmost spray of a tree near the fence line. Sometimes they bathe in the color by singing from the bending crest of a clump of weeds. Sometimes the beauty of the June fields intoxicates them and they hover above it on fluttering wings, running over with song, ringing with melody. For the bobolinks are the minstrels of the fields. They are all rapture now.

18. About this time of year we look for a visit from Eg Franklin. Driving from Chicago to Norwalk, Connecticut, to see his sister, he stops by to spend a day or two with us, much to our delight. Although Eg is well on into middle life now, he has never lost his love of games. There is a kind of whimsical sportiveness about his visits. He pops in at the door unannounced, looking exceedingly casual, and he plunges into conversation where he left off when he disappeared last year. This is a game which puckishly skirts around the main fact that we are all overjoyed to see each

other again. We all take pleasure in the game and with a glow of delight settle back into a familiar and well-loved situation. For it is Eg's genius to fall into the rhythm of any household he visits. Wonderfully perceptive, he instinctively understands what is going on. While the rest of us are working at one thing or another, he finds the things he wants to do. Without having to ask where the tools are kept he starts pottering around by himself—mowing the weeds, clearing deadwood out of trees, stringing up an aerial, finding an old kettle in the garage, filling it with a great mass of daisies and setting it on the lawn. When he has gone there are tangible evidences of his visit, apart from the glow and the encouragement which he leaves behind him wherever he travels. And since he has friends in Tennessee, Alabama, and all through the Middle West, he leaves these tokens of approval and affection over a large area of eastern United States. Johnny Appleseed's trail of blooms and fruit did not spread through so wide an area. Johnny did not have an automobile for his pilgrimages.

19. Eg is a tall, broad-shouldered man with an open face, bright and humorous eyes and gray hair cropped close and brushed back impulsively. He talks slowly with a ruminative drawl that is tinged with raillery. He believes in friendship, and his ideas of the world in general are a larger projection of his personal relations. He judges men and nations by the standards he applies to his personal life. He admires loyalty, probity and candor in nations as passionately as he admires them in the people he knows. Although he has lived for years on Michigan Avenue, Chicago, where he attends to his business, his heart has always been in the woods and fields and particularly in the duck club where he watches ducks all through the year and in the hunting season shoots a few—a little reluctantly, it seems to me, as though good taste required him to join the annual slaughter by braggart citizens. Since duck clubs are organized for shooting, he has to conform to the general usage, although it violates the friendly interest he has in ducks during the rest of the year. He has always been fascinated by Indians. The Indian woodcraft appeals to him as the triumph of a way of life; and his life in the automobile age is in many respects merely an extension of the Indians' great talent for adaptability to the prevailing conditions. In his Chicago apartment he has man-

aged to create his own way of life. He can camp on a fire escape
almost as well as in the woods, and he practices archery on the
roof of the apartment house. Accepting the world as of one piece
he understands animals as he understands human beings; and
sometimes it seems to me that his adventures among people and
places are scouting excursions motivated by an Indian-like curiosity and keenness of observation. Eg is rare and original, appreciative and approving. He is a man of strong likes. He does not en-
cumber his life much with the things and people he dislikes. He
leaves them to look out for themselves as best they can. Life is
simple for him because he dominates it and presses it into something resembling his own image. At this time of year, and again
at Christmas, we feel rich and secure because we know Eg will
pop in at any moment, picking up the conversation where he left
it the last time we were together.

20. Although only a few people realized it at the time, the
French Revolution began on this day in 1789. It has been going
on ever since all over the world. Now we can appreciate more than
the contemporary Frenchmen could how terribly crucial were the
homely, accidental things that happened on a chilly, rainy day
more than a century and a half ago. When the deputies to the
States-General went to their hall at Versailles, they found the
doors closed and carpenters working inside. The captain of the
guards officiously told the president of the States-General that the
hall would be closed for two days while the carpenters were building a platform from which the king would address the assembly.
Deliberately or unconsciously, the king, by this rude maneuver, was
indicating that the States-General, or National Assembly, as they
had just decided to call themselves, had no independent authority.
Instead of submitting to the royal whim, however, the Assembly
found shelter in a tennis court and took an oath not to disband
until it had framed a national constitution. This clash of tem-
peraments between king and national deputies began the revolution that roared on through blood and treachery for a decade and
vomited up one of the world's most cynical military despots.

The history of the French Revolution was incredibly cruel and
violent. Sooner or later the revolution murdered most of those
who led it, for the power it released was too terrible for anyone

to channel and control. But it grew out of nothing worse than a general uneasiness about the incompetent management of national affairs by an amiable, weak monarch and his unimaginative ministers. Voltaire, Rousseau, and Montesquieu had supplied the idea of liberty, which appealed to educated people. For many years there had also been a shortage of grain in France. Capitalists, officials, and privileged classes had cornered what grain there was and made a profit out of general suffering. Specifically, the economy of France had broken down and the country was financially bankrupt. The king and his controller had called the States-General to approve of tax reforms and unconsciously to appeal to public opinion. Although the States-General was on the whole loyal to the king, it instinctively began to search for causes, to reform the feudal organization of society and to fill the vacuum caused by the incompetence of the crown. Instead of making use of the brains and progressive ideas of the States-General, the crown fell back on royal etiquette, and on June 20, 1789, closed the assembly hall by royal decree in the most insulting fashion possible. *Après Louis, le déluge.* In due time the weak king gave rise to a terrible emperor who drenched the whole of Europe in blood and carnage. Nothing worked out as anyone had foreseen.

21. Summer begins today at 7:11 A.M. The sun rises at 4:28; sets at 7:34, giving us fifteen hours, six minutes of daylight in this latitude. Today, when the sun appears at its highest point in the northern sky, the sun's rays fall vertically on the Tropic of Cancer, which just about touches the northern tip of Cuba. On December twenty-second, which is the winter solstice, the sun will rise here at 7:21, and set at 4:36, giving us then nine hours, fifteen minutes of daylight—practically the reverse of today's sun schedule. In this house we gauge the swing of the sun by measuring it in the evening on the east wall of the dining room. On March twenty-first, which is the spring equinox, the setting sun just steals in through the north window for a minute or two. Today it lights eight feet, ten inches of the east wall. "Solstice" is the Latin word for "the sun stands still." For the sun does not start back to the south without an effort. It seems to stand still for one day. For all practical purposes it seems to stand still for five days, for it rises and sets at 4:28 and 7:34, respectively, on the nineteenth, twentieth, twen-

ty-first, twenty-second, and twenty-third. Having great momentum the sun takes five days to shift into reverse. Perhaps it goes south reluctantly and with friendly regrets. At any rate those are our sentiments.

Since the earth gathers warmth slowly, our hottest days and nights will not come for another month. There is this much time lag between the majesty of the sun and the response of the earth. But there is evidence on earth that the most ecstatic part of the year has already slipped by. The hawkweed, which spread a wonderful golden carpet across the fields a few days ago, has just begun to fade. The locust blooms, which were full of honey and bees a week ago, have fallen and blown away. Already the bird songs are less exultant than they have been for a month. The courting season, which is the most joyous, is over; the singing is less rhapsodic. In the morning and evening the birds sing well, but the day is filled with household cares which evidently are not worth singing about. From now on we are sliding down the year through the heat and harvest into the darkness of the winter.

22. The serenity of the evening is shattered by the radio. Congress wants to adjourn in time to attend the Republican convention in Philadelphia tomorrow, and is behaving more abominably than usual. Here on the hill where our farm is located everything seems to be under control—the garden flourishing, the grass getting thick and green, the porch painted, the newspapers read. Congress is the only exception to the natural order. Amid a storm of ignorant, bombastic oratory, it is murdering intelligence and destroying common sense. In the beginning no one foresaw that the United States would be governed in the atmosphere of a bear garden combined with a wild West show. No one believed that laws would be discussed in the atmosphere of bedlam and that our presidents would be nominated in a mood of carnival and charlatanism. No one foresaw that the biggest voice would be that of the ignorant, the vicious and the prejudiced. Democracy conducts its affairs noisily as though America were populated exclusively by wild men with no honor or intelligence. You seldom hear anything anywhere more thick-headed than you hear every day in the Capitol where humbugs concentrated in one place in-

toxicate each other and speak more cant and evil than they would think of speaking at home.

The success of representative government depends on the ability of the lawmakers to make reasonable compromises at the last moment. That was not written into the Constitution, but it is the unwritten genius of the agreement. Without reason, generated through the guts if not through the head, the apparatus of government collapses and opens the gate to anarchy. Tonight, as I listen to the savage bark of the radio report from Washington, I would happily agree to help abolish Congress which behaves as though it wanted to destroy the world out of hatred, cupidity and mindlessness. But never despair of Congress. It is not a formless assembly of knaves and swindlers as it appears to be. It represents all the people in the correct proportions—not only the worst but the best. Some day the vicious elements may get the upper hand and reduce the nation to primordial chaos, for there is no way of guaranteeing reasonable compromises *in extremis*. But over the years the record is as good as the people are, and the alternative is the government of supermen like Mussolini, Hitler, and Stalin, or the mythical sages whom Plato and Goethe foolishly dreamed about.

To believe in democracy is to believe that the collective wisdom of all the people is in the long run superior to the wisdom of any group of people. Neither labor nor capital, neither the politicians nor the lawyers, neither the preachers nor the journalists can make as sound decisions as all the people can. Not to believe this is not to believe in democracy. This is the hazard we have agreed to take in the belief that the other hazards are more dangerous. It is astonishing how many people who regard themselves as democrats do not believe in the democratic credo. Although they acquiesce in democratic government, they are not fully convinced. By being aggressively stupid, like boys recently let out of a reform school, Congress frequently seems bent on proving that the people cannot govern themselves. But the people can. Congress is seldom as irresponsible and stupid as it tries to be. At the last moment, intelligence mercifully breaks in, or there is always one more chance.

23. From any rational point of view, the nominating convention that breaks out every four years at this season, is a colossal cliché. Although it has the solemn mission of selecting a candidate who may be president of the country, the oratory is buncombe and bombast, the pretense of hilarity is sophomoric and spurious and the general tone is low. As a matter of fact, it is part of the American folklore. Rational criticism does not obtain. No one would dare alter the routine or the ritual of the political convention. It is as standard as coffee and doughnuts. The form of the oratory is more important than the content. Although no one believes that the opposition party is as crooked and vicious as the keynote orator declares, tradition requires a violent, scornful pouring out of billingsgate on this simplest of the themes. And although no one is as jubilant as the parading delegations pretend to be, tradition requires long, noisy, barbaric demonstrations by rival states, like the mummery between the halves of college football games. In fact, nothing is more traditional than this quadrennial pretense that the United States is still a wild frontier country full of clowns, braggarts, and showmen. Out of this gaudy exuberance the nation got McKinley, Harding, and Coolidge. But out of the same snake-oil milieu the nation got Lincoln, Cleveland, Theodore Roosevelt, Wilson, and Franklin Roosevelt. The convention that selected Lincoln was one of the gaudiest. The man of destiny was selected by practical politicians amid the hoopla and skulduggery of a show.

The candidate is also willy-nilly a figure in American folklore. He takes part in a masquerade. He must try to fit a traditional pattern which the American people expect, although they are not deceived by it. To play the part well, he should be presented as a former small-town boy, because American people still regard city people as unreliable. Although he may be a city lawyer, he may have small-town relatives, which are an asset; or he can buy a farm where he can be photographed. He should have a folksy hobby, like fishing, which is regarded as honest. He should be a family man of sound moral character with a presentable wife and blameless children, and a churchgoer—Protestant. He should be a good fellow with a hearty manner and homely sentiment. He should be prudent and thrifty. He should have a sly sense of humor. In some respect he should be Lincolnesque, if possible. Although he may be almost out of his mind with desire to be president, he should never acknowledge that he is seeking the office. He must maintain the fiction that in becoming a candidate he is submitting to a spontaneous public mandate. We have had some remarkable presidents whom the people have chosen with wise deliberation. But the people think they want an unobjectionable nonentity left over from the last century. They don't; they want a moderately progressive man whom they can respect. But the preliminary presidential masquerade is part of the American folklore to which, consciously or unconsciously, we subscribe every four years.

24. Thank God the phoebes have flown. They have been committing nuisance on the porch for three weeks. Every April they plaster a muddy nest over the door that opens directly into the dining room. Remembering the phoebe's filthy habits, O. wants to chase them away. But I am flattered by their sociability and I find their industry disarming; I cannot bring myself to destroy the work they have done in building up the mud foundation so slowly and persistently. At that stage of the season the phoebes are humble. But as soon as the eggs are laid they become possessive. When we use their door they fly off the nest with an injured manner that appeals to our better natures. Gradually we stop using the dining-room entrance to the house. When the eggs hatch the phoebes go one step further. They complain querulously by yelling at us. They not only want us to use another entrance; they want the dining-room door closed. If we open it for light and ventilation they scream at us until we close it again. Property belongs to whoever is using it, according to the phoebe code; and we comply with it, although sardonically.

But now the trouble begins. As the young birds grow they feel more and more contemptuous. Young phoebes especially have wonderful digestive tracts, and as they swell in size they start dropping bird lime over the side of the nest. At first it looks like an unfortunate accident, and it can be cleaned away easily. But the phoebes eat more and more, digest more and more and the volume of their elimination grows daily. It not only makes a pile on the porch floor; it runs in white streaks down the screen door and spatters. At this stage the lice begin to appear. They cover the door, and the door has to be sprayed to keep them out of the house. Meanwhile, the five young birds have grown ugly little beaks. Peering fatuously over the nest they look like gangsters. They are hideous and filthy and voracious, and we are heartily disgusted with them.

Today they flew. It took me an hour with soap, water, a scrubbing brush and rag to clear away the noisome mess, wash the screen door and woodwork, and get rid of the lice. I don't think we shall let the phoebes build there next spring. After about fifteen years I have had enough—I hope.

25. Eighty-nine degrees in town. The city is lost in fog until late morning. Throughout the afternoon the humidity is high. In the evening a wild thunderstorm attacks the city savagely with cracks of lightning, roars of thunder, and floods of rain. As usual, the people are surprised and are caught unprepared. For New Yorkers are inclined to assume that it will never rain, and certainly not on New Yorkers. Unless it is raining hard when they leave home in the morning, they go without raincoats or umbrellas. The distances are short from the house to the subway and from the subway to the office. If New Yorkers are caught unprepared they can skip along close to the buildings, which break the force of the rain; and they can hurry from doorway to doorway or from one sidewalk canopy to another, or take short cuts through buildings or walk for blocks through underground passages that feed the subway routes. They can buy cheap umbrellas at high prices in the corner cigar stores, or from street hawkers who mysteriously appear in the crowded districts almost as soon as the first rain falls, or they can buy compact cellophane bags that cover the head and shoulders and give the illusion of protection. In an emergency they can hold a newspaper over their heads. New Yorkers are never far from shelter. They do not want to be encumbered with rainy weather gear, and imagine in some mystic way that they are impervious to weather. Rain is something for the farmers. Except for a few uncomfortable moments when they have to leave shelter on the way home, New Yorkers ignore it.

Even when the rain is heavy and savage, New Yorkers instinctively belittle it. When the thunderstorm suddenly leaps on the city this evening I am talking with some friends in a mid-town penthouse. A wild gust of wind shoots through the windows and presently the rain sweeps into the room. Distracted for a moment from what we are saying, we close the windows and peer out equivocally. "Oh, I guess it's just a little cloudburst," someone says with a kind of casual superiority. Anything sturdier than a drizzle is a cloudburst in New York. But the true New Yorker is convinced that even a cloudburst would not be impudent enough to inconvenience the greatest city in the world.

26. Charter of the United Nations signed in San Francisco on this day in 1945. While the war against Japan was still being fought, the United Nations determined to save succeeding generations from the scourge of war, affirmed their faith in fundamental human rights and social progress, agreed to practice tolerance as good neighbors and to unite their strength to maintain international peace and security. It was a brave and sincere declaration. It represented the longings of every human in every corner of the world, and still does. Since the conclusion of the war did not stop the shooting and since the struggle for political victory has broken the world into two warring camps, most people would agree that the United Nations has failed. Even in wartime, political power was no more contemptuous of "fundamental human rights and the dignity and worth of the human person" than it is today. Since the armistices were signed, nations have been betrayed, statesmen and political leaders have been assassinated, children have been torn away from their homes and massed in concentration camps abroad and the world has become a nightmare of lies, treachery and violence. None of those who signed the United Nations Charter foresaw this bloodshot anarchy, and the United Nations has not been able to stop it.

Through all this postwar agony, however, something extraordinarily progressive and creative has been going on. Representatives of sixty nations have been meeting every day to discuss the problems of the world. The die is cast, the great step has been taken. For public opinion is a weapon of formidable strength, and public opinion stands behind the idea of the United Nations like a solid army with high morale. Most of us did not realize that the voice of the world was so crude and angry. The sound it makes in the U.N. sessions is shattering and alarming. But no one wants to cancel the United Nations Charter because the world talks so wildly. For the idea has conquered the minds of the people. No matter what happens, the idea will never be forgotten or surrendered or dismissed as impracticable. No one talks of filing the Charter away in the library of lost causes.

27. After the metallic clangor of the city the countryside seems quiet. To many city people on vacation the silence of the country is distracting at first; it rings in their eardrums like a preternatural void at night and is disturbing to nerves accustomed to rumble. But particularly at this time of year, which is the height of the growing season, the exultation and expansion of life keep the earth overflowing with waves of sound. The breathing earth gives off a steady murmur. Many of the individual sounds, especially at night, are too faint to be caught in human eardrums, which are less sensitive than the eardrums of highly developed animals. But in the mass the sounds of myriad insects and of the earth cooling after the heat of the day create a long, tremulous hum that overlays the sentient world and vibrates through the damp air.

The birds, being endowed above all God's creatures with the glory of song, are the most audible instruments of the daytime. Song pours out of them by instinct in the spring and early summer; from dawn to dusk they bless the earth with the joy of being and increasing. The day is interwoven with their melody. Some of the bird voices, like that of the red-eyed vireo, are so voluble that they are absorbed into the subconsciousness; and some, like that of the grasshopper sparrow, are too trivial to evoke conscious hearing; or like the chattering of the chimney swift, they seem like the common speech of the air and are not worth remarking. But the great singers transform the countryside into a mighty choir loft. The gushing ecstasy of the bobolink above the meadow, the full, round enthusiasm of the oriole in the elms and maples, the cool, lonely meditation of the hermit thrush in the depths of the woods are the charms of life on earth in the season of green and glowing abundance.

Beneath and beyond the bird chorus, however, there is the low-pitched sound of the earth preoccupied with growing. It is difficult to hear. The bird songs break into it and overwhelm it with

volume and beauty. The breeze streaming silently across the face
deadens the ears to it. The chattering anxiety of the aspens and
the deep breathing of the ancient pines are too majestic to let it
through. A man's own breathing or the pulsing of the blood in his
temples may prevent his hearing it. But occasionally there is an
interlude in the bird songs or in the fluttering of the leaves, and
then the busy stir of the growing earth reaches the ear that strains
to listen. The quivering wings of countless insects absorbed in
their affairs, the stretch of the ground in the noonday heat, the
infinitesimal bustle of all kinds of life fill the air with an under-
hum of song. Perhaps some of the sounds are the overtones of
silence; perhaps the grasses and twigs swelling up from the roots
and unfolding in the sunlight set up a wave of sound that the
human ear can catch if it listens acutely. If the music of the
spheres can be heard, the song of the earth ought to be equally
ravishing. Day and night the countryside is softly wrapped in
sound.

28. On this day in 1860 the epochal and hard-luck steamship,
the *Great Eastern*, arrived in New York after a voyage of eleven
days. She was the chief character in one of the great annals of the
sea. Built to carry 3,600 passengers, she carried thirty-five paying
passengers on her first voyage. Never did such a fine ship have
such a tragic career. She was a pioneer in longitudinal construction with longitudinal frames and bulkheads, and she had a complete, watertight inner skin. All the big ships of today owe something to her hull designed by Scott Russell who, like nearly everyone who had anything to do with her, went bankrupt. She was six
hundred and eighty feet long, and displaced 27,384 tons. It was
nearly a half century before another ship of that length was at-
tempted. She had two paddle-wheels and a propeller, driven by
three steam engines. She had five funnels. She had six masts, and
one hundred and twenty sailors to handle the sails they carried.
There were one hundred and forty-nine men in the engine room.
She was built to go East by way of the Cape of Good Hope to
India and Australia, and to carry enough coal for the round
voyage. It had been estimated that she would pay for herself in
three voyages.

But almost nothing worked out according to plan except the

engines, which were notably able. Built to be launched sideways, she resisted three attempts in three months to slide into the water. The job of launching her added £120,000 to the cost of construction. On her first trial trip, in September, 1859, an explosion in the engine room killed six men, injured several others, and wrecked the saloon. By the time she was ready to leave Southampton for New York, June 17, 1860, people were afraid of her, and only a handful of hardy and adventurous souls bought passage. On her second outward voyage she lost her steering gear and nearly foundered. Too big for any of the contemporary piers or dry docks, she continually presented huge practical problems, and she was too costly to operate. She wrecked the fortunes of everyone who at one time or another had her. Finally, she was sold at a tremendous loss to the Trans-Atlantic Cable Company. Beginning in 1865 she started laying cable; and whatever glory she had, she won in that tedious job. But naval architects respected her highly and studied her plans long after she was broken up. The *Lusitania* and *Mauretania* owed much to her design and construction; and the *Queen Mary* and *Queen Elizabeth* would doubtless be proud to acknowledge the pride and majesty they have inherited from the *Great Eastern*.

29. Strange how the academic world carries on its stooping back so much that is obsolete. In the scientific world we have gotten rid of a vast heap of dead weight, like the movement of the sun around the earth. But the academic world reluctantly yields up its cultural myths, like the perfectibility of Greek civilization. Even today the maxims of Aristotle are quoted as authority for judgments about drama, and thousands of educated people genuflect before him. Aristotle was one of the world's great scholars. He was a pioneer in the field of knowledge. But his scientific and mathematical mind was hardly flexible enough for judgments about art and his industrious attempt to codify the laws of the drama—the celebrated *Poetics*—made the obtuse blunder of putting technique ahead of creation. That may have been a valid point of view in a civilization, founded on slavery, that produced state drama, as totalitarian states do now. But it does not apply to a free society that places a high value on inde-

pendence, originality, and humanitarianism. There are no laws to which a writer has to conform today.

Take Aristotle's thoughtful and conscientious definition of the tragic hero: "A man who is highly renowned and prosperous, but who is not pre-eminently virtuous and just, whose misfortune is brought upon him not by vice and depravity but by some error of judgment or frailty." "Highly renowned and prosperous"—that is the myth of the master-man. Since we reject it in politics we should reject it in literature also. For ordinary people can suffer as terribly as kings, merchant princes and military leaders. Not to think so is to be lacking in knowledge of human nature and leaning on arbitrary authority. I personally am not moved by tragedy based on situations that I cannot accept. I am moved only by the tragedy of people. The gods of the Greeks never threaten me. But there are wild forces loose in the world today that threaten all of us, and I am purged and terrified by them. They do not inquire into a man's ancestry or bank account before they overwhelm him with tragedy. He need not be renowned or prosperous; and he does not have to have a college education to know that he is suffering. No system of thought or code of values has any validity today unless it recognizes the ideals of this century.

30. John Kieran, the talking encyclopedia, drops in with his wife, Margaret, who is handsomer. Sitting on the divan, he plunges with infectious enthusiasm into an explanation of the difference between clock time and sidereal time, tossing in some humorous anecdotes about odd people he has known. "Is the Henslow's sparrow around this year?" he inquires, getting down to serious business. The Henslow's is interesting chiefly because he is rare. He would probably be overlooked entirely except for the commonplace, snapping "fleesic" he utters when he is sitting on the stalk of a weed or a bunch of grasses. I have not heard a Henslow's sparrow all season. One field where he used to nest is plowed this year. He is not in the other field he generally occupies. Since the presence of the Henslow's is one of the few ornithological distinctions of this area, I have been vaguely disturbed by his absence this year.

After lunch John starts for the fields, preoccupied and stubborn. In the circle of the farm we see a deer, sparrow hawk, scarlet tanager, wood thrush, chewink, catbirds, Maryland yellow-throats, meadowlarks, bobolinks, and many other familiar birds. Through familiarity with the bird's habits, John locates and shows me a prairie warbler, which I have heard and tried in vain to see two or three times this year. We stroll up the road, looking for a grasshopper sparrow and listening as we go. John pulls up short. "I think I hear a Henslow's," he says. I hear nothing except a field sparrow. For about a half hour we slowly advance through the high grass a rod to the north. John is searching the grass with his binoculars. "I see him," he exclaims. A Henslow's is sitting quietly and silently near the top of some bent grass stems. After supper we are standing by the garage, talking quietly. "I hear another Henslow's," says John. In fact, three Henslow's are singing "fleesic" from different parts of the field. In the space of about five hours John has found four Henslow's sparrows within a quarter-mile of the house. He has extraordinarily keen ears. But his greatest asset as an ornithologist is persistence. No matter what other things he may be doing or thinking, there is a sensitive area at the core of his being that is constantly looking and listening. Every time he pops in for a fleeting visit, John finds two or three birds here that I have overlooked. He introduces me to my own neighbors.

John and I have agreed not to discuss politics for a very practical reason: I am invariably right, but he invariably wins the argument.

JULY

July

B Y NOONTIME the subway is choked with vacationists who are carrying suitcases and paper-covered parcels. The great hall of the Grand Central Terminal is roaring with the talk of excited people leaving the city. For this is the Fourth of July week end, and it is estimated that more than two million people will leave by bus, railway, airplane, and automobile. Tomorrow will be a frantic day, and hundreds of thousands of tired New Yorkers will be in a state of nerves. The nervous tension is mounting now. Any mass exodus from the steaming city is highly competitive. When the gates are opened for the upriver train, the crowd rushes down the platform and piles impatiently into the cars. People laboriously lift their luggage into the racks and sit down triumphantly. The excitement is infectious. Even a half-hour before the time for departure, people scurry down the platform and burst into the cars breathlessly, and some of the children are overwrought and fretful. For there is something about a long train standing in the station that seems urgent and ominous, as though it were not going to accommodate the passengers but treacherously escape them. The cars on the train are old, dirty and uncomfortable, and the plush seat coverings are hot. Although the electric locomotive pulls the train easily, the steam locomotive that takes over at Harmon has the greatest difficulty in moving it. The engine backs violently into the train to take up the slack between the cars, and then tries to get underway slowly, the driving wheels slipping on the rails before they take hold. Since the passengers are overloaded it seems logical for the train to be overloaded and for the locomotive to be hot, breathless, worried and cross. Nobody enjoys the ride along the river. The cars are dirty with soot and buck angrily when they travel fast, and the whole train bangs and clatters. Getting out of the cars with baggage at the stations is a slow and exhausting process, and the station platforms are swirling masses of bus-drivers, taxi drivers and anxious vacationists. The highways that were not crowded yesterday are clogged today with lines of crawling cars driven by hot, tired, frustrated people. The happy holiday week end has begun.

2. City is city and country is country, and never the twain shall meet. For a few tense weeks in the summer they mingle superficially. But the association seldom goes beyond tolerance. For the country has a settled society that looks after its needs twelve months a year; it is permanent and it is held together by common experience based on fundamental elements like food, water, heat, and weather. No hurried visitor from the city can enter the formidable ranks of country society, which is mobilized according to the principle of defense in depth. He cannot share the experience on which country society is founded. The experience is ancient; it has roots that go back to Adam. Many of our country people are descended from the original colonial settlers, and carry in their bones a long history of communal living. Even if he settles in the country for the rest of his life, the city immigrant can never assimilate that history or absorb the myriad, intangible thoughts, traditions and myths that hold the country people together. Most of the dead weight of country society lies, like ice, under the surface. The city immigrant never knows about it until he bumps into it.

City people are not qualified to understand the principles of country living. City life is highly organized on an impersonal basis; the various services stand between the city dweller and the raw materials of life—running water, so abundant that it appears to be valueless, mail and newspaper deliveries, deliveries from the grocery and department stores, steam heat, gas piped in from the street, painting and repairs, rapid transportation, garbage collection, professional fire fighters. The city dweller grows up amid the illusion that those things are automatic. With all this organization and equipment behind him, he is likely to patronize the country people who have to improvise these things for themselves or go without. He is ignorant of the facts of life. No one has abundant running water in the country without making a deliberate and costly choice which is beyond the means of most people. Most country people have to call for the mail, look after their own stoves or heating plants, disposing of their garbage and refuse in some way that is safe and sanitary, and bring home the things they buy at the store. Over the years they acquire knowledge, facility and self-reliance; living involves a daily routine and discipline that set them apart from city people. The pace is slower and more purposeful. No wonder they are indifferent to the casual city visitors who bumble around the country in gay sports clothing a few weeks in the pleasantest part of the year. At home in the city, city people do not commonly throw their doors open to casual visitors from the country. At home city people are preoccupied, too.

3. The cult of nature flourishes among people who live apart from nature and in countries that have succeeded in neutralizing nature with railroads, airplanes, telephones, heating systems, and water supplies. Most of the members of mountain clubs and bird clubs live in the cities. There is more popular interest in birds in countries like England and America than in countries like China and Russia, which are not industrially developed and cannot patronize nature yet. For the cult of nature is a form of patronage by people who have declared their materialistic independence from nature and do not have to struggle with nature every day of their lives. Primitive people may love nature, consciously or unconsciously, but they do not make a cult of nature because it is a fundamental part of their lives.

When I was in China during the war, I had to climb over the lofty Kaolikung mountains that bathe their green feet in the Salween River. The passes over the Kaolikungs are at an elevation of about ten thousand feet. Having climbed mountains in America and Switzerland, I instinctively approached the Kaolikungs in a sporting frame of mind. I looked forward to invading the remote privacy of the lofty ridges and standing triumphantly above the world. But climbing mountains was no sport for the Chinese. It was part of the drudgery of their daily lives. And the rocky trails by which my party ascended and descended were the normal highways from the east to the west, used every day by Chinese travelers and accepted as part of the burden of life. Rich merchants were carried over in sedan chairs. Long trains of pack animals loaded with salt were driven across, and one Chinese farmer was driving a flock of little pigs across, urging them on with the Chinese hog call, "Oo, la, la, oo, la, la." In a wind-swept hut at the top of the pass, some Chinese porters were assuaging the pain of their fate by smoking opium. My sentimental communion with the forests and the lordly heights was repeatedly shattered by natives engrossed in the unromantic toil of getting over a terrible barrier as quickly as possible. Mountain climbing is not a sport for people who have no easy way of neutralizing the obstacles of nature.

4. Independence Day. It used to be the most boisterous day of the year. We celebrated it with a midnight bonfire on the common, firecrackers, torpedoes, miniature cannon, patriotic speeches, and fireworks after dark. We behaved as though we personally had delivered a peremptory ultimatum to George III; and I suppose we assumed that democracy was irrevocable and universally admired. Nations that were not as democratic as America seemed to us rather silly; and socialism seemed like a sinister plot by evil and envious men to embarrass the prudent, the thrifty, and the virtuous. I am writing of the days when I was a boy.

If we celebrate Independence Day less chauvinistically today it may be, not only because firecrackers are dangerous, but chiefly because after more than a century and a half democracy prevails in only small areas of the world. Only a small fraction of the world's 2,231,716,000 people adhere to the Philadelphia declaration that "governments are instituted among men, deriving their just powers from the consent of the governed." Freedom does not seem so easy to us now. In our lifetime freedom has been lost in many places. If we derive our thinking from facts, uninfluenced by political and religious faith, we must recognize the tragic fact that freedom is shrinking in the world. There is a tone of anxiety in the Fourth of July speeches today. The flag looks more like a beautiful symbol of faith than a swagger token of victory.

History gets foreshortened as the years increase. The Declaration of Independence looks now like a spectacular incident in a well-conceived and ingeniously integrated design of action by heroic statesmen whose minds were clear. Now we are inclined to assume that the Declaration was unanimously adopted in the morning and that the Liberty Bell—already named and cunningly held in reserve for the purpose—started to ring in the afternoon. But the Americans of 1776 were no different from Americans today: they were not unanimous about anything; they were afflicted by doubts and many of them were reluctant to make irrevocable decisions. For eleven years the thirteen colonies had been trying to find a method of government that would be just and would also foster the development of a new, rich, vast country; and since so many of the colonists had roots in England, many of them wanted to remain inside the framework of English rule. But the fifteen months that preceded the Declaration made independence inevitable whether everybody wanted it or not. The English government had been fighting the colonists during that period, and to a large extent with German mercenaries, which was the crowning insult. In January, 1776, Thomas Paine published his fiery *Common Sense*, which could not be printed fast enough to satisfy the public demand. On April twelfth, the provincial assembly of North Carolina instructed its delegates to the Continental Congress to join other states in formally declaring the independence of the colonies. On May fourteenth, Virginia went one step further by instructing its delegates to propose a declaration of independence. Massachusetts, which had been discussing the question by means of general town meetings, came next and took the initiative with Virginia. Maryland, which had suffered little under English rule, joined the movement after public opinion had been consulted. By July first, twelve of the thirteen colonies had instructed their delegates to consider a declaration of independence. New York was the sole dissenter. It had a large Tory population; Lord Howe had already landed troops in New York, which was strategically in the front-line trenches. A trading center then as now, New York was looking after its pocketbook and convenience, although the New York delegates to the Continental Congress were personally sympathetic, as were the people of New York.

Anticipating the congressional decision, a committee in Philadelphia had been at work for three weeks framing the declaration. When the question of drawing up a declaration was taken up on July first, nine states voted for it. New York was excused from voting, since the delegates had not yet been instructed. South Carolina voted "No." Pennsylvania voted "No" by a vote of four to three. The Delaware vote was tied one to one—one delegate being absent. On July second another vote was taken. New York was still unable to vote. But the remaining twelve colonies were unanimous for the declaration. South Carolina voted "Yes." The third delegate having arrived, Delaware voted "Yes." John Dickinson and Robert Morris having stayed away, Pennsylvania voted "Yes." The Declaration of Independence was adopted by the twelve colonies on the evening of July fourth. It was not read until noon on July eighth to a crowd of people assembled before the State House. On July ninth it was read to the American soldiers in the presence of George Washington near New York City Hall, and formally adopted by New York, making the decision unanimous for the thirteen colonies. It was published in the Pennsylvania *Journal* on July tenth. It was not signed until August second. Not all who had voted for it signed, and some who signed had not voted for it, and several did not sign until two or three months later. Thomas McKean, of Delaware, who fought through the Revolution, did not sign it until 1781.

Even after so many years of conflict with the King, some prudent and earnest Americans had thought that a formal declaration of independence would be rash, and that the colonies were not yet sufficiently organized to support and carry forward a separatist movement in the face of British armed resistance. From the legal and practical point of view they may have been right. The colonies were not competently organized and the Continental Congress did everything short of wrecking Washington's leadership in the field. But when people are genuinely aroused against tyranny, practical considerations are secondary. The Declaration of Independence represented the tone and temper of public opinion. It came out of the hearts of the people. In grave and lucid prose, it expressed what they felt, though most of them were not so clear in their minds as Thomas Jefferson who wrote it in a second-story room of a private residence in Philadelphia.

5. Since human beings and animals must eat, the provender of the fields seems normal. The fields of hay and grain and the kitchen gardens look handsome and give us a feeling of security. But the fecund womb of nature not only provides food at this time of year but also blesses the earth with beauty. Out of the damp soil come delicate flower textures and splendors. Wave after wave of brilliant color sweeps across the meadows and pastures. Six weeks ago the cinquefoil made a yellow bed under the green

grass. Then came the hawkweed that banked the hills with gold. Now the buttercups and the daisies sprinkle the green fields with yellow and white. In swaley ground on the lowlands the Canadian thistle—a vicious weed—reflects the color of the sky like a lake, making pools of deep blue in the hollows. Along the hedgerows the wild grape is in bloom; and the roadsides bear lavender and white fleabane, meadow-rue and sweet clover. The milkweed, a coarse plant, is in bloom and perfumes the summer air extravagantly. The colors throughout the countryside represent the abundance and ecstasy of creation. Nature is not satisfied with necessity. As lovers are transfigured by happiness, so the fields today are transfigured by the joy of creation.

In the spruce lot the wild rose returns the daily greeting of the sun with scattered pink blossoms. The rose garden beside the house does better than that. After centuries of cultivation throughout the world the rose is the queen of flowers—soft and lustrous in texture, dainty, gorgeously colored in myriad shades and patterns. None of the wild roses can equal the abundance and glory of those that have been cultivated. Like all cultivated life, they cannot be neglected. From April to November, O. tends ours assiduously—pruning and spraying, and applying the proper fertilizer where it is needed. She knows them; she watches them day by day with a mixture of affection and anxiety. After the middle of June they reward her with a daily burst of rich blossoms, and some of the plants continue blooming until the snow settles on them.

Cultivated roses have been an ornament of civilization for centuries. Dried roses have been found in the tombs of Egyptian Kings. The word "rose" is international. It is also the symbol of all that is loveliest—to "gather roses" is to seek pleasure; a "bed of roses" represents ease and luxury; a "rose without a thorn" represents impossible happiness, an ideal that cannot be achieved. We bring roses as a silent offering to all the major ceremonies of life—graduations, weddings, anniversaries, funerals. In their grace, softness, color and fragrance they are the finest tokens we can give when words seem foolish and trifling. Although they can be cultivated and bred, they cannot be created. They stand as close to immortality as anything we know or can touch.

6. Nothing should be dismissed as devoid of interest until it has been investigated. In the ideal sense, nothing is uninteresting; there are only uninterested people.

About a hundred yards from this house lies an insignificant cat-tail swamp which is about seven hundred and fifty square feet in area. In the spring a foot of water stands there. The peepers sing there in the early spring, and the frogs take bass possession of it now. The red-wings nest there, drowned in reeds, and enjoy it. In dry summers the water in the swamp disappears, leaving a bed of ooze. Beyond taking a casual glance into it, I have never paid much attention to this miniature marsh. After supper this evening the children are searching around the edges of it for frogs. Suddenly a Virginia rail flops up from under my feet and drops back into the cat-tails a few yards away. Later I manage to put him up again and get a good look at him as he teeters on inadequate wings to the opposite end. To me this is astonishing. It moves out the walls of my universe a little further.

The Virginia rail is one of the most difficult birds to see. Small, undistinguished and thin, he commonly runs through cat-tail swamps that seem to be impenetrable. Since his wings are less developed than his feet, he rarely comes out of the obscure, slimy thicket of the swamp and is seldom seen. Years ago I saw a Virginia rail during the migration season in the outskirts of New York. But I had never seen another until this evening; and since he lives such a solitary life and is so difficult to see I have fallen in the habit of never looking for him. During the past two months, particularly at twilight, I have been hearing an unmusical, stuttering note from the swamp. It has puzzled me, but I had put it aside as a swamp mystery hardly worth the trouble of solving. Twice I have heard it from other places—from a pasture beyond the swamp to the east, and from the west-lot swale, and this was perplexing, for swamp sounds should be confined to swamps. When I caught these two glimpses of the rail this evening I quickly understood the whole experience. For the past two months a Virginia rail has been raising a family only a hundred yards from my house and, moreover, telling the whole neighborhood about it at the top of his voice. Occasionally he has wandered out of the swamp to look for seeds and locusts in the fields; that accounts for the fact that his voice has come from other

places. By being lazy I have almost missed one of the most fascinating episodes in the life of this ancient farm. Thanks to the
elastic enthusiasm of the children, whose minds have not become
routine, I discover that the swamp is one of the most interesting
corners of the neighborhood. I thought I knew the neighborhood
thoroughly.

7. During the course of the evening three planets now look out
on our hillside farm. Venus appears like a ball of white light in
the flaming glow of the sinking sun, sliding down behind the
mountain wall before ten o'clock (daylight time). Saturn pairs with
Regulus in the west as soon as the night darkens, and sets about
a half an hour before midnight. In the meantime, Jupiter rises in
the east at half past nine, becoming visible just about the time
Venus disappears.

Although Saturn is next in size to Jupiter, it looks like an ordinary star—brighter than Regulus, but nothing like so handsome as
Vega. Lying far outside the earth's orbit, it is visible only because
it is so large. I have never seen Uranus, although it is just within
the limits of normal vision, or Neptune and Pluto, which are outside it. The three flat rings of Saturn, being now end on to the
earth, are not visible through the binocular this evening. They
were in this position when Galileo first looked at Saturn through
his new telescope, and he did not see them at that time. Being
only ten miles thick, they cannot be seen at this distance. The
rings are spinning in space seven thousand miles from the equator
of Saturn and extend forty-five thousand miles into space. They
are composed of sand, pebbles and rocks—the debris of a satellite
that got inside Saturn's zone of danger, as once our sun, wandering through space, entered inside the danger zone of some big,
massive star and was broken up into the present system of planets.
Some day our moon will come inside the danger zone of the earth
and will be broken into luminous fragments, like the rings of
Saturn. This incident will be worth waiting for, because it will
give the earth continuous moonlight.

8. Criticism is parasitical. It has to have something to cling to,
since it has neither the originality nor the energy to flourish by

itself. There are good critics and bad creative writers—a fact that complicates the situation. But in any useful code of values, first things come first; and it is obvious that poets, dramatists, and novelists come before their critics.

But all writers, whether creative or critical, have one thing in common: a passion for the health and well-being of contemporary life. "Literature is big only in one way—when used as an aid to the growth of humanities," said Walt Whitman. Since all serious writers have the same goal, it follows that they need the same equipment and resources, whether they are critics or creative writers. In addition to energy ("the life force," Shaw called it) they need a wide, deep, practical experience of life. I do not subscribe to the notion that some people know what is good in art and others do not. There are no final authorities, for there are no absolute standards save the ultimate one that cannot be defined because, like God, it goes deeper than articulate human experience. But some opinions are more valid than others. I respect the opinions of interesting people who bring to the appreciation of art the same vigor, sanity and independence that they apply to the whole range of their personal lives.

Traditional opinions are full of cant. From one generation to another we carry over a lot of piety about the good and the beautiful. It clutters up our spiritual lives. Our mental furniture always needs rearranging, clearing out and dusting. Traditional opinions are hardly worth the labor of writing. There should be a large dash of the amateur in criticism. For the amateur is a man of enthusiasm who has not settled down and is not habit-bound.

Opinions are the electricity of the mind. "What do *you* think?" Is there a more profoundly social question than that? It assumes that we are all living together and have within ourselves the power to sort things out and create a civilization. It is the function of the critic to pitch in to the intellectual life of the community and express his opinion with force and clarity. His knowledge of the community, mark you, is as vital as his knowledge of art. No art can exist in a vacuum.

9. In the country peace consists of little things. They are almost too familiar to be noticed. Over the rim of the calm earth the sun rises with glory and the comfort of day wraps us in security.

This is how the world was intended to be—unhurried, full of
light, expectant, green. A slow routine frames the day and gives
it foundation. The cows leisurely appear in the pasture before
breakfast. The road gang goes off to work with a clatter of trucks
and tools. The carpenter and his assistant turn the corner on the
way to the house they are building. The putter of the tractor
comes from a valley hayfield. In midmorning the heavy milk truck
rolls down the hill. Toward noon there is a general gathering at
the postoffice for the mail and conversation, and a few people go
on errands to the store.

Nearly everything that happens can be anticipated. Even the
changes in routine, like the appearance of the truck from the mill
or the passing of a load of lumber, can be fitted into the general
pattern of a community looking after its affairs. Someone is
planting buckwheat and needs fertilizer, or someone is building
a shed. If the garage car shoots up the hill in a cloud of dust it
is certain that someone's car is desperately ailing.

In a baleful world that is booming and crashing and sick with
foreboding, these are not important things, and no one thinks
about them much. But they are the warp and woof of peace in
the country, and infinitely precious as tokens of the world as it
was intended to be. Little things have an ancient lineage that is
honorable.

10. Excepting a series of evening showers, there has been no
rain for over a month in the country. Pastures and lawns are
browned. The grass in the hayfields is prematurely dry. Although
the stuff in the kitchen garden has not died, it stands still. The
earth is parched and gasping, living anxiously on its reserves.
Today the temperature rises to 91°; and with the humidity high,
the weight of the sunlight in the fields is almost unbearable. But
every now and then a puff of breeze out of the south smells wet.
Since this has happened frequently during the length of the
drought, we dare not hope. But a rumble of thunder shakes the
heavens in the early afternoon, the clouds gather and at three
o'clock the rain begins to fall. In normal times we might accept it
casually. But today we go out on the porch to be near it, to hear
the silent rain pipes gurgling again and carrying away the dirt from
the roofs, to see the limpid rainwater collect in the hollows of the

bluestone doorstep and to see the rain wash the dusty leaves and drench the grass.

The birds serenade it joyfully. A catbird yells with more excitement than he has displayed for weeks. A goldfinch breaks out into an endless rhapsodic song that trails through one happy measure after another. Now that the flies and insects are beaten close to the ground, the phoebe comes out of the trees and perches on a stump, shouting his name and swinging his tail. The barn swallows swing low, stuttering as they skim the fields.

Although the rain lasts only three hours, it refreshes the ailing country and fills the air with merciful dampness. In the garden the peas get off the ground and stand up eagerly. I could swear that there are more blossoms on the beans. The lawn looks brighter. A baby rabbit in the road throws himself into the air for the sheer joy of being alive. A woodchuck, his fur dark and wet, climbs on a stone wall and looks around peacefully, as if he were enjoying the cool evening air. The summer haze is washed out of the mountains; and after dark the stars are brighter than they have been for a month, and Jupiter looks as huge and near as an airplane preparing for a landing. We need two days of solid rain. But the tenth of an inch that falls this afternoon relieves the strain a little and sweetens the burden of growing.

11.　In our political life nothing is more dangerous than the task of deciding whether or not a political opinion is a crime. Murder and larceny are crimes; since they are concrete acts, they can be identified and judged. But the criminal quality of a political opinion is in itself a political opinion. And the judging of political opinions is therefore a competition between opposing political ideas and is likely to be decided in favor of what is familiar, unimaginative and old. The leaders of the American, French, and Russian revolutions had one thing in common: they were all criminals.

Over the century and a half of our constitutional life we have miraculously managed to reserve the tradition of free opinion through the bloodless revolutions of the Jefferson, Jackson, Theodore Roosevelt, and Franklin Roosevelt administrations. In those instances the competition between opposing political ideas was decided at the polls and not in the courts. The polls are a franker, simpler and more flexible device than the courts for the decision of political affairs, for the polls draw on the accumulated wisdom of the nation. The courts are narrower, technical, and sanctimonious. In the courts political ideas are examined under abnormal pressure and are made to seem criminal before the evidence has been heard. In the sphere of politics the judicial process in itself has the stigma of a conviction.

Despite the Constitution and its Bill of Rights we, as a nation, are always on the verge of abandoning the principle of political freedom whenever political developments abroad threaten our security. The ink was scarcely dry on the Bill of Rights before Congress passed the Alien and Sedition acts in 1798 to outlaw the enthusiasm in this country for the reckless egalitarianism of the French Revolution. The French destroyed the enthusiasm more decisively than the Alien and Sedition acts by proposing corrupt negotiations with our representatives in Paris. A century and a half later, the power of the Soviet idea is again inhibiting our tradition of freedom of opinion. Anybody who is not an old-line Republican or who believes in hot lunches for schoolchildren is likely to find himself summoned by Congress to answer for treason.

12. Henry David Thoreau was born in Concord, Massachusetts, on this day in 1817. During most of his lifetime most people who knew him dismissed him as an irritating eccentric, for he was intolerant and antisocial. Even those who knew him well and admired him found him difficult to associate with. Emerson, his greatest champion, remarked: "Henry is—with difficulty—sweet," and that he would as soon think of grasping an oak limb as Henry's arm. To preserve his social independence Thoreau had to erect many stiff barriers around himself. But he is known today throughout America, England and France, and in many other parts of the world as one of the great American writers, as one of the great philosophers of freedom, as a man of courage, wisdom and integrity; and many of the apothegms that most of his neighbors regarded as wry whimsies have become principles of life: "The mass of men lead lives of quiet desperation." "I love a broad margin to my life." "Simplicity, simplicity, simplicity!" The core of his social philosophy is expressed with tingling strength and candor

in his essay "On the Necessity of Civil Disobedience," which is one of the fundamental papers on freedom. Gandhi regarded it as a vital part of human truth and acted on it deliberately.

It would be a mistake to assume that Thoreau fashioned this philosophy out of pure reason. He was an extraordinarily sensitive youth, hurt more by the opinions of his townsmen than he admitted even to himself. His family was eminently respectable, but poor; it lived a life of quiet desperation. Although it managed to give Henry an education at Harvard College, he was unable to make the usual social applications of what he had learned. From the social point of view, he was a failure; and he knew it, and the bravado of his writing compensated for the private agony of his soul.

From 1845 to 1847 he lived alone in a small house he built for himself on the shore of Walden Pond, and this was the greatest thing he ever did. It was dramatic, it was poetic and practical, and since it suited him perfectly, it brought him into harmony with the universe. He could understand it; after he had published *Walden, or Life in the Woods* in 1854 people generally began to understand it and him, and they still do. For this was the concrete base of his philosophy. "If you have built castles in the air, your work need not be lost: that is where they should be. Now put the foundations under them," he wrote in the last chapter. His "experiment" at Walden, as he chose to call it, perfectly illustrated that principle.

If he had not been able to express himself, the Walden hermitage might have been no more fruitful than other similar enterprises before and after his. But he was a great prose stylist—the greatest this country has produced. For he could catch in a vivid phrase or pithy sentence the illusory impressions that sweep over sensitive people and become to most people experience that cannot be described, defined or shared. Although most of his verse was rude, he was a poet. Fortunately, he was also a workman, jack of all trades—surveyor, carpenter, mason, gardener and fisherman, which are trades that are practical and some of them exacting. And his proficiency as a workman helped to make Thoreau a writer who was plain, accurate and forceful. Like a good workman, he despised sloppy, pompous or sentimental writing. *Walden* is his great work. Since many people understood and appreciated it in the last eight years of Thoreau's life, it relieved him of a good deal of his loneliness and softened the austerity out of which it had come. Thoreau had won his battle for freedom. It gave some peace to his perturbed spirit. He died in Concord on May sixth, 1862, with full knowledge of what was happening to him and willingness to add one more episode in experience to his incomparably responsive career. "There is more day to dawn. The sun is but a morning star." These are the final sentences in *Walden*.

13. Bobbing around on the flexible seat of his mowing machine, Judson Moss drives his pair of horses around the "house-lot," as he calls it, and begins the job of haying on our place. He has finished the haying on his own farm, and now comes to ours. There is a certain element of home-coming about his appearance here. For Jud was born more than sixty years ago on what is now our farm in another house that burned to the ground a quarter of a century ago. And he knows more about our farm than I shall ever know, for he has plowed it, cultivated it, and mowed it for years and has an intimate knowledge of every acre. Every part of it recalls a story or an episode, for he has sprinkled the whole of it with his own sweat.

For many years Jud was town road superintendent—an office calculated to make enemies. No one can keep the roads in a condition satisfactory to everyone, especially in the winter when all the roads are in need of plowing at the same time, and frequently are blown full of snow three or four hours after they have been cleared. Since the town's snow equipment is limited and the road gang is not large, most people have to wait to have their roads cleared. No matter how the road superintendent arranges his schedule, nearly everyone in town feels at one time or another that he is being neglected. After two particularly savage winters in succession, Jud declined to run for road superintendent again and returned to civil life. He was a good road superintendent, but the pressure of public opinion during the snow and the mud seasons wore down his resistance.

Living in the village in a small house that was a tiny bank years ago, Jud now keeps a few cows, raises a few crops, cuts and saws wood and drives a school bus. He makes out without having to yield up much of his private independence. He has a thorough knowledge of the town, a love of its history, and a wry sense of humor. It is always a pleasant morning when Jud hitches Dan and Snip to the mowing machine and cuts the first swath through our grass.

14. Despite the romantic myths that have grown up, for the most part fraudulently, about the subject of haying, let us joyfully celebrate the modern mechanization of that ancient chore. Yesterday Jud cut about half of the grass in two adjoining fields. This morning one of the neighbors rakes it in endless windrows behind a tractor. As soon as he has well started, another neighbor starts bailing it mechanically with a bailing machine that is new this season in our community. In previous seasons it has taken Jud and his son, Leslie, a week to cut, rake, stack and pitch on this much grass. But by noon today the bailing machine has gathered up, bailed, tied and tossed out all the grass cut yesterday, and no one has broken his back, strained his heart or raised a sweat. The mechanical process is less thorough than the old hand process. It does not get into the corners and it leaves grass scattered on the fields. Another load or two can be gleaned. But that is small price to pay for the merciful relief from the killing drudgery of haying by hand.

The mythical romance of haying doubtless derives from the days when a farmer could put ten men into the fields at once. They could do the work fast and probably have some fun. But it has been years since most people around here could get as many as four men at once, and the chore of haying has gone on wearisomely two months, and occasionally into September—even October. Most of the hay has passed its prime by the time two or three men could get round to it. Haying is dirty, heavy, violent work that has to be done in the hottest time of the year. Some of it has to be done in the hottest place in the region—just under the heat-crackling metal roof of the barn in a dust-laden, airless mow. Traditionally sweet as new hay is, mowing away in hot weather is a form of torture. It is one of the chief causes of heart diseases. There is nothing romantic about it. The most romantic thing I have seen all summer is the bailing machine devouring man-hours in the hayfield and rolling cheerfully away at noon to devour some more man-hours on another farm.

At this rate Jud will finish the haying on our place in another four days—three weeks ahead of average schedule.

15. *"St. Swithin's Day, if thou dost rain,*
For forty days it will remain;
St. Swithin's Day, if thou be fair
For forty days it will rain nae mair."

It does rain today, but we all know that it will not rain every day between now and August twenty-fourth. For the tradition of St. Swithin's Day, already nearly a thousand years old, has no basis in fact and never has had. St. Swithin, a bishop of Winchester, England, died on July 2, 862. Loving people as much as he loved God, he asked to be buried outside the cathedral "where the feet of passersby might tread and the rain of heaven will fall." He was buried according to his wishes. His memory was particularly venerated. People believed that miraculous cures came from visiting his grave. He became a saint by popular devotion. About a century later the clergy of the cathedral concluded that so illustrious a saint should be reburied inside the cathedral and they moved his remains inside on July 15, 971. The tradition is that it rained on that day (although there is testimony to the contrary) and for forty days thereafter and that the reburial had to be postponed for that length of time. Another tradition is that after forty days the clergy decided to let the body remain where it was and then built a chapel over it. At any rate, the body was definitely removed in 1094 inside a new cathedral.

The tradition of St. Swithin's Day comes straight out of the ignorant superstitions of the Middle Ages. But during the recent drought I have several times heard it cited as a possible solution to the most immediate calamity of the year in this neighborhood. After nearly a thousand years, St. Swithin is still regarded as one of the "healing saints." We still reach for symbols to protect us from things we cannot control and do not understand.

16. He is five years old. He weighs forty-five pounds. If he can be persuaded to stay in one place long enough, he stands three feet, eight and one-half inches. Nearly everything in the world towers grandly above him and looks down at him with a patron-

izing air. But by evening he has exhausted two adults in their mid-
fifties who are strong enough for nearly anything. For he is possessed by gods and demons of civilization; and every day he instinctively repeats the history of the human race. Like primitive
man he wakes up in full possession of his faculties with the rising
of the sun; and he goes to bed, dropping to sleep instantly, at sunset. Like primitive man, he has a dance for everything—for the
rites of rising and bathing and for the joy of being alive. His play
is largely a dance usually full of drama. He is fascinated by food;
he calls for it at regular hours; he discusses it at length, and his
feeding habits are not fastidious. Like the human race widening
its culture, he is full of wonder and inquiry. The world is his playroom, crammed with treasures and surprises. He sees them all,
peers at everything closely and tries to fit everything into the pattern of his own experience. All the things in the world are to him
terribly important—birds, dragonflies, frogs, blueberries, lawn
mowers, pumps, sawdust, grindstones, the new moon, songs, caves,
tall grass. "Wow," he says a thousand times a day when something
new staggers his imagination. Dimly aware of the stupendous empire of reading, he learns a new word every day. After supper he
reads aloud from his Polly book, squirming, scratching and wriggling, but slowly spelling out the few words he knows as he gently
lifts the heavy, mysterious curtain to learning. In the course of
the day he is likely to make a poem or two:

> "Save the icing, save the cake,
> Save the lady with the big, fat shake."

He talks to himself continuously; he tells himself long and wonderful tales. He is combative and belligerent. When he plays with
his sister he scratches, pummels, and yells, and he races through
the house, slamming doors and knocking over furniture. He has
a strong will, and he is experimentally trying to fit it into the ancient will of the race. He is also bursting with energy. His eyes
are bright, his legs are swift and sturdy and his mind is active.
This daily chore of reliving the long history of the race is terribly
exciting and seems to be a fresh experience every day. It exhausts
the adults, who have become cautious because they have learned
some of the perils of experience. But it never exhausts him. It is
not his fault that he is overjoyed to be alive.

17. Along the Hudson River flocks of white herons are assembling. Tall, slender, wary, with long legs and long necks, they paddle through shallow water, looking for fish and frogs. In some poses they look roundshouldered. When they fly they look squat and neckless. They have a melancholy appearance like something left over from primeval times. It is difficult to identify the herons accurately from a railroad train window. But they are mostly American egrets and little blue herons in summer plumage, which is white. Both species nest in the South from Florida to North Carolina or Virginia. When their nesting season is over and the hot weather settles down they start wandering north, like summer tourists, and get as far as Canada. Since white herons are a convention of Japanese prints, they are admired in this country as figures in art by people not particularly interested in birds. In Asia—in China and Java, as I know from my own knowledge—white herons are a common ornament of the hillside rice terraces and the paddy fields. Although they are less well known in America, we have them in abundance.

The heron civilization is like all swamp life, secluded and self-contained, or possibly seems so because it is relatively inaccessible. At the time when other birds are going south the herons idly drift north and relax along the Hudson River. Later in the season hundreds of great blue herons, who are majestic birds, stand like odd-shaped posts in the Hudson flats.

Our summer association with American egrets represents a triumph of conservation legislation, proposed and fought for by the National Audubon Societies. The egrets were the source of the handsome white plumes that women wore in their hats in the late nineteenth century. Thousands of egrets were slaughtered by plume hunters in the swamps of Florida. Although Florida passed protective legislation, it was difficult to enforce. At least one warden was killed, and all the wardens risked their lives policing the plume hunters. The battle to save egrets went on for twenty years, and involved legislation to make the sale or possession of egret plumes illegal. But the battle was won long ago, and one of the results is the constant increase in the numbers of egrets. Since New York took specific action to protect herons from slaughter and destruction, it is especially gratifying to see so many of them visiting the

Hudson River every summer. Nothing along the river is lovelier than those tall, white, mysterious yet self-confident water birds.

18. During the night the temperature drops only to 74°. At eight o'clock in the morning the thermometer reads 82°. The air is stale and stagnant. At breakfast time the sun is hot in the east. It burns through the trees and bushes, and the neighborhood surrenders to it. The world is dead. Nothing fundamental moves; and if nothing changes the world will get hotter and hotter, and the air will get more and more stifling until we are all prostrate. The hayfields are baking. The children are querulous. The birds are silent and morose. Even the bird bath, which usually refreshes them, has become lifeless and tepid. A robin walks around it disdainfully, looking at the house with a suggestion of reproach. Taking the hint, I replenish the bath with cool water from the pump, and the robin bathes enthusiastically. The thermometer rises steadily to 91°. In the middle of the dank afternoon, thunder begins to rumble in distant places. During the next hour the sky darkens, the thunder increases and the wind rises. The lightning strikes somewhere in the neighborhood; the black clouds open and the rain begins to spill down. Since the house is hot, we close the windows tentatively on the west. But the thunder crashes nearer all the time, the telephone bell jingles nervously, the wind rises and presently the trees are bowing and screaming with fright, and the rain beats savagely on the roof and at the windows. No rain comes through the north windows, but the wind is so cold that we close them, too. The thermometer drops to 67°. After ten minutes of crash and fury, the storm gradually moves towards the northeast, and finally the sun flames through the scattering clouds and sparkles on the wet leaves and grass. The thermometer starts climbing again towards a hot, close night. Over the radio in the evening we hear that the thermometer rose to 94° in Albany and 96° in Schenectady. Our high of 91° seems like a triumph by comparison. But the air is dead again and the upstairs bedrooms close and confining. No one escapes hot weather in July.

19. Think twice before venturing on the highway in a car on week ends this month. On Saturdays and Sundays the city drivers

are tearing along the road like gangsters. Having jumpy nerves, no knowledge of the road, and no driving imagination, they recklessly weave in and out of traffic and pass on curves. They never know what may happen to them or to us until it is too late. People accustomed to country driving have learned never to take the initiative when the Sunday drivers are on the road. Strangers to the country, they drive competitively as though it were a reflection on their self-respect to remain in line. Even though you are driving fifty or fifty-five miles an hour, they whizz by impatiently with nervous twists of the steering wheel and the squeal of hot tires. They will risk your life as well as their own to get to the head of the line.

On the way to town on business this morning, I reached a long, straight, safe stretch of road where two cars had collided. Two city cars were wrecked in the ditch. One woman, who looked dead, was lying on the side of the road while a doctor examined her, and a group of people, oblivious to the state police, stared at her morbidly. Only a week ago another woman was killed by an automobile a couple of miles north of this point; and a month ago a young man was killed five miles to the north on the same road, leaving, incidentally, a mother whose husband had died only a fortnight earlier. With these calamities fresh in mind, we who live in the neighborhood drive as carefully as possible. We do not feel like masters of the road; we feel insecure. And we regard with a mixture of fear and anger the drivers who race in and out of traffic as though the rest of us were aimless fuddy-duddies without enterprise or daring.

Last year 28,600 Americans were killed by automobiles. About one million more were injured. Americans commonly buy automobiles without counting the cost of operation, and many of them also drive without counting the hazards. There are plenty of reckless country drivers. But the Sunday drivers from the city are the most ignorant and inexperienced and have the least skill. It will not be safe to drive on week ends until after Labor Day.

20. Now is the most relaxing time of year in town. Although the oily, steaming city is uncomfortable, the mood is bland. In the perennial drive for progress and expansion this is the interlude that does not count; and the people who are not on vacation do

not pitch into their work aggressively. They dress affably. Most of the men go hatless and many go in shirt sleeves without ties, and those who adhere to the ancient punctilio wear lightweight suits in pleasant colors. The women wear fresh, washable dresses that have a holiday air. Since the temperature outdoors and indoors is practically the same, people go in and out casually as though the city were a unit and the whole area equally inhabitable. Even for those who are indoors it is an outdoor season, for the windows are open and the hiss and whirr of the traffic comes in. With the doors and windows flung open, New York seems more congenial in the summer. Everybody is caught in the same heat and feels it the same and slips through it in the same rhythm. For nothing is being settled in the summer. The great decisions are made in the autumn, winter and spring when everybody is on the job. Just now the grand executives are either out of town or dreaming wistfully of the country. They cannot put their minds on big business projects.

The evenings are the triumph of the year. After the sun sets, the temperature falls agreeably and a fresh breeze flutters across the river, trickling down the side streets and almost imperceptibly cooling the city. The Goldman band plays stirring music in Central Park. People ride the ferryboats, sit on the cramped front stoops of the dingy brownstone-front houses, or sit on the benches in the middle of uptown Broadway or along Riverside Park. Sitting quietly amid the trees and with each other, they are lost in meditation. The beating, exhausting drive of a great metropolis has subsided into an effortless holding operation. Cosmopolis has become a big outdoor town of leisurely burghers. Nothing important will happen until mid-September when the attendance will be complete again.

21. Although the thunderstorms are so violent that they drown the Independent subway system and interrupt the service for six hours, I am only dimly aware of rain and thunder outside. For Al Hirschfeld, the bearded artist, is arguing pithily on both sides of several questions, and his wife, Dolly Haas, and I are agreeing, disagreeing or introducing evidence like passages of counterpoint to the main theme. Lightning cracks all around the neighborhood; occasionally a window has to be closed to keep the wind from

driving the rain across the room. But these are only external incidents. We hardly notice them. For after an exhausting day that has left most of New York pale and enervated, Al is crackling with arguments—improvising as he goes along, and we are huddled together in a self-contained world of passion and humor on the roof of a mid-town apartment house.

There are many themes—American and Russian political relations, the theater, the futility of psychoanalysis, the basic arrogance and obtuseness of the German national character, the unworldliness of Siam, the irrational behavior of human beings. But the themes are only incidental to Al's stream of improvisations that flash more vividly than the lightning outside and flood the room with energy. Al does not argue for victory. The impulse is social. He likes the sting and pitch of ideas discharged helter-skelter around the room. Some of his resounding conclusions are not so final as they sound, but are offered as tentative points in a good-humored inquiry.

Once every five or ten years Al takes a trip somewhere to examine the world. He goes to California, Europe, the East Indies, or around the world. This refreshes his knowledge of the background and stimulates his mind. It gives him something to argue against. But his miniature apartment amid the aerials and blazing electric signs of Manhattan is a microcosm and he could live a full life without even stirring outside it. The newspapers and magazines bring him an abundance of material every day. Since his outside door is unlocked and displays a hospitable sign reading "Please don't knock," people stream in and out all day and night with recent facts, startling opinions and fresh arguments. They provide all the leg-work Al needs. What they bring, Al swiftly absorbs, adding it to the mass of material he has already assembled and revising his ideas accordingly. Ordinarily he argues until two in the morning, though sometimes until three or four. Since Nina, his daughter, commonly lifts up her voice at five or five-thirty in the morning, this raises the question, when do Al and Dolly sleep? For the argument room is also the sleeping, dining, and living room. There is no escaping the talk, which is vibrant and brilliant. This year's most furious thunderstorm goes almost unnoticed by comparison.

22. In the evening the hermit thrush sings in the woods near Mr. Dring's sheep pasture up the hill from our house in the country. Once I did catch a glimpse of the hermit in the binocular—a plain, brownish bird with a streaked breast. But usually I do not intrude on his solitude, but sit on an old hemlock stump near his choir loft and listen to his evening music. It is the finest sound in nature in this neighborhood. It is pure meditation by an inspired anchorite of the woods who lives at peace with the world, loves the fragrant hemlocks, oaks, maples, beeches, and basswoods that enclose him in greenness and loves the silence of the evening.

This is natural wood thrush country. The hermit is a more northerly species. Only an occasional pair of hermits lives as far south as this. The wood thrush is—like all the thrushes—an excellent singer, and his voice rises out of the woods everywhere in this region. It is a full, rich song with extraordinary range. But the liquid tone of the hermit has a glory beyond anything the wood thrush can achieve, and the open, rounded fluted phrasing of his central theme is the grand song of nature. Nothing more beautiful and nothing more profound can be said on this subject. Music is pure expression; it is at once more simple and more eloquent than words, and comes spontaneously from the emotions. Even the poet, who is the king of writers, cannot pierce the truth so exactly. His bow is clumsier and his aim is less sure. But the singer does not take thought; he lifts his voice and sings and the truth pours out of it.

Good and bad, pleasing and painful, there is a great deal more to life than the hermit gets into his evening song in the old sheep pasture. But as I sit on the hemlock stump beside the wood road, I marvel at the completeness and the slow, effortless beauty of what he is saying. He is looking forward gratefully to the next three or four centuries.

23. Strange how the imperious discipline of the city reaches deep into the country, setting apart those who have business to do. On the days when I go to the office, the authority of the city reaches into my home and detaches me from the country, as an army sergeant picks the kitchen police for the day. I rise an hour earlier than usual, put on a tie and jacket, which are essential

parts of the uniform of the kept man. In the village no one is working hard at this hour. But I am a man of destiny, called abroad and responsive to an alien tempo. At Andy's, where I stop for breakfast, the cooks and the cashiers are sleepily cleaning the restaurant and getting ready for a busy day. But I am busy already; I am on railroad time and eat breakfast by the clock. At the station I buy the *Times, Herald Tribune* and *News;* and when the train comes in, I find a seat in the smoking car on the river side and start to read the news of the day. Ah, yes, the news is ominous. Revolution, war, political crises, deficit financing, business recession, threats to civil liberties—the whole structure of the world appears to be collapsing. The Hudson River looks normal—brown water burnished by the sun, green hills, cat-tail marshes, black ducks, egrets and herring gulls. But the swaying train rushes on towards one of the world centers of catastrophe. Neither the river nor I can control it. At the beautiful Grand Central Terminal with its walls of lovely marble, I hurry into a squalid shuttle-train to Times Square and the office and I read the mail. It is the same mail I answered last year and the year before. In an hour or two it will be time for lunch in the air-conditioned dining room.

24. There is one star of minor magnitude that we can see by daylight. The sun, which is pouring in like a stream of gold through this west window, is one of the innumerable stars of the Milky Way, which is a great trailing luminous cloud that we are inclined to regard as something far away although we are in it. The sun is the major fact in our existence. It warms the earth. It supplies the water vapor we breathe. It has given us the store of coal and fuel that supply us with energy. It provides the plant life on which we and the animals are dependent. We are living off the accumulated energy that the sun laid down before the days of man. By our modest standards, the energy of the sun is incredible. Its interior heat is upwards of forty million degrees, centigrade. For millions of years it has kept the earth's temperature within relatively few degrees of what it is now. Everything alive desperately strains towards the sun. Plants grown indoors reach towards the windows where the sunlight shines. No one knows how much energy the lordly sun radiates, since the earth absorbs only a small part of it. By raising or lowering the temperature only a few de-

grees, the sun could destroy all the life on the earth. It is a blazing holocaust, but so benign on the earth that we gratefully bathe in its rays. No wonder men worship this majestic ball of fire that seems to cross our world every twenty-four hours and turn the terrible darkness of night into the beating glare of noon. For there is nothing we know that can compare to the great king of the skies in whose radiance we humbly wear out our little lives.

But the sun is only an irregular variable star of minor magnitude, hardly worth noticing amid the colossal treasures of the universe. It is so close (93,000,000 miles) that it looks bright to us. But if it were removed to the distance of Aldebaran, it would look only as bright as those celestial pin points of life in the Pleiades, charming, exquisite but insignificant. Aldebaran gives ninety-five times more light than our sun. Canopus gives thousands of times more light—perhaps hundreds of thousands of times more light. Although the sun is one hundred thousand times bigger than the earth, Antares is four hundred and fifty times bigger than the sun. To keep us warm the sun consumes itself and shrinks two hundred and fifty feet a year in diameter. In seven million years it will be half its present size, and you and I shall not be nearly so comfortable. There is not much time left to straighten out the world before a new ice age crawls down from the Poles. The last one had New York worried. On a clear day it could have been seen from any of the tall buildings.

25. It is Sunday. Although the stock has to be fed and the cows have to be milked, all the enterprises of the fields are suspended and the countryside takes a deep sigh of relief. For six days the work has been heroic. Haying began every morning as soon as the dew was off the grass; once or twice it continued into the evening after the chores were finished. But now it is Sunday and a man can see what he has done and, behold! it is very good.

Most of the fields have been cut; they look clean, crisp and tidy. There are a hundred things to be done in the next two months. During haying the crop lands are never worked as thoroughly as they need. But on Sunday, after the chores have been done and the milk cans sent down to the creamery, it restores a man's strength to walk leisurely over the farm, seeing how gloriously the corn has tasseled out this week and how heavy the potato tops have become.

All through the town there is a pleasant ritual on Sunday. Although the store is officially closed, the proprietor will emerge if a car draws up at the gas tank, and a few of the village cronies are lounging inside. The post office is firmly closed; letters can be dropped in the slot in the door, but the curtains are drawn. The door and the windows of the church have been open for some time. Presently the chairwoman of the flower committee will hurry down the street with blooms from her garden and an armful of wild flowers to decorate the pulpit. At ten o'clock the bell begins to ring. The sound is a little brazen close by and the machinery in the tower rasps and groans, but up on the hill the ringing of the bell is the loveliest note of the day. Now the preacher and his wife walk down the street together. Cars draw up from all parts of the town and the neighbors, who are scarcely recognizable in their scrupulous Sabbath dress, chat at the door and disappear inside.

The newsdealer is busier than usual until early afternoon, and the village inn looks for a heavy run of outsiders for dinner and supper. But the rest of the town accepts Sunday with the gratitude of a community that has been working hard during the most exhausting time of year. The afternoon is good for visiting and the evening is long enough for sitting under the trees. Although the sun and the sky and the hills are just as they have been all week, they look fresher on Sunday. A man has time to look at them with admiration in his heart.

26. George Bernard Shaw, born July 26, 1856, died November 2, 1950. Our most illustrious ancient was the world's foremost man of letters. Let it be recorded of us as a permanent distinction that we were contemporaneous with G. B. S. Although he wrote in a hard, sparkling, iconoclastic, comic style he was a profoundly serious man—an eminent teacher, a great and original scholar, a much finer artist than most intellectuals are, and a brilliant stylist. No pedant knew more than he about the social sciences, religion, and art. But unlike most students, he played out his life in the role of a knock-about comedian—enjoying the spectacle of G. B. S. in performance. On the spur of the moment he said a million things, most of them witty. His only consistency was the radiant and sardonic image of an intellectual clown. He liked to *épater le bourgeois*, as he phrased it. No doubt there was a lot of humbug in the part he played, for no clown can be pertinent in every improvisation. But he was no trifler; he, too, had a passion for the wellbeing of the race and faith in vitality, evolution, and creation.

"Never believe anything a person tells you about himself," Shaw said. "A man comes to believe in the end the lies he tells about himself to himself." The brassy part Shaw played became second nature to him during half a century. But he, too, had his humilities, though he did not make a point of them in public. He believed in art. "God created the world as an artist," he said, and concluded that artists are the world's only qualified interpreters. Although he was a pioneer in the scientific analysis of human nature, he declared: "I would rather be led by a poet than a scientist any day." And despite the mask of crackling omniscience he wore when he discussed public questions, he had this to say about his venerable career: "I am ending as a sage with a very scrappy and partial knowledge of the world." No man knows enough. Even the Jovian Shaw had to rely on faith to piece out his inadequate knowledge.

27. No one's judgment is worth much unless it is well seasoned with humility, as Shaw's was in the last years of his long life. For humility becomes people who are only human. The profoundest reason for humility is obvious: we inhabit a tiny corner of the universe, and as a race we have lived only about a second— hardly long enough to be sure of survival. "After all, ours is a very minor little planet," as some astronomer has remarked drolly. But the practical reason for humility is easier to understand: no man knows enough to set the affairs of the world straight. For knowledge is not enough. It is only a way of laying foundations, leaving all the creative work still to be done. Since every man's knowledge is incomplete and may be erroneous, it may not even lay a sound foundation.

Knowledge impregnated with love and faith grows into wisdom which is something worth respecting. For the wise man, steeped in knowledge, is lost in hope and wonder over the things that pass his understanding. Wisdom and humility are synonymous. Even God may not know all the answers.

28. Something of extraordinary interest happens this morning. A fisherman near the Seventy-ninth Street yacht basin catches an eel. Such things happen now and then. But it is the first time I have happened to see a fish caught in the stinking, polluted river at Riverside Park. Since some New Yorkers insist on fishing, however dim the prospects may be, the paternal Park Department has closed off a brief section of the walk for fishermen and women. At this time of year about twenty-five or thirty of them lean thoughtfully on the rail, staring at their lines, or sit gossiping on the benches in the sunshine, cooled a little by the river breeze. Life is very relaxed at the riverside; the rhythm is slow and easy. Only about fifty feet back of the river, automobiles are streaming along at thirty-five or forty-five miles an hour. Planes roar overhead on the southern course to Washington and Florida, and the bedlam of the city fills the sky. Except on this thin margin of the river, people are sweating and looking anxious. But the river loungers, dressed in their old clothes and battered hats, move slowly if at all. Occasionally one of them winds in his line to look at the bait and sinkers and then casts it out into the foul water again. Sometimes a man pulls his pole up sharply, fancying that the bait has been nibbled. This quick motion is instantly remarked in a group of people who normally do not move at all. The talk stops. Everyone looks eagerly or skeptically at the man who has moved quickly. I have seen this sort of incident innumerable times. But today is the first time I have seen a fish come out of it. Amid general excitement a man pulls out a fat eel about fourteen or fifteen inches long. The other fishermen stand around it, looking and discussing for about ten minutes. Despite the sewage in the river and the obscene trash that floats on it close ashore, fish do come in here. One was caught today, his senses possibly dimmed by the sewage that pours in to the lordly Hudson at Ninetieth Street.

29. At the conclusion of every thousand miles, take your automobile to the garage for greasing—"servicing" some people call it

in the language of bulls. I am always glad when the thousand miles
terminate when my car is in the country. For I like to have it
greased in Hyatt Field's garage. It will be thoroughly greased, no
doubt of that; and I can watch it and talk about it, which are impossible in a city garage. But I also enjoy loitering around Hyatt's
garage which is the mechanical center of the community. Some of
his friends call him "Dr. Field" because he is always on call and
looks after the mechanical health of the neighborhood—not only
the automobiles and trucks, but tractors, mowing machines, baling
machines, gas engines, buzz saws, lawn mowers and any machinery.
Hyatt has a genius for machinery. He can diagnose mechanical
troubles and cure them if there is anything healthy to build on.
At any time of day, and occasionally at night, you can see Hyatt
driving his repair truck to the home of some ailing machinery.
Complaining happily and swearing affectionately, he looks it over
and either applies the proper remedy on the spot or undertakes the
preliminary measures of an extended convalescence. This town
could not operate without Hyatt. He knows it and acknowledges
statements to that effect with a wry grin and a good-natured blast
of obscenity.

Don't go to Hyatt's garage for any dilettante services like wash-
ing a car or scrubbing whitewall tires. He and his assistants, surrounded with the mechanical calamities they normally work on,
will look at you with an air of horrified incredulity. They do not
like to have their manhood impugned in this fashion. Hyatt is so
conditioned to old machinery that he has a prejudice against new
cars. Drive a bright, gleaming new car to his garage with all the
gadgets the salesman has loaded on to it, and Hyatt will look up
from his greasy work with scorn and contempt. All automobile
manufacturers he regards as crooks and fools; there is something
incredibly wrong about every brand of cars currently manufactured. But go to him with mechanical trouble of some kind and
he will listen to you, examine the ailing member and cure it. A
man of honest character, he takes pride in charging an honest
price. He never takes advantage of the innocents who need his
services. I'm not sure but that Hyatt is the most important man
in town.

30. For the first time in my memory the exact boundaries of our nine-acre wood lot have come into question. Stanley Ingalls has bought all the standing saw timber in the wood lots of Arthur Dring and Potter Scott, whose lands abut upon ours. The timber consists of hemlock, maple, basswood, and oak. Since Mr. Ingalls wants to be sure that he cuts none of our timber, which we want to keep standing, he asks me to show him where our north and west lines are located in the thick of the woods. Now, this is quite a problem. Except for a little cutting for stove wood, these lands have not been used for years, and never by the three families who now own them. The lands have not been surveyed for at least a century, and the present owners know the boundaries only as their predecessors pointed them out from memory. There has not been a new name in my deeds for seventy-five years. At the time of every transfer the county clerk has slavishly copied the descriptions in the original deeds which mention Pharez Chittenden, Emeline Chittenden, Edwin Hubbard, and Zelotes Brand—all of them dead long before we ventured into this country. All the Chittendens were descended from Captain Jairus Chittenden, a Revolutionary War veteran, who took up four hundred acres on this hill in 1787 and founded a dynasty that lasted more than a century, cleared land, and built numerous houses and barns. The one romantic note in all the deeds refers repeatedly to "lands occupied by Emeline Chittenden" and "to a stake in the north line of said Emeline's garden." The stake and garden have long since disappeared. Alas, "said Emeline" has disappeared also with her spades, forks, rakes, hoes and sunbonnets, for I have a deed of October 29, 1890, signed by Arlane H. Chittenden, "Executor of the Estate of Emeline Chittenden, deceased." I wonder if the deer, woodchucks, coons, and rabbits poached on her garden as they do on mine.

Since the deeds refer to worthy people long since dead and stakes long since rotted away and stones indistinguishable from other stones, they do not help much in defining the boundaries of our wood lot. Only the measurements in chains, links, roods, perches, and acres are valuable now. But Mr. Scott knows a beech tree that marks one corner. I know a maple that marks another, and there is Mr. Dring's barbed-wire fence that defines the west boundary. Pooling our respective bits of folklore, we agree on a north boundary that, as the deeds say, is "more or less" satisfactory

to everybody and saves us the expense of surveying. I hope Emeline
Chittenden will forgive me if I have made a mistake. I am sure
she never made a mistake when she occupied these lands.

31. Now is the dead center of the summer season. Nothing
grows perceptibly. The birds are molting and are almost silent.
There is no dawn chorus this morning comparable to the endless
roll of happy melody in April, May, and June. Soon after five
o'clock a robin sings, and catbirds, meadowlarks, song sparrows and
a Henslow's sparrow shake the indolence out of their voices. But
the bobolinks have not sung for a fortnight or more, and probably
are drifting south already; and although the Baltimore oriole visits
the bird bath regularly he has not sung for a long time. Young
bluebirds, robins, catbirds and phoebes—comically tailless—are
blundering and cheeping around the house, causing their parents
considerable anxiety. But the ecstasy and radiance have evaporated
from the country, and the spirit of the world has dropped to the
low point of the year. We are going mechanically through the
motions of living.

AUGUST

August

H ERMAN MELVILLE was born at 6 Pearl Street on this day in 1819. At the age of thirty-two he finished the great American epic *Moby Dick* at his farm in Pittsfield, Massachusetts. A wild, terrible dance on the rim of chaos, it was, he said, "broiled in hell-fire." It gutted him and wrecked his health. It was also a complete publishing failure. Two years after he had finished this mighty work, all the plates and unsold copies were burned in the fire that destroyed the Harpers' publishing plant. That was the final stroke of evil that killed the genius of Melville. He lived for forty more years like a ghost—a quiet, solitary man, walking in limbo, perhaps haunted by dreams more malefic than Captain Ahab's obsession with the white whale. Nothing else he wrote found a public, and he was not wanted as a lecturer. In 1866 the man who had wrestled with the angry sea got a routine clerk job as a custom's inspector and walked every morning down Gansevoort Street to an office at the waterside. For nineteen years he kept his blameless accounts as a petty bureaucrat and drew his stipend—a man damned by the indifference of other men, but denied the consolation of death. Finally death did deliver him in 1891 at 104 East Twenty-sixth Street. About a quarter of a century later America woke up to the grandeur of his achievement.

Inhuman as the sea is, it gave him the only comfort he ever had. His father died when he was twelve. A bitter, austere woman, his mother hated him. He went to work as a clerk when he was fifteen. Two years later he went to sea as cabin boy in the *Highlander*, bound for Liverpool, and for eight adventurous years he lived with the exultation of a man who had joined the universe on its own terms. In 1841 he sailed out of Fairhaven, Massachusetts, in the *Acushnet*, bound for whaling in the South Seas. That was the transcendent experience of his life. After eighteen months in the *Acushnet* he deserted in the Marquesas Islands, and lived with cannibals. He escaped from them to the Australian whaler, *Lucy Ann*, and deserted from her at Papeete, and worked as a farm laborer on Tahiti. On August 17, 1843, he signed on as ordinary seaman on the frigate, *United States*, and was discharged at Boston on October 14, 1844. Out of these rude and roving four years came *Moby Dick, Typee, Omoo* and *White Jacket*—books of wonder and knowledge. With one final outburst of energy and passion, he poured everything that he had into *Moby Dick* a decade after the *Acushnet* put out from Fairhaven. After that supreme effort he was burned out, although he had not yet reached middle age. He had nothing but flesh and bones to hold him together for the forty long years he stayed above ground in the uncharitable light of the sun.

2. A tiny red-haired girl of three comes for a visit. Up to this moment our boy of five has been the baby, since he is four years younger than his sister. But now he suddenly acquires the dignity and prestige of the conquering male. His sister exudes maternal patience. She is elaborately sweet and kind. After a day or two the boy accepts the responsibilities of a courtier, and he, too, is sweet, kind and responsible, squiring his red-headed tot almost obsequiously. "Don't you want to do this or that?" he inquires with a solicitous air. But his first instinct is to exhibit his prowess; he runs and jumps with superhuman bravado; he struts extravagantly. He dazzles his redhead with feats of daring, riding his tricycle round and round a tree, calling attention to his speed and skill by rolling his head joyously and trumpeting a bizarre tune. He audaciously breaks a few household laws to establish his male independence. It must be confessed that his gallantry is a little unreliable. For he also teases the little girl by tickling her; and once in a while he hauls off and bats her one that makes her squall and run to her mother. This bewilders him; he had not realized that a cuff is not so winning as a tender overture. He is genuinely sorry, for he sees that his redhead is not to be subdued by a beating—or rather, not by a beating alone. It takes a little time to learn how to be a gallant. But not much time—two days are long enough.

3. No, realism is not the solution to the problems of art and philosophy. The truth escapes realism, too. For realism does not lead to the ultimate objective reality. There are as many realistic truths about New York as there are observers. Which is the truth: that the citadel of skyscrapers downtown is beautiful or that it is monstrously inhuman; that the city is stimulating or exhausting; that New Yorkers are cosmopolitan or provincial; that the Broadway drama is enlightened or decadent and depraved; that the *Times* is the greatest and most thorough newspaper in the country or that it is boring; that Greenwich Village is bohemian or bogus? There are no definitive answers to these questions. There are only valid points of view.

Some of the abstract facts about New York are definitive and truthful. Manhattan is twelve and a half miles long, and two and a half miles wide at the broadest point; it comprises an area of 31.2 square miles, and has a population of 1,906,000 (according to a Board of Health estimate). But these facts, although realistic, do not indicate whether New York is a success or a failure, whether life in New York is good or bad, and whether New Yorkers are happy or wretched. There is no realistic way of arriving at truthful answers to these fundamental problems. There are only opinions, based on experience.

In art, the realistic method therefore has no special virtues. After the austerity of classicism and the emotional extravagance of romanticism, realism in art looked like a divine deliverance from formalism and distortion. But realism merely continued in another style the perennial expressions of opinion and character. The realism of Strindberg expressed his psychopathic suspicion of women, the realism of Ibsen expressed his pessimism, and the realism of Chekhov expressed his compassion for the limpness of Russian society. For realism is only one of the artistic methods. Neither the artist nor the thinker can escape the warmth, vigor, hope or despair of his personality.

4. Free Press Day. In 1735, John Peter Zenger, publisher of the *Journal*, was tried and acquitted of libeling the governor of New York in articles that had criticized the administration. According to tradition, this verdict by a jury established freedom of the press

in America. But the tradition was a long time in the making. Governors and members of governments were slow in acknowledging the right of the press to criticize them. Even in the administration of John Adams, sixty-one years later, editors were jailed or put out of business by ruinous fines under the Sedition Law.

Despite the guarantees in the Constitution, the freedom of the press is not a natural right, like the use of air, but a gift from the people, who can withdraw it whenever they think it has been misused. Contrary to common assumption, the most powerful threat to the freedom of the press does not come from political, economic and religious groups who would like to control it. It comes from the cynicism and ignorance with which many newspapers get through their daily task. For let us admit that a large section of the free press is irresponsible and some of it pours a horrifying stream of malice and stupidity into the life of the country. Not many newspapers make a conscious attempt to give an honest, balanced report of the day's activities. These are negative failings, based on a willingness to conspire for gain with the most unenlightened people in the community. But some of the press is more vicious than that. It assassinates the characters of people it does not like. It harries people. It slants the news in its own interest. It creates public hysteria by accenting the statements and opinions of hysterical people, and then lives off the hysteria it has helped to foment. Given two choices, it selects the more unworthy. For business reasons it assumes an omniscience that it does not have; and having once made an error, it persists in error to protect its reputation. Some newspapers, taking a leaf out of the propaganda books, are more concerned with the effect of the printed word on the mind of newspaper readers than about the truth of the printed word. Many newspapers give free rein to a few journalists who are personally ambitious or corrupted by power to influence the mind of the public. No wonder that the public generally repudiates the political leadership of the press, the press sets the public such a bad example.

The Constitution guarantees a free press on the assumption that an informed public can govern itself and that truth will destroy error in an equal competition. But the responsible newspapers that make a sincere attempt to print the truth objectively, and thus fulfill the code of journalistic morality, are few in comparison with the newspapers that operate on the level of demagoguery and huckstering. Honest news and responsible opinion have to compete with the venom and dishonesty of ignorant and evil people.

Where there is a free press there is hope. Where the press is controlled there is none. But the paradox of the situation today is that the principle of the free press is endangered most by the ignorance, prejudice and irresponsibility of many successful newspapers and magazines.

5. After an absence of several weeks, I visit Pier 43 at the foot of Barrow Street in the hope of seeing Captain Bill Westervelt, retired skipper of his own tugboat. A huge barrier and peremptory police signs block the entrance of the pier. But all pier barriers can be penetrated. Although two policemen are dozing in their car at the corner of the barrier I slip around it with no trouble. The police can usually be circumvented. Except for seven Italian boys fishing successfully for crabs, the crumbling pier is deserted and the dock beside it is empty. The metal shack, where for more than a quarter of a century Captain Westervelt has dispatched his tugboat, is a fire-blackened, empty relic, with a burned account book or two abandoned in the wreckage. Some of the piles have rotted off at the water level. Some of the dry, splintering string-pieces have come loose, and the decking is full of dangerous holes. Only a few weeks ago Bill and his associate, George, kept their daily vigil here—talking, quarreling, playing poker and answering the telephone; and tugs were constantly tying up to the old bollards to take water or receive orders. But now Pier 43 has finally collapsed and the watermen have abandoned it, and I have lost my last personal association with the water front. Standing incredulous amid the wreckage I realize that an epoch has ended, and that another section of our battered water front has died—killed by high shifting fees, gangster tyranny and graft. It took Pier 43 over a quarter of a century to die, but now even the corpse is disintegrating—the lesions open, the bones poking through, the limbs dropping off one by one.

A quarter of a century ago the Royal Mail steam packet, *Ohio*, fresh from the builder's yard, berthed at the adjoining pier; and some splendid vessels have lain here—German liners in their heyday, white naval sloops from Denmark and Brazil, the huge Luck-

enback freighters from the West Coast, and refrigerator vessels
from South America. Once this dock was so congested that a junk
boat could hardly find room enough for petty pilfering. Every day
a river boat from Catskill arrived in the morning with upriver
produce, and left in the evening with city freight. The Farrell
barges bunted in and out with coal brought downriver from Edgewater. The *Rosalie May, James Watt, E. P. Haley,* and N. *John
Barrett* lay here with steam up or fires banked according to the
volume of harbor business; and droves of Barrett and Meseck tugs
hung on to the pier between jobs or at mealtimes and a noisome
gang of water-front vagrants slept off their "smoke" jags in the
corners.

6. Sitting at a disheartened desk by the dirty windows, with an
old straw hat on his head and paper cuffs to protect his wrists
from the soot, Charlie Volk kept track of the tugboats, and hospitably relayed orders to their skippers, and sometimes he signaled
with a huge white cloth to the N. *John Barrett* puffing solemnly
along the distant Jersey coast. But the business began to melt
away almost imperceptibly twenty years ago. The Catskill Night
Line closed down. The *Rosalie May* and the *James Watt* (worth
$100,000 each when new) were silently towed away to the bone-
yard; and in a year or two the *Haley* followed. Stealing and rack-
eteering drove off the freight ships from the adjoining pier, and
eventually the Farrell Coal Company abandoned its barge traffic.
During the war Charlie retired, shrewdly picking the best time to
get some of his money out of the business; and Captain Bill
Westervelt sold his last remaining tugboat to Meseck. For another
four or five years, the Meseck tugs lay their rope-bound noses
against the crumbling pier and George sat in Charlie's chair,
monitoring the telephone and dreaming of the days when he
cooked in schooners out of New York in the coastal trade. But
Pier 43 was obviously doomed and the Dock Department no
longer patched the holes in the decking. Now the old metal shack,
which was stifling in the winter and baking in the summer, is
gutted and deserted and Pier 43 has succumbed to economics.

Fishing through the great holes in the planking today, the
Italian boys have caught enough crabs to half-fill three wriggling

gunny sacks. The police are still sleeping in their scout car when
I slip around their barrier on the way to my office.

7. In 1942 the U. S. Marines on this day landed at Guadal-
canal, and thus began the three-year assault that drove the Japanese out of the Pacific islands. There has never been such an
implacable and stupendous naval and army assault over so wide
an area and against so many fortified positions. In their advance
analysis of fighting the Americans, the Japanese had counted on
superior spiritual resources. They dismissed the American civilization as materialistic. In the sort of tedious, intricate personal
combat that conquest of the Pacific islands would entail, the
Japanese believed that personal bravery and spiritual tenacity
would win and that the Americans, dependent upon materialistic
superiority, would not have the heart for exhausting and mur-
derous physical combat. Being largely Asiatic, many Russians now
believe the same thing.

But the Japanese analysis of American civilization proved to be
superficial and calamitous. Older cultures, like those of the Orient
and some of the European, frequently make the same mistake. For
the materialistic variety and abundance of the American civilization are not the American spirit but one of the products of the
American spirit. Machines are the products of ideas and imagination. They have to be conceived, invented, made, and operated
by man. And the material of a civilization is not an end in itself.
Its function is to conserve and to free human life. We hold the
life of our people dear. We do not believe it should be debased
or wasted.

Contrary to Japanese expectation, the Pacific war vividly proved
the point. It was won by free spirit. During the three years, the
manufacture of war materials at high speed seemed incredible
even to Americans accustomed to industrial operations. Ships
were built at high speed in tremendous numbers, and goods of
all kinds were produced in staggering quantities and delivered
thousands of miles away. The supply service was so perfected that
on Okinawa some lucky marines under fire in advanced positions
had hot meals of steak and French fried potatoes. But all this
should not be regarded as the mechanical ingenuity by robots. It
was the expression of the American spirit. For the whole of

America had been enflamed by the savagery and treachery of a
barbaric civilization that was ignorant enough to think it could
conquer the world. Behind the deadly fire power that swept the
Pacific was the tenacious spirit of free men who will never submit
to tyranny. It is tyranny that is decadent and degenerate. That
was decided long ago.

8. Suddenly in the midst of summer there is a foretaste of
autumn. For today is exactly midsummer—forty-seven days since
the summer solstice and forty-seven days before the autumnal
equinox. Yet there is more autumn than summer in the look and
feel of things. Last night the thermometer dropped to 51°, and
stands at 59° at nine in the morning. The oil burner, set at 65°
in the dining room, automatically comes to life. There is a fresh
wind out of the northwest that is buoyant and tonic, that blows
the summer haze out of the mountains and drives the clouds
swiftly through the blue sky. In the fields some of the grass is
already brown, and would not be worth cutting if the corn crop
were not so short this year. The ox-eyed daisies have lost their
luster; the yellow petals are drying up. Some of the Queen Anne's
lace blooms are folding into frayed and dried skeletons. Locust
leaves are beginning to scatter on the grass. Most of the birds have
either gone away or lost their enthusiasm. The red-winged black
birds, who flew around so anxiously when we crossed the field a
fortnight ago, have gathered in flocks and patrol the neighborhood
together. The Henslow's sparrow keeps up his monotonous chatter
in the tall grass. But the household birds are few and desultory—
a robin or two, a catbird or two, and the bluebirds still loitering
around their box where the last brood is ready to fly. The song
sparrows are virtually silent. The goldfinches have lost their yellow
splendor although they still toss out a cheery note or two as they
swing across the meadows.

On June twenty-second the sun set at 7:34 (8:34 daylight-saving
time) and we came home from our evening walk when the sun
was just slipping behind the mountains. Now we have lost nearly
a half hour at the time of day when we notice it. Tonight the
sun sets at 7:08 (8:08 daylight-saving time), and we come home
in the twilight. Although we are midway in the summer, there is

less of June than of September in the texture of the day. The
pitch and lean of the seasons are forward.

9. People from abroad listen with some incredulity to the commercial advertising on the American radio. Since we are accustomed to it, we are less astonished. To a considerable extent we
listen to it without hearing it. We are constantly acquiring a
degree of immunity to this most loathsome of the commercial
diseases. But complete immunity is impossible. For as people
acquire immunity the disease becomes more virulent. In order to
leave some impression on the toughening consciousness of the
listener, the advertising writers grow more desperate and resort to
baser means. They have long since prostituted their self-respect.
"L.S.M.F.T. . . . L.S.M.F.T.," shouts the Lucky Strike tobacco
announcer with an excitement that is purely bogus. "Lucky Strike
Means Fine Tobacco!" he concludes on a note of spurious triumph. If he is normally fastidious, he is ashamed of himself—
balancing his shame against the bribe the advertising company
gives him. The radio listener is ashamed to be within earshot of
such tasteless adolescence. But the "L.S.M.F.T." slogan sinks
into the listener's consciousness, nevertheless, and justifies the
antic.

There are radio advertising devices that are more obnoxious
than "L.S.M.F.T.!"—singing commercials in a nursery-book style,
bizarre sound effects; and on the lowest rung of a very short ladder
there are the "give-away" programs that bribe listeners with a
fabulous junk heap of unrelated products. Advertising cannot go
lower than that, and the radio cannot more candidly adopt the
midway charlatanism of the fly-by-night carnival show, nor is the
greed of human beings ever much more obscene or swinish than
on the nights when "give-away" programs clog the airwaves. Since
the radio as an industry performs a number of admirable public
services, like the transmission of news, discussions and music, the
whoring mentality of its commercial spiels is revolting—especially
because it is deliberate. The alliance of radio and advertising is
a malignant one; they debase each other.

10. Not the narrowness of hackneyed men but the bitterness of enlightened men is the disheartening thing in politics. There is something in politics that seems to poison judgment. Last evening I dined with a congressman of unusual ability and exceptional experience. He has been well educated and he has lived abroad. Since Congress is naturally overwhelmed by professional politicians with narrow interests, the country is fortunate when it acquires the services of unusual men whose experience has shaken them out of provinciality. But the congressman with whom I dined is imprisoned within a hard shell of rancor. His judgment is distorted by hatred of the other party, and he talks like an educated charlatan. For hatred acts in opposite directions against him who hates as well as those he hates. Hatred walls him around with dark barriers that kill his independence.

The success of the two-party system assumes the existence of men independent enough to think for themselves and cross the party lines. If all men were party hacks, nothing would ever change; there would be no need for argument, investigation, thought and discussion; and all the decisions would be mechanical in the interest of party instead of people. Since neither of the two great parties holds a monopoly on ideas, the vitality of the nation depends on the judgment of men who are intellectually disinterested and courageous enough to break party discipline. They have to risk their party future for the good of the nation, and usually they succeed, for people admire courage and integrity.

But the congressman I sat with is no longer a free agent. He lives in a world of negations. He believes that nothing can be done on most of the vital problems of today because of the stupidity or malice of the opposite party. He even votes against measures in which he believes because his political opponents have sponsored them. Party regularity is his platform. His triumphs are petulant. His pleasures are acid. He is more polished than a hack, but no more useful.

11. The shower of Perseid meteorites occurs every year after midnight on the tenth, eleventh, twelfth, and thirteenth of August—or for about a week at this time of the summer. Enthusiastic astronomers spend the morning hours from midnight on, staring towards the constellation of Perseus in the northeast where these meteorites streak across the darkness like "shooting-stars" when they enter the earth's atmosphere. There are likely to be three or four an hour, and sometimes fifty or sixty. Since a shooting-star or two can be seen almost every night, the Perseid shower appeals to me more in theory than in practice because, in the first place, I like to be in bed by midnight and, in the second place, I have never been lucky enough to see more than four or five meteorites on the nights I have stayed up to look for them. The word "shower" to describe the Perseids is overdramatic.

I prefer reading about the Perseids to staying up all night to see them. They are, it is supposed, the debris of a comet that was destroyed by either the sun or Jupiter in 1862—Tuttle's Comet that passed close to the earth at that time and was never seen again. The debris—meteorites about the size of a grain of sand— is still traveling in the same path. In its annual cycle around the sun, the earth moves through this orbit for several nights at this season. Every year many meteorites are caught in the earth's atmosphere about seventy miles up. Since the meteorites are traveling fast, the resistance of the earth's atmosphere is like friction that heats them to a white heat that, in turn, burns them up. The streaks of fire across the black sky are the funeral pyres of the meteorites, which are reduced to the size of cosmic dust. None of the Perseids reaches the earth. They burn out before they fall that far.

The air we breathe is, we usually think, so light as to be almost imperceptible. "Light as air" we regard as the symbol of nothing-ness. But the air has enough body, structure and texture to set a fast-traveling meteorite on fire. And although the meteorite is only as big as a grain of sand, the fire is brilliant enough to be visible thirty or forty miles away.

12. On this day in 1941, when the scourge of Nazis was over-running Russia and sweeping south into the Mediterranean, Franklin Roosevelt and Winston Churchill drew up and signed the Atlantic Charter on board the U.S.S. *Augusta* anchored off the coast of Canada. It is difficult now to recall the emotions of terror and sadness with which we had watched the Nazis advance. Memories of pain vanish quickly. But I can easily recall the grate-

ful enthusiasm with which I read the Atlantic Charter. It was one
of the victorious moments of the war. The grass has grown over
the graves that received those who died on the battlefields of
August 12, 1941. But the hopes of the Atlantic Charter live in the
minds of men who still believe in a better world. Good ideas
penetrate deeper than bullets. Bullets cannot kill good ideas.

For so memorable a document, the Atlantic Charter is modest
and simple. It is not an agreement or a treaty. It is only an informal statement of certain common principles on which two
statesmen based "their hopes for a better future for the world!"

FIRST, their countries seek no aggrandizement, territorial or other:

SECOND, they desire to see no territorial changes that do not accord
with the freely expressed wishes of the peoples concerned:

THIRD, they respect the right of all peoples to choose the form of
government under which they will live; and they wish to see sovereign
rights and self-government restored to those who have been forcibly
deprived of them:

FOURTH, they will endeavor, with due respect for their existing obligations, to further the enjoyment by all States, great or small, victor
or vanquished, of access, on equal terms, to the trade and to the raw
materials of the world which are needed for their economic prosperity:

FIFTH, they desire to bring about the fullest collaboration between
all nations in the economic field with the object of securing, for all,
improved labor standards, economic adjustment and social security:

SIXTH, after the final destruction of the Nazi tyranny, they hope to
see established a peace which will afford to all nations the means of
dwelling in safety within their own boundaries, and which will afford
assurance that all the men in all the lands may live out their lives in
freedom from fear and want:

SEVENTH, such a peace should enable all men to traverse the high
seas and oceans without hindrance:

EIGHTH, they believe that all of the nations of the world, for realistic
as well as spiritual reasons, must come to the abandonment of the
use of force. Since no future peace can be maintained if land, sea or
air armaments continue to be employed by nations which threaten,
or may threaten, aggression outside of their frontiers, they believe,
pending the establishment of a wider and permanent system of general security, that the disarmament of such nations is essential. They
will likewise aid and encourage all other practicable measures which
will lighten for peace-loving peoples the crushing burden of armaments.

The United Nations as war allies never forged a mightier weapon
than this unrhetorical statement of principles which shook more

of the earth than an atomic bomb. Echoes of it reverberated back almost immediately from remote places, and the whole earth is still impregnated with it.

The principles of the Atlantic Charter have not been established in the practical relationships between nations. They were first violated when England and the United States handed Poland over to the Russians in 1945, thus traducing a valiant ally. In the materialistic world the whole structure of the Atlantic Charter began to topple then, and all that remains of it lies in the charter of the United Nations. But in the world of human spirit the Atlantic Charter is still strong and vital. From now on it establishes a moral standard by which the actions of nations will be measured. It cannot be repealed. Every nation—including the United States—that violates it stands guilty before the world. There is no way now of escaping the high moral judgments of the Atlantic Charter.

13. The marshes along the river have come into their supreme glory. The purple loose-strife is in bloom. Probably it has been blossoming for two or three weeks, without being conspicuous. But now the profusion of purple spikes fills the marshes with royal color that represents the inexhaustible vitality of nature. The summer heat of the sun produces the boldest colors of the year. There are other flowers along the railroad track. The goldenrod is in its prime. Joe-Pye weed lifts its domes of crimson flowers four or five feet above the mud and rocks, swaying with terror when the heavy train rushes by. But the purple loose-strife is the king of the river swamps. It rules an extravagant empire that reaches deep into the city as far as the Bronx River, and turns the Hudson Valley into a long corridor of splendor. The loose-strife blossoming in August is like a second spring. In abundance and color it is more imposing than the daintier flowers of May and June.

14. The genius of America is growing and ripening now throughout the country in the cultivated fields, the pastures, and the kitchen gardens. Although the wayward genius of America has many sources, the chief one is the abundance of food grown

here every year. Good food produces energy: energy produces enterprise, independence, and a self-confidence that verges on bumptiousness and irritates the rest of the world. If these are creative virtues, thank God for the food we are able to produce.

The people of most nations have to live on slender margins. Anxiety about the food supply always hovers somewhere in the back of their minds. The dread of famine permeates their thinking. In many nations a crop failure goes beyond disappointment: it is a major and immediate catastrophe. People have to go through the long, harrowing, demoralizing ordeal of starvation, which in extreme instances induces the horror of cannibalism. All through the growing season people in these countries watch the weather and the crops apprehensively, for their lives depend on this year's harvest in their neighborhood. People who are afraid of famine cannot plan boldly or dream great dreams.

For more than two hundred years Americans as a nation have never had to worry about the food supply. There is always enough food somewhere in the country to keep all the people fed. When starvation occurs here it comes from other causes, chiefly the lack of money; and this can be remedied, and generally is. To judge by the current state of the crops in the Catskills, this is going to be a disastrous year for the farmer here. Because of the drought, the crops that mature the last of August and in September are probably going to be failures. No one here worries about starving, however. For the national grain harvest this year is now estimated at 3,506,000,000 bushels—more than a quarter of a billion bushels above the last record crop, which was only two years ago. Despite the crop shortage in the drought area, there will be more food than Americans can consume, and more than ever will be shipped to the English, the Europeans, and the Asiatics. The whole world will be better nourished next year and better able to establish a good future. Food is the primary source of civilization and spirit. I imagine it ranks ahead of freedom. People may die for freedom in battles and revolutions, but I doubt that they starve for freedom. In time of starvation, freedom is a slice of bread.

15. After living in a room-and-a-half in Astoria, a young man with his wife and child has moved to the country in a house with twelve rooms and two barns. He is jubilant; his hope and confi-

dence permeate the neighborhood. He says that he will never go
back to the city to live. His mother, a pleasant woman with excellent manners, is janitress of a building on Thirty-fourth Street;
and he stayed there two nights recently. "I couldn't sleep," he
said. "The busses kept going by—whit, whit, whit—all night." In
the country everyone in the family has a separate room; there is
a big kitchen, a separate pantry and a large living room. During
the summer the family eats on the porch where there is a glorious
view of the mountains. The mother, the brother-in-law, and
friends are now assisting in the enjoyment of space, quiet and
good air.

A city lad, the young man does not know much about the
country yet. The maple is the only tree he knows by name. It
never occurred to him to notice birds or flowers. He does not
know the difference between a cross-cut and a splitting saw. In
the country he is an alien; he must learn a new way of life. But
he has a sunny disposition, a good head and a strong back. He is
not only willing to work but anxious to work; and since he is infatuated with his house in the mountains, he is determined to
succeed in the country, and he will. At the moment he is working
like a one-man army. From 8 P.M. to 3 A.M. he waits on table in
a bar for summer people about fifteen miles from here. On Tues-
days and Saturdays he comes to our house for five hours of labor.
He is also painting a house for people near by, borrowing my
extension-ladder to get at the high places. His brother-in-law is
working in a lumber yard ten miles from here. In their spare time
they both work on the house where they live and have great plans
for the future. Already they have given the old, dry siding one
coat of white paint with a jaunty red trim.

Everybody in the family is very happy.

16. She is nine years old. She stands four feet, five inches and
weighs a plump eighty-four pounds. She has blue eyes and golden
hair, a fair skin and a large, grinning mouth. She is a solid chunk
of happiness, good nature, and vitality. At the moment she cannot decide whether to be a sophisticated lady or an uproarious
child. This confusion leads her into grotesque paradoxes. She
dresses up in her grandmother's fur coat, a smart hat and a veil,
which is a jaunty and worldly outfit, but she flaunts it while riding

around the yard on her tricycle. The maturity is a masquerade.
The genuine part of her is childish. The world was made for her;
she is in a rush to enjoy every part of it between sunrise and bedtime. When she wakes up she has time to read in bed, which is
exciting. It is exciting to dress, for she likes dresses and shoes,
both of which are colorful. Breakfast is one of the meals she likes
best. The morning is full of games with her brother, outdoors by
the swing or in the playroom, where she has posted a sign: "Art
Room. Keep Out. Thank You." She likes to ride to the post office
in the luggage compartment of the station wagon. She reads the
comics in the newspaper on the way home. She plays all afternoon, takes a walk in the evening, and reads again after dark while
she is drinking a glass of milk and munching cookies.

All day long she is sharp and alert. She knows and sees most of
the wild flowers and the trees. She watches the birds. Every now
and then she has terrific obsessions: she searches the countryside
for garnets, which she imagines are strewn around in abundance,
or she wants to name all the stars and constellations in one night.
At intervals she imagines herself in very important roles—as a
housekeeper, which requires a tidy band around her hair, or a
nurse, which requires the dedicated white costume of a sister of
mercy; and when she plays these roles she is grave and suspiciously
responsible. Whatever she does involves a flow of noisy conversation, for everything is novel and unprecedented and has to be described, analyzed, or explained at high speed. The conversation is
strewn with expressions of disfavor. Last year, it was "Goush!"
This year it is "Glub-glub" or "O murder!" She hates to go to
bed. Getting her to bed is a long, nerve-wracking, tiresome ordeal—
a half hour of mounting torture for every member of the family.
She drops to sleep almost as soon as she gets upstairs, and generally sleeps on her stomach with one leg hanging out of the bed.
Nothing wakes her at night. Life is very busy and fascinating. God
does not provide time enough to keep abreast of it.

17. On this day in 1807, a huge cloud of aromatic smoke
belched out of the stack of a macabre-looking boat on the Hudson, steam hissed at the pipe joints, gears thumped and groaned,
and Robert Fulton's *Clermont* set out on her celebrated voyage
to Albany. The paddle wheels, being uncovered, very quickly

drenched the passengers. The helmsman, standing aft of a deck-house, had difficulty in seeing the bow. But the *Clermont,* burn-ing pine wood, made one hundred and ten miles to Chancellor Livingston's country seat, Clermont, in twenty-four hours, and the full one hundred and fifty miles to Albany in thirty-two hours—at an average speed of nearly five miles an hour. The *Clermont* was an ugly, noisy, frightening vessel. But she fulfilled the conditions for a voyage to Albany and established the monopoly of Fulton and Livingston for steam navigation of the Hudson. In 1809 she was refitted into a gay, beautiful, and more comfortable ship and she established regular passenger traffic to Albany and back.

Steamboating had been going on twenty years before Fulton got the *Clermont* underway—powered, incidentally, by an engine built in Birmingham, England. Twenty years earlier, James Rum-say of Maryland had sailed a steamboat on the Potomac at four miles an hour. She was propelled by a jet of water driven by steam through a pipe at the stern. In the same year John Fitch, the original steamboat man, made a successful trial trip at Phila-delphia in a steamboat propelled by six oars on each side. In 1795 Samuel Morey built a screw propeller boat that made five miles an hour on the Connecticut River. In 1796 Fitch equipped a yawl with a screw propeller and drove her in the Delaware. In 1802 Symington operated a steamboat on the Clyde, and Fulton had made sketches of the design and equipment. Fulton had also seen Fitch's experiments in the Delaware and had had in his possession for several months Fitch's drawings of another proposed steam-boat. With the financial backing of Livingston, Fulton built a suc-cessful steamboat that ran in the Seine in August, 1803. Mean-while, John Stevens had built a screw propeller steamboat that made nine miles an hour in the Hudson. In 1807, when the *Cler-mont* was under construction, Stevens and his son built the paddle wheel, *Phoenix,* which was completed only a few days after the *Clermont* had made her voyage to Albany. Since Fulton had won the exclusive rights to the Hudson, Stevens took the *Phoenix* out around Sandy Hook and along the New Jersey coast to the Dela-ware River. The *Phoenix* thus became the first steamboat to go to sea, and only a few days after the *Clermont* navigated the Hudson.

Robert Fulton, who was born in Pennsylvania, was a profes-sional mechanic and inventor. In the development of the *Cler-mont* he had the financial and political backing of Livingston, which seem to have been the decisive factors in his competition with other inventors. He had the advantage of studying other experiments in steamboat construction. No doubt, all the inventors learned from each other. The *Clermont* was a large, practical craft. The one that steamed to Albany was the second model. The first model was one hundred and fifty feet long, thirteen feet wide and drew two feet of water. But she proved to be too weak to hold the machinery, and she had to be scrapped. The second and successful model was one hundred and fifty feet long and sixteen feet wide and was much stiffer. She carried two masts and sails, but the sails were not used on this first round trip to Albany. The *Clermont* established steam navigation upriver; that was her great achievement. She was not the first successful steamboat.

The river steamers now make Albany in nine and one half hours. But there have been many faster voyages than that. The *Mary Powell*, still remembered as the most brilliant Hudson River steamer, reached Albany in seven and one half hours.

18. As soon as the farmer has finished cutting his hay he and the hired man take a hand at the brush. Beside the road and along the margins of his fields it is stubbornly crowding his free domain. For the land is trying to return to its original state; and cultivation of the fields, like cultivation of the mind, is an endless labor. Both the fields and the mind go rapidly to seed when they are neglected. Wildness hems in the areas of cultivation; it flourishes on the edge of deliberative growth and it never relaxes.

In America it is not long since the fields were forests. Only about two centuries ago they were cleared by men of heroic strength. Out of the sinewy wilderness the hackers and hewers created fecund land. They cut down the great trees, burned most of them in impatient bonfires and let in the sunlight to land rich from centuries of natural compost; and for many years it bore abundantly. Although two centuries is a long time in the sweat and muscle of men's labor, it is only an incident in the eons of the earth; and already the wilderness is fiercely marching back into mountain pastures and closing in on tired fields. Garden roses now bloom amid the brambles where a pioneer once put his shoulders against the forest. Broken apple trees wistfully blossom in the tight loneliness of the second-growth woods.

But the brush does not restore old fields to their original forest majesty. The gray birch, the black locust, the wild cherry, the ash, and poplar are quarrelsome interlopers who waste their vitality on competition, and the thorn apple—a haw—makes petty infernos wherever it grows. Long before America came into the pages of history, King Solomon knew that neglected fields let in the evil of nature as well as the decay of man: "I went by the field of the slothful, and by the vineyard of the man void of understanding; and, lo, it was all grown over with thorns, and nettles covered the face thereof, and the stone wall thereof was broken down."

Even nature suffers from wildness. The worn fields will not return to their original glory without cultivation. The future forests have to be planted. And so the descendants of the pioneers are hopefully planting seedlings where once the giant trees stood; or with ax, bush-hook and brush clippers every year they try to drive the brush back to the stone walls. It is wretched work. Armed with a million savage barbs, the locust sends up aggressive shoots from every root. By this time next year there will be five vigorous shoots to every one cut down today. For the farm brush is never discouraged. Where there is cultivation it fights to get in.

19. Travelers returning from abroad should not expect much attention from New Yorkers. In the great ships that dock along the Hudson, travelers are now coming back by the thousands, burdened with baggage and gifts, their heads full of the strange and fascinating things they have seen, heard, or done. But they had best not expect to find anyone in New York who is willing to listen. In the first place, New York has scarcely been aware of the fact that they have been away. No one is genuinely missed in New York. Leaving New York is suspected of being bad taste, and is passed over in well-bred silence by those who remain. In the second place, many New Yorkers have already been abroad and regard themselves as authorities on dining at odd places in London and Paris and finding original accommodations with particularly unspoiled lower middle-class innkeepers in Italy. Your New York traveler is never a tourist; he is a connoisseur of European customs; he has cosmopolitan tastes and invariably sees things that escape the notice of ordinary Americans. His only interest in returned travelers is confirmation of his own experience. He inquires

about an exotic dish that, so far as anyone can tell, he discovered
by the sheer brilliance of his international knowledge of food, or
of a charming little place that he discovered on the Left Bank
where the concierge took a personal interest in his comfort.
Oh, everybody was completely charming and obviously felt honored to have so rare a visitor in charge. Only a New Yorker can
command so much loyalty from the grateful natives of foreign
countries.

The returned traveler can expect a fifteen-minute audience from
his friends. It is good to have him back. He looks well. The gifts
he has brought are not only thoughtful but beautiful. Did he
dine in that odd little place in Soho? No? How are things at the
Dome? Did he see any interesting New Yorkers abroad? Alas, it
is to be feared that he is a very naïve traveler—practically a tourist,
in fact; and he might as well have stayed in New York. The returned traveler is no hero to people who have been everywhere,
seen everything and know all about it. He has only one consolation: he didn't miss a thing in New York.

20. At noon on the Bowery the thermometer reaches 95°. The
musty, shabby stores and rookeries are saturated in stagnant heat.
On one store front a fresh bold sign with azure lettering says:
"Sign Up Now for Snow Shoveling on the Long Island." Today
this attractive invitation goes unnoticed, and the wilted clerk inside stares vacantly at the hot street. Turned out of the flophouse
for the day, vagrants are sleeping on the sidewalks or standing at
the curb, lost in boredom, weary, burned-out, deserted. A sign on
a mission inquires: "Are You an Alcoholic?" Some of them are.
Some of them are already staggering along the sidewalk, muttering to themselves or flinging their arms around the shoulders of
buddies in a glow of boozy devotion. The Bowery is dirty, noisy,
foul, and ugly. The terrible heat scorches the little life that is left
in it. In this catch basin of a wasteful metropolis, vagrancy looks
seedier and blearier than ever.

The day is terrible everywhere, partly because New York mechanically goes through the routine motions of a normal day,
driven to suffering by mindless habit. Crumpled and sweating,
people look exhausted on the streets. Many offices close at two
or three, and mercifully send their people home before the sub-

way crush becomes unbearable. Coming in proudly from the cool Atlantic, the *Queen Mary* discharges her passengers with thousands of heavy bags and trunks into the inferno of a heat-stricken city. The official thermometer crosses the 98° mark at three o'clock; and the thermometer at my window, with its back to the baking wall, reads 105°. My sweaty arm sticks to the limp paper as I write these notes on a gritty desk.

An hour after sundown, a pleasant breeze comes in from the ocean, and by nine o'clock the thermometer falls to 86°. Hundreds of tired people in shirt sleeves or off-the-shoulder dresses saunter down to the river promenade and, in the darkness, sit on the benches, talking or lost in wretched dreams. The brightly lighted yacht-basin has a carnival look with the flags lazily moving in the breeze and silken reflections wavering beautifully on the black water. People are spending the night in the yachts that are large enough to provide accommodations. It will be a stifling night for people who live back from the river. But it will be refreshing for those who sleep with the river breeze pouring in through the scuttles or down the open companionways. For the breeze that sweeps in from the Atlantic gathers strength and enthusiasm and is purified with sweetness as the land recovers from the fever of an infected day.

21. Towards midnight Arcturus, one of the beacons of June, sinks towards the western horizon; and Capella, one of the beacons of January, rises in the east. The season of ice and snow is already chasing the season of blossoming out of the sky. The whole cycle of the seasons is etched in fire and spread out before our eyes. Six weeks ago Vega stood directly overhead at midnight. Now she is half-way across the western sky, following the Corona towards the mountains. But until Sirius rises at midnight towards the end of October, Vega will continue to be the jewel of the night—a clear, sparkling diamond with a drop of translucent blue. In our latitude only Sirius is brighter, but Sirius and Vega are seldom on view simultaneously. Fourteen thousand years ago Vega was the pole star, and will be again. It is in the south position of the circle around which the north pole travels every twenty-six thousand years. A star of first magnitude and conspicu-

ously beautiful, Vega will make a much lovelier pole star than the
dim Polaris with which we are now temporarily associated.

Now the stupendous luminous banner of the Milky Way bisects
the sky and sends a flood of pearly light flowing lazily through the
world's darkness.

22. Ernest and Bertie Ford have the rare gift for general storekeeping. For operating a good country store is much more than
a business. It is a constant test of character. Mr. and Mrs. Ford
keep a good store where you can buy groceries as well as cloth,
shoes, hardware, paint and gasoline; and this is the basis of storekeeping in the country. But they are also people of good will; they
are hospitable and friendly; they are tolerant and obliging and
have gentle dispositions. In a small community a man with a
mean streak cannot keep it to himself. Everyone is always under
observation. But in all the years we have lived in this community
I have never heard anyone speak ill of the Fords. I have never
known anyone who felt that he had not had a square deal. By
tact and wisdom they have avoided unpleasantness and misunderstanding. No one can find a flaw in their characters.

Not everyone can be a good storekeeper. Ernest learned the
trade from his father. It was "Ford & Son" when he was a young
man. An itinerant sign-painter put that lettering over the door in
1901. It still stands there intact and unblemished after all these
years. After his father's death, the store became "E. E. Ford."
Now it is "Ford & Ford," for several years ago Ernest took his
nephew into partnership, and has taught him the tradition as
well as the trade. For storekeeping is immensely personal. The
storekeeper is the center of community life. Almost everyone
"trades" in the store nearly every day, and many people drop in
for talk and relaxation. No one knows more than the storekeeper
about the lives of the townspeople—not only their finances, but
their tastes and foibles, and no one is the custodian of more personal secrets. You are always welcome at Ford's store. You can
buy what you need and depend on the service, and you can pay
as conveniently as possible. You can get a check cashed, no questions asked. And you can be sure that neither Ernest nor Bertie,
nor their nephew, Leo, will betray a confidence. Without ever
leaving the store they know everything that is going on in town.

Don't expect any gossip from them. They maintain a benevolent
neutrality in all the village feuds. They will talk about themselves,
if necessary, but they are reluctant to talk about other people. By
now they should be comfortably wealthy. I hope so. For they deserve it. Their general store with its bizarre stock of goods is the
most enterprising institution in town. Anyone can walk in there
any hour of the day, certain of a civil reception and help if possible. I think Ernest Ford is the finest man in town, although he
would be surprised to find out that anyone thought much about
him, one way or another.

23. On this day in 1927 Nicola Sacco and Bartolomeo Vanzetti were executed in the electric chair by the Commonwealth of
Massachusetts for murders which, there are the strongest reasons
for believing, they did not commit. On that fateful night (the
executions were after midnight of the twenty-second) people all
over the world collected in the streets seeking the comfort of numbers in the agonized hope that this monstrous perversion of justice might not be true, or that a delay of sentence might prevent
the awful finality of execution. While the officers of court and
state hid behind their little formalities, the shoemaker and the
fish peddler were taken to the death chamber and legally murdered in the electric chair. Thus ended the blackest tragedy in the
history of our courts. Although Sacco and Vanzetti magnani-
mously forgave their executioners in advance, thousands of us who
followed the seven-year ordeal of the trial will never forgive the
police, prosecuting attorneys, jury, judge, and governor who took
part in the savage betrayal of justice, nor the three distinguished
laymen who blandly assented to it as aids to the governor in
the end.

Sacco and Vanzetti were charged with the murders of a pay-
master and his guard in a robbery in South Braintree, Massachusetts, on April 15, 1920. The State never established their
identity as the murderers or connected them with the crime. In
fact, the crime was probably committed by a gang of professional
thieves from Rhode Island, one of whom confessed. But Sacco
and Vanzetti were Socialists in a period of history when Socialists
—particularly foreign-born Socialists—were violently hated. They
were tried before a poisonous, vindictive judge—Judge Thayer—

who poured his personal hatred into the public rancor of the day. Once the evil was started no one could deflect it or stop it, even when the prejudice was exposed and the probable criminals discovered. After seven years the judge, officers of the law, the State, and people of conservative political principles had a vested interest in the deaths of two ignorant and obscure Socialists, and dared not relinquish it. Never has a democratic state set itself so malevolently against the processes of legal justice, and never have men in a democratic society trifled so recklessly with the honor of the state. Sacco and Vanzetti paid with their lives for the evil and terror of the State's advocates. Nothing could have confirmed so eloquently Sacco's and Vanzetti's political doubts of the state's integrity.

24. As evidence of progress towards realism and sanity, note that poverty is no longer a social disgrace. Both Hawthorne and Melville were ashamed of being poor. It ate into their souls. They segregated themselves from society, as though they were infected with some horrible disease. See Melville's "Poor Man's Pudding" with its bitter record of the meekness of the poor, and its companion-piece, "Rich Man's Crumbs," with its horrifying description of charity. In Melville's day, and also in Hawthorne's, poverty was regarded as one of the unpleasant facts of life—ugly and pathetic but necessary. "The poor we always have with us." Poverty was regarded as a disgrace for cultivated people because it reduced them to the level of people of low station.

We know too much about poverty now. During the great depression, millions of able and intelligent people were haunted by the specter of poverty. For poverty is not wholly a personal failure. It also represents the failure of an economic system. And the remedy is not wholly one of charity, but of political and economic action. Poverty is a reflection also on those who are not poor. I am skeptical of simple solutions. The simple solutions, like state socialism, have been tried and have not succeeded remarkably. But since the time of Hawthorne and Melville the stigma of social disgrace has been removed from poverty. Poor people no longer have to cringe. They are citizens, too.

25. These are the "dog days." The term refers to the "dog star"—Sirius in the constellation, Canis Major. This hot, sticky, stagnant period is identical with the seasonal rising of the "dog star," which from now on becomes one of the friendliest sentinels in the sky. Sirius rises at about 5 A.M. today. It will rise earlier every day until April. From the point of view of Sirius we are already on the threshold of winter.

Since New York is an ocean port the dog days have special significance. They are likely to bury us in a thick blanket of fog. Today is a case in point. Sirius is not visible this morning, nor is anything else. For the cool air from the sea moving into the heat of the city has made a dense fog that extends as far north as Westchester County. The sun comes up like a reddish gold disk. But the fog is so thick that I cannot see the river from the front windows and can hardly see across the street. Planes are grounded. Trains are late. Automobiles move slowly through a white blanket of nothingness. By midmorning the fog is gone. But the damp heat stands in the canyons of the streets. "It must be in the nineties," a sweaty taxi driver remarks as he keeps his cab crawling through the choked and irritable jangle of Times Square. It is 85° on top of the Whitehall Building, where the temperature of New York is officially recorded. But it is probably 90° or more in the streets where New Yorkers have their being—sweaty and dirty and limp.

In the evening, I attend a theater performance in a tiny, airless auditorium near Washington Square. Little beads of sweat run down the faces of the actors. Sweat melts the starched collars of the men actors, who are impersonating elegant English society people, and the frocks of the actresses stick to their necks and shoulders. Sitting in shirt sleeves, the audience stares at them listlessly through the moist heat of a steaming auditorium. When I reach home at one in the morning the candles in the living room have flopped over in the heat and are resting their tired heads on the table.

26. The most spectacular feature of a Broadway sign in Times Square is a waterfall, one hundred and twenty feet wide and thirty-five feet in depth. Fifty thousand gallons of water pour over

it every minute with a cool splash that can be heard above the metallic grind of traffic. There is no logical connection between the waterfall and the product it is advertising, which is Bond's clothes. But people love to look at moving water. And since every day 1,500,000 people walk up and down Broadway between Forty-second Street and Fiftieth, Douglas Leigh, ballet master of the Great White Way, believes that a manufactured waterfall attracts their attention and is worth $10,000 a month to Bond. This is carrying eccentricity to gargantuan proportions—showmanship gone over the borderline into insanity. But the Bond waterfall is the most popular spectacle on Broadway today. To people suffering from the heat (98°) it looks cool. Thousands—hundreds of thousands of people—glance at it with interest and perhaps with gratitude in this fiery canyon. Standing on the steps of the Astor Hotel I feel cooler when I gape at it. I imagine that I can feel a breath of freshness and coolness crossing the baking street. This is pure illusion. The water is not fresh out of the city mains. It is the same water pumped back and used over and over and over, and during the day it gets heated to the temperature of the air. But water looks cool because by the association of ideas our minds have made it so. The Bond waterfall on the roof of a squat building looks to most of us like a merciful oasis in the dry, wilting heat of Broadway.

27. The country also is wincing from the heat. Everything except the cicada has withdrawn into its private misery; there seems to be no universality in nature. During the night the thermometer got no lower than 76°, and it stands at 84° when we assemble for breakfast. The lawn is burned brown, and is strewn with bleached locust leaves, and the trees look parched and wilted. The dirt is white and powdery. Even the chipping sparrow and the Henslow's sparrow are silent. Where do the birds go in the heat? Since we keep the bird bath freshened with cool water, we expect them to use it freely, but only an occasional robin, catbird, or goldfinch appears. Two fields to the north the lumbermen are cutting hemlock logs to standard lengths. I can hear the steady putter of their gas motor and the whine of the chain saw.

By noon the thermometer has swollen to 94°. I have to drive ten miles through the valley to a woodworking shop where Lester

Storey is going to turn some pieces of oak into table legs for a job
I am doing. On his porch a thermometer in the sun has reached
120°, and another in the shade three feet away is 110°. Inside the
shop the temperature is 90°. The shop is old and unpainted; the
clapboards are like tinder, and it is a wonder the whole thing does
not go up in flames. "The witches' oven," the children call it.
Standing in the sun the car is like an oven; the leather seats burn
my back when I get in, and the plastic steering wheel is hot.

As usual people are saying that this is the hottest day they can
remember. The high for the afternoon is 95°. I have a record of
103° on July ninth, 1936, but no one wants to believe it. On the
hill there is a steady breeze from the west, but it is hot and dry,
for it comes from a continent that is baking. Over the radio we
hear that the high for the day in town is 100%₁₀°. After sundown
we sit on the lawn in the breeze which seems merciful, since the
house is close and warm, and the upstairs rooms heavy and stagnant with heat. We put the children to bed downstairs. The
summer sky looks pleasantly familiar tonight as we let the cool
breeze flow around us—Jupiter a steady beacon in the southwest,
Vega overhead, Arcturus, a yellow lamp in the west, and the Great
Dipper flung boldly in the northwest. At eleven o'clock the thermometer is down to 79°. But the night leaves us unrefreshed.

28. Photography is the poor man's art, and it is practiced
feverishly all summer—an essential part of the equipment for a
vacation. For those who can see pictures but cannot paint or draw
them, the camera will do the job efficiently. First a man sees the
picture in his mind's eye. After composing it and studying the
lighting, he makes it with the camera on film. In the darkroom he
selects the picture he wants from all the detail caught on the film,
and finally produces a photograph. It is a piece of art because it
represents the impact of a mind on a fragment of nature, and occasionally it is very beautiful. But the range of photographic art
is limited—there is more nature than mind in it, and much less
mind than in a painting or drawing. No one can exhaust the resources of painting; no painter can reach the absolute peak of perfection. But many photographers can very nearly exhaust the range
of their medium. For modern films are wonderfully sensitive and
the cameras ingenious and versatile; and the man who has mas-

tered the film and his camera has mastered most of the art of photography. Look at a photographic exhibition: all the pictures are masterpieces. They vary in subject matter, but they are all technically brilliant—the modeling is deep and round, the tones soft and varied, the surfaces beautifully portrayed and produced, the figures full of life. There are millions of variations in this impact of mind on nature in camera art, but they are all uniformly excellent. Master the camera and you have mastered the most essential areas in camera art.

It is not a great art, but it is marvelously stimulating and it gives a man the priceless gift of seeing. "Beauty is in the eye of the beholder," said Emerson, thus endowing man with the supreme power of creation. Everything is beautiful to the man who is sentient enough to see it. Light is the master painter; light can transform a dingy brick wall into a warm and buoyant surface, a battered rusty chimney pot into a friendly image, a worn, dirty cobblestone pavement into a bold tapestry, a rusty steamer into a romantic argosy, a tired face into poetry. And the virtue of the camera is not the power it has to transform the photographer into an artist, but the impulse it gives him to keep on looking—looking speculatively at faces in the street, raffish corners of the water front, clouds above the sky line, reflections on the water, shadows across the buildings—restoring to visible beauty the million things that have been lost and forgotten or discarded. Everything is alive to the man who can see light transfiguring material into beauty.

29. If you are navigating a steam vessel in the Hudson River through fog, mist, falling snow or heavy rain, be sure to sound a prolonged blast on the whistle at intervals of not more than one minute. If you are navigating a tugboat with a tow, sound three blasts in succession; namely, one prolonged blast followed by two short blasts. These instructions come directly from a masterpiece of prose composition that governs the lights and signals prescribed by law for all vessels in the harbor—*Rules to Prevent Collisions of Vessels, and Pilot Rules for Certain Inland Waters*, published by the United States Coast Guard. I dote on it. The prose is explicit, ominous and pitiless. The tone is Jovian. Woe to the skipper who does not faithfully submit to it, for, in case of an accident, he may as well retire to a farm.

The inland waters pilot rules generally follow the international rules of the road. But there are some entertaining variations. For example, the international rules make exceptions that do not apply here: "In all cases where the rules require a bell to be used, a drum may be substituted on Turkish vessels." We do not permit Turkish vessels to substitute drums for bells here. Nor do the harbor rules specify the lights required on "a vessel employed in laying or in picking up a telegraph cable." We are not over-burdened with cable ships in New York harbor. But this severe little book is the voice of authority on lights and signals for big steamers, small steamers, sailing ships, tugs, ferries, barges, dredges, motor boats, rowing boats and everything that floats. If it is obeyed by everybody, there will be no accidents caused by confusion in navigation.

But to one who is skeptical about the omniscience of any authority there is something very disarming about the *Rules to Prevent the Collisions of Vessels*. Lo, it goes to pieces at the crucial point. A note of panic creeps into the sections concerned with vessels that cross the courses of other vessels. For these are situations that require judgment and calculation on the spot and test the ingenuity of the mortal men who are in immediate charge of moving vessels; and no rule composed in the cool detachment of the coast guard headquarters can be much more than an anxious and hysterical warning. Note the confusion in the following rule when the lords of the Coast Guard break down and confess their muddled humanity: "When two steam vessels are approaching each other at right angles or obliquely so as to involve risk of collision, other than when one steam vessel is overtaking another, the steam vessel which has the other on her own port side shall hold her course and speed; and the steam vessel which has the other on her own starboard side shall keep out of the way of the other by directing her course to starboard so as to cross the stern of the other steam vessel, or, if necessary to do so, slacken her speed or stop or reverse.

"If from any causes the conditions covered by this situation are such as to prevent immediate compliance with each other's signals, the misunderstanding or objection shall be at once made apparent by blowing the danger signal, and both vessels shall be stopped and backed if necessary, until signals for passing with safety are made and understood."

Although the prose style is calm on the surface, close readers will perceive that the Coast Guard is worried. Just how worried appears in Article 27 which reveals the ultimate collapse of Jovian authority and a return to human chaos: "In obeying and construing these rules due regard shall be had to all dangers of navigation and collision, and to any special circumstances which may render a departure from the above rules necessary in order to avoid immediate danger." This is the "escape clause"; the Coast Guard says in effect: "Brother, you are on your own!"

Even in the most majestically regulated harbor, there comes a time when a man cannot lean on authority, but has to use his head. Every man has to be his own master, and the Coast Guard washes its hands of him.

30. If only we could look into children's futures! If only we could help prepare them for the outrageous fortune that some day will knock them off balance! Now they live in the golden shell of a magic world—fed, sheltered, clothed and tenderly cared for. They are radiant with happiness. They are healthy and imaginative. Their good will is not merely disarming: it is curiously pathetic because it is founded on innocence and faith rather than experience. In the next ten or fifteen years they will have to venture outside the borders of the magic world that now envelops them; and large areas of the great world outside are harsh, bitter and treacherous. Will good will preserve the children when they leave their world of innocence? Or, shall we ruefully be cherishing memories of a soft and dewy beauty that the poisons of the adult world have destroyed?

Even though we are with the children all day long, there is no way of communicating with them. No adult can tell them anything decisive, for their understanding is limited. They believe but they do not know. At best, there are only two things that would be worth saying. Be honest. That is the keystone in the arch of life. There are millions of us; we have to live together. But we can live nothing except a ghastly nightmare if we do not have a hard core of honesty at the base of our life. Be kind. Be kind, not only to friends, but to strangers. Preserve in the soul a kindly incandescence so that wherever you go a kindly glow passes through the streets and fills the home with light. There is nothing more that anyone can say. None of the poisons of life can rot the characters of human beings who are honest and kind. If only it were possible to tell children these simple things!

31. On this day in 1837 Ralph Waldo Emerson delivered his Phi Beta Kappa address at Harvard, "The American Scholar." It expressed an attitude towards scholarship that was revolutionary at the time ("our intellectual Declaration of Independence," O. W. Holmes called it). It is still pertinent, and it still needs to be said. In Emerson's day American scholarship was dominated by the Germanic idea of research in books. By exhaustive reading the scholar correlated the writings of others; and scholarship became an accumulation rather than a creation, and the scholar became isolated from life. "Meek young men," said Emerson, "grow up in libraries, believing it their duty to accept the views which Cicero, which Locke, which Bacon, have given; forgetful that Cicero, Locke and Bacon were only young men in libraries when they wrote these books." Emerson believed that books should be used only for inspiration and for scientific and historical facts, and that the chief function of the scholar is to study life. "Life is our dictionary," he said. "There is virtue in the hoe and spade," he said (although he personally was all thumbs outside the library). "I embrace the common," he said. "Give me insight into today, and you may have the antique and future worlds."

In America, some students even now meekly acquire learning out of books in an airless, sunless world of scholarly authority—obsequiously memorizing and accepting. Count them out of the age-old battle for the brave new world that is always dawning but never reaching high noon. And count out any unreconstructed Germans who, like the pedants of Emerson's day, are still building systems of order which they expect to obey. "A little injustice is better than disorder," Goethe remarked complacently, anticipating Bismarck, Kaiser Wilhelm, and Adolph Hitler. A little skepticism is better than the monolithic order that has twice driven the world to war. For the fruits of scholarship are not merely lectures and a new series of scholarly books but national attitudes and behavior. Those who do not practice freedom in their education will not understand freedom in the world.

The value of education is not the knowledge it imparts but the wisdom it helps to create. Genius looks forward, according to Emerson. Books and knowledge are the things from which the scholar departs into the realm of life and creation. It takes most men five years to recover from a college education, and to learn that poetry is as vital to thinking as knowledge. Any hack can accumulate knowledge methodically.

SEPTEMBER

September

ERMANY INVADED Poland on this day in 1939, thus setting
off the catastrophe that brought down the roof and walls
and shook the foundations of the world. Life will never be the
same as it was on August 31, 1939; we can never recover the feeling of continuity that kept us oriented at that time. Since this
was obviously one of the decisive days of the world, I set down a
record of the weather, my thoughts and my activities on that date
so that I might not forget the texture of the first day of a new and
angry era. It was a beautiful, warm, late-summer day illuminated
by translucent sunlight. There was a chance that on that day I
might finish a shed I had started building two months before. I
got out of bed early, chiefly to get to work without delay, but also
to hear a seven o'clock radio bulletin, since we all knew that
momentous decisions were being made abroad. "Germany has invaded Poland," the radio announcer said laconically. After listening for a few sorrowful moments, I went outside with the trash
to burn in the incinerator, grateful for the comfort of the old,
domestic routine. As I looked around at the fields and hills (hoping as usual to catch a glimpse of a deer in the orchard), gradually
it dawned on me that the news was true and evil. For one hundred and fifty years men had stood on our fair hill studying the
morning and contemplating the work of the day, as I always do
when I am in the country. But on this day the morning was
silently ringing with alarms and portents. Somewhere thousands
of miles away bombing planes were screaming, tanks were clattering along the roads and over the harvested fields and men in steel
helmets with rifles in their hands were marching to the first course
of a banquet of death. As I gazed into the mellow sky I, as one
member of the human race, felt somehow guilty of the bloodshed
and violence that were staining the loveliness and fragrance of the
first of September. At breakfast we all felt shrouded down in the

misery of a broken world. I went to work on the shed without enthusiasm but grateful for the concreteness of measuring, sawing and nailing. Although the shed turned out to be reasonably workmanlike, I took little pleasure in finishing it, for this world of destruction was not the one I had planned it for.

It is perhaps symbolic of something that the shed was burned to the ground less than two years later. All that remains of it now is a bulge in the grass where the foundation was made, and even the foundation now is unintelligible and useless.

2. After six harrowing years the war came to an end on September second. Japan formally surrendered at a severe ceremony on board the U.S.S. *Missouri,* lying at anchor in Tokyo Bay. I was in Moscow that day. The official surrender of Japan was accepted there joylessly by a people exhausted by the war and perhaps too broken in spirit to believe in their bones that a brave, new world was beginning. Some ancient wisdom must have instructed them that wars are not concluded by official agreements between heads of state and that the pompous celebration in Moscow at night was only another official festivity, signifying nothing. For wars go deeper than reason. Even Jesus said: "Think not that I am come to send peace on earth: I came not to send peace, but a sword."

I have never known a war-monger anywhere, although perhaps some do exist. I have never known a general who believed in war, although probably there are some. Everywhere in the world people want peace as passionately as they want love and happiness and rest. For the arts of peace are the glorious ones. Why, then, are we unable to muzzle the guns, ground the bombers and lay up the battleships? Why do we go on marching our young men to camp at the time when they are hungriest for life and best able to beautify it? Why? Even those whom we have come to regard as our enemies want to dwell at home and raise families. Why cannot we exorcize this last of the primitive evils? Perhaps the idea of peace is too revolutionary for an earth drenched in blood and fertilized by the bones of dead warriors ever since the angry dawn of civilization.

3. After a week of crushing heat in the city, a northwest wind makes life tolerable again. At eight in the morning the thermometer stands at 58°. There seems to be a grain in the air. The sunlight is bold and firm. For a week the river has been hot and glassy. But this morning it is tumbling with a lively blue. The waves break into whitecaps and drench the east shore with spray. The small boats moored at the yacht basin are lively. A cabin cruiser headed upstream is pitching rapidly, and the helmsman on the bridge teeters back and forth like the eccentric-rod of a steam engine. Flowing through the gasping streets, the brisk wind quickly revives the whole city which is coming to life again with a rush. Yesterday New York looked worn, dirty and dispirited; it smelled of sweat and decay. This morning it looks fresh and energetic and the impulse is forward. Somewhere in Canada the father of winds has sent us a message of deliverance and overnight we rebuild New York into the sort of youthful and dynamic city we wish it were.

During the past month the herring gulls have been reassembling and are now, I should think, in full winter strength again. By their presence in great numbers through the autumn and winter they keep the choked and ramshackle port of New York related to the open beaches and the sea outside. On a day like this one they sit facing into the wind, gracing with their wonderful beauty the rotted piles that stand in the river. The laughing gulls—still in their black-headed plumage—are the ones that enjoy the harbor. They are smaller than the herring gulls, and they are much livelier and noisier. Whirling above the tide rips they scream almost hysterically with excitement and enthusiasm. They will drift away during the next two months. But the herring gulls will remain. They are scavengers. I wonder whether they may not be more numerous now than they were in the days when the Indians lived here. Although the Hudson River was much purer then, it probably fed fewer herring gulls. Fortunately for us, they are not so fastidious as they look.

4. While prowling around on the shore of the Gilboa Reservoir this afternoon O. picks up a stone imprinted with the delicate patterns of thirty-two sea shells. It is the most sensational thing I

have seen for years. It proves dramatically what the textbooks say: that once the Catskill region was drowned by the sea. The Taconic Mountains on the boundary between Massachusetts and New York were the eastern shore of an arm of the ocean and the Adirondacks were the northern shore. Ocean waves rolled over the Catskills. Gilboa Reservoir is now so far inland and so high above sea level that I have always had difficulty in believing the geology books. But here is the evidence! This stone, eight inches long, two wide and two thick, has modestly preserved millions of years of geological history and has innocently passed the record on, specifically to us.

Even in those dimly known years before the plants flowered, sea shells had delicate traceries and beautiful designs, as they do now. Some of the larger shell-prints look like peacock plumage, fully spread. Most of the impressions are from small shells no larger than the head of a wooden match. Tiny and exquisite though the radial lines of these shells were millions of years ago, this eloquent stone has scrupulously retained sensitive impressions of them, and passed on to us their beauty, like an ancient parchment from some long forgotten civilization. I wonder whether O. may not be the first human being in some millions of years to have seen this relic. Now the Cambrian era does not seem so fabulous as I had imagined.

After O. picks up her stone, I start looking seriously in the litter for others. The only thing I find is a copperhead snake curled up in the sun. He lifts his head to look at me. Frankly, I do not feel inclined to disturb his rest. We part amicably, forever I hope. On principle I respect the privacy of poisonous snakes.

5. In the woods that shelter the creek below our farm the crows and jays are screaming. Although crows are wary as a rule, these do not take off when I move up quietly towards their forum, for they are seething with anger and possibly hope that for once I am on their side. By good luck I catch a glimpse of the thing they hate. I see the brown back and short tail of a huge owl perched close to the trunk of a hemlock. He is facing the other way, but he knows that he is being observed. Leaning down he is peering in front of him, and then slowly turning his head he looks behind him. As he turns towards me I see his ear-tufts, and finally

his baleful eyes and savage beak. He is a great horned owl, the most rapacious and inhuman bird in our neighborhood. Nearly two feet tall with a wingspread of three feet and equipped with strong, razory talons, he could slaughter any one of the crows and jays that are besieging him; and unless he were hungry he would eat the brains of his victim and drop the rest to the ground. Crows are part of his diet, along with other birds, woodchucks, opossums, skunks, rats, and rabbits. Although the crows mob him, they do not bother him. Perhaps he hardly notices them, since he does not begin to hunt until dusk.

But he feels uneasy about me and keeps looking everywhere. Having watched him through the binocular for about ten minutes I try to circle stealthily through the woods to a place abreast of him for a better view of his face, breast and talons. While I take my eyes off him for a split second to see where I am stepping he silently disappears. It is as though he were a wraith and had never been there. The crows and jays pursue him, their screams increasing in volume and virulence to the place where he perches again in the seclusion of the woods. But nothing they can do invades the malevolent isolation of the bloody empire in which he dwells. When he wants food he will take it swiftly, coldly, noiselessly.

6. Labor Day. The last public holiday before the children go back to school and the city people settle down to work again. If Memorial Day opens the vacation season, Labor Day closes it. The highways today are choked with automobiles on their way back to the city, and the railroad trains are packed with tired, nervous people sullenly going home. By tomorrow evening the country will be purged of çity people.

Originally Labor Day was intended to show the strength and ésprit de corps of trade and labor organizations. Peter F. Maguire, an active Knight of Labor and president of the Carpenters' and Joiners' Union, proposed a Labor Day resolution at a business meeting of the New York City Central Labor Union on May 8, 1882. He asked that one day a year be set aside to honor laboring people; and since there was no break in the working week from July Fourth to Thanksgiving, he suggested the first Monday in September. The resolution was adopted. On the first Labor Day, union and trade groups marched in an imposing parade in New

York. The idea spread to other cities and states. Labor Day was established as an official national holiday by an act of Congress in 1894.

It has lost most of its original significance. With the adoption of the five-day work week, it now assures nearly everyone of a long week end and the final excursion to shore or country, and it marks the civilian end of summer. May first has superseded it as the day for labor demonstration, for May first has a militant significance that suits the more aggressive spirit of modern labor organizations. May first was set aside in 1889 by the Second International in Paris for demonstrations by socialist labor and radical groups. Soviet historians, accustomed to making history conform to Soviet policy, say that it commemorates the Haymarket massacre of labor people in Chicago on May 4, 1886. Whatever the specific motive may have been originally, May first has political meaning now all over the world. It has a defiant attitude far beyond anything Peter F. Maguire had imagined. May first is now the labor day that means revolution. Our Labor Day means the last fling of the season for all Americans, whether they regard themselves as workers or not.

7. None of the elaborate machinery thrown together to reconcile capital and labor can succeed, nor is it worth the trouble of improvising. For it is political sophistry. Laws, Supreme Court decisions, conciliation boards, and collective bargaining do not get to the heart of the problem. Nor does socialism; when the motive of private profit is removed, people are no more virtuous than they were before. The innumerable schemes for keeping the industrial peace are doomed because they preserve the alignment of two hostile forces, each of which wants to exploit the other. There is a good deal of solemn cant about the common interests of capital and labor. As matters stand, their only common interest is that of cutting each other's throat.

Believe it or not, workers are people and respond to the usual stimuli. And if a worker had a direct stake in the profits of the industry that employs him, the alignment of hostile forces would be broken. His motive is the same as his employer's; he wants to make money, and for the usual legitimate reasons. If his income expanded with the prosperity of the industry and shrank with the curtailment of production, he would have a motive for working efficiently, for expecting his associates to work efficiently and for accepting responsibility in the affairs of his employer's enterprise. At least in theory, stockholders share directly in the fortunes of corporations. Since the workers do most of the work, they are morally entitled to participation, also. For they, too, are human beings and respond to the normal human motivations.

Labor is no longer a raw material as it was a century ago when factories were comparatively new. It is a human force, nearly but not quite so powerful as capital, and intelligent enough to know the difference between bargaining and co-operation. All the present schemes for regulating the relationships of capital and labor are versions of power politics. Power politics do not lead into but, on the contrary, away from democracy.

8. Broadway theater season opens. "Night's black agents" assemble for the first time since June. Since the evening is warm, everyone loiters outside the theater in the dusk until curtain time, shaking hands and catching up on gossip. The gang never looks better than at the first autumn assemblies. The first-nighters are tanned and rested and fresher in spirit than they will be again all winter. For the mechanical routine of gathering in a theater two or three nights a week is not in itself the basis for abiding friendships. Within a few weeks the conversation will be familiar and desultory and much of it will have the false gaiety of desperation.

Since they are hired rather than voluntary theatergoers, the first-night people are hard to conquer. They have seen too many plays, most of which were bad, and they know the actors too well to be surprised, astonished, or fascinated. And since the world of the theater is fairly self-contained, the first-night crowd brings very little intellectual curiosity to the theater. It is sharp without being keen or dynamic. The producers feel frustrated by the hardness of first-night responses, and from time to time try to invent schemes for breaking up the square phalanx of critics, agents and talent scouts.

But there is no audience that knows so much about the theater and that so thoroughly appreciates good theater work. In the theater an audience is as essential as a playwright and a company of actors; for theater is a communal experience in which everyone is caught up in an extraordinary incandescence. An acted play that is not appreciated never comes to life. Although the first-night audience has certain intellectual and spiritual limitations, it appreciates good work more intelligently than any audience I know. It responds to genuine talent instantly. Other audiences seem to me sluggish and obtuse by comparison.

N.B.—The new season opens with a bad play that is badly acted and that survives only until the next Saturday night. It loses $44,000. There is something ironic in the fact that the first American play on record bore the prophetic title, *The Disappointment*.

9. When Americans are abroad they are inclined to regard foreign bureaucracies as evidence of foreign stupidity, resistance, and inefficiency. Irritated by the lethargy and the complicated paper work of foreign bureaucracies, Americans complacently assume that things are brisker at home. That is one of the common illusions. Bureaucracies are the same the world over—slow, complicated, timid, unimaginative, routine and inhuman. The perfect bureaucrat everywhere is the man who manages to make no decisions and escape all responsibility. All the triumphs of bureaucracy are negative.

Bureaucracies are designed to perform public business. But as soon as a bureaucracy is established, it develops an autonomous spiritual life and comes to regard the public as its enemy. Instead of serving the public, which pays the bills, it devises ways in self-defense of thwarting the public. For the past year we have been trying to get an R.F.D. route established on our hill in the country. We are the only community in this region without R.F.D. service. Since we pay equal taxes we do not feel humble about expecting equal benefits. But the Post Office Department in Washington has wrapped itself up so securely that it is almost impervious to the public. It takes three months to answer a letter and then contemptuously sends nothing but a mimeographed form. To preserve its freedom of action it conceals its thoughts and decisions behind a curtain of secrecy. It says or does nothing that commits it to any program. It is monolithic—tall, imposing, and free of detail. Pressed by a senator and a congressman, who belong to related classes of society, the Post Office does murmur something that is apparently intelligible in Washington, where nearly everyone happily conspires to keep the public away; but then the Post Office again retires into ponderous silence, contemplating its navel. When goaded into answering a letter by an especially sharp inquiry, the department sends a curt reply that would be considered inexcusably insulting in private business. The Post Office Department is paid for by the public, but it regards the public as a nuisance, and contacts with the public as dangerous intrusions on its private life. In Soviet Russia, victims of bureaucracy write for relief to Stalin and frequently get some. Our bureaucracies are no more democratic than his. We shall have to write to the President.

N.B.—We got the R.F.D. without having to appeal to the President.

10. At last the rain has come. There has not been a soaking rain since June, and this has been a stricken territory. The hay crop was light. The corn is a failure, lacking energy enough to form kernels on the ears. The potatoes have squandered their strength on luxuriant tops; there are virtually no potatoes in the ground. Everything has been looking worn and haggard—the grass and pastures brown, the lilac leaves withered, the locust trees thin and desiccated. The creeks have been rivers of dry stones, and some of the wells have gone dry. Alarmed by day after day of burning skies, people have been anxiously saving water and devising ways of using it three or four times—first for the hands and face, then for the cooking dishes, then for slop pails, and finally for a corner of the kitchen garden. If necessary there are countless ways of saving water. With the fields and woods dry, we have all been in dread of fire. There have been three grass fires on the hill, one of which was just creeping towards a pine lot when the swiftly assembled members of the volunteer fire company put it out. We have never before been so grateful to the members of the fire department, who drop whatever they are doing when the alarm is given and rush to the place where help is desperately needed.

Yesterday the southern sky was heavy with haze. In the middle of the afternoon thunder rumbled and presently a brief shower swept down from the mountain. This has happened several times during the summer—a shower so scanty that it hardly laid the dust

in the powdery road. There was another shower in the early evening. But during the night the blessed rain came, falling straight
out of the black sky—drumming joyously on the roof, rattling on
the dry leaves, and soaking the baked and crusted ground. By
morning the air is buoyant with moisture. The thermometer drops
to 65°, and the barometer, which has hardly moved away from
the thirty-inch mark for three months, is at 29.40. All morning
the rain pours down with a great weight of sweet water—cleansing
the trees and bushes, dissolving the hard surface of the ground,
bringing the dead ditches to life, dyeing the brown grass with
greenness, and relieving the tension of life on the hill. More than
three inches of rain fall in nineteen hours. It will be many months
before the earth is filled with as much water as it needs. But the
long, agonizing drought has been mercifully broken.

11. In our modern office building we are grandly sealed against
the uncivilized chaos of nature. In wet weather we are dry. We
are warm in the winter and cool in the summer. Most of us are
also spared the rawness and inefficient variability of sunlight,
which is not satisfactory for sound newspaper work. My desk faces
a dead window of opaque glass. Since the ventilation of the building is scientifically planned as a unit isolated from nature, the
window is not supposed to be opened. Once I did recklessly open
it. I was horrified to find myself looking into an alien office about
ten feet across a dark alley and populated by strangers who were
absorbed in some absurd business which obviously had to be conducted in private. It looked furtive. That was about two years ago.
Shocked by the glimpse into the catacombs I have never upset the
sensitive balance of our organization by opening the window
again.

The window is so dark and useless that, in point of fact, I rarely
notice it, although it is only a foot in front of the desk at which
I work. My office is cheerfully lighted by electric globes that make
midnight indistinguishable from midday and eliminate the capri-
ciousness of nature. On a shelf beside the desk, a philodendron
lives (I cannot say that it grows). A jungle plant, it is used to hiding away from the sun, although it would probably enjoy a tongue
of sunlight at noon. It looks etiolated. But the scientific lighting
is obviously better than sunlight for working. It makes it possible

for us to go on hour after hour into the early morning without realizing that the day has gone to rest. I imagine that the working arrangements in hell are similar—steady, uniform, detached, and permanent.

Although we are scientifically isolated in our office, we are in constant touch with the world by telephone, and get frequent bulletins from the outside. Also, there is a kind of human variation. The people bring in color and freshness from the outside. After the long periods of vacations, people look tanned, rested and good-humored, and their minds are pointed towards the months ahead. They introduce a grateful element of the seasons into the standard uniformity of our modern office building.

12. After lying at anchor for nine days between Sandy Hook and Staten Island, Henry Hudson sailed through the Narrows on September 12, 1609, and anchored for the night off Manhattan, a sweet-smelling vineland. He was in the *Half Moon* of eighty tons burden and had a mixed crew of sixteen or eighteen English and Dutch sailors. When he left Holland he had headed for Nova Zembla, where he had been before, to resume the quest of finding a passage to the Far East. Baffled by the ice he had turned south. For two weeks he and his crew laid up in Maine to make a new mast to replace the one lost in a storm. Resuming his coasting he got as far south as the Virginia Capes and then came north to Sandy Hook. He and his men spent nine days making soundings from the small boat and also fishing. After one night off Manhattan Island, which had green slopes and many "great and tall oaks," they started sailing up "the river of the mountains" on the thirteenth. By the twenty-second they reached beyond what is now Troy. Finding only seven feet of water there, they turned back downstream, and left the river on October fourth. Hudson admired the river and the lush country through which it ran, and wrote the first workmanlike and appreciative report of the region. The grapes were almost ripe and the vines heavy. The trees were just turning. Herons and black ducks were patrolling the river, as they do today. Most of the Indians he found civil and friendly, although some of them were hostile. Near what is now Catskill, his mate went ashore to accept the hospitality of an Indian chief who prepared a feast for him, including wild pigeons. The Indians

were well supplied. They had stocks of corn and beans ample enough to fill three ships, in Hudson's estimation. Hudson traded with the Indians of the river for oysters, beans, corn, pumpkins, and tobacco.

Although Hudson is regarded as the discoverer of the glorious river that now bears his name, other Europeans had seen it and some of them had sailed up it as far as the region that is now Albany. In 1524, eighty-five years before Hudson, Giovanni da Verrazano, out of Dieppe, dropped anchor off Sandy Hook and took notice of *"una grandissima riviera."* The next year Estovan Gomez, a Spaniard, saw the Hudson. Around 1540 French skippers built a fort near Albany to trade in furs with the Indians, and presumably French ships used the river now and then to reach and stock the fort, which stood for a number of years. The Flemish geographer, Gerard Kramer, better known by his Latinized name, Mercator, showed the Hudson as the "Rivière Grande" on a chart he made in 1569. The truth is, no one knows how many Europeans used the Hudson before Henry arrived in 1609. The traders probably were not interested in exploration and kept no records apart from their business affairs. Although Hudson came at least eighty-five years after whoever discovered the river, he was an able and large-minded navigator and explorer, and appreciated what he saw intellectually and emotionally. He was a man of character. It is an honor to have his name commemorated in the grand river that washes New York's doorstep.

13. Mass calamity strikes at our community in the country today. School opens. At eight-fifteen the bus goes by after collecting the victims in the neighborhood. They look cleaner than at any time all summer, but grave and resigned. Something too big for them to handle has overwhelmed them, and they are offering no resistance. Abandoned toys can be seen along the village street and children with notebooks and pencils in their hands are loitering somewhat gloomily by the store. The school is clean and shining and the teachers are in their places. A veteran of five grades, Heather takes her place in good humor, after squawking, "Ah, nuts!" ever since she was routed out of bed. But Andrew is taking his place in educated society for the first time. Accustomed to the nervous vagaries of adults, he has gone off to school quietly and apparently with no apprehensions. He enters school politely and takes his place in the first grade as obediently as he goes to the movies or climbs into a bus. But he was not counting on being completely deserted and turned over to the care of strangers. He looks panic-stricken when he is left in the classroom. His eyes are big with terror. His mouth is tense. Clutching the stub of a pencil in one hand, he sets out to conquer the world alone. He had not imagined that going to school would be so heartless. For the first time in five bewildering but not cheerless years, he is on his own.

After the children have left, the house looks dazed and wilted. All the vitality has suddenly evaporated from it, leaving a very audible vacuum. No screen doors slam. No feet go clattering through the living room or pounding the stairs, and no one is pushing, shoving, slapping, gouging, shrieking or working up refinements of fraternal torture. Most of the energy from all over town has been transferred to the school, which is made of steel and concrete and is manned by a large staff of guards who are strong, swift, and vigilant and know how to make good citizens out of natural terrorists.

14. Beware of pure intellect. It is cold, inhuman and fanatical; it is unbalanced and mischievous; and as in the instance of Goebbels, it can bring down a civilization in destroying itself. Unless it is supported by a good heart and purged in the bowels of compassion, it is a form of insanity. For we have to live in a society, not of brains, but of men and women, and they are animated as much by love and passion as by reasoning and learning. And life is not logic but *mish-mosh* and muddle, which reflect the tolerance by which we live together in a community. Until everybody is graduated from the university as a doctor of science, life will not follow the straight line of logic, and men of pure intellect will be inadequate counselors.

Beware also of the syllogism by which logicians reason that if two things are true, a third thing must be true, also. If a normal human being has anything to do with it, the third thing will turn out to be nothing of the kind. Let's face it: life is not a science. Human beings are not scientific animals. The human sciences are incomplete—being baffled, in fact, by the wayward and unscientific behavior of human beings. By and large, men act according to what they like. They like Roosevelt or Willkie, as they like the Dodgers or Sunup in the fourth race at Aqueduct. At the very most they like the partisan logic presented to them by the Republican or Democratic candidate for president. For both candidates make a cunning pretense to logic, i.e., they make the most of the arguments for their side. Acting strictly according to logic the Soviet Politburo gives the people only one candidate to vote for. That is the absolute peak of political logic. Since the people and the politicians want only one thing, the Soviet logicians say, and since the party invariably nominates the best man, there is no need for more than one candidate.

Beware of pure intellect. But give some wondering heed to the ward politician. He knows something that is valuable; he can get along with people.

15. Everyone in our country town seems to be in a mood of rapture today. We had forgotten that the outdoors could be so nearly celestial. The air is soft. The harsh flame of the summer has burned out and the sting of winter is far ahead. After two or three torrential rainstorms the hard earth has softened and the withered grass is again green and luxuriant. Except for the locust groves, which withered a fortnight ago, the trees are still in full foliage and look gratefully refreshed. There is a cordial pinkish tint in the maple leaves and some of the ash leaves have been dyed dark red in the vats of early autumn. There are purple asters flourishing at the doorstep. The chickory strews flakes of the heavens beside the road and through the fields, and Queen Anne's lace is still full of neat embroidery. The golden-rod that is now in bloom is especially rich—soft, thick minarets of gold nodding in the waste places. Some of the birds have already left for the south. A few strangely faded warblers from the north are drifting silently through the thickets. But birds that kept to themselves during the nesting season have joined the residents of the house-lot and now boldly appear in the dooryard. Two brown thrashers— probably the pair that nested discreetly down the hill—enjoy splashing in the bird bath. There are two bluejays in the bath at one time—an audacious autumn adventure. A towhee has come from the spruce lot to be near the house. The chickadees and

bluebirds are drifting through the neighborhood in amiable flocks—singing absent-mindedly now.

This is a happy day for all of us. Whenever we meet on the road or in the village we remind each other that we are blessed. Perhaps we cherish it because we know that it is one of the last echoes of the summer. For under the rapture a stillness is collecting. Crickets are murmuring in the fields. Grasshoppers are leaping on dry wings through the meadows. But the life of the last five months is drawing to a close and a hush is spreading over the woods and gathering around the house and stealing into our hearts. There will not be many more pretty days this year.

16. In the western sky Jupiter is the steady beacon that fills the night with unearthly majesty. Even Times Square, a gash of savage light in the autumnal darkness, does not outshine the radiance of Jupiter that is swimming silently in space hundreds of millions of miles away. Venus is much nearer the earth and sends us more light on that account, for even in the heavens neighborliness creates a brighter feeling. But Jupiter is the grandest of the planets, and sometimes casts a shadow. It has an equator of 88,700 miles, in comparison with ours of 25,000 miles; in volume it is 1,300 times greater than the earth. It is so far from the sun that it takes nearly twelve years to make one revolution—a journey we are able to accomplish in one.

Thank God the earth is solider. That is the reason I am able to scribble these random notes. For Jupiter is a ball of clouds and vapors that are never settled or stable. It is remarkable for a tremendous red spot, about 30,000 miles by 8,000 miles in width, that changes over the years in color and intensity—sometimes brick red, sometimes faint gray, sometimes almost invisible. The red spot was first noticed in the latter quarter of the nineteenth century. After fading gradually it started forming again and became brick red once again in 1927. Jupiter is also plagued with a "south tropical disturbance" that shows dark fingers poking through the vapors. The red spot and the tropical disturbance wrestle with each other ponderously. Jupiter is a sun of low density and brightness. It has a temperature of $-100°$ C.—more than it could receive from solar radiation, but not enough to burn the skies of our solar system.

In 1610 Galileo, acting on information he got from Holland, invented a telescope and discovered that Jupiter had four moons. Three of them are about the size of our moon and could be seen with the naked eye if they were not so close to the planet. Five more moons have been discovered since 1892 on photographic plates. But more than two centuries passed before astronomers discovered more than Galileo had seen. There may be greater news about Jupiter still unpublished. The affairs of Jupiter in the western sky may be more complicated than we know at the moment. Why so calm, Jupiter? Are there no wars between the gasses? Are you not rumbling with discord, too?

17. Constitution Day. It would not be difficult to argue that conservative or reactionary ideas are un-American. Under the Constitution a man has a right to any opinions that do not foster violence. But the Declaration of Independence, on which our national life is founded, is a liberal document that was written by an illustrious liberal. And the Constitution, adopted this day in 1787, is a liberal charter that has influenced the political ideas of the world. Although it is known as a great people's contract, it was written by fairly conservative men who represented property, and it was ratified by officials qualified by property. The liberal ideas in the Constitution were not the immediate inspirations of the individual delegates but were swept in by the practical necessities of the times. In fact, the Bill of Rights was quickly added to answer criticism that individual rights had not been sufficiently clarified in the original document. Faced with the solemn duty of drawing up a national contract, public men of generally conservative character found liberal ideas essential and inevitable.

There is no need at any time for conservative or reactionary ideas. They merely repeat the stupidity and torpor of the times. They perform lip service to dullness. Thought is not static but dynamic. No ideas are good for anything unless they are enkindled with vitality—unless, in short, they are liberal.

18. The United States has 6 per cent of the world land surface, 7 per cent of the world's population and produces 50 per cent of the world's goods. These facts are regarded as evidence of

the triumph of the American system. But they seem to me sus-
ceptible to different interpretations. In the first place, they should
make us profoundly grateful to God for the abundance of land,
water, forests, and minerals on which our materialistic triumph is
founded. Living amid God's plenty, it has been easy for us to
avoid some of the ancient evils, like conquest for plunder. In the
second place, we should be alarmed by the recklessness with
which we have squandered national riches—wrecking the land as
though it were worthless, hacking and burning away the forests as
though they were weeds. All these years we have been living off
capital and treating it contemptuously. In the third place, we
should be chagrined in a land of plenty by the poverty that still
gnaws away at our standard of living. Millions of Americans still
live in ramshackle houses without running water, heat or sanitary
improvements. The system of public education is starved. Hospitals, mental institutions, public libraries and universities are either
inadequate in number or impoverished or both. All of the public
arts, like orchestras, opera, theater and dance, are poverty-stricken.
There are still a lot of nightmares haunting the American dream.

19. *O wild west wind, thou breath of Autumn's being.* Not
wild today. In two or three months it will begin to seal the earth
in ice and wildly whistle down the hills. But now it is the good
genius of the prelude to autumn. It sweeps the last remnants of
summer out of the torpid landscape, putting a firm grain in the
air, cleaning the sluggish surface and restoring the spirit of the
earth. That aromatic odor comes from the wood fire kindled on
the hearth to take the chill off the house in the morning. For the
west wind, particularly when there is a little "northing" in it, has
a cool breath. After the languid heat of summer it is active and
bright. The sun is no longer a disk of hot ferocity. The flame has
died down remarkably and pours a gentle warmth against the
south side of the house. A pleasant, dry heat radiates from the
south meadows where, for the first time in months, the earth
seems warmer than the sun. Although there is less sunlight day
by day, the quality of the light is more flattering, for the angle is
longer and more revealing. The flow and ripple of the grassland
were lost in the glare of the summer, but the autumn sunlight
rediscovers them and brushes them with shadow. Look at the

meadows that seemed to be flat a month ago: the light has found
their natural rhythm. The declining sun distinguishes the texture
of the earth. Wind to freshen the air, long rays of sunlight to
warm it benignly and illuminate it beautifully—that is the blend-
ing of geniuses worth cherishing at this lovely time of year. The
west wind will be wild quite soon enough.

20. Throwing all caution to the winds, the bluejays have become boisterous again. They behave as though no other birds in-
habited the trees and thickets. I hear them screaming in Riverside
Park, along the roads upstate, and in the dooryard of our home in
the country. A bluejay is trumpeting truculently in a plane tree in
the middle of Broadway at One Hundred and Tenth Street this
noon. This is a seasonal augury. For despite his handsome and
ostentatious plumage, his size and his swagger bearing, the bluejay can be the most inconspicuous bird in the neighborhood if he
happens to be feeling discreet. During the nesting season he keeps
his mouth shut and, somehow, he can manage to slip through the
landscape unseen. All this time he may be stealing the eggs from
other nests and possibly murdering fledglings, but his surface behavior is circumspect. You have to hunt for him to see him; you
are lucky if you find his nest, for he conceals it amid the foliage
and never goes to it directly. He steals up to it behind a screen of
leaves and branches. But as soon as the nesting season is over and
he has finished molting, he resumes his cheap, noisy, braggart
manner, bullying every bird that does not object. He collects in
gangs and screams in concert as though he were leader of some
superior race of birds. He comes boldly around the house, eating
nuts and suet with a mixture of guile and bravado. Oh, yes, he is
lord of creation when his family has flown and he is on the town.
He screams belligerently at hawks and owls. But he is not likely
to scream at them unless he has either prepared a safe retreat or
is inside a thicket that they cannot enter. The bluejay, like the
crow, will always be with us because he is cautious, shrewd, wary
and intelligent. He is a notorious thief. Among the things he
steals are the notes of other birds. The catbird you may think you
hear mewing today may be a bluejay mimicking a catbird. You
cannot trust the bluejay. He is a rascal. His dashing appearance,

with such glorious blue feathers and a smart crest, has gone to his head. He thinks he must strut and yell.

21. Date of the disastrous hurricane of 1938. To most New Yorkers, hurricanes had been rather coarse phenomena that periodically terrified people who were unintelligent enough to live in other parts of the country. That attitude came to an end in 1938. After nine days of consecutive rain that year, a tropical hurricane swept across the bottom of Manhattan on the afternoon of September twenty-first and then went on through New England and Canada and disappeared into the Arctic and permanently changed New York thinking. It killed 494 people, injured 708 more and destroyed 4,500 buildings, to say nothing of hundreds of thousands of trees. In New York City it killed ten people and injured five others, uprooted thousands of trees in the parks, tossed hundreds of small boats on the rocky shores of the Hudson and on the beaches of Staten Island, destroyed a bungalow colony at Gravesend Bay, and flooded the Hudson Tubes. Most New Yorkers did not realize that a hurricane had struck them until they read the newspapers the next day, but the evidence was overwhelming when it was finally assembled.

The hurricane had first been reported off Porto Rico on September seventeenth. Instead of passing off to the east, it was caught between two high-pressure areas and funneled up the Atlantic Coast to New York. The center or "eye" passed close enough to Manhattan to leave a record in the Weather Bureau in the Whitehall Building near the Battery. The wind velocity was eighty-seven miles an hour at three-fifteen and then dropped to five miles an hour until 4 P.M., while the "eye" was passing northeast, and the pressure dropped to 28.72 inches. Not realizing that a hurricane had struck us, I thought my barometer was out of order. The rainfall was 2.78 inches in the twenty-four hours, added to the 7.75 inches of rain that had fallen in the preceding one hundred and twenty hours. Between four and five o'clock, when the second half of the storm struck, the rain blew horizontally across the city.

The tide rose 8.6 feet above mean water, tore through the water front, and made ferryboat navigation perilous. A gust of wind and waves struck the ferry *Knickerbocker* just as she was entering the

South Ferry slip and drove her port side over the iron guard on the bumper that is secured to the piling. She hung there at an angle of thirty degrees for twenty minutes until tugs, a fireboat and a coast guard cutter pulled her off. Fifteen passengers on the Clason Point—College Point ferry were kept afloat from 7:20 P.M. to 2:15 A.M. because the high tide had flooded the slips. The ferry finally landed them at Atlantic Avenue, Brooklyn. Unwilling to be caught in a narrow, crowded channel during a hurricane, the master of the *Queen Mary* delayed sailing until the next day. New York thus learned to respect hurricanes, although, as usual, the Weather Bureau minimized the storm by calling it a "whole gale."

22. Once a month I visit the tobacco counter of a nervous, soulless chain drug store on the corner of Eighth Avenue and Forty-second Street. Looming up out of a bizarre array of cheap and irrational goods, Mr. Johnson gives me a pound of Wild Honey smoking tobacco which he stocks for me regularly. It takes him two or three minutes to wrap it and make change. Business moves so fast at his corner that in two or three minutes four or five people crowd up to the counter to buy candy or cigarettes, and the tempo is so swift that a delay excites their nerves, and they start squirming, grumbling, and tapping the counter with their coins. But Mr. Johnson likes a few words of gossip in the midst of the day's tensions. He is a tall, blond gentleman from Minnesota, where he owns "a little acreage" and where he imagines one day he will build a house and retire. Having obligingly mailed tobacco to me in the country, he knows that I, too, own "a little acreage." Amid the brassy hubbub of Eighth Avenue, we imagine ourselves to be farmers, which distinguishes us from unenlightened city dwellers. But his brother-in-law farms his acreage; and my farming consists chiefly of keeping my mouth shut when the neighbors slice the grass in the hayfields or tear up the sod to plant corn or buckwheat.

"Have you finished harvesting?" he inquires, although obviously I have just come from nothing more rural than the composing-room. "Such as it is," I reply enigmatically, hoping not to reveal the fraudulence of my position in a huddle of impatient tobacco smokers. "How was the hay this year?" he asks politely. "Thin. It's run out so long it's hardly worth cutting now," I answer defensively. "Do you raise alfalfa?" he asks with the authority of a specialist. "No, mine's all timothy, June grass, clover with a fine underpinning of trefoil, which is a wonderful legume that seeds itself and spreads rapidly." "My brother-in-law sold enough alfalfa off my eight acres to make seven hundred dollars this season," he says triumphantly. A tall, rough, gravel-voiced assistant who has never been farther from the city than Van Cortlandt Park interposes sentimentally: "Boy, I'd love to go to sleep on some sweet-smelling hay right now." That remark makes him a fully accredited actor in our romantic fantasy. Meanwhile, the customers for cigarettes have piled up and are growing rebellious. But Mr. Johnson and I, being make-believe farmers, are calm and substantial citizens with property and we have great, national responsibilities on our hands.

23. Autumn begins. Sun rises at 5:47 and sets at 5:57. Night is black at 7:31. According to the almanac, the axis of the earth is today at right angles to the direction of the sun, and day and night are supposed to be of equal length, as the word "equinox" indicates. As a matter of fact, the day is ten minutes longer than the night which is a welcome token of the inefficiency of the solar system. Nothing is absolute, fortunately. But the sun is in a hurry away from us. We lose three minutes of daylight tomorrow, two minutes the next day, three on the third, and so on, in irregular units, rapidly. Next Sunday we shall lose daylight saving—the benevolent hoax that for six months gives us an illusion of brightness and gaiety. Today it is still light when I go to the theater and the occasion seems informal. After next Sunday it will be night, and the earnest season will have settled in for a long time.

There is an old wives' tale that predicts the "line storm" today or within a day or two. When the sun crosses the equator the heavens are supposed to open and drench us with cold rain. The weather bureau predicted rain for today and tomorrow—after consulting the instruments and weather map rather than the crystal ball. But today is cold and sparkling. The thermometer stands at 52° at 9 A.M., and for the first time since May I change into a woolen suit. There is no scientific basis for the traditional "line storm." But the great hurricane of 1938 occurred here on September twenty-first, and today a tropical hurricane is tearing savagely through Florida. People who believe in the "line storm" have enough evidence here to support their conviction. For a superstition has to be confirmed only about once in ten times to acquire the authority of an absolute fact to the human mind. People like to believe superstitions. It gives them the illusion of leaning on some great supernatural force, which they cannot control and to which they must submit. It seems to save them from the necessity of thinking for themselves.

24. At about breakfast time eight naval ships come up the river and tie up to buoys off Riverside Drive. The Navy always steams in with dignified austerity—all ships perfectly spaced and aligned, all etiquette meticulously observed. When a ship lets go her anchor, the flag comes down from the gaff and another flag goes up at the stern simultaneously. It probably takes four men to execute this ceremony accurately, but the Navy considers it worth-while, and so do I. In their neat blue-gray paint the ships look clean and handsome, especially in the sharp morning sunlight which gives everything the appearance of eagerness and vitality. Every day is a fresh beginning; the keen morning sunlight makes it so.

The task group consists of the carrier, *Mindoro*, and seven destroyers. The *Mindoro* takes more than an hour to turn around and put two cables to the buoy opposite my window—alternately stopping or reversing the propellers, and apparently using the gale churned up by airplanes on deck to guide her into position. After maneuvers off Bermuda this task force has come in for four days to give the men shore liberty and to receive the public on board during visiting hours.

Normally, the Hudson is a quiet interlude cutting through the jangle of the city. But the Navy overwhelms it with noise and bustle. Opening the window, I can hear the public address system of the *Mindoro* rasping out orders continuously, and the ship's bells striking the hours more crisply than the bells on merchant ships do. Within a half-hour the river is alive with barges racing to shore landings with crowds of men in blue uniforms and immaculate white caps. The admiral's barge glistens in the sunlight; the metal work shines and the varnish sparkles. The admiral's barge, which throws up a bulging wave, seems to regard the water disdainfully as something beneath the notice of a smart craft. At this time of year the Seventy-ninth Street yacht basin is generally lost in wistful dreams of the departed season. But it crackles with activity today. The Navy has brought a freshly painted landing float alongside, and small boats are coming and going in a steady stream, sailors with bundles are climbing ashore and the shore patrol is in command of Riverside Park. Sailors are perched on the railings, eying the civilians, and eating ice cream cones. A slatternly old crone, who is sitting on a bench and sewing, is exchanging banter with some of the sailors off the *Mindoro*. "She looks like a damned old scarecrow," the woman says good-humoredly in reference to the eccentric design of a carrier. The boys laugh. Addressing the other civilians on neighboring benches, the woman exclaims: "I don't know what the hell got into me to speak to them. I never speak to anybody. I guess it's because they are sailors."

Everyone is pleased to see sailors off the ships. After a tour of duty at sea, they have an enthusiasm for New York that is stimulating.

25. "Some of my friends tell me I ought to take up writing," a veteran sailor once remarked to me during the summer languors of a long voyage home. "Man, I've had a bookful of experiences! If I only knew how to write I could tell about them." Well, there was nothing to prevent him. He could hold a pencil in his hand, as the log-book bore witness, and he had literally oceans of time. But something was troubling him. He was thinking of writing as a trained profession. To many people who live but do not write, writing seems like a highly technical art or science like medicine, engineering, architecture, or the law.

It would be foolish to maintain that some people do not write better than others, or that professional writers do not improve their technique by practice. In the first instance, some have a natural aptitude for writing, like Shakespeare, to use the supreme example. In the second instance, everyone learns about writing by the simple process of writing more and more and by constantly thinking about writing—jotting down phrases that illustrate aspects of daily life, searching for the exact word (generally it is a verb) that catches some of the vitality of living. Observe how Sinclair

Lewis developed from a mediocre writer by discovering a subject—Main Street—and by crystallizing a point of view toward American society as in *Babbitt, Arrowsmith* and *Ann Vickers*. The craftsmanship of writing can be learned by constantly writing.

But to regard writing as a trained profession is to put secondary things first. For the only important thing a writer needs is a subject. Thousands of people who do not write have lively subjects already at hand and are thus better equipped to write than many writers. For writing is primarily an aspect of living. At its best, it is a vivid record of experience. What the reader hungers after is not accomplished craftsmanship nor even correct grammar but a frank report of the things a writer has done, seen, and thought. None of these things can be learned in the library or classroom. They have to be learned in the unsheltered world of living where men get slivers of the truth beaten into their heads. *Moby Dick* tumbled out of the wildness of the universe. It recorded the tragic awakening of a man brought up amid the snobberies of middle-class life and then let down into the damp, stinking squalor of the fo'c'sle. Melville's prodigious scholarship in that novel was incidental to a glimpse of the elemental fury that had possessed his soul.

26. "Style is the man himself," Buffon said. A man writes according to what he is. There is a kind of fatalism about it. Good writing expresses a man's experience, character and personality—particularly his capacity for passion. Since the shelves are packed with good writing in variegated styles, it would be myopic to celebrate one school of writing as the best. But let today's essay stand in praise of plain writing by men who have had experiences outside the library and who have written without literary flourishes—like Franklin, Thoreau, and O'Casey.

When Franklin wrote his incomparable *Autobiography* in a sound, modern idiom, the orotund Johnsonian style with its ponderous, balanced periods was fashionable. Since Johnson wrote it, he must have been that sort of man—heavy in accent, pompous in attitude. Steeped in books and learning, he wrote a style that became him. Living the life of a man of letters, he had no personal knowledge of the practical trades. But Franklin was a printer, which is at once a practical and very intelligent trade. And look how he wrote a plain, salty prose in modern sentences when even his democratic American contemporaries wrote in their best clothes with obtuse, formal phrases.

Although Thoreau was a bookish man, he was redeemed as a writer by his working knowledge of surveying, masonry, carpentry, and pencil-making, to say nothing of his romantic love for nature. He wrote sentences that had the strength and simplicity of journeyman building. To a large degree Emerson was Thoreau's spiritual teacher. Although their philosophy was similar, Emerson, the library workman, recognized that Thoreau, the outdoor handyman, expressed it in a bolder, more daring style that had an earthy foundation.

Or take the instance of Sean O'Casey, whose mastery of singing English amounts to genius. He dug ditches and worked on the docks before the world accepted him as a writer. In one passage in his autobiography he describes in whirling prose the agony of digging ditches. That passage, small as it is, is a contribution to human knowledge. Being a genius, O'Casey is a subject in himself, particularly since he fuses mysticism with knowledge. But here it is sufficient to point out that his experience as a laborer has bred in him contempt for pretentiousness. For he knows that pretentiousness in art discloses pretentiousness in the artist's mind; and that the fault to condemn is not false style but false humanity.

There is much that can be learned about writing. But it is not one of the learned professions. No one can teach a writer the primary essentials of subject and attitude. First of all, a writer needs something to write—not the art, but the life; not the words, but the experience. Given those things, anyone can "take up" writing.

27. Unilateral conversation with a nine-year-old girl on a calm, wide autumn day: "It would be a shame to go to school on a beautiful day like this," she says.

"Uh-huh."

"There ought to be a rule that there would be no school on beautiful days like on bad days. We don't go to school when it rains too hard or when there's too much snow. I think we ought to be outdoors on the good days. We ought to go to school only on the kind of punk days when it's cloudy or discouraging."

"Uh-huh."

"It would be easier on the teachers, wouldn't it? They wouldn't have to go to school so much."

"That's true."

"There ought to be a rule that we would only go to school when we want to. I would go now and then."

"Uh-huh."

28. In the pleasant coolness of a September evening, with Jupiter hanging in the sky over Eighth Avenue, the Columbus Circle forum is well attended tonight, under the benign supervision of policemen who are profoundly uninterested in what the speakers say. The policemen show good judgment. For the cradle of New York liberties rocks some pretty infantile discussions. Tonight there are four speakers, mounted on boxes and braced on one side by the American flag. One of the speakers is an old-timer who loves the authority of addressing a crowd and fancies himself as a wit. Tonight he is bandying personal insults with a drunk. The crowd is delighted; in fact, his crowd is the biggest and the most responsive in the Circle. Adjoining him is a morose meeting that listens stupidly to a thin, bespectacled young intellectual arguing about Soviet Russia with an earnest young Negro. The argument seems to be private. It is garnished on the edges by ill-tempered wrangling among the adult adolescents—"You ain't got no brains." "I got more brains than you got," etc. To the west stands another one of the regulars—a thin, dirty, bearded icono-clast who is discussing philosophy and the stars and the solar system, unhappily oblivious of Jupiter, which is burning with a clear flame above his left shoulder. A hobo ("My address is 24 Central Park") is screaming for independence on the adjoining soap box. "Don't take your hat off to anybody," he says. "If the boss offers ten dollars, demand twenty; he ain't doing nothing." The only hot argument is at a rump meeting a few feet away. It is about conflicting interpretations of the New Testament and it provokes fiercer difference of opinion than any of the other arguments. "All right, you take your circumcision and I'll take my baptism. Good-by!"—is the concluding shot in that exchange of hatreds about the doctrine of love. Although our Columbus Circle open-air meetings look picturesque they are the asylum of crackpots. They prove nothing much except that there is one man who loves the intoxication of public speaking to a hundred who have nothing to do but listen.

29. In comparison with the screen, the theater is poverty-stricken and chaotic. People in the theater live from one production to another. Most actors do not get one part a season; most of those who do are out of work again after a month. Nobody knows how most of them live. Although the theater is reckoned a glamorous profession, actors in the mass are a threadbare group of people, desperately hanging on to a gay illusion. As a way of earning a living, the theater is treacherous and cruel to most of its people and it seldom returns the love they have for it.

In these circumstances, many theater people naturally dream enviously of Hollywood, where employment on a contractual basis is more regular and salaries are high. Whatever their personal devotion may be, many theater people have no choice; they have to go where they can earn a living. For the screen is a genuine industry. It has long-term financing, a tangible product that can be shipped around the country, and a vast organization of outlets. Like soap and refrigerators, it fits into the industrial pattern of the age, and it can be administered on scientific business principles.

But big industry in art has one crushing and destructive infirmity—the dead weight of controls. Long-term finance likes safety and security and it feels uncomfortable in the presence of ideas. Hollywood's cowardly repudiation of its own writers under political pressure from a congressional committee is the stigmata of big industry in an art field. That is a stubborn, basic fact that cannot be altered, no matter how passionately the artists in Hollywood want to circumvent it. The bankers will not underwrite art that challenges the myths and folkways of the past, nor can they distinguish between an enemy of the state and a poet. As a group, bankers and industrialists have no capacity for sitting in judgment on an artist's ideas.

Although the theater is economically wretched, it is still free. It is not afraid of ideas and does not meekly submit to institutionalized morality. The freedom of the theater derives directly and perhaps solely from its poverty and anarchy. It is the last refuge of individuals. From the point of view of modern industry, that fact may be obsolete and chaotic, but it is the greatest single asset the theater has. The theater has no master except the public.

30. Farther up the hill, where the view is long, deep and capacious, lives the happiest man in our country neighborhood, and he knows it. In his middle sixties he has retired with his health and spirits intact, and, as he says, he has enough jobs on hand to keep him busy until he is a hundred. He is George Dahl, who began his career as a ship's engineer, and retired as company superintendent for the repair of ships in New York. He hunts and fishes; he raises a garden and looks after the flowers that bank the house. What he likes most is to tinker in his workshop a few yards uphill from the house, and he is one of the ablest tinkerers now extant in New York State. He can do anything. He can even make his own machine tools out of parts accumulated on the shelves of his shop. He has made a saw that cuts a true edge through planks four inches thick. He has just made a sander that can miter joints and also dress rough lumber. Alert to new preparations that come on the market he is forever discovering new glues and new wood fillers. He enjoys devising schemes for solving small problems in woodworking. Like a true mechanic he invariably spends more time in preparing for a job than in doing it. When it is done, it is done right. There are no mechanical flaws in his craftsmanship.

No wonder George Dahl approaches everything with a twinkling, amused expression. Of all the people I know he is sitting the prettiest, for he knows that he is having a good time. He is surrounded with things he has made—tables, cabinets, a porch, a grease-trap in the kitchen drain, an outdoor fireplace on a terrace; and his mind is wrestling with the things he is going to make when he has a few moments. Last year he built a tiny cottage in Florida where he can tinker all winter. Life is very congenial to Mr. Dahl.

OCTOBER

October

I N THE COLD of the midnight darkness, the song-birds streamed through the black sky last night on one stage of their panicky migration south. Standing under the fiery heavens I could hear an occasional bird note falling out of the darkness, for the migrating birds talk to each other—possibly to keep together as they rush down the cooling latitudes. No one knows why they go south on these annual journeys that are fatal to millions of them. It is not solely the cold: many of them left in July when we were still suffering from the heat, and there will be many warm weeks yet before the winter is icy. For equally inexplicable reasons some of the migratory birds will remain all winter. There are always song sparrows, meadowlarks, myrtle warblers, and a few robins that stay with us through the ice and blizzards. Sometimes a mockingbird audaciously reverses the process by coming north for the winter. Nor is it solely the food supply that sends the birds south, for millions leave when the food supply is still abundant; and for several species, the food supply is never completely exhausted. Is it the sunlight? But again, many of them go when the sun is still in the north, and some remain when the sun has dwindled towards the south. There is a theory that the migratory birds repeat every year the history of their race during the glacial epoch. During the glacial period the birds were driven south by the ice; in consequence, it is suggested that this epochal rhythm still lives in their annual migration, though I can hardly believe it.

But the cold, still nights of the autumn bring them south in stupendous numbers on a long, exhausting, dangerous journey. Some of them will cross the Gulf of Mexico into South America in one headlong leap, or will go down through the islands. This morning the woods and thickets are full of newly arrived transients from the north country. I see a stubby winter wren in a brush-heap. Hermit thrushes are feeding among the leaves and white-throated sparrows in the raspberry bushes. Search the tree-tops and you will find warblers and vireos darting in and out of the leafy branches. I see the first ruby-crowned kinglet of the autumn. Most of the birds are silent; their season is over and they are caught unhappily in the grip of an elemental passion that is pulling them down the curve of the earth. Being in a hurry they have little to say. Tonight most of them will take off again on another leg of this strange odyssey. Tomorrow another group of song-birds will probably rest here for the day.

2. The panic is on. Before I get out of bed I hear the white-throated sparrows conversing. They have arrived during the night, and the rose garden is full of them. Twenty-five or thirty sparrows—most of them white-throats—leap into the hedge when I step into the garden. All the migratory birds seem excited, like travelers refreshing themselves for the next part of the journey. The lilac hedge is full of white-throated, song, field and chipping sparrows; and myrtle warblers are flitting through the locusts. There is a red-breasted nuthatch in the rock maple. The thirty-acre lot has just been plowed and harrowed in preparation for a crop of wheat that will be sowed tomorrow. There must be five hundred birds running over the newly turned sod, and a quarter of them are pipits, freshly arrived from the far north, perhaps from the Arctic. In the panic of the fall migration they rest where they alight and take food where they find it; and as the sun comes up, they run lightly over the damp furrows, looking for the nourishment that will sustain them on their next flight. The field has been plowed only a week. How do they find it so quickly and recognize it as the freshly turned ground that they need? For there are no pipits in the adjacent woods and fields.

Nearly every year people in our village tell each other that the autumn foliage has never been so gorgeous. Nearly every year that neighborly remark seems to me to be true. Nature is massing the colors with a careless richness that startles and awes everyone who lives in the country—pinkish maple leaves, bronze on the ash trees and gold on the lindens and hickories. On this hill we are heaped around with gold. But there are towers of gold on Cheese Hill and Pisgah and flakes of gold strewn through the dooryard. Most of the year's work is finished in the country. The treasure

that surrounds us today is priceless. Everyone with eyes is as rich
as the richest man in town.

3. Fall migration of the storm door. Although the earth has
four seasons, we have two—both of them decisive. When the
storm door comes off in May, the world indoors and the world
outdoors have begun to flow together in a triumphant flood of
warmth and brightness. The removal of the storm door indicates
that we are joyfully joining it. When I lug it out of the shop in
the autumn and twist the rusty-headed screws into their familiar
holes, we have already begun to withdraw from the fields and hills
and to restore the house to its primitive use as shelter against the
wind and cold. This is a decision we always dislike to make because it is final. There are days in September when the door would
be useful, although the world outdoors still seems to be too hospitable to be shut out deliberately. But a time comes when everyone agrees that the summer has finally slipped away over the
mountains to the south and the winter is building up behind
Cheese Hill. Last night the wind slapped the woodbine against
the rear walls of the house and sang in the throats of the chimneys. The thermometer touches 33° this morning. Although the
sunlight is generous, the mercury is reluctant to rise. At breakfast
time about one hundred crows settle with composure to feed in
the Alger lot. When crows fly in huge flocks and boldly come near
the house, we can tell them from a handsaw and we know what
time of year it is. Like an intelligent husbandman, I put the lawn
furniture in the garage, remove the screen doors and hang the
storm door on the rear entrance to the kitchen. A heavy object,
made of matched fir, it blocks the window in the kitchen door,
darkening the room and shutting off the view up the Preston
Hollow valley. It is solid and blank, unlovely but firm in its resistance to the weather. Now we are moving in a smaller, gloomier
orbit. This is one of the two most decisive days of the year.

4. Rosh Hashana, or the beginning of the Jewish New Year.
Today and tomorrow the Orthodox Jews, refraining from work,
pray in the synagogues. The Jewish New Year begins with the new
moon in the autumn in accordance with the ancient agricultural

origin of most Jewish festivals. Beginning with the sounding of the Shofar, or ritual horn, at sundown on New Year's Eve, Rosh Hashana opens ten days of penance and ends with Yom Kippur, the holiest Jewish day of the year. On Rosh Hashana all the inhabitants of the earth pass before God in judgment. They are divided into three classes—the wicked, who are blotted out of the book of the living, the righteous, who are sealed in the book of the living, and the middle group, who now have ten days in which to repent. The traditional greeting on this day is, "Mayest thou be inscribed for a good year." Prayers are held in the synagogues for the recognition of God's power, restoration of the Jewish state (now accomplished), the reward of the righteous, the punishment of the wicked, and for universal theocracy.

Rosh Hashana, coming at the harvest time, is a day for feasting. "Eat the fat and drink the sweet," said Ezra. Pumpkins, leeks, carrots, beets and grapes were traditionally regarded as good omens when eaten on this day. In modern times grapes, fruits and honey are the usual festival foods.

The ten High Holy Days begin today and will be reverently observed throughout the city. Today the garment and furriers' districts are as deserted as if this were Sunday, and a large part of the city's business stops. Since Reformed Jews observe Rosh Hashana for only one day, there will be a little more activity in New York tomorrow; but the city will not resume full operation until the day after tomorrow when all Jews will be able to return to work. May all of us, non-Jew as well as Jew, be inscribed today in the book of the living for a good year!

5. It would be easy to be sure of basic principles if our political choices were simple. If we had to choose between holiness and evil, we would all be on one side, and the future would be serene and golden. But political decisions are by their nature the result of compromises between people of different minds and interests. No one is thoroughly satisfied because everyone has to yield something he wants. In the mighty struggle between democracy and Stalinism, the choice of sides would be easy if one or the other were perfect of its kind. If American democracy in practice matched its idealism—if there were not millions of second-class Americans, disenfranchised by prejudice and custom, if justice

were the same for all, if workers could always find work when they need it, if every family had a house, if university education were free to all who can make use of it, if the choice of candidates for the highest office represented the free choice of the people, if all the press were honest and omniscient and sincerely dedicated to the people—if our democracy represented in practice what we believe, the choice would be easy and unanimous. And if in foreign affairs we could be indifferent to governments and politics and pour out food and goods to people without discrimination, we might not violate our own codes of ethics by shoring up governments we really despise. If the world were composed exclusively of saints and sinners we could live in the spirit of our dreams. But the world is broken and hungry, and our imperfect democracy loses a little more faith and a little more idealism the further it travels from home. The great dream looks soiled in the noisy, cluttered streets of the great cities and it is thoroughly bespattered abroad. The choice is not between holiness and evil. It is between good will that blunders and a fanatical conspiracy for power.

6. In the final analysis there are only two sides—right and wrong. All the other divisions are ambiguous and confusing. Republican and Democratic, Socialist and Communist, Protestant and Catholic—these are not opposite sides of anything, and I could not reject any of them or give to any of them my complete devotion or loyalty. These divisions are not real. You have to argue about them or summon historical, political, or economic evidence to show how they differ. In point of fact, I do not believe that they do differ. But right and wrong differ radically. You and I know in our bones that they do.

Talk to the people, hear their evidence, investigate the trouble personally; then you will know what to do. The troubles may be superficial and the divisions unreal. Probably they are not as serious as we had been imagining. There is more time than we had supposed.

7. World Series begins. Although the business of the city continues without interruption, the opening game at the Yankee Stadium supplies a sort of taut, exciting counterpoint. Every pitch

in the ball park instantaneously echoes through the city. No one
in our office is specifically listening to the broadcast of the game,
but word passes at intervals from desk to desk that the score is
"o to o at the end of the fourth," or whatever the inning may be;
and everyone lets out a whistle of approval. There are only a few
customers in the barbershop in the Statler Hotel, and most of the
barbers are crouched over a radio set in the corner. While he is
cutting my hair, Harry is listening to the broadcast. "A pitchers'
battle," he keeps muttering in awe and wonder as the game goes
through the seventh and eighth innings without a score. Returning to the office, I walk up Seventh Avenue through the garment
district. It looks normal; the streets are choked with enormous
trucks; the curbs are blocked with trucks loading merchandise, and
the sidewalks clatter with the metal wheels of the primitive hand-
carts in which garments are transported from factory to factory.
As usual, the garment district is pandemonium, sharpened today
by the shattering stutter of riveting in a new loft building. But
suddenly a shout of triumph drowns the other sounds. "Heinrichs
gets a homer," the loaders of a truck at Fortieth Street yell, stopping work and pounding each other on the back. For thirty sec-
onds or so, everything seems to stop as the word passes swiftly
to people on the sidewalk, the traffic cop in Seventh Avenue and
the drivers of the trucks. There is a moment of mass jubilation.
Then the garment district settles back to its normal, mechanical
work and confusion; but no doubt refreshed by the fact that a
brilliant baseball game has been won in the last half of the ninth
inning by the only smashing hit of the afternoon. The spirit of
the city, as well as of the entire nation, has been lifted by a fast
baseball game played with great skill and drive by two excellent
baseball teams. All sorts of Americans everywhere are today
united in their admiration of a fine game.

8. Drawn by the celestial magnetism of the sun, everything
leans toward the south. The myrtle warblers have reached Riverside Park. Resting between two stages of their long journey, they
busily search along the limbs of the plane and pin oak trees, oblivious of the house sparrows and starlings that regularly inhabit
this city greenery.

No one notices the yellow-spotted myrtle warblers, although

their dry "Cheep" constantly penetrates the muggy river air. But everyone notices the white two-masted schooner, *Constellation*, out of Grand Rapids, which is tied up in the yacht basin in the course of a long voyage down the coast through the islands to South America, thence through the canal and up the west coast to Alaska. She is the stoutest seaboat we have had this season— ample in the beam and solidly settled into the water. Tenderly cared for by the lucky people who are sailing her, she is shipshape in Bristol fashion—clean, tidy, the gear neatly stowed away, the sails smoothly furled and protected against the city grime with spotless khaki covers. Enviously gaped at by a throng of gawky city dwellers, the people on board have no privacy above decks. Every move they make is silently studied by fifty pairs of hungry eyes. They could hardly have less privacy in a show window. Standing with one foot on the string-piece, some of the bolder city dreamers engage them in conversation—ask questions about the ship and the voyage and listen open-mouthed to the saga of the *Constellation's* rough crossing of the Bay of Fundy in a blow and through four massive tide changes. The *Constellation* has some business ashore. A shy messenger girl delivers a telegram. There is a telephone call in the yacht basin shack, and the attendant bellows: "*Constellation*, ahoy!" through the megaphone. But the meeting of the ship and the city is meager. Nothing is really exchanged. To those who are staring at the *Constellation* in a sort of melancholy reverie, New York seems less and less real and desirable, like some horrible accident that can never be repaired. But the *Constellation* looks substantial, sensible, beautiful, free, poised, and confident. Nothing else that is in sight from the pier looks as if it had such a happy future.

9. Since he is eighty-seven years of age, his step is not so firm as it used to be. A tall man with a big frame, Mr. Kartevold has to look to see where he is going. Perhaps the air is thinner so close to the summit of the years. But he is clean, bright, intellectually restless, and shining with friendliness. Now he spends only about four hours a day at the watch and jewelry shop that he founded over sixty years ago. Having time on his hands he is reviewing his life, trying to discover the truth about it. On the table of his living room he has laid out some of the documents of his long

career—letters written in Norwegian to his sister in Norway in 1881, letters received from Norway, a pamphlet concerning his father, his diaries back to the time when he first came to America to work for six dollars a week in the watch business, and most vital of all, his philosophy. He is a pantheist. He loves everything that grows.

Although his business is watchmaking, he has long been a student of thought. At various periods in his career he has studied Herbert Spencer, Robert Ingersoll, Henry Ward Beecher, and Norwegian thinkers whose names are unfamiliar to me. He is not a theatergoer. But two plays that he read in Norwegian have been the most profound influences on his intellectual life. Björnstjerne Björnson's *The Bankruptcy* helped him to understand his father and prompted him to send money home from America to lift the mortgages from his father's property and to bring his brothers and sisters to America. Henrik Ibsen's *When We Dead Awaken* changed his whole life. "It was my life," he says. "Ibsen was writing about me." Suddenly he realized that he had been foolishly in love with clocks and watches, which are mechanical and sterile things. That angry play was his resurrection. He married and was blessed with children. He had been a melancholy youth, but "joy" is a word that is now very conspicuous in his vocabulary. When the whole family is assembled, usually in the summer, it numbers ten—his wife, three daughters, two sons-in-law and three grandchildren in addition to himself. He can hardly believe that all these good things have happened to him. Surrounded with the records of his lifetime and the records of his thoughts, he is now trying to find out how it all happened.

10. In China this day is known as "the double ten" (tenth day of the tenth month) and is celebrated as the beginning of the revolution against the Manchu dynasty in 1911. As a result of the revolutionary teaching of Sun Yat-sen, an inspiring idealist, China was rumbling with discontent against the inflexible, doctrinaire rule of the Manchus. On October tenth, a mutiny broke out among troops in Wuchang, who seized the Wuchang mint and the arsenal. Simultaneously, there was a rebellion among the stockholders of a proposed railroad in Szechwan. Cities everywhere began to declare against the old imperial government. On

February 12, 1912, the Manchu emperor abdicated, and General Yuan Sheh-k'ai became head of the provisional government and China became technically a republic.

Although the Manchu dynasty was destroyed, China has never been able to establish the humane and progressive government that Sun Yat-sen dreamed about and planned with considerable concreteness. For China is too old to change rapidly in any direction. Steeped in an ancient tradition of family loyalties, composed principally of peasants who devote most of their energy to the exhausting labor of raising their own food and to evading as much as possible the intrusion of predatory government officials, China has a ponderous momentum that can hardly be changed; and the momentum leads in the direction of endless repetitions of the past. Since the past has been heavily laden with work, suffering, ignorance and oppression, the resistance to change is tragic. Enlightened Chinese with modern and progressive ideas are hardly more than a flimsy veneer on the massive structure of the peasantry; and the whole life of the peasantry is bound round with the immutable turn of the seasons across the rice fields and villages.

The life of the peasantry is bondage; but the great and heartening paradox of China is that the peasants are not bondsmen. They are sharp-witted individuals—ingenious, industrious, alert, strong, humorous, and sociable. They have the mettlesome character of indomitable people who are wholly alive. Westerners are impatient, and cannot wait until the Chinese conform to one or another of the Western political patterns. But none of these patterns fits the Chinese, who hardly have time enough between sunrise and sunset to look up from the cold muck of their rice-paddies. They will not need the ballot for many years. Their needs are more basic—roads, transportation, improved seeds, education. Political revolutions are too superficial to get to the great heart of Chinese life.

11. For the past few days, there has been sickness in our family. Quite apart from the anxiety and the physical and mental discomfort involved, I have been thinking of the petty personal inconvenience. Like ripples in a pool it extends in ever widening concentric circles—inconveniencing those close by first, then inconveniencing secondary people and finally upsetting the routine

of the social system. The sickness of one person is visited on people who are several stages removed.

For society is based on the assumption that people in general are in good health. The household routine, the office and plant routine, and particularly the routine of the farm, where animals are dependent upon people, are all based on the assumption that good health is normal and that everyone will be able to discharge his daily obligations. Can we go one step further? In addition to good health, are good intelligence and good conduct normal also? And are the evil and savagery of the world abnormal? In other words, is the constructive way of life the normal standard? Maybe we had better think about this theory a little longer—for two or three centuries, at least.

12. After a voyage of seventy days in the *Santa Maria*, Columbus sighted land on the evening of October 11, 1492, and on the next day landed on what is now known as Watling's Island. The *Santa Maria* was about ninety feet long and twenty in the beam, and was decked over. Columbus had hoped to sail west to Japan and was looking for a short route to the wealthy East Indies, rich in gold and spices. "Gold is excellent; gold is treasure, and he that possesses it does all that he wishes to in this world, and succeeds in helping souls into paradise," Columbus believed, and he was looking for a short way to get it. When he explored the Bahamas on the first voyage, discovering what are now Santa Maria, Haiti, and Cuba, he thought he had, indeed, found the shortest and most direct route to the East, although he never located the Great Khan, to whom he had a letter from Ferdinand and Isabella. Cuba he mistook for the Asiatic mainland. He made four voyages through the islands, touching the mainland of South America at Trinidad and the Bay of Honduras, but he never realized that he had discovered a new continent. John Cabot landed on the mainland two years before Columbus got west of the islands. Columbus died in poverty after eighteen months of sickness at Valladolid in northern Spain on May 20, 1506.

What Columbus had discovered was not regarded as a new continent for many years. To the other voyagers, of whom there were many, it seemed to be rather an interminable, incomprehensible barrier to the East. After sailing along the northern coast of South

America in 1501, Amerigo Vespucci tentatively remarked that it "may be called a new world since our ancestors had no knowledge of it." In 1519 Magellan found a way around it and was the first man to learn the astounding distance to the East Indies that still had to be sailed. But knowledge that a new continent had been discovered permeated very slowly into the mind of the world, and for more than a century after Columbus' first voyage, explorers were still trying to find an open strait around North America to the more glamorous and luxurious treasures of the East.

13. Yom Kippur, or the Jewish Day of Atonement, which is the holiest day in the Jewish year. The fast began at sundown yesterday and extends until sundown today. All Jews who have not renounced their faith attend the synagogue services on Yom Kippur: "For whatsoever soul it be that shall not be afflicted on that same day: he shall be cut off from his people."

To "atone" means to become "at one." Religious atonement assumes that there is a natural relation between God and man, that man has broken it by ungodlike behavior and that it can be restored by communion between God and man. On Yom Kippur the Jews observe, either literally or symbolically, the laws set down in Leviticus and Numbers: forming a holy convocation, afflicting their souls, making offerings to God. Leviticus provides a very precise ceremony that includes entering the holy of holies and transferring the iniquities of men to a sacrificial goat who is sent into the wilderness, bearing with him the sins of mankind for the year. (This is the origin of the word "scapegoat.")

"And it shall be a statute for ever unto you," says Leviticus. "Ye shall afflict your souls and shall do no manner of work, the home-born or the stranger that sojourneth among you: for on this day shall atonement be made for you, to cleanse you: from all your sins shall ye be clean before Jehovah. And this shall be an everlasting statute unto you, to make atonement for the children of Israel because of all their sins once in the year." "In the day of atonement shall ye send abroad the trumpet throughout all your land."

These laws were written by the prophets for an agrarian people who cultivated the fields and tended their flocks and herds and lived in the open halls of nature. But the holiest of the laws are still faithfully observed in the brick and steel fortress of New

York which has all but forgotten the lore of the fields. The commerce of the city is rigidly planned on a precise schedule of hours and days, and throughout the year people adhere to it scrupulously. Most religions have complacently adjusted their calendars to the work schedule of the profane world, putting the day's work first. But on Yom Kippur one-fifth of the population of New York is absent from work, and the subways and business districts are strangely empty. In the twentieth century in the heart of a callous city the Jews obey the everlasting statute of the ancient prophets and on the Day of Atonement make their peace with God.

14. Outward bound! On an ebb tide she is sliding down the river at eight or ten knots, already sure of herself and of where she is going. With the sun in the west, the light pours at an angle around her hull and housing and seems to separate her from the shore, the Weehawken cliffs, the elevator warehouses, apartment buildings, church spires, and the whole apparatus of land. There is a lively southwest breeze. It cuts the brown smoke sharply from her single funnel and spreads it lightly over the steel-blue river. At the speed she has already picked up she is throwing up a vigorous white bow wave and little geysers of white water along her black hull and she leaves a column of confused white water astern. A small American flag flutters at the gaff. On the foremost yard she carries the national colors of Brazil, where spring is just beginning. The pilot, in civilian clothes with a felt hat, stands in the port wing of the bridge, and the captain, in uniform with a white cap, stands beside him. They are both looking straight ahead, no doubt watching the Forty-second Street ferries that cross the channel at frequent intervals at the rush hour. Once a white burst of steam tears out of her whistle, followed by a detached bellow of deep sound. For she intends to pass on the portside of a tug which might cross her course. The tug answers with a sullen blast and straightens upriver.

At the speed the outward bound vessel is traveling, she will be free of the land in another forty minutes. After slipping past the Forty-second Street–Weehawken ferries, she must steam clear of the Hoboken ferries, which are packed at this hour with New Jersey commuters, and the ponderous Staten Island ferries, which are running on their busiest afternoon schedule and keep crossing the channel. But at eight or ten knots a blue-water vessel ought to be through the channel and the Narrows before the steward is ready to serve dinner in the saloon. After threading the Narrows she will steam into livelier water that will begin to slap the hull, and the cold of the open ocean will start pouring across the bridge and through the scuttles. She will approach the Ambrose Lightship slowly and will ring off the engines for a few minutes while the pilot climbs down the ladder and jumps into the bobbing pilot boat. When he is clear she will give him a blast on the whistle. Signaling for the engines again she will plunge into the grand loneliness of the sea and settle down happily on the long south course to the green magnificence of Brazil.

15.

Taxi driver: "This is good weather for your health."

Myself: "It sure is a wonderful day. I'm on my way to the country, which makes me feel very happy."

Taxi driver: "Going to see all those colors? Those colors are worth a million dollars. I wish someone would drive me up to Connecticut. You know that country in New England? I'd kiss the man who would drive me up there today."

These breezy conversations about the country have to be taken with a grain of salt. They seem to suggest a deep, nostalgic longing for the country. But most of the citizens of New York, I fancy, are very happy to be where they are. No matter how meager their lives may be, they acquire a sense of importance from living in New York and they regard themselves as distinguished Americans on that account. Although they may be routine clerks, working in obscure offices and living in stale flats, they take personal credit for the wonders of New York—the Empire State Building, Rockefeller Plaza, the giant forest of skyscrapers downtown, Broadway, and the water front where the royal liners of the world come and go every week. They happily ignore the ignoble aspects of New York—the dirty streets (dirtier than the streets of any major city in the world), the broken-down school system, the ancient, slatternly city hospitals, the inhuman subways that haul human livestock as most transportation systems haul freight. Since New York is the largest city in the world, most New Yorkers regard themselves as important people. The aura of a great city shines through them and sustains them. Longing for the country is largely city folklore. Most New Yorkers feel restless and insecure outside the city.

16. *"John Brown's body lies a-mouldering in the grave,*
John Brown's body lies a-mouldering in the grave,
John Brown's body lies a-mouldering in the grave,
But his soul goes marching on.

"Glory, glory, halleluia,
Glory, glory, halleluia,
Glory, glory, halleluia,
His soul goes marching on."

Most conservative men were ashamed of John Brown when, on this day in 1859, he and eighteen others recklessly attacked the United States arsenal at Harper's Ferry, Va., captured it and took sixty leading citizens of the community as hostages. Conservative people regarded this wild insurrection as madness. From a rational point of view it was. The slave insurrection that Pottawatomie Brown hoped to foment did not take place. After two days of siege, the United States Marines, commanded by Captain Robert E. Lee, of the U. S. Army, took Brown and his men prisoner. Brown was jailed at Charlestown, Va., convicted of "treason, and conspiring and advising with slaves and other rebels, and murder in the first degree," and was hanged on December second. From the practical point of view the insurrection was a disastrous failure.

But as the verses above indicate, John Brown is now a folklore hero, mentioned in song every day by thousands of people who may not know exactly what he did. And his fierce, quixotic blow for the ending of slavery, together with the artless nobility of his character, won the respect of many of his adversaries. He was a simple man—so simple, in fact, that he believed in direct action for the moral cause to which he was spiritually committed. "These men are all talk," he said after attending an antislavery convention. "What we need is action—action!" He took it. His motives were upright. He acted from principle. Reasonable men equivocated. The State was cautious. The churches were prudent. But John Brown and a handful of adherents struck a blow for a principle and awoke the nation. Since he was a religious man he put on the armament of the Lord. The logic and dismay of the conservative people who repudiated him do not matter much now. For John Brown's soul goes marching on.

17. Soon after sunrise I am awakened by a banging on the screen of the little window at the head of my bed in the country. It is a bluebird vainly trying to take a hornet that is on the inside of the screen. I don't suppose I have ever seen a bluebird so close—only a foot away. His red breast is paler than in the spring, and the blue on his back is lighter. But his eyes are bright and his attitude is alert and belligerent.

In the spring we feel happy to have a pair of bluebirds modestly nesting in the old box in the locust tree. There have been seasons when the box has been empty, for every now and then the race of bluebirds is decimated by late blizzards. But in September bluebirds begin to gather in companionable flocks. Today there must be more than a hundred of them—old and immature birds—dancing through the trees around the house. There are bluebirds everywhere—on the ridge of the garage, on the twigs near the bluebird box, on the telephone wires, in the roadside bushes, and all around the house. During the nesting season they never seem to use the bird bath, which is probably too near the house for such quiet birds. But today they besiege the bird bath. Five of them stand on the edge of it at one time. Two of them bathe in it together enthusiastically. They are so numerous, active and light-winged, that they look superficially like a scattering of falling leaves. In the autumn when they no longer have secrets to hide, bluebirds are gay and sociable.

Some other birds have joined their company. A robin, who looks clumsy in comparison, is traveling with them. A song sparrow tries to keep up with them, although he seems ground-borne rather than tree-borne. A myrtle warbler, small and light, is as swift and buoyant as the bluebirds. He, too, is a handsome bird, with yellow on the sides of the breast, a yellow spot on the base of the tail and white tips on the tail. He can follow them anywhere. But the bluebirds have taken possession. They chatter, tumble through the landscape and whirl down from the tree branches like blue leaves. They are never so light-hearted as in the early autumn just before they turn south.

18. "Canst thou bind the sweet influences of Pleiades, or loose the bands of Orion?"

Not in the summer, when the Pleiades and Orion are invisible or visible just before sunrise when most of us are not star-gazing. But that sparkling cluster of diamonds, which is Pleiades, is now high in the east at eleven o'clock, and the mighty constellation of Orion is boldly flung across the eastern horizon. The pleasant summer sky has trickled away down the west. Vega, which used to be overhead in the evening, now guards the northwest with a beautiful beam of light, but Arcturus and the Corona have dropped over the mountain wall. The Great Dipper, which stretched wide and grand across the sky all summer, now snuggles low on the northern hills. Cassiopeia, rocking her chair on the star dust of the Milky Way, is directly overhead, having climbed high since August. Sirius, the brightest beacon in the heavens, does not clear the horizon until nearly one o'clock. It will be a month before we can lie in the light of Sirius in the evening. But the winter sky, which is more vivid than the summer sky, is beginning to stretch its glittering garment over the earth. Castor and Pollux, the heavenly twins, are back. Rigel has returned. Capella sparkles on the rim of the Milky Way. And Aldebaran, that mighty pillar of red fire, is glowing in the constellation of Taurus. The sweet influences of Pleiades have been unbound indeed, and the bands of Orion have been loosened by the autumn night. As the earth swings away from the sun, the richly jeweled sky of the winter fills the vast cavern of the night with splendor. The less light there is in our corner of the earth, the more light there is in heaven.

19. There is a wild clamor in the sky. The geese are flying south in search of marshes free of ice all winter. This is the most ancient and the most dramatic of the portents—the long, wriggling V spreading back from the leader and the noisy conversation among excited birds. I have seen enemy planes flying this bold formation. But the Japanese were more grimly disciplined than the geese, who keep breaking formation and shifting restlessly from one leg of the V to the other. They have accepted a leader, but they have not renounced their individuality. There are forty-

nine geese in one of the flights that go over at breakfast time. In spite of central heating, paved roads and motorized snowplows, the geese desert the north when the frost settles on the lakes and travel the air routes laid out by their ancestors to the Gulf—just high enough to clear the mountains that for centuries have blocked the south. To judge by this morning's weather map, the geese are running ahead of a cold snap that is moving down from Canada.

Most of the leaves have fallen now, and make a crisp, deep, aromatic carpet in the woods. On the neighboring hills we can see houses that have been hidden by trees for several months. It is as though we were all coming out of hiding and drawing near to establish a visible community for comfort during the bleak savagery of the winter. Some of the trees still cling to their leaves— notably the beeches, which are pale yellow, and the aspens, which pile their gold along the margins of the woods. The birds are scarce; but the partridges, perhaps alarmed by the hunters, are nervous and appear to be more numerous than in the summer. The slate-colored juncos are trickling back. A northern shrike— the butcher bird—has moved into the neighborhood. Perhaps that is why the birds are so scarce in the house-lot. For the shrike is a wanton killer who murders small birds for the ecstasy of slaughter. He casts the dark shadow of death over any community he in- habits. Overhead the honking geese are uttering the poetry of the seasons. But the solitary shrike on the maple top has brought us the hooked beak, the razory claw and the rapacious heart of natural evil—rousing us from the sweet drug of wistful dreaming.

20. Just before Indian Summer is due to set in, Maurice Schwartz annually blows the dust out of the Yiddish Art Theatre in Second Avenue and opens for business. Not many young people speak Yiddish in New York today. Since the immigration quotas were established in the first quarter of this century, fewer Yiddish-speaking people have entered the country. Most of the New Yorkers who understand Yiddish are in or approaching middle age now, and most of them speak English most of the time. Many of the actors in the Yiddish Art Theatre appear on the English-speaking stage, where their accent is virtually indistinguishable from the accent of native-born actors. And the sociable audi-

ences that loyally support Mr. Schwartz's theater speak English
to each other before the play opens and between acts. Since our
Jews are completely American, and since the young ones scornfully
prefer Broadway, there is no need for Yiddish theaters in this community. They have dwindled in numbers to two or three. The
patrons of the Yiddish Art Theatre are loyal to a tradition, but
the tradition is empty. It does not represent a need.

But New York would be the poorer without it. For the Yiddish
Art Theatre preserves in our midst some of the customs and attitudes of the old European and Russian theaters. It is an institution with cultural integrity. It opens its doors hospitably to a
homogeneous group of people who want to be together to have
their memories stirred and their faith awakened or confirmed. The
plays are not classics. But they have a classical look and sound—
flowing costumes of the Middle Ages, beards, religious ceremonies,
plaintive music, romantic scenery. The acting is rich, wide and
imposing. The voices are musical. The staging is flamboyant. Since
the tradition is now slightly factitious, the flowing style is more
a habit than a conviction. Mr. Schwartz is going through the motions of an art that is no longer pertinent. The art has a grandiose
surface, but no content. For a few more years he will draw into
his open-hearted theater audiences who have warm and bright
memories of their native lands, and who like to assemble now
and then to meet old friends. But the glorious days of Yiddish
culture are over in this country. Second Avenue is only a little
cozier than Riverside Drive.

21. This is the first item I have written on a new table that I
have built to my own specifications. It replaces one of a similar
model which for ten years has annoyed me by jiggling. The new
one has red oak legs, which are solid; the top and side pieces are
cherry. Both woods are beautiful. The oak has a pinkish tinge and
a straight grain. The cherry, which I sanded day after day monoto-
nously, has whorls, mottled areas, eyes, and wave designs in the
grain, more daring and imaginative than anything a human artist
could create. This is the most inviting and convenient table I have
ever had; and I look back with gratitude on the unconscionably
long period I devoted to bringing it into existence out of rough
lumber.

But it stands here as a monument to something else: to a basic
lack of mechanical dexterity. Nothing puzzles me so much as the
fact that I cannot do a sound professional job in woodworking.
Although I have been pottering around with wood for years I
have never yet done a first-rate job. This is the more puzzling
because by experience and observation I know the hazards of
amateur work—imperfect joints and corners that are not exactly
square—and I also know that a basic mistake has to be carried all
through the construction and can never be corrected. One rotten
apple infects the whole barrel. Since I have learned these primary
truths of craftsmanship, I took meticulous pains on this occasion
to make everything accurate and square. Aware also of my temperamental deficiencies, I guarded against my own weaknesses by
stopping work whenever I was tired and never going to work when
I was not fresh and did not know exactly what I was doing.

In the making of a table there comes the great critical moment
when all the parts have to be put together—the side pieces pegged
and glued into the legs, the top pieces doweled and glued together
and fastened to the frame. This is the operation that tests the
quality of all the preliminary work. Now you discover whether or
not you have done what you thought you were doing. Alas, this
table is only microscopically better than its bungled predecessors.
It is square; even the drawer, laboriously and crudely dove-tailed,
is true. But there is only one perfect joint in the whole job. The
mark of the bumbling amateur is scrawled over every fitting. I can
never pass the pitiless judgment of a piece of wood.

Don't tell me that it is because I am not a trained artisan and
have never learned the techniques of handicraft. I know that, and
do not regard it as decisive. Don't tell me that I lack tools; I have
a number of good tools, some of them superior to the tools used
by celebrated artisans a century ago. No, this knack for imperfec-
tion is more basic than that, and I confess, apart from my disappointment, I do not understand it. All I know is that I cannot
work with the easy mastery of Bill Palmer, Ad Showers, George
Dahl, all of whom can do fine wood work without having to fret
about it. They have the magic dexterity—not because they have
learned it but because it was born in them. Shoemaker, stick to
your last. Writer, stick to your pen. That is practical and sensible.
These imperfect joints on the top of this writing table are going
to be under my eyes for years—a constant, baleful reminder of

mechanical incompetence. Why is it? I shall never know. More than that: no one else knows.

22. Toward stage comedians people are inclined to have a slightly patronizing air. "Yes, he is amusing!" they say grudgingly as though they were ashamed to admit it. Far from being a pardonable foible, the art of low comedy is a triumphant creation and the exuberant mountebanks who set the audiences to roaring are masters of make-believe. They rank with writers, painters and composers as imaginative creators who are not earth-bound but free spirits and geniuses.

"Life is a tragedy for those who feel, a comedy for those who think," said Horace Walpole. Yield yourself freely to the mindlessness of the universe and you surrender yourself to anguish and loneliness, for the universe is not interested in you. "Who, if I were to cry out, would hear me among the angelic orders?" asked Rainer Maria Rilke. The universe swallows up your cries and wheels on through space, obeying the inhuman orders of the spheres. Ultimately, you die, which is the supreme tragedy because everything that is you slips mockingly away and all that you have tried to become is wasted. Life has no form if you submit to it emotionally. But you can create a form and build a design with the tools of the mind. You become the captain of your soul by thinking. You can irradiate the blackness of the universe with the shining light of thought and knowledge.

The clowns are triumphant, too. Comedy is ugliness without pain. The clowns translate the ugliness of life into the fantasy of roaring sound and exultant motion—dancing and shouting like mischievous supermen. They have more gusto than other people have. They can run and sing, turn handsprings, tumble and bellow, and distort the ordinary materials of life into something rich and merry. By excessive skill and enthusiasm they can conquer like poets and music-makers. Bless them! They are the royal minstrels—the antic comics, the skipping fools, the masters of the revels. For an hour or two in the evening they push back the walls of the universe.

23. The last of the coastwise liners has come in from her last
voyage and concluded an interesting port era. Trucks, busses, railroads, and planes have absorbed the coastwise business. Even the
small ships that used to trade along the Atlantic coast are now
too expensive to operate. The coastwise sea traffic is obsolete.
Before the war it brightened the port every day with the busy
arrivals and departures of smart little steamers that plied on
regular schedules between New York and Boston, Providence,
New London, Norfolk, Savannah, Jacksonville, Miami, Mobile,
New Orleans, Galveston, and Vera Cruz—carrying passengers,
automobiles, fruit, and mixed cargo. Although the ships were
built for coastal waters, they boldly crossed the North Atlantic
during the war, and most of them were lost in submarine warfare.
Even the bulging, waddling *New York* and *Boston,* built for use
in Long Island Sound in the summer, crossed the stormy North
Atlantic. The ships that were lost will never be replaced. In the
motor age they are outmoded and superfluous tonnage.

For intercity traffic they were slow and cumbersome. You can
ride to Boston on the railroad in four and a half hours with no
more fuss than for a subway ride, or fly in an hour. The steamer
to Boston left at six in the evening and arrived at eight in the
morning. Except in the summer there was not much to be seen
from the deck, for the steamer left after sundown, passed through
the Cape Cod Canal in the darkness of early morning and docked
before the day was really started. But I loved the little water
excursion these steamers provided. The long blast of the whistle
when the ship started sliding out into the North River was the
prelude to a miniature sea voyage with all the privacy of escape
from the land. The deep, steady throb of the engines, the smell
of oil and tar, the hiss of the water at the stem, the soapy, bub-
bling wake where the screw churned up the water, the pleading,
lonely bells lazily marking the buoys in the channel, the solitary
lighthouses bright and alert in the darkness, the exchange of whis-
tles with passing steamers, the rumble of the steam in the funnel,
the silence and darkness of the wheel house—we were never far
from land but I relished those old sensations of life at sea. Sometimes, rounding Point Judith, the ship caught the wildness of the
open sea and pitched and rolled like a blue water vessel. In the

days of the coastwise liners, we all had quick and casual access to the sea.

24. In a miraculous, golden October, people take their outdoor leisure in a mood of exaltation that is almost a trance. Every day we expect autumn to settle in with a sharp breath from the north and a tumble in the temperature. But every day the air is soft and tropical. Men go hatless and coatless on the street, and strollers along the river dwell in a kind of timeless interlude—enjoyment of the summer having been exhausted, but endurance of cold weather not having begun. The amateur watermen are still pottering around their holiday boats. In the summer they pitch feverishly into the business of having a good time as though an hour could not be wasted. But time is standing still at present; time is borrowed from the winter, and people luxuriate in it by gazing at the river and idling along the riverbank. Today's temperature is 84°, which is a record for the day. Normal for this day is 60°.

25. While most of us are surveying the river with landsmen's eyes, the small-boat basin shelters two yawls that have braver plans in mind. One is the white yawl, *Gaucho*, that flies Brazilian colors and is preparing to sail back to Rio. Manned by two young Brazilians, she bustles with competence. The other has a shining blue hull and immaculate brightwork. A heavy-set man of middle years is taking water in the forepeak tanks and supplies on the afterdeck. His crew consists of a slender woman in burly slacks and a rough turtle-neck sweater who looks at me, I think, for a little appreciation and encouragement. "You've got a fine boat," I tell her, quite honestly. "Thank you," she says as though I had complimented her on the health, beauty and good-nature of a six months' old baby. Her attitude radiates pride, as though she were a particularly lady-like shellback. "You should have seen her when we got her last year," she continues, "all covered with thick, brown paint. We scrubbed her and painted her ourselves." They are headed for South America. "Can you two handle the sails?" I inquire. She blushes and bridles inside her raffish sweater: "It's pretty hard, sometimes. We are going to get a man to ship with us down through the Caribbean," she says shyly.

With the weight of the world on his shoulders the man looks glum and keeps on working silently. He means to suggest that everything is against him in a landlubber's city.

26. We imagine that we want cautious government. Since we as a nation do not trust government, we imagine that we want government kept on the level of clerking, safe and unimaginative. But cautious government cannot keep abreast of the needs of the people, which are dynamic always. The modern world with its high mobility and quick communications requires enterprise and boldness. Even our current concepts of freedom in our own country have hardly been fulfilled, and certainly not for all our people. The people are entitled to the benefits of modern knowledge, not in some future life, but now while they are still alive. Science, industry, business are all bold and energetic; government cannot cautiously lag behind. There is a calculated risk in everything. There has been a calculated risk in every stage of American development. The nation was built by men who took risks—pioneers who were not afraid of the wilderness, business men who were not afraid of failure, scientists who were not afraid of the truth, thinkers who were not afraid of progress, dreamers who were not afraid of action. When there is no risk, but only prudence, the American way of life may be regarded as finished. For progress in liberal institutions, as well as in material things, takes courage, drive and conviction. Nobody's revolution is ever finished, including Washington's, Jefferson's, and ours.

27. Theodore Roosevelt born on this day in 1858 in New York City. On the panels encircling a vigorous equestrian statue of Roosevelt at the Museum of Natural History, he is described as "patriot, soldier, humanitarian, historian, author, statesman, naturalist, conservationist, scientist, explorer, scholar and ranchman." These offices are not of equal rank, and several of them overlap. But they fairly represent the exuberant vitality of the most popular president of the United States—advocate of "the strenuous life" in his personal career and of "the square deal" in political affairs. Since he strove with great force for democratic reforms inside the framework of capitalism and without repudiating the party dedi-

cated to business interests, his dynamic administrations look a
little naïve to contemporary logicians; and his incitement to rebellion in Panama for the explicit purpose of digging the Panama
Canal violated American political morality. "I took Panama," he
boasted in later years. He was never overscrupulous about the
methods he used to promote the health and well-being of his
country. But it is difficult to recall now the progressive excitement
of his administration when he ran roughshod over political enemies, corporations and financiers, loosened old habits of thought,
reaffirmed the principles of democracy and put the interests of the
people ahead of business laissez faire. Now we do not have much
faith in the permanent values of reform. The cures to public diseases must strike deeper than reform. But reform seemed to most
people to be sufficient in Theodore Roosevelt's day. And he was
an aggressive reformer—an educated man of independent mind
with a good heart, a rugged constitution, amazing self-confidence
and a love for moral crusading. An aristocrat by birth, he acquired
the common touch in the rough-and-tumble of politics by association with woodsmen, ranchmen, and soldiers in the open; and his
restless, impetuous, keen personality invigorated the entire country and quickened the tempo of the whole world. Impatient with
"pussy-footing," as he contemptuously called it, he irritated pedes-
trian people who could not move fast enough to suit him. No one
ever denied that he was an egotist. But realizing that the power of
the president came directly from public opinion and not from the
lawmakers, he repeatedly went to the people with picturesque
fighting speeches and won their support. They loved him. They
were "dee-lighted." As usual, their instincts were right. He was a
"bully" man to have in the White House at a time when the
power of wealth was beginning to alarm responsible people.

28.   On this day in 1886 the Statue of Liberty was unveiled on
Bedloe's Island in the Bay. Like the Hudson River and the Palisades, it is now accepted as one of the natural glories of New
York. We who are used to it seldom see it consciously, but it is in
our souls and governs our attitude towards the contemporary
world. It is a work of art beyond criticism now, for no one knows
how deeply it has penetrated into the life of America and of the
world, nor how much it has strengthened the ideal of liberty by

standing there year after year and holding a lighted torch in the sky. The Constitution is no more explicit than this silent colossus that rises three hundred and five feet, eleven inches above low water in our harbor and greets every ship that steams through the Narrows.

Now that it has become part of our heritage, it is difficult to realize that once it was planned deliberately. Edouard René de Laboulaye, a friend of America, called together a group of French artists and writers at Versailles in 1865 to consider some way of commemorating the first century of freedom in America. Author of a number of political studies of America he had once written: "The folly of love and the madness of ambition are sometimes curable, but no one was ever cured of a mania for liberty." This perceptive statement shows how genuinely he understood the American principle. The men meeting in his house decided to give America a huge statue of Liberty as a gesture of friendship from the French people. Frédéric Auguste Bartholdi, the sculptor, drew the sketches and chose the setting on Bedloe's Island (then Fort Wood). He wanted to design the largest statue in the world, but harmonize it so completely with the harbor that the size would not be conspicuous.

In the course of years more than a million francs were raised by popular subscription in France. It was not easy to raise the whole amount, but in time the people gave it, and the Statue of Liberty is genuinely a gift from the French people. It took the United States nine years to collect three hundred thousand dollars to build the pedestal. An immigrant to America, Joseph Pulitzer, raised a large part of that sum through an active campaign in his newspaper, the *World*. More than 80 per cent of the money raised came in contributions of less than one dollar. Like Laboulaye, Pulitzer fully understood the truth of the project, and perhaps also foresaw what it would mean to the world. The inspired sonnet by Emma Lazarus, a pioneer Zionist, was contributed to the *World* as part of the campaign, and is now inscribed on the statue:

> *Not like the brazen giant of Greek fame,*
> *With conquering limbs astride from land to land;*
> *Here at our sea-washed, sunset gates shall stand*
> *A mighty woman with a torch, whose flame*
> *Is the imprisoned lightning, and her name*

Mother of Exiles. From her beacon hand
Glows world-wide welcome; her mild eyes command
The air-bridged harbor that twin cities frame.
"Keep, ancient lands, your storied pomp!" cries she
With silent lips. "Give me your tired, your poor,
Your huddled masses yearning to breathe free,
The wretched refuse of your teeming shore.
Send these, the homeless, tempest-tost to me,
I lift my lamp beside the golden door."

Everything about the Statue of Liberty is enlightened, honest and noble. It has become everything it was intended to be. It is the Statue of "Liberty Enlightening the World," to use Bartholdi's original title for his heroic work. Out of good will and imagination some French people created a statue that has become one of the most priceless of our natural resources.

29. Now Sirius, the "dog star," rises at midnight like a fire balloon in the sky. The entire constellation of the Great Dog is not visible until early morning, but the royal luminary sits on the black throne of the night and rules the heavens. More than six thousand years ago—a length of time that cannot be imagined— the Egyptians and Babylonians gazed at Sirius and wondered what influences he had on the affairs of mankind. Looking up through the dry, crisp air of the desert, the Egyptian soothsayers based their forecasts on the position and radiance of Sirius. The Romans also respected Sirius. The hot, humid weather of August, when Sirius begins to rise with the sun, they described as *dies caniculares*—the "dog days"—a bit of folklore that has come down through twenty centuries and crossed the Atlantic to a new city that remains in the same band of latitude.

Sirius is the brightest star in the sky and one of the nearest. It is fifty-one million million miles away, in comparison with the ninety-three million miles to the sun. Sirius is about twenty-eight times brighter than the sun. The light it throws down on our nightly affairs is whiter than the light of the sun, for Sirius is hotter. The surface temperature is 10,000° in comparison with the 6,000° of the sun. Sirius means "scorching." The Greek astronomers who gave it that name knew that it is incredibly hot,

although they had none of the instruments for measuring heat
that are available today.

In 1844 one astronomer noted that Sirius does not move through
the sky on a uniform route. He guessed that a star he could not
see must be pulling it off into some subsidiary orbit. Eighteen
years later another astronomer confirmed this speculation by discovering a companion star so overpowered by the great light of
Sirius that it can hardly be seen. That great light is still pouring
down on us out of the winter empyrean. Like the Babylonians and
the Egyptians, we are stirred and reassured by it. It relates us to
the history we know, as well as the history that has been lost in
the careless shuffle of the centuries.

30. Walking down One Hundred and Sixty-eighth Street, I
hear a chickadee singing above the rumble of the traffic. It is difficult to locate him by ear, but after walking up Fort Washington
Avenue two blocks I find him whisking around the branches of a
plane tree and singing as sweetly as he does in the country. In
fact, the bustle of the city may be stimulating him a little so that
he is singing more enchantingly than he does in the country at
this time of year.

In the country he is the friendliest bird and one of the most
delightful. In the city he is a distinguished visitor who alters all
the normal values. His purity of spirit is more nearly priceless
than the ground value of the surrounding real estate. Since this
part of New York has been heavily built up for at least a half
century and has become a solid part of the steel and brick Cosmopolis, it is remarkable that the chickadees still appear. But
during the autumn migration they come, sometimes in droves,
appearing on rooftops and in window boxes until the air seems
full of their innocent "chick-a-dee-dee." I have seen them in the
privet hedges in the center of Broadway with the traffic angrily
whizzing by on both sides. It must be something racial in their
memories. They haven't yet learned that the shores of the Hudson are no longer covered with woods and wild bushes and that
the Indians no longer live under the big tulip tree near the bay in
the Bronx River.

31. Bill McDermott, critic of the Cleveland *Plain Dealer*, and
his wife, Eva, come to dinner. Everyone feels a little brighter and
more comfortable when Bill is around, for he is interested in
everything, takes time to mull it over and comes up invariably
with wise and generous conclusions. The presence of one man like
that would be reason enough to live in Cleveland. Our association
with the McDermotts reveals one of the inequalities of New York
life. When we visit Cleveland on business, we stay in the Mc-
Dermotts' house, which is a large one, take breakfast, luncheon
and dinner with them, go to the theater with them and sit up
and discuss it with them at midnight. After two or three days
like that we cover a wide variety of topics and arrive at a number
of conclusions. Apart from the glow of friendship, we accomplish
a great deal. But when the McDermotts come to New York on
business, only the most careful sort of planning makes it possible
for us to spend one evening together. Since we live in an apartment and not a house we cannot put them up in comfort. And
since they have a number of plays and people to see they are
pressed for time, and my working schedule is likely to be inelastic.
A visit to New York is generally under pressure; a visit to almost
any other city in America is a release from pressure.

Compute this on the basis of a lifetime and it is evident that
most New Yorkers are permanently deficient in the sort of seasoning that comes from conversation at leisure. Life is too rigidly
organized. Not to have frequent opportunities for sitting down
with Bill is in my case a denial of life. Bill is a small, compact,
crinkly eyed man who smokes ten or fifteen cigars a day (he de-
nies this), likes bourbon and ginger ale, is animated by the spirit
of pure inquiry and talks with humorous, friendly deliberation.
Widely read, widely traveled, he has prodigious knowledge of
many things. But his ultimate standards of judgment are based
on good will. They are flexible according to the integrity of the
people he is trying to assess; he values good will a notch or two
above ability and accomplishment. It is hard for a man of this
quality to be wrong about anything.

NOVEMBER

November

Last NIGHT was Halloween. The young men who labored hard and valiantly to make appropriate mischief probably did not realize that they were carrying on traditions that originated with the Druids in ancient Gaul thousands of years ago. Our sleepless young neighbors in the country dragged a heavy privy a mile up hill to the village street, where they left it in the midst of other incongruous objects. Using soap as a writing element they scrawled rude though friendly messages on the windows of the store and the post office. In the morning the villagers observed the results of the midnight mischief with equanimity, and in due time put everything to rights again. No one was surprised. No one was annoyed. Some enterprising young men, who could be identified without too much trouble, had loyally performed the rites of the eve to All Saints' Day. For it is traditional that the night should be filled with unseen impishness, performed by witches or hobgoblins, riding either broomsticks or jalopies in the darkness. Our neighbors learned it from their parents, who in turn learned it from their parents, and so on back through the centuries to the superstitious Druids. We all carry in our souls the heritage of primitive days.

October thirty-first was the last day of the Druid year. On the eve of the new year, Saman, the lord of death, gathered the souls of those who had died during the year and who had been condemned to enter the bodies of animals for punishment. On the night of October thirty-first, Saman decided what to do with these souls during the next year. The Druids believed that the punishment could be lightened by gifts and prayers.

All folk observances also accumulate other ideas from succeeding civilizations. And so October thirty-first acquired other rites from the Roman festival of Pomona, who presided over harvests. The early Christians, who were a minority sect, were disposed to

lay claim to holidays that were already established. They named
the evening "All Hallows Eve"; today is All Saints' Day, which is
a legal holiday in France and other European countries.

In America Halloween is the young people's masquerade, slightly
formalized nowadays with traditional parties and mummers' parades. From primitive religious superstitions it has developed into
licensed hooliganism. Elderly people are supposed benevolently to
acquiesce in foolishness in the night.

2. Election Day. Temperature 36°. The day begins cloudy, sere
and somber—the haze hanging white in the hollows and blue
across the mountains. By ten o'clock the sun comes through,
warm, cheerful, still. Our village votes in the Odd Fellows Hall
where an American flag hangs at the entrance. Two or three of
the town politicians are lazily gossiping on the porch. About ten
cars are parked outside. The hall, as usual, is over-heated, which
always makes it seem especially hospitable. The election officials
are dressed in their best clothes, which makes them at first unrec-
ognizable. Having been on duty since six o'clock they are feeling
relaxed and facetious on the surface, although they preserve a
certain gravity and sincerity of office underneath. Coming in to
vote is like entering a good-natured neighborhood club. About six
hundred townspeople are registered to vote in this district. But
this is a presidential election at which no town officers are to be
chosen. In the circumstances the election officers do not expect
more than four hundred voters. Next year when we choose the
town supervisor and road commissioner the local politicians will
take greater pains to bring out the vote.

I think I enjoy Election Day more than any other day in the
country. A little undercurrent of excitement skips through the
town, emerging in the form of guying and humor. After O. and I
have voted—each of us scrupulously canceling the other's selection—we see more people and have more conversation with all of
them than at any other time of year. Socially, this is the most cordial of the seasons, for the urgent work of the year has already
been accomplished and people have time to loiter and talk. Also,
on Election Day every man and woman is as good as the next, and
equally valuable to the community. This is the egalitarian spirit
that gives the day so much common exultation. Although we

hardly realize it, there is a rebirth of freedom in America on this day.

When I was in Russia I was envious of the solemn grandeur of their election day. The election was held on Sunday. The workers at the Stalin automobile plant voted in their social center. A brass band played in the lobby. Ushers received the voters at the door and guided them upstairs to a long, carpeted hall which had been decorated with national flags, patriotic slogans, boughs and blooms and the standard busts of Lenin and Stalin. One of the posters said: "The USSR is a thousand times more democratic than the most democratic nation in the world." Dressed for a great ceremonial occasion, the voters were guided to the proper registration desk, checked off on the list and given a ballot. The greatest difference with American elections came at this point. For the Russian voters had only one candidate to vote for, and their only choice lay between voting for him or crossing out his name and dropping a blank ballot in the box. Although the Russians ridicule our democratic elections as "formal," theirs is the apotheosis of "formality"—substituting the form for the deed. Their elections are a travesty on the democratic process. Nevertheless, I envied them the reverence with which they have taught their people to participate in the election. The form may be tragically empty, but it breeds respect for the election institution. By comparison, we take the institution cheaply. Only about half of the Americans entitled to vote will cast ballots today. Throughout the country only about two-thirds of those who have registered will vote. This is the most shockingly wasteful aspect of a nation that is congenitally wasteful. Whatever methods the Russian communists use for getting out the vote, they have a right to be proud of the number of people who come to the polls. But I would not trade the respect their people have for the polls for the breezy, genial camaraderie of our annual visit to Odd Fellows Hall where both the temperature and the good humor are high.

3. At eleven this morning enough votes have been counted throughout the country to decide the election for President.

Naturally there is great rejoicing in the headquarters of the successful candidate. But the headquarters of the defeated candidate collapses swiftly and silently in an atmosphere of pessimism and gloom. Since the election has been close, nearly half of the forty-eight million people who voted are disappointed with the result. Political feeling is so strong that many of them are bitterly disappointed and imagine that the next four years are going to be disastrous for the country. But no one suggests that they should question the nation's verdict or resist it or try to circumvent it. For the people have spoken with finality, and the country instinctively obeys. During the last six months the two parties have fought each other violently, getting as close to personal libel as they dared. Each party has tried desperately to convince the voters that the other party is stupid, vicious, treasonable, crooked, sinister, ignorant, and un-American. The whole nation has been enflamed by political argument and animosity, day by day and night by night. But now the people have decided. The decision is final and unassailable; and the defeated candidate, who was a tremendous public figure yesterday, is a private citizen today, spectacularly repudiated by the country. Although he appeared to have a dazzling future yesterday, he has none today.

Elections of Presidents have been resisted. When Lincoln was elected in 1860, southern states began at once to secede because there was obviously no possibility of settling the slave problem politically. In 1876 the close vote between Hayes and Tilden aroused the nation because five southern states returned double sets of electors. A special electoral commission of five Supreme Court judges, five senators and five representatives decided all the disputed factors in favor of Hayes, and the nation resented the obvious partisanship of the commission. As one wag said at the time, the Democrats stole the election and the Republicans stole it back again.

But I believe the national elections of 1860 and 1876 were the only ones ever seriously challenged. For everyone regards the decision of the people as final; and perhaps unconsciously many people regard it as inspired. Despite the closeness of yesterday's election and the apparent gravity of the issues that have been decided by a narrow margin, the country has already settled down to conforming to the result—rather amused on the whole by the excitement.

4. After serving as a war transport, the *Nieuw Amsterdam* makes a triumphal re-entrance this morning as a passenger ship. She is dressed with signal flags, as are the tugs that push her into her Hoboken dock, and everything is gala. She is a beautiful modern ship with trim and sturdy lines, broad, sweeping decks, and powerful propulsion machinery. Inside she has been redecorated at a cost of twelve million dollars, although she cost only nine million dollars to build nine years ago. Except for the headroom between decks she looks like the Waldorf-Astoria—luxury, pomp, and showy splendor. I would as soon go to sea in the Waldorf-Astoria.

Luxury in the fitting of ship interiors is traditional. In the old sailing ships the captain's stateroom was made of costly, carved woods, although the captain may have been a drunk and thug. I suppose the motive of such landside luxury was to create the illusion of security and permanence. It must have been reassuring to timid passengers. That may be the underlying reason for luxury in modern steam vessels. Entering the carpeted deck by the purser's office, no one would imagine that the *Nieuw Amsterdam* can sink. She seems as solid and permanent as a modern steel building, and the gorgeously decorated bulkheads of her public rooms keep the wild seas far away.

The real luxury of ocean travel is the freight ship that keeps you close to the ocean and steeps you in the main business of the sea, which is mixed cargo for foreign ports.

5. From this window, the sun sets—usually in a red burst of glory—six minutes early over the purple hills of Weehawken. To-night it drops into the flaming kettle of declining day at 4:42, although the calendar sunset is put at 4:48. The time differential is a little surprising. The Weehawken hills are about three hundred feet high, and my window on the fifth floor is about one hundred feet above the level of the river, which is practically sea level. If I lived about twenty-five stories higher I could have six minutes more daylight in the afternoon and live accurately according to the almanac. If I lived higher than twenty-five stories I could have more daylight than nature provides for earth-bound human beings. That would be one way of lengthening life. Two

minutes more sunlight a day than the almanac allows would increase life more than twelve hours a year, or thirty-five days in the
traditional lifetime of three-score years and ten.

6. Since the entrepreneurs of the new Children's World Theatre would not admit a critic today without an authentic child,
I improvidently invite two fair-weather friends—Heather, age 9,
and Andrew, age 5. This turns out to be a full-time project. Since
they have never attended the theater before, they started to get
ready yesterday afternoon, and could easily have appeared at the
Barbizon-Plaza playhouse, neatly dressed, at 9 o'clock this morning to see *Jack and the Beanstalk*, a tale with which they are thoroughly familiar.

It is like sitting on top of a volcano to keep them away from
the theater until 2:15, which is fifteen minutes before the adver-
tised curtain time. They are extremely well behaved, if you don't
count wriggling, constant leg motion, and the natural tendency of
a child to sit in a chair backwards. Until 2:45, when the curtains
finally part, the conversation, as scribbled on my program, is as
follows: "What time will it begin?" "How many minutes now?"
"Why don't it begin?" "It should be starting now. Why isn't it?"
"Why don't you make them start?" Unilateral conversations of
this kind always establish my personal responsibility in the end.

By 2:45 the theater is jammed with gabbling children who
spend about five minutes impatiently clapping. Finally the curtains part, revealing a prop cow and Jack. The theater is suddenly
silent. "There's a man in that cow," Heather declares. Behind us
sits a six-year-old skeptic. After studying the situation for a few
minutes, the skeptic asks: "In that man real?" Her mother assures
her that he is. Since the child has started with the assumption
that everything is fraudulent, she is totally confused by this evidence of honesty. She begins to suspect that everything may be
honest. "Is the cow real?" she asks, trying to get a little logic into
the proceedings.

When Rafe Heywood, a villainous character, swindles the cow
away from Jack and his disconsolate mother, a pair of twins in
front of us bursts into tears and weeps copiously. There is an
especially spirited youngster across the aisle. When Rafe makes
his exit, the boy angrily shouts: "Go away and stay away!" Pres-

ently the act is over and the house lights come up. Irritated by this arbitrary theater convention, Heather inquires: "When will it begin again?" Questions by the young apply constant pressure, like the Chinese water cure, and result in making everything in the world look hopeless.

In the second act, Jack climbs into the giant's kitchen and things get really tough. "Fee, fie, fo, fum, I smell the blood of an Englishman," he says with regrettable racial intolerance as he sharpens a long, savage knife. After gazing cherub-like in silence at this sanguinary scene, Andrew sits back in his seat and turns his head from the stage. "I don't want to see the giant hurt Jack," he whispers. But presently Jack is chasing the giant around the kitchen, minute by minute getting the upper hand in an astounding contest of good and evil; and the audience bursts into highly partisan cheering and shouting. "Look out, Jack, he's right behind you!" one piercing voice screams above the pandemonium.

Jack makes his escape safely. In the last act, anybody can see that the giant is coming down the beanstalk, which is shaking violently. Children all over the theater warn Jack to get the knife and cut down the beanstalk, but Jack seems incredibly unaware of the danger. After shouting repeated warnings, the little boy across the way can contain himself no longer. He leaps violently out into the middle of the aisle. Wielding an imaginary knife, he starts fiercely whirling around, growling under his breath: "I'll kill the giant. I'll kill him."

It is one of the most dangerous theater performances I have ever sat through. We make our way through the revolving doors (there's a nice hazard for small children) into the quiet peace and composure of the New York streets that look like heaven. Does Heather like the play as much as the movies? "Better." Why? "Because the people are real." That settles that. Andrew listens quietly to this long, profound, and penetrating discussion. "I don't like the giant," he says. Why? "He's bad." Why is he bad? "He wants to hurt people."

That seems to cover the episode of *Jack and the Beanstalk*, except that Heather and Andrew are obviously the neatest, best-looking, and best-behaved children in the audience.

7. On this day in 1917 the Bolsheviks seized power in Russia, overthrowing the provisional government, establishing the Soviet regime and introducing into the life of the entire world the most unsettling idea of a century. Lenin, who had just slipped into Russia from exile, Trotsky, Zinoviev and a few others, including Stalin, who was then a minor figure, overcame the resistance and torpor of other political parties by being prepared, organized and ruthless. What they lacked in numbers they supplied out of determination and knowledge of the technique of revolution. Two weeks previously Trotsky had organized the War-Revolutionary Committee, which brought under one head military, political, communication and industrial groups. Being the only energetically directed organization in what was then Petrograd, they controlled the government and the city even before they demonstrated their control. On November seventh at 2 A.M. they silently occupied the railway stations, bridges, power plants, telegraph offices and the Bank of Russia. They seized the telephone offices at 7 A.M., and at 10 A.M. were able to proclaim the overthrow of the government.

The government, under Kerensky, was in the Winter Palace, guarded by two hundred Cossack infantry, one thousand cadets, a women's battalion and four guns from the Michael Artillery College. Kerensky escaped at 7 A.M. to procure troops to defend the government. In the afternoon the Bolshevik forces attacked the Winter Palace. Fighting began at 9 P.M. and lasted about an hour before the Bolsheviks broke in and started fighting from room to room. They were in complete physical control of the palace and the government about 2 A.M. on November eighth. Lenin addressed a joint meeting of the All-Russian Congress of Soviets, the Petrograd Soviet, the garrison and other Bolsheviki in the afternoon and in the evening proposed the first fundamental law of the new regime. It was unanimously accepted without discussion—foreshadowing the august subservience of the Supreme Soviet today where everything is unanimously agreed upon, generally without discussion.

The Bolsheviks were not secure until they could dispose of the Constituent Assembly which met for the first time on January 18, 1918. It had been elected in November. The Socialist-Revolutionaries had polled 20,893,734 votes; the Bolsheviks, 9,023,963; other parties, 6,340,263. The members elected were: anti-Bolsheviks, 535; Bolsheviks, 168. That overwhelming majority against them did not deter the Bolsheviki. Being in control of the garrison forces, they surrounded the assembly hall with their own men and filled the galleries and anterooms with their own people, many of whom were armed. When the assembly opened at 4 P.M., the Bolsheviki lost the first two motions by overwhelming votes. The Bolshevik members quickly left the hall. Bedlam broke loose. The gallery visitors overran the floor. Some of those in the gallery leveled rifles at the members on the floor. Nothing could be heard from the rostrum. By five o'clock the next morning the meeting had become hopelessly disorganized. A sailor approached the chairman who became visibly alarmed; and suddenly the members of the Constituent Assembly got up and left the hall, and that was the last and only meeting it ever held. After the destruction of the Constituent Assembly, the leaders of the Bolshevik party were completely secure in their position and have remained so ever since.

This was a revolution by able men who no doubt sincerely believed that they could give Russia and eventually the whole world the sort of enlightened government that would be best for all mankind. They also knew that they could never win power in a free election. The dogmatic socialism they proposed was too repugnant to the groups of people that would have to be dispossessed and also to the peasants who wanted to own the land in their own right—not as serfs of the state. Lenin and Trotsky had no choice of methods; they had to overcome disorganized resistance with small but compact and rigidly directed force. They had long ago concluded that the ends, which were good, would justify the means, which were treacherous and barbaric. Perhaps that is the basic fallacy of bolshevism—the false assumption that has undermined the whole book of dogma of communism. To stay in control and to organize a vast, backward country of emotional people, the Communist leaders have had to jettison the democratic process permanently and build up the police force more and more efficiently; and lying and conspiracy have become permanent and deliberate techniques. The history of communism has been one crisis consecutively following another, progressively requiring more and more force to deal with it. And the cruel irony is that a regime founded on the moral principle of liberating the masses from bondage has had to put them deeper and deeper into bondage and to spread the principle of bondage into contiguous countries too weak to resist it. The basic moral fallacy of the first day of the revolution has spread like a cancer through the body of communism everywhere. The ends do not justify the means. In time the means destroy the ends, and only the means are left. "The evil that men do lives after them; the good is oft interred with their bones."

8. The long, soft-textured, drowsy autumn has come to a sharp conclusion. Last night the temperature dropped to 31°; and when the sun lifts over the rooftops at quarter to seven this morning it seems to have a slightly detached relationship to us, as if it were no longer personally interested in this climate. A hard breeze out of the northwest pours around the corner from Riverside Drive, and the flinty blue of the river water is cross-hatched with white patches where the wind breaks the surface. The day begins tersely. After six weeks of benign indolence, the season is striking its first trial balance.

9. Brilliant and powerful though the *Queen Elizabeth* is, she, too, must conform. She cannot cleave the fog; she cannot spurn the tide. She was due at her pier at one o'clock yesterday afternoon with 2,249 patrician passengers. But the fog smothered her off Ambrose Lightship. The *DeGrasse* and the *Batory*, handier vessels, came up to their piers later in the day. But the *Queen Elizabeth* could not come up until ten this morning. Hundreds of people thronged the water front to greet friends and relatives. But the royal *Queen* had to anchor in midstream for four hours until the tide came to full and subsided to slack water. The prestige of the finest liner on the Atlantic and the important connections of her passengers could not add four feet to the water level of the North River and could not hurry the turn of the tide.

At sea she is a swift sentient being—all speed, lightness, and grace. But she is a ponderous mass of steel in port and incredibly dangerous if she is out of control. In addition to her own engines, it takes eleven tugs to cant her slowly into her berth and lay her gently against her pier. To the landsman it looks like a perilous maneuver. But the docking pilot far up on the bridge and the tugboat skippers take it phlegmatically. When the water is slack the bow anchor rises heavily out of the river and the forepeak bell rings frantically. There is a shattering blast from the steam siren, the water boils over the screws, and the tugs, massed five on the port bow and six on the starboard quarter, lay against her and help keep her steady as she swings and moves slowly into the berth. She looked enormous as she lay stretched at anchor in the stream. But as she comes closer she looks colossal. Creeping in the berth towards the shore she is a great wall of steel that blocks the sun. The wings of the bridge hang in the air. The great, razory stem towers high above the street. After a clatter of signals, the lines are ashore, the steam whistle blows a sweet, musical "all clear," and the red-and-white pilot flag is lowered and at long last the _Queen Elizabeth_ is ready to discharge her passengers. She will be off to England tomorrow. A line of food trucks is already waiting in the pier to restock her larder, and four oil barges are moored to the other side of the pier to replenish her fuel tanks. She is uneasy inside the cramped river. She needs the open ocean for dancing and racing and steaming.

10. Why do preachers address God in a pompous whine? To anyone who believes that God extends through all forms of human nature as well as wild nature, the whining tone of the professional dominie is intolerable. It is also insulting to God, who needs no protection. It is professional cant, like ham acting. In case God is interested in manners, He would probably enjoy having men behave like men instead of like obsequious valets. I have no objections to churches so long as they do not interfere with God's work. "Any old woman can love God better than a Doctor of Theology can," said St. Bonaventura.

11. Armistice Day. At eleven o'clock on the eleventh day of the eleventh month in 1918, the warring armies in Europe mercifully laid down their arms. We innocently believed we would never again take up arms against a foe. Although Armistice Day was one of great carnival and rejoicing in 1918, it has become a minor Memorial Day now.

I vividly remember the original Armistice Day. I was corporal of a development battalion at Camp Upton, Patchogue, Long Island, where the winter was just beginning to settle in. There had been a premature or false "Armistice Day" that had raised and dashed our hopes two or three days before. But on November eleventh the report was official and true. It spread through that drab, sandy camp with joyous speed. Since we were not and never had been in danger, it did not bring to us the miraculous release that it brought to the muddy, cold troops in the field. But for us it brought the promise of early relief from the unutterable boredom of life in the Army. As normal people we hated everything about it—the herding of men like animals in ugly barracks, the segregation of men according to rank, the brutal impersonality of army life, the tedium of drill. It seemed almost too good to believe that soon this brassy tyranny would break up and restore us to civil life. The news of the armistice angered our commanding officer, a New York lawyer, who wanted to lead his company into battle and become a hero. "Sergeant McClinsky," he roared out of the orderly-room window, "take the company and drill hell out of them." We celebrated Armistice Day with a couple of hours of close-order drill. But our commanding officer could not repeal the armistice, and three weeks later we began to break up the company and go home.

Armistice Day is no longer a day of rejoicing. Every military observance inevitably becomes a time for mourning. The 1918 armistice only interrupted the war, which broke out again in 1939 and has not yet led to peace. In the bottom of our hearts we are no longer sure that the ancient madness will not seize the world again.

There are services for the war-dead today at the Eternal Light in Madison Square.

12. "It won't be long now," the neighbors in the country say with a kind of humorous resignation. They mean winter, which is the next fact of any consequence. The temperature is 30° at nine o'clock, and never gets higher than 36° all day. The hill is ruled with a wicked lash by a roaring northwest gale. Although the temperature is not low yet, the gale is the advance guard of winter and drives its shrill warning into the eyes and ears. The road gang, well wrapped up and bending into the wind, is driving the stakes

and putting up the snow-fence—an annual and ominous chore. The marsh hawk makes use of the gale. He rides buoyantly as he beats back and forth across the meadow in search of mice. While I am eating breakfast, I see a long flight of at least five hundred crows coming out of the valley and heading west. It takes them nearly an hour to fly past in ragged groups of five or six. Probably they come from a crow roost in the valley.

I have greased the tools in the shop to keep them from rusting and put them away for the winter. That is another annual chore, and a melancholy part of the annual retreat and withdrawal.

13. Deer-hunting season begins. This is the day when mass madness possesses a large section of the human race—mostly male. Extravagantly attired in jackets with "blood proof" pockets, red caps with long visors and knee-length boots, they start chasing the deer over the hills as though it were a civic duty and as though they somehow acquired heroism by killing the most enchanting and universally loved creature of the woods. There are three cars parked by the road on our farm; and while I am working outdoors I occasionally see pairs of solemn men tramping across lots, looking as though they were about to be swindled. No deer are "taken," as the euphemistic phrase goes, here today. But I hear two pairs of frantic shots off towards Cooksburg, as though a hunter had been scared, and I hear two separate shots from up towards Pisgah. There are some good hunters in town and I suppose they are entitled every year to prove that man is a triumphant animal. But most of the hunters are incompetent and bewildered. Last year unknown hunters killed two cows in Brink's mountain pasture. It's a pity the hunters were not caught, if only to humiliate illustrious woodsmen who cannot distinguish a cow from a deer.

14. During a search of about two hours on the north side of the hill I see four deer browsing in the wheat field, three partridges in the woods, also one rabbit and two gray squirrels. Their lives are in danger. The open season for deer has just begun. But partridges, rabbits and squirrels have been shot at around here for a month. The hunters have been industriously cannonading at

them throughout the neighborhood. The hunters do not hate any of these birds or animals. On the contrary, they are fond of them. Throughout the year they watch the game with interest, pride and admiration and are likely to know a good deal more about the habits of wild life than the people who do not hunt. This passion for killing is a curious perversion, bringing evidence to bear on the cynical observation that "each man kills the thing he loves."

Naturally it has had a decisive influence on the temperament of the game. To people who are familiar with the hysterical flight of partridges when they are flushed, it is difficult to remember that once the partridge was the friendliest bird in the fields. He was known as the "fool hen" because he naïvely trusted men, could be knocked over with a stick, and frequently was. This was probably a century ago. But I can remember as a boy coming on partridges in the White Mountains who did not take off in a panic when human beings happened along. I photographed them at six feet. Probably these were the Canadian spruce partridges—a more northerly species than the one that lives in the woods of New York State. But the partridges that did not protect themselves by thundering off into the thickets were killed. The only survivors were those that regarded men as mortal enemies and kept themselves hidden; and all the partridges who raise broods now are descendants of the wary ones who staked everything on the chances for survival. All partridges now have developed elaborate techniques for protecting their chicks during the breeding season and protecting themselves during the gunning period. Of the three I flush this afternoon, two leap into the thicket so swiftly that I catch only a glimpse of them through bare branches. The third is on the edge of a pasture and has to fly one hundred feet through the open before he plunges into the pine lot. Since he lets me come within twenty-five feet before he takes to his wings, he may not survive the season. He is one whom the species is probably eliminating.

15. She is as fat as a hen's forehead. She weighs about ninety pounds. But her energy is like a series of electric sparks that dart through the office; and she has one of the biggest hearts in the organization. In the beginning we did not want a woman in the office; we were afraid that a woman would formalize our cheerful

though untidy working relationships. But now we wonder how we managed to get through so many years without her. Once she was grudgingly admitted, she unobtrusively organized the office for the conduct of business on a convenient schedule, and now we all impose on her with the most thoughtless good will. She has a mind like a steel trap. She never forgets names; she can pull forgotten facts out of the files, and she has all our business at her finger-tips. She anticipates what some of it is going to be and has the material ready. She manages the office with such silent skill that I live in a dreamworld, unaware of half the things that go on and frequently receiving credit for things I have not done.

The priceless thing about her is her good nature. She likes people. She is cordial and patient with people on the telephone, which is something we never thought of being. She is thoughtful. Formerly we had only the meagerest relationships with the adjoining departments, which are also preoccupied with their daily affairs. But now there is a good deal of friendly visiting back and forth and a wholesome exchange of gossip. Things go fast in our office under a certain amount of tension at times, for most of our staff is temperamental. But under the tautness of the day's work she has time for other enterprises, like a wedding gift to a secretary in another part of the building, a greeting card to a client in the hospital, a house plant for the shelf by the window, cakes and cookies for holiday observances. There is no end to her good will. Although she is tiny and unobtrusive, she radiates all through the building and has friends and admirers among the high brass. Officially, she is the secretary. But actually she is the office manager. It is a pleasure to go to work now that she is in charge.

16. No culture is vital if it leaves people in ignorance and poverty and permits them to go on living a life of serfdom. When I hear people speaking reverently of Chinese culture, which derives from several thousands of years ago, I think of the four hundred million or more Chinese peasants who are living in the modern world without modern enlightenment. The old works of art and the old glazes and Confucius's venerable maxims mean nothing if they have not enriched the lives of people who are trying to live today. Old wisdom like that of the ancient Chinese sages supplies a cultured defense for corruption, lethargy and bondage of the

people. You can always find a picturesque old saw in any culture to excuse or defend intolerable conditions. It is like a shrug of the shoulders. Stuff a man's mind with old sayings and he will never wrestle with a new idea. There is no honor in traditions unless they represent something vital to modern life.

17. Of all the week days, Thursday is the brightest. *The New Yorker* is amiably leaning against the door when I open it before breakfast. *The New Yorker* is the most brilliantly edited weekly in the world. What we did before the first number was published on February 21, 1925, is a little hard now to remember; and whatever we did then we probably kept on doing for some time. For in the beginning *The New Yorker* was hardly brighter than a college comic. The art it published was trite and crude. But *The New Yorker* has long since settled down to a coherent pattern of tolerant satire that accepts the foibles of New York without sharing them. The art is superb—witty and skillful. The prose is impeccable. *The New Yorker* enjoys and on the whole approves of New Yorkers, but maintains an attitude of dazed incredulity about the irrational things they do and say.

If *The New Yorker* were only a comic magazine it would not be, as it is, indispensable to New Yorkers. There are jokes in other magazines and on the radio. Since the page design of *The New Yorker* accents the giddy drawings, the prose looks casual by comparison, for the personal manners of *The New Yorker* are conservative. But the prose that *The New Yorker* prints so unostentatiously is uniformly excellent. It is so silken in style that the occasional piece of humorous claptrap it prints from old masters, like Mencken, looks spurious and old-fashioned. None of the regular *New Yorker* writers reaches out after gaudy words. Their taste is temperate.

In the writing of narrative *The New Yorker* is incomparable. Its reporting is factually accurate, but also unique in the value it places on human beings and the nuances of human living. *New Yorker* reporters have covered obscure corners of New York and have traveled around the world, particularly during the war. Newspapers and the radio cover the news of the world systematically and cannot afford to be highly selective. But with plenty of time at their disposal and all the space they need, *The New Yorker* reporters translate life into prose with astonishing completeness and truth. The truth goes beyond facts into impressions, moods and characters. It gives the facts depth and perspective. Fresh and receptive, *The New Yorker* reporting has added a new dimension to modern journalism. Scratch the jester and you will find a serious reporter wearing motley.

18. Today our housekeeper, Sue, has left us. Her baby will be born in a few weeks and she can no longer do regular housework for us. Although a new and more cheerful housekeeper is replacing her, we are unhappy about losing the big, black, silent woman who has been keeping our house in order and cooking for us efficiently with patience, with skill, with undemonstrative good will. I think Sue is sorry to leave us, for this has been an agreeable job and we have never knowingly imposed on her. But I imagine we are more regretful than she is; losing her means more to us than losing us means to her.

Sue represents the sorrowfulness of the Negro race in a white man's world. Although she is pleasant and gentle there is a core of blackness in her soul. She expects nothing but work and unhappiness for the rest of her life. She is lost in some strange, melancholy reverie. Occasionally, I have passed her on the street when she did not see me. These chance glimpses are revealing. She walks to work with resignation, seeing nothing, absorbed in her thoughts, detached and bemused. In the house she is silent although never sullen or bitter. It is only because she has nothing to say—at least to us. Sometimes she talks over the telephone with a friend and then she seems interested and almost jovial. I have occasionally heard her talking in a lonely voice to herself or humming a mournful song when she did not realize I was at home. But apart from her quiet friendliness as a human being she has hardly ever communicated with us or taken anything more than a functional place in our home. Although I respect Sue's detachment, we would have enjoyed a more intimate association.

Sue faces the prospect of motherhood without enthusiasm or curiosity. "I had a little bad luck," she told my wife shyly when she announced that she was pregnant. The father of the child has married her. At present he is employed. Probably for the first time in her adult life Sue will now be supported. But deep in her heart

I imagine she feels that bringing a child into the strident world of Harlem increases the general misery and carries it on to one more whipped generation. Perhaps the physical and spiritual shock of motherhood will bring her at least a few hours of joy and triumph. Nothing less vital can invade the great shadow of sorrow that engulfs her. Good luck, Sue!

19. "The world will little note nor long remember what we say here," Lincoln remarked on this day in 1863 in his dedicatory speech at the National Cemetery at Gettysburg. That was the only error in these valiant and sorrowful words that have since been etched deep in the heart of the world. No one remembers Edward Everett's formal speech of the day which lasted one hour and fifty-seven minutes. He had been writing it for six weeks in the classical style of its time. It filled two closely printed newspaper pages; it had been distributed in advance in proof to the people and newspapers that wanted it.

After coming by special train from Washington, Lincoln retired with pen and paper upstairs to his room in a Gettysburg house at ten in the evening. At eleven he showed the finished manuscript to Seward who, presumably, approved of it. After Everett finished his address on the battlefield the next morning Lincoln rose, holding the two pages in his hand, and uttered the remarks that have since stirred and nourished the faith of the world: "That this nation, under God, shall have a new birth of freedom; and that government of the people, by the people, and for the people, shall not perish from the earth." To the thousands of people assembled on the battleground, the speech seemed to be over before it was begun. According to one observer, the applause was "formal and perfunctory." The hostile press, whose contempt for Lincoln extended to everything he said and did, seized on the speech to revile him. "Silly remarks . . . bad taste . . . foully traduced the motives of the men slain at Gettysburg . . . Lincoln acted like a clown," they said. But others, hearing it for the first time, understood its nobility and artistry. "A perfect gem," the Springfield *Republican* exclaimed. The Chicago *Tribune* declared prophetically: "The dedicatory remarks of the President will live among the annals of man." Edward Everett modestly remarked that Lincoln had gotten closer to the heart of the occasion in two minutes than Everett had in two hours. For Everett had written out of his library, and Lincoln had consulted nothing more recondite than his memory of suffering and his religious hopes for mankind. In his head and heart he bore the anguish of the democratic dream.

20. "Simplify, simplify," Thoreau exclaimed in *Walden.* "Instead of three meals a day, if it be necessary eat but one; instead of a hundred dishes, five; and reduce other things in proportion." Since he was a romantic poet first and a moral philosopher second, Thoreau did not intend his instructions to be taken literally. He was also humorous and enjoyed amazing people with hyperboles. Although his call for simplification proceeded from a cozy house on the shore of a woodland lake, it applies to New York, more particularly than to Walden, for New York is intricate, complex, and powerful. If the whirling nervous energy of Cosmopolis is not resisted or renounced, it can destroy a man of normal strength and character. For the drive of New York is wild. No one is strong enough to accept combat on New York's own terms. We can only be intelligent enough to escape it.

To simplify is to decide what we want and what we do not want. If we make no decisions we are overwhelmed with the sheer mass of New York's manifestations—social and political, artistic and commercial, for separate civilizations coexist here, touching at the boundary lines but independent at heart. The high-pressure organization of the city wastes time and energy, for New York consistently goes through the motions of solving problems or promoting ideas without accomplishing anything concrete. People go from one committee meeting to another or from one conference to another with a virtuous feeling that they are founding a new order of human beings, although they are only meeting a few pleasant friends on the wing and reading a few pieces of paper. One of the most efficient cities in the world wastes time and energy on a colossal scale, for it can never distinguish between the bland gesture and the deed.

The free people are those who have made up their minds. For they are not distracted, and they have all the time and energy they need to minister to their own dreams. They have mastered a titanic city. Like the Sermon on the Mount, the doctrine of simplification is a revolution that any man can begin here and now without joining an organization. It is also a revolution that can be won in five minutes or a half hour, and costs less than the morning newspaper. Misanthropy is the philosophy of abundance.

21. The West and Middle West are today recovering from a savage blizzard that has blocked the railroads and highways and caused the deaths of eight people. By some sort of merciful dispensation, a sweet-smelling south wind caresses this gritty, littered city and brings us a mellow day and a temperature of 72°. Massive cumulus clouds shimmer in the sunshine. The Riverside Drive benchers silently drowse in the warm light, reading books and newspapers or staring out over the river, suffused with dreams and melancholy.

A beautiful new tanker drops anchor off Seventy-ninth Street and keeps open house all day to festive visitors who go aboard from two busy launches. She is the *Olympic Games*, 18,000 tons, flying the blue-banded flag of Honduras and designed for the Persian Gulf trade. Fresh from the Sparrow Point yards of the Bethlehem Ship Building Corporation, she is painted an immaculate white with red-boot topping, which glows clear along her hull, and a sand-colored stack which is smartly raked and tapered. She will make fifteen knots service speed. This is a gala day on her clean decks. The officers in white hats crowd around the gangway to welcome their guests. Some of the crew lean lazily over the rail of the afterhouse; and occasionally the cooks, in white aprons flying in the soft breeze, hurry along the catwalk to the bridge house where the owners are no doubt serving refreshments, hot from the galley.

This is the crowning day in the career of the *Olympic Games*. She will never be so gleaming and spotless again. Presently she will be steaming across the cold and sullen Atlantic, through the Gibraltar gate into the long, blue Mediterranean that stretches 1,920 miles to Port Said, slowly and cautiously farther through the eighty-seven miles of the Suez Canal, and then through 1,400 miles of the blazing Red Sea, around Aden, into the Arabian Sea and Persian Gulf to a hot, stinking oil port in the caldron of the world. If she makes six or seven round trips a year she will be doing well. And since even a huge tanker can fill and discharge

her tanks in much less than twenty-four hours, the men who tend
to her needs have no time to stretch their minds and legs ashore.
They live suspended in space, detached from the world, dropped
from the rolls of society. Sailing the *Olympic Games* will be
drudgery.

22. Possibly the building agent is good to his family and his
friends who like him. There is some good in nearly every man if
you search deep enough to find it. But from nine in the morning
until six at night he stands between the owners and the tenants,
absorbing rancor from both sides. The tenants want heat and hot
water, clean hallways, convenient elevator service, and clean paint
on the woodwork and walls. The owners are jewel merchants who
have bought real estate as an investment and to spread the risks
of capital. They want to cut expenses to the bone and make a
profit. Like the tenants, they are full of hatred and scorn. The
building agent is their man. He collects the rents, pays the service
employees and haggles over the expenses. The job is impossible.
In nearly every human relationship, someone is satisfied at one
time or another. But in the relationship between tenants and
landlords no one is satisfied ever, and no one is ever in good
humor. Good humor is a tactical weakness that is exploited by
the opposing side. Caught in the middle of this eternal, furtive,
destructive hatred, the agent moves silently through a secret
world, hoping to keep out of sight. He does not answer letters.
Nothing less than a court summons brings action from him.
From one work day to another he sees nothing good, hears nothing good and speaks nothing good. There is bitterness in his soul.
"Make no friendship with an angry man lest thou learn his ways
and get a snare to thy soul."

23. "Wood-burning fireplaces," the apartment advertisements
enticingly declare. Although steam heat is infinitely more efficient
and economical, the fetish for fireplaces endures from the primitive past. Living among the mechanical comforts of today, apartment dwellers are reluctant to sever the link with past ages when
fire enclosed in a chimney was the center of living. Not many fires
are built in the fireplaces included in the appointments of new

apartment houses. Fires are superfluous; the wood, bought in lots of a dozen thin sticks, is expensive and a nuisance, and the dirt adds one more chore to the problem of keeping clean. But even in the modern age a fireplace is the customary focal point for the decoration of a living room. And particularly on snowy nights a crackling fire on the hearth is the supreme social luxury. It is fascinating to watch. It draws everyone close together in an atmosphere of timeless privacy and simplicity, as though the husbandman had collected the wood and brought it in from the woodpile in his arms. Call it a token offering to the gods who attended to the needs of primitive man, and still linger somewhere in the sleeping memories of apartment dwellers.

"I had to move into an apartment without a fireplace," an acquaintance mournfully declared the other day as evidence of hardship and a sharp drop in the social scale. He felt that his life among his peers was finished. There seemed to be nothing he could do to make his living room look comfortable. If worse comes to worse he can buy an imitation fireplace in any department store with grate and mantel and, if necessary, imitation logs that glow when the switch is turned on. That will propitiate the household gods and maintain unbroken the link to his forgotten ancestors.

During the autumn migration a chimney swift once dropped down a five-story flue into our apartment on the ninth floor of a new building and clung to the curtain beside the window. If a chimney swift does not know the difference between a perfunctory and a practical flue, who are we to be liberated from ancient superstitions? For many centuries the chimney swift has been working at flues. He ought to be able to distinguish between the genuine and the decorative.

24. Basically the Broadway theater is not an art, but an unsuccessful form of high-pressure huckstering. There is little continuity of management and no continuity of employment among actors, playwrights and allied artists and craftsmen. The operation of the industry is rigid. The business is conducted in an atmosphere of crisis, strain, and emergency. It is dependent chiefly upon a few established playwrights and a few established stars who have proved in the past and in most cases go on proving that they are good risks. If the Broadway theater survives, it will have to develop

new talent. But the crisis organization of the theater practically eliminates new talent. No one person and no particular groups of theater people are responsible for this tightly knotted situation, which is something that has been forming through the years; and there is no simple way of releasing it. Despite the huge sums of money involved in every production, not many people get rich out of the theater. Most of those who do are merely lucky for the moment. The Broadway theater is so firmly blocked on all sides that it has no freedom of action. It is a wonder that anybody stays in it. The present is intolerable; the future is very gloomy indeed.

Broadway theater people normally think in terms of the abnormal Broadway situation, and rarely in terms of variations from the Broadway norm. But if we ever have a theater that is versatile and flourishing, it will come by encouraging variations from the norm and making it possible for them to operate. Granted that the technical accomplishments of the Broadway theater are the best, not everything has to be held to those exacting standards. Half way between the tense perfection of the best Broadway stuff on the one hand and nothing on the other, there ought to be a more relaxed and informal theater where new playwrights, new actors and new audiences can enjoy themselves. There ought to be something between a feast and a famine. For the plight of the professional New York theater is not merely economic. It is much more serious than that—the fun has gone out of it. It is high-strung and sterile. It is not developing playwrights, actors or directors. It is doing the best it can to commit suicide.

25.   *"We gather together to ask the Lord's blessing.*
He chastens and hastens His will to make known,
The wicked oppressors cease then from distressing,
Sing praises to His name; He forgets not His own."
—Netherlands Thanksgiving Hymn, 1597.

Thanksgiving Day. Temperature 42° when we get to the country at 2 P.M. Pale but cheerful sunlight. This is the beginning of a holiday season that lasts until after New Year's Day. Although we usually date Thanksgiving from the first feast at Plymouth in November, 1621, the tradition of feasting and making merry at the darkest period of the year probably goes back much further into ancient history. At that time farmers did not have barns big enough to store grain for all the animals they had raised during the growing season. They slaughtered those they could not feed, and in order not to waste the meat, they celebrated with a feast. In ancient times people celebrated for one reason or another all through the dark, cold weeks at the bottom of the year. Although the organization of modern life gives us a certain immunity to the tyranny of the season (i.e., electric light compensates for the darkness and central heating for the cold) the impulse to celebrate still lies in our subconscious. From Thanksgiving through Christmas until New Year's Day is our annual holiday season. In length of time it coincides with the ancient pattern.

In modern history, days of Thanksgiving go back to 1574 when the Netherlands legislature proclaimed a day of prayer and thanksgiving for the liberation of the city of Leyden from the Spaniards. There was another day of Thanksgiving in 1609 when Spain signed a treaty of peace with the Netherlands. The English Separatists, who came to Plymouth in 1620, were in Holland at that time. They could give thanks for having found a refuge from religious persecution in England. It was natural for them to declare a Thanksgiving period in 1621 in Plymouth at the end of their first harvest. The first Thanksgiving lasted several days. Apart from giving thanks for the pathetically meager success of their first year in North America, the Plymouth pilgrims were able thus to make friendly overtures to the Indians and, craftily, demonstrate the superiority of their weapons. Throughout the Colonial period there were many days of Thanksgiving, and also throughout the Revolution. When Washington was President, he proclaimed a day of Thanksgiving on the last Thursday of November, 1789: "A Day of Public Thanksgiving and Prayer to be observed by acknowledging with grateful Hearts the many Signal Favours of Almighty God, especially for affording them an opportunity peaceably to establish a Form of Government for their Safety and Happiness." Thanksgiving did not become a regular holiday until Lincoln issued a proclamation in 1863, having been urged to do so by Mrs. Sarah J. Hale, editor of *Godey's Lady's Book*, and for many years an advocate of a national Thanksgiving Day.

My personal enthusiasm for Thanksgiving derives from the gargantuan celebration at my grandfather's house when I was a boy. My sisters and I had to get up in the early morning darkness to make the long journey by railroad with my parents to my grandfather's house in Weymouth, Massachusetts, within sight of the great Fore River Shipyard in Quincy. My grandfather's house looked enormous to us. It had two hot-air furnaces—a mark of luxury on a grand scale. The kitchen range was enormous. It had three ovens—the central oven for the turkey and the side ovens for ducks. The house was filled with the savory odors of roasting when we arrived, and the aunts were cheerfully busy with the huge task of preparing dinner. In addition to grandfather and grandmother and my parents there were three uncles, five aunts, one cousin, my two sisters and, later, my brother. Smoking was not permitted in the house. The uncles and my father went down cellar to sit on the settees, which had been brought in from the lawn, to smoke cigars and talk politics, rather petulantly and acidly, until dinnertime. The male gathering in the cellar was a very lordly ceremony while the women were scurrying around upstairs. Their nervous footsteps could be heard hurrying between the kitchen and dining room overhead. As nearly as I can recall, dinner consisted of soup, turkey and duck, mashed potatoes, onions, yellow turnip, cranberry sauce, plum pudding with hard sauce, apple, mince, pumpkin and cranberry pie, nuts and raisins. After dinner the entire company played "Stagecoach" in the parlor—probably to entertain the children, although we imagined that the adults loved it as passionately as we did. There were also toys and games in a closet for the children to play with after the adults had had enough. Everyone reassembled at the table about five o'clock for supper, which, I trust, was a light meal. It was dark when my parents, sisters and brother walked down the short hill to the railroad station to start the long, sleepy journey home. That journey lives in my memory as sheer torture. We children were thoroughly exhausted, as my parents may have been also. Thanksgiving will always be to me a romantic and exciting day because of these annual feasts when I was a boy.

Even now Thanksgiving dinners in a restaurant seem to me like a profanation of one of the glorious days of the year, and I find myself unreasonably intolerant of any intrusion on the privacy of family life on this day. But I shall always be especially grateful to a company of American missionaries in Foochow, China, who invited me to their religious service and Thanksgiving dinner during the war. That was a mournful time in a baleful coastal city with the Japanese not far away and spies and informers everywhere in the city. There was no turkey for that dinner. We ate goat. But most of the missionaries had been driven in by the enemy and they were keeping a hospital open and in use in the one coastal city not occupied by enemy troops. Their Thanksgiving Day was devout, cheerful and hospitable; and the humble sentiments and the noble melody of the old Netherlands Hymn of Thanksgiving, quoted at the head of this entry, stirred my memory and devotion on that lonely day in Foochow.

26. At this time of year the brown south shoulder of Pisgah Mountain snatches the sun out of our sky fifty-five minutes before the calendar sunset. On this eastern bastion of the mountain we have almost an hour less daylight than the late autumn sun is willing to provide. According to the almanac, sunset is scheduled for 4:37 this evening. But the sun slips down behind Pisgah at 3:42, which seems to me almost like mid-afternoon as I sit here writing by the west window. The hills to the north, which are not blocked by Pisgah, are lighted by the sun until 4:17, when the first shadow of evening rises from the valley and reaches the crown.

Since we live under the influence of Pisgah, our winter nights are as long as those in higher latitudes where Arctic influences are more austere. For at this season Pisgah rules the afternoon and evening. In the summer the sun sets further north and over hills that are lower and therefore do not snatch the sun so impatiently. In June the sun sets at about 7:15, standard time, which gives us three hours and thirty-three minutes more afternoon than we have now. But we are on daylight-saving time in summer, and the sun appears to set at 8:15, and the afternoon appears to be four hours and thirty-three minutes longer than it is today.

This is a tremendous time differential—much greater than I had imagined until I started just now to compute it. It accounts for the fact that at this time of year the afternoon seems to vanish before it has started, and it also accounts for the fact that I do a lot less work out of doors in November than in summer. The community as a whole is obviously that much less productive. And winter is to the same extent a grimmer season here than it is even a few miles farther north. Pisgah is only 2,900 feet high, but it rules our winter like a dour and icy giant.

27. After a night of rain, a gale comes roaring out of the north-west, and wind-torn clouds scud over the rim of the mountains and race in a panic across the blue sky. The sun is weak. The sun-light is white; and even at noon the shadows lie deep across the earth. Since the trees are bare, an occasional white birch draws a slim, glaring line that is conspicuous a half mile away. The silvery trunks of the beeches reflect the light gently. The mown fields are grayish yellow; the fields that have just been plowed are red with moist fertility. Well-watered for the past month the lawn is brilliantly green, and two misguided dandelions are in bloom. This is the majestic season for the evergreens. Blackish green after the growing season, the Norway spruces look hardy and massive. The red pines glow extravagantly, and the stand of young white pines at the bottom of the pasture now dominates the whole landscape. When the ancient deciduous trees are in leaf, the pine lots look promising. But this is the season of triumph for them. They are the liveliest patches on the hill. Relieved of the summer contrast with old elms and ashes, they look big. They are going to in-herit the earth. They were planted thirteen years ago. In contrast with the disorder of a natural forest they have always looked a little too proper, like a convention of latter-day converts. But now it is plain that they are acquiring a natural disorder of their own. They range in height from three feet to fifteen. They have devel-oped their own groupings; they have left open spots, and the deer have made twisting corridors through their ranks. The pines toss and twist in the gale. But their motion has the grace of a dance, and as the wind sweeps through their long leaves, they make wild music. For this is their season, and they are happy about it. They assume that they have a long, exultant future.

28. In the valuation of art, the judgment of artists is virtually infallible. Even professional critics, whose business is the giving of considered judgments, have a less secure grasp on the subject of art. They do not arrive at decisions so spontaneously. In the first place, the artist is the only free man in our society. He is not an artist primarily for the purpose of making money. He is fascinated with art of all kinds—whether graphic, literary or musical; his pri-mary motivation is artistic. Although some artists earn large sums

of money, most of them do not, and have no personal stake in commercial success. They are free to enjoy what they see without regard to its commercial value or its influence on the political structure of society. They do not care who gets hurt by an artistic creation. In the second place, they are accustomed to working directly with individual men and women, who are the raw materials of art. Nothing comes between. The artists cannot paint the mass-man, nor the Republican, Democratic or Communist party, nor capital or labor. They can paint only individual people in a characteristic or revealing environment. Accordingly, they have a keener understanding of human beings than any other group that I know.

People with a stake in our political or economic society are timid judges of art. Art terrifies them, or at least gives them an elusive feeling of insecurity. In the back of their heads they nurture a hope that art can be pretty, charming and innocuous. They feel happy when the artist makes no comment on anything vital to society. They want art that is familiar, rich in texture, joyous and satisfied. Hedged about with so many inhibitions, they are poor judges of art, for their minds are not free.

Being free, the artist is clairvoyant. Whether it is a painting, drama, dance, poem, symphony, or jam session, he assimilates it without confusion or alarm, knows whether it is genuine or spurious and knows whether it has achieved what it set out to do. His sense of values is uncorrupted. Since society consists of a series of compromises in which no one can be wholly satisfied, the artist is not an ideal social mentor. He cheerfully throws out the baby with the bath. But no one is as sound a judge of art as he is. To him it is the most essential thing in life, and he brings to it spiritual honesty and extraordinary artistic awareness.

The function of art is not to promote a code of standards or to establish social ideals but to tell the truth. What is, is; and if we are ever to get anywhere with enlightened civilization we must know the full truth about it. Whether it is flattering or distressing, inspiring or depressing, moral or immoral is beside the point; and the need is not for temperate speaking but for complete frankness about everyone and everything. For none of the maladies of humanity can be cured until it is understood.

29. In our civilized metropolitan life the most barbaric institution is the smart cocktail party. It herds strangers together like animals, pours liquor into them and expects them to perform. Noisy and cramped in a choking room, it is notable chiefly for its hysterical clatter. "Yatata, yatata, yatata, yatata," is Oscar Hammerstein II's parody of cocktail-party conversation.

Like buffet lunches and dinners, the cocktail party is basically insincere. The guest is cheaply valued, hurriedly greeted and thrust among strangers, serviced in passing and dismissed with a minimum of inconvenience to the host. The conversation is desperate and mechanical amid the bedlam and hubbub of a graceless social occasion. The cocktail party has the form of friendship without the warmth and devotion. It is a device either for getting rid of social obligations hurriedly en masse, or for making overtures towards more serious social relationships, as in the etiquette of whoring.

I always know how contemptuously I am valued when I am invited to a cocktail party. My value to society is easily computed—two drinks and half an hour.

30. On this day in 1835 Mark Twain (Samuel Clemens) was born in Florida, Missouri. In his own time Americans enjoyed him, but did not take him seriously as a great man of letters. Now we do. The life of the frontier having passed into history, we have pride of ancestry in it now and we honor Mark Twain as one of our cultural progenitors. In his early years he shared the life of the frontier, not as a critic but as a natural believer. He was filled with the vigorous optimism of the West. Son of a land speculator he, too, hoped to strike it rich—and even in his mature and sober years in New York he still gambled for high stakes like a frontiersman. At the impressionable period of his life he was filled with gusto, daring and animal spirits and enjoyed the excitement of being foot-loose among wild and adventurous men opening up a new country and mining it for big profits.

No one else who was also articulate knew so much about the root and muscle of America. He went to work when he was twelve, apprenticed to a printer in Hannibal, Missouri, on the unruly banks of the fabulous Mississippi River. He tramped through the

Middle West and East as a journeyman printer—the most learned of the vagabond professions. For four wonderfully impressionable years he served the Mississippi—first as an apprentice pilot and then as a licensed pilot on river steamers that were saturated in the floods, mud, and commerce of America. He went to Carson City and Virginia City which were roaring mining towns, and then on to California which was turbulent with men gambling, dreaming and sweating for fortunes. He was part of the raw material of literature. He had the extravagant humor of undisciplined men full of mighty enterprises; and he wrote the epic of America in the racy, braggart style of frontier Americans. *Life on the Mississippi* and *Roughing It* preserve the lustiness of his era, and *Tom Sawyer* and *Huckleberry Finn* retain the natural youth of the Mississippi civilization.

He did strike it rich, after all. When his short story, "The Jumping Frog," aroused the enthusiasm of the whole of America, he became a successful author, and secured his reputation by writing *Innocents Abroad* in the vein of Yankee irreverence and hyperbole. His vulgarity was honest and young. Like those who struck it rich in the mines, he settled down in the East and submitted to the discipline of being a wealthy celebrity. But there was nothing so enriching in the East as the mother of waters and the mining camps. A man of abundant energy, he kept on writing furiously, using his head more and more as time progressed. But the living magic trickled out of it. A native son had become a professional writer, rich, famous and influential. No wonder that the black clouds began to form in his soul and that in his declining years he despaired of America.

DECEMBER

December

WHEN THEY COME to work this morning, two typists on the sixty-seventh floor of the sleek R.C.A. tower in Radio City do not expect to find a long-eared owl at the window. But one is there. Screaming for protection against the untidiness of nature, the typists are comforted by a fearless window-cleaner. He captures the owl and summons the A.S.P.C.A., which consistently mediates between nature and civilized people. Drawing on his city store of folklore, he formally pronounces his captive "a barn owl." Photographers come rushing from the newspapers to record this impertinent invasion of a city person's prerogatives.

It is a long-eared owl. At this time of year long-eared owls drift southward. No doubt this one is more astonished by the slim grandeur of Radio City than the typists are by him. He refuses cheese, thus arousing the scorn of his captors. Doubtless he would enjoy a mouse, beetle, snake, or spider if Radio City restaurants were able to provide him with such simple field fare. The long-eared owl also eats small birds, of which there is a conspicuous lack at Radio City, but he might kill and devour pigeons, of which there is an abundance. If he can eat a partridge he ought to manage a pigeon.

Although birds of prey are not usual in New York City they are not unknown. A great-horned owl once spent a profitable winter season in Wall Street, living off pigeons. He had a better winter than the brokers. The duck hawk—swiftest and most deadly of our birds of prey—nests in the Palisades near the city and occasionally takes up residence in the city, also feeding on pigeons. I once happened to see one perching on the top of the Park-Sheraton Hotel roof sign at Seventh Avenue and Fifty-sixth Street. He was as detached, poised and lonely as if he were perched on a tree beside the river. The clattering, gritty hubbub of the biggest city in the world seemed somehow to escape his attention.

2. "Foreigner" is a word I have come to dislike. It preserves ignorance and prejudices that are obsolete in the modern world, and draws distinctions between natives and outlanders that are not genuine. The word derives from the Latin "foris," which means "outside"—purely a geographical distinction that applies as logically to other towns and other states as to other nations. The word itself is legitimate; we need a word to express the idea of "outside" places. But all national cultures, like ours, preserve a number of primitive and tribal attitudes. Primitive people feared and distrusted outside groups of people. Like the American Indians, who fought tribal wars, primitive people regarded other people as their natural enemies, and fought them instinctively.

After living in the blinding glare of international events for a number of decades, we have learned many things that primitive people could not know. Through the sensitive instrument of the United Nations, we have access every day to the problems of other nations and can begin to understand the sources of international troubles. But the word "foreign" still carries with it implications of fear and distrust; and, in the bumptious American point of view, it also carries implications of inferiority. When I first went to work abroad, I felt humiliated to discover that I, too, was a foreigner. In the remote provinces of China I was, in fact, *yang-kuei-tzu* ("foreign devil"), or *ta-pi-tzu* ("big nose"). American ignorance of foreigners is not as primitive as that, but it is steeped in the ancient superstition that strangers are enemies and that unfamiliar ideas are vicious. We do not accept foreigners as individuals.

This is a strange attitude for a country that, with the exception of a few thousand red Indians, is entirely composed of foreigners. No nation in the world has drawn so heavily on the rich human resources of foreign nations.

3. First snow of the season in the city. For about an hour in the morning it drifts by the windows and whitens the long roofs of the steamship piers. Although the sky is low and sodden, the roofs are fresh and immaculate. By noon the snow turns to rain, and by midafternoon the familiar dirty gray and brown repossess the city. New York is not in the mood for a decisive snowstorm yet.

4. After I have finished writing my theater review about midnight at my desk in the office I walk upstairs to the composing-room to correct the proof and stand by while the type is put into the drama page. This concludes the long day with at least one concrete and satisfying triumph. For the composing-room, which is warm and bright at midnight, is a model of efficient organization by trained men who know what they are doing and enjoy it. By the time I reach the make-up table, the proofs of the first two sections of my review are waiting. I correct them, give them to the copy-cutter who pastes a "rush" slip on them and gives them to operators of the type-setting machines. Within a few minutes the last paragraphs of my review, gleaming in white type metal, reach the assembly-bank and are whisked through a slot to the proof boy. He pulls a proof and hands it to me. By the time I have finished reading it, the "Colonel" or Harold, who makes up the page on alternate nights, has the type in its proper place on the page and is waiting for the corrected lines to come from the machines. Occasionally we are late by a few minutes. Since the mechanical departments of the paper are thoroughly organized, we can be a few minutes late if we notify the key man who, in turn, notifies the stereotypers and pressmen, who adjust their schedules accordingly. Almost anything within reason can be done because the men are masters of their jobs and work with esprit de corps.

Their skills are flexible. They are not confused by sudden changes. Five minutes before closing time last night, Harold, who was studying the type of my one-column story, remarked: "I'd like to see that under a two-column head." "So would I," I replied. "Let's do it then," he said, beginning to move fast. While I scribbled a two-column head on the back of a proof sheet, he broke up the page and rearranged the type. The new head, accurately set and spaced, came off the machine the instant he was ready for it. He dropped the type into place, stuffed in a few leads, and locked up the page. It was rolled off to the stereotyping table on the exact second of official closing time.

I wish the world were operated a thousandth part as well, and that the men of the world knew their jobs as well and worked together with anything like the good will and good humor of our night composing-room.

5. Gaped at by a silent crowd of two or three hundred people, the service employees of Radio City raise a ninety-foot Christmas tree in the plaza today. This annual and cheerful rite formally opens the holiday season in this neighborhood. The tree is a giant Norway spruce cut in Mt. Kisco and hauled to the city in a trailer truck that blocked traffic all the way. It was brought inside the city in the dark of the morning before the day traffic had fairly begun. Chester Arthur was President of the United States when this tree was a seedling. It is a forest monster, sixty-five years old, with a colossal butt, and it is thick with long, heavy boughs that canopy the street. It took seven hours for a twelve-ton derrick to raise it into place, plant it securely in a timbered base and secure it with guy wires. It will take several days more for a crew of electricians to decorate it with festive light bulbs, imitation snow flakes and other traditional baubles. When it is formally lighted it will be the most glorious sight in the neighborhood and will give thousands of people a few moments of elation and wonder. After sixty-five years of reaching for the sky, this spruce has achieved an enviable triumph. In its old age it will bring happiness to thousands who will admire it, understand it and be grateful. Not many human beings conclude their lives so honorably.

The R.C.A. Building rises eight hundred and fifty feet of cold, slender, arrogant steel, glass and masonry. Measured against the seventy-floor spire that efficiently houses a busy city, the forest giant is factually insignificant. But in spirit, it is the most royal thing in the busy plaza—rugged, dark green, dignified, detached. Radio City is one of the world's most distinguished real-estate developments. It is a monument to modern design and engineering. But a ninety-foot spruce tree with its forest of branches and spire of green leaves outranks it. Amid all the chromium appointments and metal splendors of Radio City, there is nothing to see today but a lone spruce tree that graces the plaza with natural form and beauty.

6. St. Nicholas Eve. When New York was a Dutch colony, gifts were made secretly on the eve of St. Nicholas in accordance with the European tradition. The association of St. Nicholas, or Santa Claus, with Christmas is not much more than a century and a

quarter old. In fact, the institution of Christmas set aside as the grand climax of the calendar year is comparatively modern. You do not find much about it in old diaries and journals.

St. Nicholas, bishop of Myra, in Lycia, lived in the fourth century. The tradition is that on three successive nights he tossed bags of gold into the windows of an impoverished nobleman who did not have doweries for his three daughters and was proposing to make prostitutes out of them. The gifts of St. Nicholas, bestowed secretly, provided doweries and the girls were properly married. This is the origin of the custom of making gifts anonymously at night, and stuffing them in stockings hung outside the door or by the chimney indoors. St. Nicholas is the patron saint of Russia (no doubt, unrecognized today), and the special patron of children, scholars, merchants, and sailors. In 1087 the citizens of Bari, Apulia, seized his bones and took them home to Bari, where there is one of the many churches that are dedicated to him.

Since folklore does not get into print while it is spontaneously forming in the fancies and customs of people, there are no records of the transformation of *San Nicolaas*, as the Dutch called him, into the modern Santa Claus—who, incidentally, is standing on corners of Fifth Avenue today, ringing a cheerful bell and collecting money for good causes. But at Christmastime in 1822 Dr. Clement Clarke Moore, a somewhat pedantic divine who lived in the Chelsea district of New York, put the myth of Santa Claus into verse, "The Night Before Christmas," and described him at length. For the first time, as far as printed records go, Santa Claus drove reindeer over the rooftops and entered the house by way of the chimney. For the first time he wore a fur hat and a coat trimmed with fur; and very nearly for the last time, "the stump of a pipe he held tight in his teeth." Also, observe that he came prancing over the rooftops on Christmas Eve—"Happy Christmas to all, and to all a good-night." Dr. Moore's model for Santa Claus was not a saint of the Middle Ages, but a little, round, jolly Dutchman who did odd jobs around the Moore house. His Santa Claus was, accordingly, rougher, dirtier and smellier than the snowy-bearded, sanitary Santas who cozen children in the department stores today.

Dr. Moore wrote several scholarly works, among them being a two-volume *Compendious Lexicon of the Hebrew Language*. But nothing he ever wrote contributed so much to joy and good will as "The Night Before Christmas," which is Santa Claus's first portrait, drawn in particularly festive rhyme. The good doctor wrote it for his own children. Somewhat to his annoyance, a friend of the family sent it to the editor of the Troy *Sentinel* who published it anonymously on December 23, 1823. Naturally, it was popular, and republished every Christmastime. In 1829, the editor of the Troy *Sentinel* described the author as a New York scholar, but did not name him. The poem was included in *The New York Book of Poetry* in 1837, still anonymously. By this time many people knew who had written it. On Christmas Day, 1838, the Troy *Budget* named Dr. Moore as the author. Dr. Moore included it, under the title of "A Visit From St. Nicholas," in his collected poems in 1844.

Dr. Moore died on July tenth, 1863. He was first buried in St. Luke's churchyard in Hudson Street. When that property was sold, his bones were transferred to Trinity Cemetery, Broadway and One hundred and Fifty-fifth Street. Every year a fresh wreath is laid on his grave and carols are sung there. For Dr. Moore is the patron saint of Santa Claus. Not even Dickens has contributed so much to the festive mystery and good cheer of Christmas.

7. December 7, 1941, will go down in infamous memory. Sweeping out of the benign Hawaiian skies, about one hundred Japanese bombers killed more than three thousand American soldiers and sailors and crippled the American fleet lying in Pearl Harbor. Thus, the Second World War wrapped the world round with the shroud of death. Although most Americans had felt subconsciously that sooner or later we would be drawn into a war that was being fought to defend freedom, most of us tried not to think about it logically. We were dwelling in an uneasy but pleasant dreamworld. December seventh was a Sunday—clear and cold (high temperature 34°; low 25°) and the newspapers were heavy with Christmas shopping advertisements. We were joyously slipping into the holiday season. The leading news story reported that Roosevelt had made a personal appeal to Hirohito to call off Japanese aggression in Siam and at the Burma Road, which governed the defenses of the Malay Peninsula. Two other stories on the front page indicated that America was valiantly trying to feel secure. The Secretary of the Navy declared that the United States Navy had no

superior in the world: "I'm proud to report that the American people may feel fully confident in their Navy," he exclaimed. Another somewhat truculent story announced that Australia, Great Britain, the Netherlands Indies, and the United States had completed preparations "to match Japanese action, move by move" in the Pacific.

While we were indolently glancing at these complacent news bulletins, the Japanese were whining murderously out of the innocent sky and inflicting on Pearl Harbor the worst naval disaster in history. In the next few weeks and months Hong Kong, Manila, Malaya, the Netherlands Indies, and Burma fell with sickening softness. Until the Battle of Midway on June third to sixth, the mighty powers of freedom fell back farther and farther before the superior fighting strength of a small but bellicose tyrant. That was the blackest period in the history of the United States. On this terrible Sunday in 1941 I don't suppose there were more than a few people in the country who knew how feeble we were and how vulnerable to the savage and hysterical warfare of a trained, organized, fanatical little enemy. Not many of us realized that it would be nearly four desperate years before we could breathe more easily and read the Christmas shopping advertisements leisurely.

8. In the country. Where do the birds hide on days like this? The temperature is 26°. The northwest wind that cuts across the hills has icy fingers now. Thick, grayish clouds wallow ponderously in the sky. Occasionally the silvery sun breaks through. Squalls of snow, whirling in the wind, brush through the woods absent-mindedly. Reasoning that the birds may be lying in the south pasture under the lee of the spruce-thatched hills, I go down there and swing back towards the northwest, looking and listening. Although the giant white oaks have shed their rounded leaves, the young oaks are still clinging to theirs, and they rustle dryly in the wind. But there are no other sounds. Coming out of the pasture I cross the boggy field where the deer drink, just south of the freshly plowed hill. In a sheltered bay, a chickadee calls once feebly, as though he were frostbitten, and flutters off without enthusiasm through the bare trees. But he has no companions. There are no other birds in this area, and no deer either, although I saw two yesterday when I was driving in the car.

Thinking that the birds might be in the old hemlock woods on the north side of the hills, I climb over and come into the wood-lot from the east. This is a favorite woodpecker neighborhood. The hairy woodpecker lives there in the spring and summer, gouging holes in the dead hemlock stumps. I have never seen the pileated woodpecker there, although some of the deep, oblong gashes torn out of the trees are his work. But the hemlock grove is birdless today. I go over it thoroughly, crunching the beech and red oak leaves, then stopping, listening, and looking. There is nothing—no song birds, no partridges, no deer, no squirrels, no rabbits, no woodchucks, no hedgehogs. Across the narrow valley to the steep north, a fox barks once. Otherwise the frosty woods are barren. Somewhere in this township there must be fifteen or twenty species of birds. Probably they are huddling together for companionship, waiting for the snow. But I cannot find them on my hill today.

9. Although the country looks bleak and dour there is a spot of Christmas cheer in one of the two windows in Marshall Bell's store in the village. There is also a tiny Christmas tree with colored lights in the window of Mrs. Hastings' ice cream store. Mrs. Matthews, our postmistress, has hung holiday decorations in the post office, and simulated a snowstorm with daubs of white soap on the windows. The village street is empty and the village trees are barren. Doors and windows are closed in the cold weather, and no one loiters outside. The village would look desolate except for the holiday red and green glowing in the store windows. Even in the country there is a human need for living colors on which to store up strength for the bitter season ahead. No doubt this is how the holiday custom of green boughs and red berries originated among farmers and husbandmen shut up for the winter thousands of years ago. As a species the pine is one hundred million years old. During the winter green boughs and evergreen trees keep intact the image and fragrance of life; and during the congealed winter season men and women like to remember the glory of spring and the abundance of the summer and the harvest weeks.

Since Marshall Bell keeps a general store, he cannot wave a magic wand over the whole of it and devote himself exclusively to holiday trade, as the department stores do in the city. But one corner of his store is festive. He and John Crotty have added personal enthusiasm to merchandising guile in the Christmas transmutation of their store. In the center of the show window there is the model of a red fireplace with two birch sticks on the hearth and candles with red bows on the shelf. A hunter's red shirt fills one corner of the window with fiery color. Inside the store, the holiday goods include toys, perfumes, Christmas wrapping paper, ribbon, Christmas tree lights, candles and decorations and practicable goods like shirts, underwear, socks, shoes and rubber boots. Most of these things will probably turn up in the neighborhood farmhouses on Christmas Day. "If we have some snow, I'll sell this stuff," Marshall says. "You mean, people don't remember Christmas unless there is snow on the ground?" I ask. "No," he replies. "I mean that they will not buy their Christmas stuff here unless the snow keeps them from driving to Albany or Catskill. If the driving is bad they will not stir out of the village. Well, we'll wait and see," he concludes with the sigh of a merchant resigned to the follies of the public.

In the meantime, everyone who walks up the street or comes into the store knows that Christmas is only sixteen days away. That is a genuine poetic contribution to the spirit of the community—almost as necessary as groceries and hardware.

10. It seems to me we always close the house for the winter on one of the most lustrous days of the year. Temperature 22° today. A fleecelike snow of bright particles has dusted the hill. The road is pure white, curving up the hill between white-powdered fields. The hills are steel-blue with white patches where the plowed fields lie. The shaggy woodlots have become a crisp design of black and white; the woodlots have acquired a finely groomed appearance. But, alas, this is the day when Chris Ehlers and I rob the house of its hospitality and return it to the loneliness of an abandoned dwelling. There is too much work to be done in the city now. And sooner or later the winter will have the hill so firmly locked in ice and snow that we cannot casually open our part of it on week ends.

It is disheartening to observe the speed with which the house withdraws into itself. We have to put the shutters on the big windows, close the blinds, store the cushions in a metal chest, drain the water out of the plumbing system, and empty the tanks and boilers. For the two of us it is hardly more than an hour's work, we have done it so many times. But before we have finished, the house has begun to keep its own counsel and retreat into some remote, inscrutable mood of its own. It becomes dark, cold and disinterested. It gives me a feeling that it is eliminating me, and never had any confidence in my loyalty. All winter it will snap with the cold, and the snow will whirl down off the roof and pile up to the eaves of the porch. But it will be entirely self-contained. I have seen it in the winter after it has been closed, and I have felt like a stranger to it. Closing the house is the one melancholy chore that has to be done every year. I am glad to leave the last rites to Mr. Ehlers, who actually turns the key in the lock.

In March the red-winged blackbirds will be calling "congaree" in the swamps, and the robins and bluebirds will be singing in the dooryard. I shall not be singing but, *deo volente*, I shall be there.

11. Like public office, newspaper reporting is a public trust. If anything else is to be right in the tumultuous life of the city today, the facts in this morning's newspaper must be accurate and judiciously selected. The vital news must be reported honestly and the community must be fully informed about its affairs. For several million people are now reading yesterday's record over breakfast or on their way to the office; and the whole world is at their mercy, because they are forming impressions on the basis of a headline here, a paragraph there, a photograph or the gag in a column. In the course of time the world will be shaped in the image they form in their heads. For information, whether right or wrong, creates the basis for judgment; and the whole structure of our lives rests on judgments that are sound. Every word in a newspaper is vital to someone, and every word must be right. Contrary to the familiar phrase, it will not be all the same in a hundred years, for what is evil in today's newspaper will be visited unto the third and fourth generations.

Facts are essential, but they are not enough. Facts can be dug out of the files—those morgues of dead or dehumanized information where errors, too, are embalmed—and facts piled on top of facts can crush the truth out of anyone. You can slit a man's

throat with a fact—even with a fact that is accurate. It is a fact
that he was once charged with espionage, but the basic truth is
that he was exonerated. It is a fact that he was suspended from
the service; but the basic truth is that he was reinstated and pro-
moted. No single fact conveys the whole truth, and all the known
facts put together still may be misleading.

There are three sides to every story—what you think, what he
thinks, and the truth. Get the facts, but get the truth before you
print them. For public opinion founded on gossip, rumor or suspicion has the capacity of a plague and will wipe out civilization.
The atomic bomb is not a millionth part so destructive. The evil
that men do lives on the front pages of greedy newspapers, but
the good is oft interred apathetically inside.

12. Relax your vigilance for a few days, and the news becomes
bureaucratic. It consists of facts and figures, declarations, speeches,
decisions. "The President said—," "the Chinese General Assembly
today elected—," "the Russian representative declared—," etc.
You would think that the world were populated by automatons
who went through a prescribed series of motions and responded
mechanically to mechanical situations. But there is a reason for
everything, and behind the reason stands a human being—doing
or thinking. Most of our news is dehumanized. It gives the fact;
it ignores the people. One of the reasons why people are fascinated by crime stories is that crime news is violently full of
human nature.

Some facts are vital, like the election of candidates and changes
in the income tax, and they have to be reported as facts. But most
news is dull because it is reported tersely without reference to the
people who made it. And most foreign news is reported as though
the French, the Russians and Chinese were indistinguishable from
Americans and arrived at their decisions by American methods.
You would think that people behaved like Americans everywhere.
You would think that they all lived on cement highways and had
oil burners in the cellar.

The basic news seldom gets published. It is the news of people.
How do they live? In what kind of houses and eating what kind
of food? What sort of work do they do? What do they do with
their idle time? What are their problems? What are their hopes?

Why do they behave so abominably? There must be a reason, and it is not a fact, but a condition. For that sort of news you need correspondents who put on their shoes and get out of doors. Most news lacks warmth and flavor, for it is written as though human beings were statistics.

13. In one of the few empty ceremonies of our national life, the electors of the Electoral College meet today in their respective states to elect the President of the United States officially. The governors of the states must report today's results to the Secretary of State. On January sixth, the presiding officer of the Senate will open the ballot box at a joint meeting of Congress and supervise the counting of the electors' ballots. Although we have all known since November third, how many electoral votes the various candidates have won, the Electoral College still goes through this ancient mumbo-jumbo, and the President is not officially chosen until it has acted.

American official life is comparatively free of obsolete formalities. We pride ourselves on being blunt and progressive. But the institution of the Electoral College preserves the most conspicuous blunder the Founding Fathers made in the venerated Constitutional Convention in 1787. Liberal as circumstances made them about most things, they did not trust the people to choose the chief executive. Even after the Revolutionary War, they were afraid of populism and thought of the President in terms of the crowned heads of Europe. Hamilton was inclined to think that America should choose a King and found a royal family. Others believed that the President should be chosen for life. There were several other points of view. Accordingly, the Founding Fathers compromised by deciding that the President should be chosen by electors in the various states, and that the electors, in turn, might be chosen as each state independently decided. In any event, the President would not be elected directly by the people.

At best this ceremony is bogus now. At worst it can elect a President who is not the people's choice. In 1824 it elected John Quincy Adams, although Andrew Jackson had 40,000 more votes. In 1876, it elected Rutherford B. Hayes, although Samuel J. Tilden had 250,000 more votes. And in 1888, it elected Benjamin Harrison, although Grover Cleveland had 100,000 more votes. And even when the Electoral College chooses the President whom the people have chosen, it monstrously distorts the election by the arbitrary system of unit votes by states. In 1912 Woodrow Wilson received 42 per cent of the popular vote but 82 per cent of the electoral vote. In 1936, Franklin Roosevelt won 60 per cent of the popular vote but 98 per cent of the electoral vote.

In our national life there is nothing more sacred than the election of a President by the people. This is the most vital process in the democratic system. Nothing penetrates so deeply into the heart of democratic government. Yet we stupidly preserve an archaic election machinery that always arbitrarily distorts the proportions and may again subvert the will of the people. We are stupidly preserving the one dangerous error in the democracy of the Constitution. Although the United States has three times accepted a President it did not elect, it would be foolish to do so again. There is too much at stake today, and any law that subverts the will of the people is an invitation to violence and revolution. Doubtless the electors are feeling foolish today—going through an empty ceremony as mechanical and specious as the annual meeting of the stockholders in large corporations. But they are dealing with something of first importance to the well-being of the nation. If the nation were really alert to its own interests, it would withhold even this formal authority, and insist upon choosing the President directly. To elect the President through the ritual of the Electoral College is to conspire in an old and dangerous fraud.

14. Whenever I am required to define my religious beliefs I write "Transcendentalist." This is not entirely frank. Transcendentalism is not a religion and in fact is not a vital element in thought today. It was the philosophy of Emerson and Thoreau and grew out of the aspiring and heady optimism of that period in American culture—"the Newness," some people scornfully dubbed it. It was basically a religious philosophy that saw God reflected in every aspect of life and placed the divinity of a tree on an equality with the divinity of man. It did not isolate God on some exalted throne in some remote and invisible heaven, but found Him here and now in the midst of the workaday world, the animating force behind every creative impulse. Where there is life

there is God. He is not condescending or snobbish; He is not censorious or fastidious.

Since transcendentalism had no dogma and no intellectual structure, it escaped out of our civilization, like mysticism which is in turn an escape from reality and therefore an evasion of life. But I like the warmth, brightness, confidence and hope of the transcendentalist universe in which I am related to all men and all growing things and am not shut off from anything except by my own ignorance or the feebleness of my own vitality.

15. On this day in 1791 the Bill of Rights went into force as a living part of the Constitution. Like the Magna Carta and the Declaration of Independence, the Bill of Rights is among the great state papers of all time. For almost a century and a half after their ratification by the original states, the various rights were generally taken for granted as finished business. But when the creeping paralysis of totalitarianism began to spread across Europe and Asia, we awoke to the value of these ten amendments to the Constitution which specifically guarantee the independence of ordinary men and women. For now we realize that the guarantees cannot be preserved without a deliberate and vigilant effort. Individual freedoms are not the law of nature, but the will of man. In a fiercely competitive world they cannot be taken for granted.

When the Constitution was presented for adoption to the states, the Bill of Rights rose out of a fierce popular determination to be free from the tyranny of states and masters. The authors of the Constitution had thought that a Bill of Rights was superfluous. They believed that individual freedoms were sufficiently implied in the Constitution. And since each state had its own Bill of Rights, they modestly believed that they had no authority to write a national Bill of Rights: that to do so would be, in fact, an unwarranted invasion of the sovereignty of the states. For they, too, were thoroughly aware of the vital importance of freedom for individuals, and that too much national authority might murder the freedom they were endeavoring to preserve.

But when the Constitution was submitted to the people, the absence of a Bill of Rights alarmed the citizens of every state.

The Constitution was variously described as "haughty" and "imperious," and as a cunning charter for delivering liberty into the hands of a few men. Patrick Henry declared that all rights "are rendered insecure or lost" by the Constitution. It was "unworthy of free men," he said. Public opinion then, as now, controlled the course of public affairs. Although many states were reluctant to ratify the Constitution without a Bill of Rights, they were also aware of the perils of delay in putting the Constitution into force. There was, accordingly, a gentleman's agreement that a Bill of Rights would become the first piece of business of the first Congress. It was. The first Congress assembled in New York in 1789, and wrote twelve amendments to the Constitution guaranteeing individual freedoms. The first two amendments were not ratified by the states, and the third amendment thus became the first of the ten amendments now known as the Bill of Rights. They have never been altered. No one has ever proposed that they should be altered, and no one would dare affront the American people with so cynical a proposal. Our Bill of Rights has served as one of the models for the Universal Declaration of Human Rights adopted by the United Nations in December, 1948. On the other hand, our Bill of Rights is descended from the Bill of Rights written by the English Commons in December, 1689, reasserting ancient rights and liberties that had been destroyed by James II. Note that December appears to be the month when people act on the principles of individual rights, thus pouring light out of their minds to compensate for the light that nature does not supply in this hemisphere.

16. On the top floor of a ramshackle building on the west side of Columbus Circle dwells a man of independence and integrity. You puff and groan up three flights of battered stairs. At the top you enter a series of ancient rooms that seem spacious, warm, and inviting. For Boris Aronson and his wife, Lisa, are artists who make a world of their own inside the visible universe that leaves most people at loose ends. With a few pots of paint and abundant imagination they have transmuted a forgotten rookery into an immaculate drawing room with a working studio attached. The up- and downtown traffic hurries petulantly through the Circle. The lighted display signs for all sorts of pagan enterprises glow and flash through the bay of windows—a chop-suey joint, a television theater, the General Motors giant enterprises, wearilessly reminding New York of their size and success, and Coca Cola, the beverage of millions who have only a minute or two for relaxing. Boris' drawing room with its green plants, comfortable furniture, and its paintings hanging on the wall or stacked in a corner is the focal point where the bizarre competition of the Circle's affairs falls into order and perspective. It becomes a picture—vulgar, crude, humorless, grotesque, but vivid and interesting, for it emits a kind of wild, self-confident vitality.

Boris sees it. He sees it all the time and is fascinated by it. Standing thoughtfully at the window, he looks for the forms that compose it. It is a constant challenge to the artist in him. Sometimes he will shyly show you a sketch or a painting in which he has tried to resolve the raw materials of Columbus Circle into art—drawing your attention most insistently to places where he has failed. Somewhere in the back of his head there is a dream of what a painting of Columbus Circle should be, but he never feels that he has recaptured it on canvas. The great truth, he believes, always just eludes him. This is the problem of his life—not only Columbus Circle but America: how to perceive the truth and express it. "This is the greatest unexplored country in the world," he says with enthusiasm. "If writers and artists would only find out what is going on every day in the lives of the people, the whole world would be astonished and excited. But writers and artists never seem to get beyond the little forms of art. All we get really are the little forms that become fashionable."

I know the answer, and it is not encouraging: God has the only welkin eye; He is the only complete master of form. All the forms we know are merely parts of the whole. But this will not keep Boris from gazing ruefully out of his window at Columbus Circle and wondering why he cannot put the whole truth on canvas. For the truth is there, his eyes are good and his mind is both judicial and receptive. He has a passion for art. He is not much interested in himself.

17. In the country everyone begins the day by idly consulting the thermometer. It is one of several weather auguries—like the clouds, the wind, the temper of the sun, and the general tone of

the morning. But from a fifth-floor window in a tall city apartment house one morning looks exactly like another, except for occasional days of fog, rain, or snow. The physical structure of the city takes no interest in the weather; in fact parts of the city do not even recognize the sun. Unconsciously the city imagines that it has eliminated the weather. In the city, therefore, the thermometer has an independence and integrity that have to be especially respected. It has its finger on the sensitive pulse of nature; it cannot be controlled for the convenience of the citizenry. Faithfully, unemotionally it gives the raw facts of the day, whether you like them or not. The thermometer sensitively responds to the only wild thing left in the city: the free air that rises or falls in temperature according to the weather that inexorably rolls across the Hudson from Canada, the merciless plains of the West, or the balmy Gulf of Mexico. Every day it measures a part of America accurately. Unlike the barometer, it is simple and direct and needs no interpretation. I am especially devoted to the thermometer in the city; and I consult it, humbly and inquiringly, the first thing every morning.

It is 28° F. (−2.22° Centigrade) this morning. Brisk, but not aggressive; "seasonable" in the sociable vernacular of the Weather Bureau. I learn, with a mild sensation of local pride, that our weather in Eighty-fourth Street is one degree colder than the weather on top of the Whitehall Building near the Battery, where the Weather Bureau takes the official temperature of New York. Uptown and downtown do not agree on many things. We are farther north. We are accustomed to a harsher climate. We are hardier people. We do not have to be pampered by the weather.

18. The holiday has begun. There is a quiver of excitement around town today—postmen making three deliveries of mail instead of two, children a little keener than usual in the otherwise dismal subway, porters unloading crates and barrels of turkeys in the meat-market section of Fourteenth Street, automobiles speeding up West Street with Christmas trees on the running board, on the roof or poking out of the luggage carriers.

Along the water front two steamships are loading cargoes of trucks and busses for Caribbean and South American ports. The guards are warming themselves at fires of broken boxes, which are snapping and smoking in empty oil drums. Otherwise, the water front is locked up tight. But there is one cheerful oasis in the week-end blankness—the green and aromatic Christmas tree mart in the middle of West Street. Hundreds of fir balsams from Nova Scotia are stacked there in neat bundles. Already a carpet of evergreen needles has begun to soften the black pavement, as though West Street were an incipient forest. Customers of all ages are critically examining the trees for height, symmetry and fullness of branches, and carrying away the ones they choose on their shoulders or on their autos. It seems to me that this is privileged merchandising—dealing in a great folk legend that is bigger than any of the clerks or customers; and the clerks appreciate it. The customers look wary and driven, eager not to get cheated. In spite of the impatience of the crowds, however, the two brothers who are selling in the booth I visit seem to enjoy the occasion. When I pay for the pair of wreaths I have selected, they both say: "Hope you have a Merry Christmas." I must remember to patronize them next year.

19. *"Good my lord, will you see the players well bestowed? Do you hear, let them be well used; for they are the abstracts and brief chronicles of the time; after your death you were better have a bad epitaph than their ill report while you live."*

For Shakespeare had been among actors and knew their worth. When he inserted these fond remarks into *Hamlet* he was more concerned with writing than with acting, but he was still full of affection for the people who had helped bring him up. Observe Hamlet's delight when the arrival of the actors is reported. He has been deep in melancholy. The life of the court stinks with corruption. Among the politicians and palace guard he is a lonely man, for they reek with treachery, scheming, sycophancy, and deceit. He does not trust them. But when the players enter, the clouds lift from around his soul and he feels gay and secure. "You are welcome, masters; welcome, all," he says joyfully. "I am glad to see thee well: welcome, good friends." For the first time in the play he is radiant. In company with the actors he knows that he is on firm ground.

Players did not have much social prestige in those days. In

Molière's time actors ranked with peddlers and rat-catchers. *Une vie sans soucis et quelque fois sans six sous*, some noble punster said. Although individual stars were respected in later years, like Betterton, Garrick, and Fanny Kemble, actors as a group were classified as rogues and vagabonds through most of the nineteenth century.

20. But they are first-class citizens now. Ironically enough, they are admired and appreciated for their spirit and skill at a time when most of them are unemployed: they have most prestige at the time when most of them are not working. But everyone knows how willingly actors have risen to their responsibilities as citizens. No other group has so consistently and successfully taken leadership in good causes that deserve public support. No group believed more passionately in the moral principles of the war or did more to arouse the public or to assuage the loneliness of the soldiers. During the war actors were literally the abstracts and brief chronicles of the times as well as the keepers of the public conscience.

There are plenty of bad actors. Like people in general, many actors are ignoble. Their jealousies, vanities and professional whims provide, in the formal phrase of Dr. Johnson, "the most risible scenes in the farce of life." But by nature acting provides a unique training for citizenship. It is a group art that comes alive only in association with other artists. When he is at work the actor performs as one of a team. And since acting is performed for the delight of the public, the actor acquires a remarkably quick and sensitive awareness of the spirit of ordinary people. No one knows better how to get on with people, and no group has won so much of the public's confidence. No wonder Hamlet rejoiced when the players arrived at his stepfather's castle. He could trust them. Their motives were clean.

21. Winter begins at 11:43 A.M. Sun rises at 7:21; sets at 4:36. The axis of the North Pole is tilted 23° 27′ away from the sun, which is the maximum for the year, and the rays of the sun now reach New York at their maximum, therefore their weakest, angle. Although the North Pole starts tilting back towards the sun at

11:44 A.M., if not before, the earth will continue for several more weeks to lose more heat by night than it receives by day. Although the solar system begins almost at once to make our life brighter, the earth is sluggish. It is as though the tilting earth, like a torpid and dull-witted human being, could not change direction easily, and through inertia tended to keep going in the old direction. There is a lag here, the cold increasing several weeks after the sun has started coming back again. But even in the solar system the improvement will be more scientific than practicable for a long time. The sun, which rises today at 7:21, will rise at 7:22 on the twenty-fourth, at 7:23 on the twenty-sixth, at 7:24 on the twenty-ninth and at 7:25 from January first to January eighth. It will not again rise as early as it did today until January seventeenth. But the sunsets will be more cheerful almost immediately—a minute later on the twenty-fourth, two minutes later on the twenty-sixth, three minutes later on the twenty-seventh. On January eighth the sun will set thirteen minutes later than today. Today is the bottom of the year.

22. A friend drops into the office after returning from two years in Shanghai. To me his return looks like a happy deliverance from a wretched and crushing ordeal. For Shanghai—a stricken city—has been short of food, fuel and living quarters. Blockaded by Nationalist ships, it has been isolated from the rest of the world. It has been repeatedly bombed by Nationalist airplanes. Although Americans have been unable to leave Shanghai, they have been harried and victimized by the Chinese communists, who have systematically added personal abuse to privation and misery. I am full of sympathy for a friend who has survived and finally escaped from a nerve-wracking experience.

But he is a little taken back by my sympathy. The facts were grimmer than the realities, as is often the case, and he is not aware of having suffered physically or mentally. "It is true that things have been hard," he says with some surprise, "but we have managed somehow. In fact, we have occasionally had some pretty good times. Don't forget that there were a lot of us and we did a lot of laughing when we were together. When you're there, it doesn't seem so bad."

For human beings are tough and flexible; and when they are together they can stretch their powers of endurance wide enough to encompass almost anything. In assessing most bad situations, the margin for error should be thrown on the positive side. There was a dark time in the last war when the British were beaten. They did not realize it. They carried on and won. Life is seldom as unendurable as, to judge by the facts, it logically ought to be.

23. "We may be having a white Christmas," one of the men in the office exclaims triumphantly this afternoon. The rain has turned to snow. Although the streets are slushy until dinnertime, they are white with ice and snow tonight, and automobiles are moving cautiously.

Although the city's work dutifully moves forward today in office and shop, it seems temporary and unimportant. A great pressure of excitement is building up under the work day and will explode tomorrow evening. Nothing we do today is going to make much difference. For the work looks uninspired in comparison with the cheerful beauty of the holiday-wrapped packages that are going out of and coming into every office and home. The mail is overwhelmed with Christmas cards. They make a glorious festival of art out of the familiar traditions. If Christmas had no other delight or meaning, it would still be memorable for the great flood of red, gold, blue, and green prints that come with a note of good wishes from friends and acquaintances who still have "in their souls some images of magnificence." The mail includes some business letters on ordinary paper. They look astonishingly pallid today; and the ideas set down in them are irrelevant, peevish, selfish, and superfluous. For today the affairs of the workaday world seem like a kind of remote and meaningless affliction—an incurable St. Vitus dance. Nobody with any imagination would intrude his wretched affairs on the bountiful and joyous Christmas mail.

Everything today falls into a grand design that expresses the exultation of the community at Christmas—the sparkling trees, the shivering Santa Clauses with their bells and their collection pots hanging on tripods at street corners, the holly wreaths and lights in the windows of apartment houses, the people carrying bundles in the subways, the carols sung over the radio. The beautiful ideas are unconquerable. The dream of Christmas cannot be torn out of the human race. At the bottom of the year, when things are blackest, people all over the world are overflowing with good cheer and neighborly sentiments.

24. Christmas Eve. Temperature 22°. The moon is white and cold. This is the night towards which the whole year is directed—the summit of human happiness and hope. All the tension of a year of living is released in the dark, cold and mystery of this blessed evening. Christmas Eve is less roisterous and more humble as the years go by. Remembering a garish, huckstering Christmas Eve in Fourteenth Street about fifteen years ago, O. and I go down there after dinner to enjoy the excitement of a pushcart bazaar. We have always kept in grateful memory the picture of that eager holiday street where vendors in the harsh light of gasoline lanterns were shouting their wares and people were nervously buying toys, decorations, cheap gifts, and plaster images of the Virgin and Child.

Nothing could better illustrate the change in public manners than Fourteenth Street this evening. There is not a pushcart in the street. Most of the shops are closed. A few people are hurrying through the street with bundles under their arms, but Fourteenth Street is virtually empty. Eighth Street, another shopping mart, is also deserted—the shops closed, the sidewalks clear and the street free of traffic. A Christmas tree sparkles like a pillar of gems in Washington Square arch and the Christmas trees outside the Fifth Avenue churches are shining with celestial light. The only crowds we see in the neighborhood are those of people going to the Christmas Eve services in the churches. For Christmas Eve is a religious festival now. Although Christmas is deliberately commercialized by the department stores, the people, as usual, have made their choice. They obey the slogans, buy gifts extravagantly and join the carnival. But they cherish Christmas Eve as the holy, silent night of the year. The business carnival is over when the cold stars climb up the dark walls of the night, bringing tidings of comfort and joy.

25. *"Nor war, or battle's sound,*
Was heard the world around.
The idle spear and shield were high uphung,
The hooked chariot stood
Unstained with hostile blood,
The trumpet spake not to the armèd throng,
And kings sat still, with awful eye,
As if they surely knew their sovereign Lord was by."

Christmas. On one day of the year we live at the peak of our spiritual strength. We surround our friends with love and joy; we are tolerant of those who are not our friends. Historically, this is probably not the birthday of Christ. Four centuries went by before the church deliberately chose to celebrate the sacred birth on this day—possibly in part as a rebuke to the wild and licentious pagan revels common to the end of the Roman year. For many years after the fourth century Christmas celebrations ended in drunkenness and coarse mummery. But gradually the gentle spirit of Christ has possessed the day set apart in honor of His birth. And on one day of the year we behave towards our neighbors as we wish that they would behave towards us—with kindness if not with generosity.

Although Christ never had a white Christmas, we prize it in this latitude for some elusive sentimental reason. We are having one today. The temperature is 24°. The Weehawken cliffs are crisply white and Riverside Park glistens in the pale winter sunshine. Some children are happily sliding down the snow-packed walk that enters the park. Before noon O. and I take the bus out to New Jersey to carry a basket of gifts. The bus is crowded, people with bundles standing the length of the narrow aisle. But the bus is a community vehicle today. Whether they know it or not, the passengers are taking a holiday from the million irritations that normally afflict them. They are aware of each other and look at each other with a gleam of unaccustomed friendliness. Strangers are talkative, which rarely happens. People instinctively help each other with bundles or hospitably try to make more room in the seats. And the sullen torture of trying to squirm through the crowd to the door becomes almost a game when we reach our destination. Today people are abnormally interested in other people. It is as though a multitude of the heavenly host had actually blessed the Public Service Corporation, which on every other day of the year is better known for its boorishness and short temper.

"Glory to God in the highest, and on earth peace, good will toward men" are the most radiant words in our language. The light they give mysteriously transfigures everyone it brushes across. On the most joyous day of the year, people live by the laws of their greatest dream. The dream began long ago when the heaven-born child, all meanly wrapt, lay in a crude manger because there was no room in the inn. On one day in each year, the dream comes true.

26. With the help of God, we have made history today. More snow has fallen in one day than ever before here since records have been kept—25.8 inches. When I get up, the air is whirling with whiteness. It has transmuted the sullen brick canyons into immaculate aisles, edging the hundreds of window-sills with snow and animating the whirls and flutings of iron grillwork at the windows and along the fire escapes. The river is swallowed up in the soft cloud of snow.

It seems like a pleasant freak of nature at first. But by noon-time a quiver of excitement begins to possess the city. For this is no ordinary whim but an epic snowstorm, and we begin to acquire historical importance. At last we are going to have something with which to challenge the survivors of the renowned blizzard of '88, who have been tyrannizing New York for years. Riverside Drive is solidly blocked by noontime. Truck-drivers, bus drivers and automobilists abandon their machines to the drifts that have already swallowed the cars parked by the lost curbs. Busses stop running all through the city. Some of the subways begin to falter by midafternoon. The vivid, dynamic city is paralyzed. By dinner-time the Times Square district is virtually abandoned—no traffic is moving, the bus stations dark, and only a few people slowly pick their way along the curved, narrow footpaths. A taxicab has been abandoned criss-cross in the middle of Seventh Avenue.

The mood is festive on the street and in the offices. Everyone has a story to tell of frustration or defeat. The man who can prove that his own defeat has been the greatest is inevitably the hero. In some curious way we have greater respect for a triumphant snowstorm than for the ingenious, complex organization of the city. We enjoy being defeated by a natural adversary. Incredibly enough, there is a full house at the theater for an opening performance. The composing-room at the office is also fully manned; and although the delivery trucks have to be massed in the one lane that is open in Forty-third Street, the papers are printed and loaded. That is the only activity in Times Square after midnight. When I go home, Broadway uptown is full of traffic that is blocked and deserted and the side streets are cluttered with abandoned automobiles. The snow is drifted in a wind-sculptured mass four or five feet deep in the middle of Eighty-fourth Street. Not even a footprint mars the immaculate surface of this silent city lane.

27. Now that the snow has stopped falling, the cliffs of Weehawken have reappeared across the rippled surface of the river. On Christmas Day they were outlined with snow. But now they are magically transformed into a long, gigantic snowbank—the gleaming surfaces broken by blue-tinged shadows where the sun does not reach. The city is paralyzed. Riverside Drive is still blocked by the dead busses and cars abandoned yesterday. Our own street is still a long, deep snowdrift, although someone has now broken the hard surface with a pair of ski tracks down the middle. The highway beside the river is open. A few cars are picking their way between the plowed banks, and some wind-bitten figures of men are laboriously digging out the cars they deserted yesterday. By afternoon paths have been shoveled along the sidewalks of our block—the snow having been thrown up in piles higher than a man's head. As I stumble downstreet I cannot see the other side. Children have begun to appear with their sleds. But Riverside Drive, which is normally a busy and noisy thoroughfare, is still deserted, as though some great calamity had suddenly struck the city and the inhabitants had dropped everything in a panic and fled for shelter.

The thermometer rises to 30° by midafternoon. But the west wind still howls around the corner, rattles the windows, whines in the dumbwaiter shaft and tears up the surface of the snow.

28. The arrival of the morning newspapers at the door is like a message of assurance and friendship from abroad. Although Riverside Drive is still blocked and one enormous bus at the corner is as dead as it was when it was abandoned two days ago, three people have managed to retrieve autos after the exhausting labor of digging, pushing, and shouting. Nothing has moved yet in Eighty-fourth Street. It is deeper in snow than ever because the people who have been digging their autos out of the snowbanks have thrown the snow in the middle of the street. People are also burning garbage and trash in niches melted out of the snow. It will be several days before the refuse trucks can come through this district. It will be impossible for some time to get coal or fuel oil. Although this is only the third day of the Big Snow we are already living on our reserves. Some apartment dwellers have had no heat for two days.

The snow gangs, fortified with mechanical equipment, start breaking a lane through our street in the afternoon; it takes them two hours to open a narrow passageway between snowbanks six to ten feet high. The Weather Bureau estimates that ninety million tons of snow fell in New York. Thirty thousand men are now working in eleven-hour shifts to open paths through it, clear it away from fire hydrants, dump it in truck-load lots into the North or East rivers, or sluice it down the drains.

For New York becomes more vulnerable according to the increasing intricacy of its organization. We would have been helpless if there had been a big fire, a subway accident, or a break in the water system. We live on a narrow margin in these efficient modern apartments. In similar circumstances in the country I could at least chop wood and burn it in the stove and fireplaces.

29. Although this book is presented in the form of a journal, I hope that is not what I have written. Few people's lives are worth daily recording, and mine is certainly not one of them. I hope that this is a book about America, and that these pages contain raw material that helps to illustrate life in America, and that it composes one of the countless patterns of life in a democracy. Not everyone is enchanted by birds and ships, but there are countless other familiar things worth equal devotion. Although we have fallen into the habit of thinking in large, general abstractions, our daily life is composed of millions of familiar things that affect us intimately and keep us patiently making the rounds from year to year.

The annual cycle of the seasons is the common experience. No one escapes the grand march of the year—winter, spring, summer and autumn, which are four of the five proper nouns in our grammar book. We all shiver together or mop our brows together according to the season we are sharing. "Good day," "*bon jour,*" "*guten tag,*" "*dobryi den*" express the common interest everyone all over the world has in the temper of the seasons. But within the golden rim of the wheel of the year there are incalculable riches that can be drawn upon freely. No one can sample a thousandth part of the treasure that is available. "Men may choose different things, and yet all choose right," said John Locke. For there are no masters who know everything or respond to everything that crowds the universe. The most we can do is to create out of the innumerable things that are available a congenial environment for ourselves.

We live not only in the present, which is vivid, and either ominous or beautiful according to the mood we are in, but on the crest of the past, where people with hands, backs, minds, and souls have been working at the things that vitally concern us. Fortunately, some great things have been done, like the cultivation of seeds and the invention of the wheel, and some great decisions have been made, like Magna Carta and the founding of the United Nations. We do not have to do everything for ourselves. People of good mind and principle have been working on our problems for centuries. In view of the things that still have to be done, it is heartening to realize that many great things have already been done by men and women who have hated ignorance and injustice and believed in the possibility of a good life for everyone. Down through the centuries so many dreams have come true that we can still go on cheerfully dreaming without feeling supercilious. The practical man is the one who has faith in the valor of the human race.

I am not forgetting that everything may end disastrously. Dreams have come true, but terrible things have happened, too— Buchenwald and Dachau, Hiroshima and Nagasaki. In the pavement of a walk in Riverside Park, a granite marker reads: "This is the site for the American memorial to the heroes of the Warsaw Ghetto battle April-May 1943 and to the six million Jews of Europe martyred in the cause of human liberty." Six million! Even God must have difficulty in assimilating so monstrous a catastrophe and in going about His affairs as usual. No, we can never be innocent again. Our dreams will be troubled ones—even in the grave, where some that we have loved are lying.

But look at the record—the grand cycle of the seasons year without end, the sun that warms and lights us, the triumphant snowfall that has just transfigured the gritty city, the dramas and symphonies played here every night, the songs that are being sung in theaters, schools and churches, the friends who are talking, arguing and laughing, the men and women pitching in to the clutter of work day and night at the office. To know these things is to believe in them and in the whole magnificent panorama of daily life they help to compose. Nature supplies the unity. We supply the vast array of sentient details.

30. *"These times (though many a friend bewail)*
These times bewail not I."

Speak the most brutal truth about this era in history. Remind us of the ghastly incinerators for human beings in Germany, the barbaric work camps in Russia, the lynchings and primeval race animosities in America, or count the war dead by the millions. Never has there been a time of evil and violence on such a colossal scale. But these times bewail not I for one mighty reason: our allies and ourselves rose in defense of freedom at the time when the honor of the world was degraded. Even if we had lost the war, which we damned near did, I would not in my heart bewail a time in which so many million people dropped the things they liked to do and marched to battle for freedom. They knew in their bones what the issue was; they understood the peril and they did not hesitate.

For let's not forget that we could have evaded the war by equivocating and compromising. Both the Germans and Japanese were anxious to make it easy for us. The Germans did not attack England, France, or the United States, but Poland, which was in the other direction; and in the beginning the Japanese did not

attack the United States, but China and Indo-China, which were
in the other direction also. On the surface it did not look like our
war. Many of our own people explained it away and warned us
against it because we could not hope to win it so many thousand
miles away. There were a million plausible and inviting reasons
why we could go on living cozy lives, why tyranny was inevitable
and perhaps desirable abroad. We could have drugged ourselves
into a state of insensibility and lost our freedom, bit by bit, without knowing it. There is always a way out for craven people who
do not care.

But the French and the English—especially the English—did
not take the easy way out, even when they were already defeated
on paper; and our ships and munitions, as well as our moral support, were on their side until Japan and Germany could no longer
pretend that we were neutral. Freedom is more than a pleasant
word now. It has sensory properties, like sunlight and sweet air,
like the eagle circling in the sky, like music and worship and
revelry. I cannot bewail a time in which men know what freedom
is and believe in it.

31. In terms of daily experience the last night of the year has
no significance. It is only a calendar date, about ten days too late
to mark the low point in the physical world, and more than two
and one half months too early to mark the arrival of spring, which
is the physical and spiritual beginning of the new year. Until the
sixteenth century most Christian countries celebrated the new
year on March twenty-fifth. Ending the old year tonight is an
accident left over from the introduction in 46 B.C. of the Julius
Caesar calendar which divided the year into 365 days. Although
the Julian calendar has been once modified and once revised, and
ought to be again, it is the basic element in the arbitrary system
we still use and which brings us to the end of the year tonight.

Since the latitude of Rome is only a few degrees farther north
than New York, the winter nights are only a little longer there
than here. That is probably the fundamental reason why our
attitude towards this time of year coincides with the attitude of
the ancient Romans. The dark time of year was their carnival
season, too: they defied the long nights, the cold weather and the
dead fields with festivals and topsy-turvy revelry. In one of Shaw's

plays Caesar remarks ruefully that his own age always increases, but the age of the crowds in the Appian Way is always the same. The age of crowds is always the same the world over in all centuries. Anyone who had heard the roars and squeals of the Appian Way crowds on the night of the Roman Saturnalia would probably be able to recognize the noisy pandemonium of Times Square tonight. The sounds are probably the same. For we, too, are celebrating the end of the winter holiday season and we are consoling each other for the dark and chill by being together and cheering.

On the day after tomorrow we have to go to work in earnest with nothing gay to anticipate for a long, dreary round of weeks and months—work and routine, worry, petulance and anxiety. But tonight let's drink and joke with our friends, wear fantastic carnival hats and blow horns at midnight, throw colored streamers across the room and devour the first feast of the new year. Drop the last year into the silent limbo of the past. Let it go, for it was imperfect, and thank God that it can go. Let us discard it as rapidly and thoroughly as possible. Let us remember it only as something that must never be repeated. Tomorrow comes to us untarnished by human living. No human eyes have seen it and no one can tell what it is going to be. The Chinese word for tomorrow (*ming-tien*) means "bright day." There is the wisdom of sages and the rapture of poets in that cheerful image.